An Agenda for People

An Agenda for People

The UNFPA Through Three Decades

Edited by Nafis Sadik

NEW YORK UNIVERSITY PRESS

New York and London

NEW YORK UNIVERSITY PRESS
New York and London

Library of Congress Cataloging-in-Publication Data
United Nations Fund for Population Activities.
An agenda for people : the UNFPA through three decades / edited by Nafis Sadik.
p. cm.
ISBN 0-8147-9782-2 (cloth: acid-free paper)
ISBN 0-8147-9783-0 (pbk.: acid-free paper)
1. United Nations Fund for Population Activities—History.
2. Population assistance—History. 3. United Nations—Population assistance—History.
I. Sadik, Nafis. II. Sadik, Nafis. III. Title.
HB884.5 .U55 2002
341.7'66—dc21   2002000322

10 9 8 7 6 5 4 3 2 1

TABLE OF CONTENTS

LIST OF TABLES

LIST OF ACRONYMS AND ABBREVIATIONS

ACC	Administrative Committee on Coordination
ADR	alternative dispute resolution
AIDS	acquired immune deficiency syndrome
ALACODE	Latin American Development Journalists Association
ANU	Australian National University
APLIC	Association for Population/Family Planning Libraries and Information Centres
ASEAN	Association of South-East Asian Nations
ASRH	Adolescent Sexual and Reproductive Health
BSSA	ACC Task Force on Basic Social Services for All
CBD	community-based distribution
CBO	community-based organization
CCA	Common Country Assessment
CCP	Center for Communication Programs
CCPOQ	Consultative Committee on Programme and Operational Questions
CEDAW	Committee and Convention on the Elimination of All Forms of Discrimination against Women
CEDPA	Centre for Development and Population Activities
CERD	Committee on the Elimination of Racial Discrimination
CESCR	Committee on Economic, Social and Cultural Rights
CIS	Commonwealth of Independent States
CMA	Commonwealth Medical Association
CPA	Country Population Assessment
CPD	Commission on Population and Development
CRC	Committee on the Rights of the Child
CSO	civil society organization
CST	Country Support Team
CTA	Chief Technical Adviser
DAC	Development Assistance Committee
DALY	disability-adjusted life year
DAW	Division for the Advancement of Women
DemoGraphics	Demographic Software for Population Education package
DemoTables	Demographic Software for Population Education package
DESIPA	Department for Economic and Social Information and Policy Analysis
DHS	Demographic and Health Survey
DIESA	Department for International Economic and Social Affairs
ECA	Economic Commission for Africa
ECLAC	Economic Commission for Latin America and the Caribbean
ECOSOC	Economic and Social Council of the United Nations
ESCAP	Economic and Social Commission for Asia and the Pacific
FAO	Food and Agriculture Organization of the United Nations
FCI	Family Care International
FGM	female genital mutilation

FP	family planning
FPA	Family Planning Association
FWCW	Fourth World Conference on Women
FY	fiscal year
G-77	Group of 77
GCCP	Global Contraceptive Commodity Programme
GDI	Gender Development Index
GDP	Gross Domestic Product
GEM	Gender Empowerment Measure
GIS	geographic information systems
GNP	Gross National Product
GPD	gender, population and development
GPS	global positioning system
GRAD	Gender, Reproductive Health and Advocacy
HABITAT II	Second United Nations Conference on Human Settlements
HDI	Human Development Index
HDR	Human Development Report
HIV	human immunodeficiency virus
HRC	Human Rights Committee
IATF	Inter-Agency Task Force on ICPD Implementation
ICOMP	International Committee for the Management of Population Programmes
ICP	International Conference on Population
ICPD	International Conference on Population and Development
ICPD+5	five-year review of the implementation of the Programme of Action of the International Conference on Population and Development
ICRC	International Committee of the Red Cross
ICT	Information and Communication Technology
IEC	Information, education and communication
IERD	Information and External Relations Division
IFAD	International Fund for Agricultural Development
IIASA	International Institute for Applied Systems Analyses
ILO	International Labour Organization
IMF	International Monetary Fund
INSTRAW	International Research and Training Institute for the Advancement of Women
IOM	International Organization for Migration
IPPF	International Planned Parenthood Federation
IPU	Inter-Parliamentary Union
ISI	International Statistical Institute
IUD	intrauterine device
IUSSP	International Union for the Scientific Study of Population
IWHC	International Women's Health Coalition
JCGP	Joint Consultative Group on Policy
JHU	Johns Hopkins University

JOICFP	Japanese Organization for Cooperation in Family Planning
KAP	knowledge, attitudes and practices
LIP	Local Initiatives Program
MCH	maternal and child health
MIS	management information systems
MVA	manual vacuum aspirator
NGO	non-governmental organization
OAU	Organization of African Unity
ODA	official development assistance
OECD	Organisation for Economic Cooperation and Development
OHCHR	Office of the United Nations High Commissioner for Human Rights
OOE	Office of Oversight and Evaluation
PAI	Population Action International
PDS	population and development strategies
PIACT	Program for the Introduction and Adaptation of Contraceptive Technology
POA	Programme of Action
POPIN	United Nations Population Information Network
POPLINE	bibliographic database on population
POPMAP	Computer Software and Support for Population Activities
PP&E	population, poverty, and environment
PPU	population planning units
PRB	Population Reference Bureau
PrepCom	Preparatory Committee
PRSD	Programme Review and Strategy Development
RAPID	system showing effects of rapid rates of population growth
STD	sexually transmitted disease
SWAP	sector-wide approach
SWOP	State of World Population
TBA	traditional birth attendant
TCDC	technical cooperation among developing countries
TED	Technical and Evaluation Division
TFR	total fertility rate
TPD	Technical and Policy Division
TSS	Technical Support Services
UNAIDS	Joint United Nations Programme on HIV/AIDS
UNCED	United Nations Conference on Environment and Development
UNCED+5	five-year review of the implementation of chapter 5 of Agenda 21 of the United Nations Conference on Environment and Development
UNDAF	United Nations Development Assistance Framework
UNDG	United Nations Development Group
UNDP	United Nations Development Programme
UNEP	United Nations Environment Programme
UNESCO	United Nations Educational, Scientific and Cultural Organization
UNFPA	United Nations Population Fund
UNHCR	Office of the United Nations High Commissioner for Refugees

UNICEF	United Nations Children's Fund
UNIFEM	United Nations Development Fund for Women
USAID	United States Agency for International Development
WEDO	Women's Environment and Development Organization
WFP	World Food Programme
WFS	World Fertility Survey
WHO	World Health Organization
WISTAT	Women's Indicators and Statistics Database
WPAW	World Population Awareness Week
WPC	World Population Conference
WPPA	World Population Plan of Action
WPY	World Population Year
WRI	World Resources Institute
WSSD	World Summit for Social Development

ACKNOWLEDGEMENTS

The editor of this work would like to acknowledge, with gratitude, the contributions of several persons who helped to make the book a reality. First and foremost, I would like to thank the authors, both from within UNFPA and outside, who graciously agreed to undertake the task of researching and writing their various chapters. The breadth and depth of their experience and learning is evident from the quality and scope of their contributions. They are listed at the end of the book and my heartfelt gratitude goes out to each of them for undertaking their tasks through commitment to the fields of population and reproductive health and their appreciation for the work of UNFPA.

The idea for this book came from Mohammad Nizamuddin, at that time Director of UNFPA's Technical and Policy Division. His suggestions and those of one of his predecessors as head of that division, Jyoti Shankar Singh, were instrumental in shaping the list of contributing authors and the direction of their essays.

In addition to the authors cited in the table of contents, several staff members at UNFPA contributed at different points to the writing of various parts of the book. I would like to especially note the contributions in that regard of Alexander Marshall and Stan Bernstein of the Fund's Information and External Relations Division; Richard Leete and Ann Pawliczko of the Technical Support Division; and John Herzog of the Country Technical Services Team in Addis Ababa.

Several copy editors, including Dan Baker and Gail Cooper, helped in clarifying ambiguities and smoothing out the text. Radha Bhattacharji helped to track down some elusive references and to standardize their presentation.

The overall coordination of this project required the assistance of several persons, including Mr. Nizamuddin and Ugur Tuncer. They were ably assisted, at various stages, by Yunae Yi, Christine Czarnecki, Madeleine Sacco and Flavia Roche. Throughout the process, Sharyn Sohlberg conscientiously kept track of all editorial changes and worked diligently to maintain consistency of style and presentation. To all of these persons, I would like to give my heartfelt thanks.

Dr. Nafis Sadik
Editor

PREFACE

The 1970s saw the first of the international conferences on the great issues facing humankind; the pace and frequency of these meetings accelerated in the 1990s. In 1994, the United Nations Population Fund (UNFPA) was the driving force behind the International Conference on Population and Development (ICPD), held in Cairo with 184 participating countries. This gathering produced the Programme of Action, a seminal document on population and development, which has become the "bible" for population activities by UNFPA, other members of the United Nations system, governments, and non-governmental organizations (NGOs). The ICPD has given tremendous impetus to strengthening reproductive rights. Most important, it explicitly recognizes that women's rights *are* human rights — the two are one and the same.

It is now recognized that reproductive health is affected by such socio-economic factors as education, employment, living conditions, family environment, social relations, gender relations, legislation, and cultural and traditional practices. As the Cairo consensus further emphasized, poverty and social and gender inequity influence and are influenced by population growth, structure, and distribution. Efforts to slow population growth, reduce poverty, achieve economic progress, protect the environment, and reduce unsustainable consumption and production patterns are mutually reinforcing. Investments in social infrastructure — basic education, sanitation, drinking water, housing, food supply, and health care, including reproductive health and family planning — will speed up sustainable development and poverty alleviation and help realize population objectives and improve people's quality of life.

The composition of the world population is changing. The percentage of older people is increasing. While the percentage of people under 15 is shrinking, the actual numbers of young people continue to grow. These changing demographics are bringing about changes in such areas as family structures, housing, transport, labour, employment, and migration.

Population, sustained economic growth, and sustainable development are inextricably linked and interrelated. Sustained economic growth within the context of sustainable development — along with improvements in education; in health care, particularly reproductive health, including family planning and sexual health; and in the status of women — is needed to alleviate the extreme poverty that affects about a billion people in developing countries. Such human-centred development is likely to slow population growth and reduce related pressures on the environment stemming from cultivation of marginal lands, overuse of water resources, and rapid urbanization.

Furthermore, these issues are linked in complex ways and at different levels of development. For example, most environmental damage is done by the richest people: industrialized countries contribute to environmental degradation through higher resource consumption and large-scale use of polluting technologies. At the same time, industrializing countries are rapidly increasing their contribution to environmental stress. The world's poorest people have few options: population growth and uneven population distribution can overwhelm traditional sustainable land use practices, and for the poor there are no other options.

Too often, however, we have focused on the economics without a sufficient understanding of the social, political, environmental, and cultural aspects of societies. We must set forth objectives to ensure environmental and human sustainability, and these are issues that must be dealt with on a global level. At the same time, we must ensure that the culture of each country is nurtured and enriched so that development is firmly based and historically grounded. Development is about putting all the component parts in place — together and in harmony.

We must think of global strategies to achieve the global public good. We must have a new approach to partnership: partnerships that are led by governments but include civil society and are joined by the private sectors and by the international community. And, of course, in responding to population and development needs, the question of resources is critical. Mobilization of resources is an essential component if we are to achieve the goals laid out in the ICPD Programme of Action.

We cannot afford to be complacent about population and development issues and their implications for the future health of our planet. The consequences of complacency come at an alarmingly high price and will be legion: a crisis of world population that could add 3 billion more people to the planet over the next 25 years; chronic water shortages affecting 2 billion people by 2025; urbanization that will mean that the population of cities will triple over the next 30 years; and a food security problem that will require doubling food production over the next 30 years if everyone is to have adequate nutrition.

It took all of time for the world's population to reach 2 billion in 1927, then less than a lifetime to arrive at 6 billion. Yet 6 billion marks a success: people today live longer and healthier lives than any generation in history. Six billion is also a challenge, as the billion-plus young people determine how many persons will inhabit the planet by 2050 and beyond.

There is nothing accidental about either past or future trends in population growth. We have arrived at our present position as the result of tremendously hard work on the part of many thousands of people the world over, and, above all, by the women and men who have exercised their right to choose the number of their children responsibly.

The year 1999 simultaneously marked the end of the 20th century and of several significant international events: the five-year anniversary of the ICPD; the 30th anniversary of the founding of UNFPA; and the year that world population passed the 6 billion mark.

The 21st century will present the international community and the United Nations with a unique opportunity to dramatically expand the economic and social progress of the past thirty years. The challenge before us is to have the courage and the vision to create an environment that is conducive to the equal participation of both women and men in society. The fundamental concern here is the depth of our commitment to this issue; we must firmly resolve that our children and grandchildren will live in a more equitable world. We must have the will to actively pursue and to achieve this goal. Through our desire to understand and grasp the issues and through stronger political and personal commitment, we can be agents of positive change.

In the last analysis, only an integrated, comprehensive approach to development can achieve the required results. In formulating and implementing population policies, we should be mindful that there must be changes in all areas of societies. Equal responsibility, equal participation, equal opportunity, and mutual respect of individual rights are imperative to meet the goals of ICPD and to lay the foundations for sustained and sustainable development.

Our children's future is in our hands, just as surely as the world's will be in theirs. The combined efforts and decisions of the international community will determine how future generations will live — in poverty or prosperity; on an environmentally secure earth or one degraded and devastated by human activities; with hope for a better future or with the bleak prospect of trying to accomplish the daunting task of correcting the short-sightedness of their forebears.

Population in the 21st Century

The last thirty years have seen a transformation in the field of population and development. The most obvious outward sign is that modern methods of family planning have become widely available and widely used. In many developing countries, family planning has become part of everyday life, and users expect it and other reproductive health services as a normal part of their primary health care.

One result has been falling fertility, smaller families, and slower population growth. Desired family size has fallen rapidly in Latin America and most parts of Asia and has recently begun to fall in sub-Saharan Africa, creating considerable demand for family planning and other reproductive health services.

The less obvious but fundamentally important change has been in the perception of population issues and the way in which the international community, countries, and individuals act on their perceptions. Thirty years ago, it was barely possible to discuss population activities in an international forum. Even at the World Population Conference (WPC) in 1974, there was a sharp division in perceptions, broadly between the developed and developing countries. Many developing countries were adamantly opposed to international support for family planning.

UNFPA's approach in the 1970s was to offer assistance in the areas where countries expressed concern. In Africa, UNFPA supported the United Nations African census programme in 36 countries. In Latin America, UNFPA supported demographic research and population education. In Asia, UNFPA's role was frequently to support existing family planning programmes and to offer assistance in integrating family planning with maternal and child health (MCH) programmes. In West Asia, and in fact in all countries, UNFPA supported the integration of population concerns into development programmes. An important part of this support was data collection and analysis, providing expert advice and training for government statistical offices, and strengthening the capabilities of universities for training and research.

At the international level, UNFPA's contribution was to build awareness among policy makers of the complexity of population issues and their relationship to other areas of development. Simplistic "population control" solutions were inappropriate for developing countries whose perceived problems were colonial-era economies, slow economic growth, and pervasive poverty. The relationship between rapid population growth, poverty, and economic growth was still not clear: in the 1970s, opinions were more readily available than facts.

A related contribution was UNFPA's insistence that population problems had to be seen in the national context and that unique solutions had to be found for and by each country. This struck a chord with countries emerging from colonial dominance, whose first desire was to establish their unique national identity.

UNFPA understood early on that women's rights and status were not only important in themselves but would be critical to the success of population and development policies and programmes. Women's organizations were welcomed as partners of UNFPA, and governments were urged to involve them in the development process.

Better understanding of population issues led to more dialogue within and among countries. The consensus of 1974, the World Population Plan of Action (WPPA), was a compromise document reflecting a very wide range of attitudes and approaches, but it marked an historic shift in the international discussion. After 1974, it was possible to offer and accept assistance for population in its many aspects as a recognized part of development programming. The result was a surge in interest in, and rapidly rising demand for, UNFPA's services.

One important aspect of the population and development agenda was notably missing from the 1974 consensus document: an acknowledgement of the importance of women, not merely as agents and actors in the population drama, but as individuals with their own development needs, notably for education and for reproductive health. This omission was only partially repaired at the International Conference on Population (ICP) in 1984, and it was only in the 1994 Programme of Action of the ICPD and the key future actions that were agreed on in 1999 that women would take their appropriate place on the stage.

It would be hard to overestimate the significance of the global consensus on population and development reached at the ICPD in 1994, now reviewed and strengthened by the ICPD+5 Special Session of the United Nations General Assembly in 1999. The 1994 consensus made possible a surge of activity in population-related areas on all levels, comparable to the surge after the WPC in 1974. More important than that was the sense that in this vital and most contentious area of development, the entire family of nations had at last found a secure ground for determined action now, and for constructive dialogue in the future.

This transformation offers the strong possibility that the ICPD goal of universal access to family planning and related reproductive health services will be reached by 2015; that fertility will continue to fall sharply in countries where population growth rates are still high; and that gender equality will become a practical possibility.

The key future actions approved by the Special Session of the General Assembly in 1999 vindicate the exhaustive and inclusive process of consensus building at the United Nations. If constructive consensus in this area is possible, even in an atmosphere of uncertainty over so many global issues and at a time of rapid changes in international relationships, then it should be possible in many other areas of social development as well.

Population and Development Policy

Countries in all settings have re-examined their policies in light of the ICPD, in the areas of population and development; environment and natural resources; urban growth and urbanization; ageing and social security. The re-examination has included areas not previously understood to be population-related, such as, for example, economic policy, education, and gender-related issues, including the political participation of women.

The Special Session confirmed the consensus of the ICPD and previous conferences that policies on population size, rates of growth, and distribution were matters for decisions by sovereign states. Globally, it is agreed that population stabilization is the aim. Nationally, countries wishing for slower population growth will attain it by purely voluntary means, not by setting numerical targets and, by extension, targets for family planning use, contraceptive prevalence, and quotas for service providers to meet. The evidence is that women and men in general wish for smaller families than previous generations, and that national governments wish to extend to them the ability to choose the size and spacing of the family, as has been guaranteed by human rights and population agreements since 1968. Increasingly, they are doing so.

Freedom of choice, backed by the information and the means to make choices, will result in smaller families and slower population growth overall.

Gender Equality, Equity and the Empowerment of Women

The body of law related to gender is undergoing review and change in many countries in light of the ICPD and the Fourth World Conference on Women (FWCW). This includes, for example, laws on marriage and divorce, property, inheritance, and political and economic participation. Existing law and constitutional protections are being more strongly enforced; for example, the right of girls and women to be treated equally under the law, laws related to child sex and marriage, and laws related to child labour, health, and education. The practice of allowing customary law on (for example) marriage and inheritance to take precedence over constitutional and statutory provisions is being questioned; and traditional harmful practices, such as female genital mutilation (FGM), that fly in the face of human rights are increasingly outlawed. Practices that have no legal or even customary protection but have been sanctioned by inattention are also coming under scrutiny. These include the relative neglect of girl children, and the secondary status suffered by both girls and women compared with boys and men in the areas of education, health, and nutrition. All of these understandings were reinforced by the Special Session, which insisted, for example, on "zero tolerance" for harmful and discriminatory attitudes towards women. Violence against girls and women — including rape, incest, trafficking, sexual violence, and exploitation — were explicitly condemned.

The Movement to Reproductive Health

The ICPD agreed on a package of reproductive health services that should take the place of stand-alone family planning programmes. The challenge for most countries is how to implement these understandings on reproductive health, given their resource constraints and the complexity of reform.

Most developing countries have a system of separate programmes to deliver services for preventive and curative health, often separately administered and with their own protocols for staff training, delivery, supervision, and reporting. Moving to an integrated system, in which all primary health-care services will be delivered under one roof by the same cadre of providers, would challenge most countries, rich or poor. Reorganization must also ensure that neglected areas such as family planning and safe motherhood are given the appropriate attention. Shortage of resources colours any attempt to make such integration and reorganization respond to the needs of the people being served.

Nevertheless, countries are taking the challenge, and many have made good progress in putting integrated systems in place. The priority for the next five years, as the Special Session confirmed, is enabling all countries to do the same. The aim is to ensure universal access to a full range of reproductive health services by 2015 and to rapidly close the gap in unmet demand for family planning.

Partnership

To implement the agreements of ICPD, countries need the strong leadership of governments. To mobilize the united efforts of all elements of society in favour of the ICPD consensus, strong advocacy by political and parliamentary leaders is required. At the Special Session, governments agreed on further action to draw into partnership elements of civil society, including NGOs, religious groups, educators, and the private sector.

Resources

Alone among the international conferences of the 1990s, the ICPD attached costs to its recommendations, and included funding as part of the consensus. The agreed total to fund the ICPD Programme of Action was $17 billion a year by the year 2000. Of this, two-thirds, or $11.3 billion, was to come from developing countries themselves, and the remainder, $5.7 billion, from donor countries.

The developing countries are about two-thirds of the way to their target, although much of this expenditure is accounted for by some twelve large countries. The donor countries, however, have reached only one-third of their target, or $2 billion. Some donors are indeed fulfilling their commitment to transfer 0.7 per cent of their gross national products (GNPs) to development assistance, with some 4 per cent going to population and development programmes. However, several of the largest and most important donors have fallen seriously behind.

This shortfall is a threat, not merely to the ICPD Programme of Action, but to global stability and security. In the broadest sense, meeting the ICPD goals, including the transfer of resources, is in the best interest of *all* countries. The Special Session endorsed the ICPD resource goals. It is to be hoped that the consensus of ICPD+5 will give all countries a powerful impetus towards meeting them.

Areas of Debate

Adolescent reproductive health

The proposed key future actions adopted by the Special Session in 1999 include some sensitive topics; one of these being the reproductive health of young people. Such topics include some associated areas, such as the respective roles of parents and of the family and society in general in protecting adolescent reproductive health. This is a legitimate area for international discussion: just as the global community concerns itself with the health of children and adults, so it should address the health of the generation aged 15 to 24 — reproductive health is very much a part of this discussion. The first priority is to protect the health as well as the human rights of the billion young people whose decisions will determine the demographic future.

As with all other areas of population and development, adolescent reproductive health is a matter for national discussion and decision, according to each country's situation and priorities. However sensitive, it is a discussion that must take place, both as a matter of human rights and as a matter of necessity. We cannot afford to let our young people grow up in a rapidly changing society without offering some guidance and practical help in coping with the changes, including changes in family formation, structure, and roles.

As the Special Session agreed, these discussions will take place on the basis that the family is the basic unit of society and should be strengthened. A sure way of strengthening the family is to ensure the health and well-being of all its members, including young people. We should also remember that there are many young people outside the purview of the family, and their needs and aspirations must also be taken into account.

Abortion

The ICPD spent nearly three days discussing one paragraph, the one dealing with abortion. It was the last issue to be decided at the ICPD+5 Special Session. Abortion is and will remain a contentious issue, but agreement on a rational approach is closer than at any time in the past. As the Special Session underlined, unsafe abortion is a serious health problem in many countries. It affects millions of women and kills 70,000 each year. It follows that all efforts must be made to eliminate the need for abortion, notably by expanding and improving family planning services.

The Special Session agreed that women with unwanted pregnancies should receive reliable information and compassionate counselling, and where abortion is not against the law, abortion should be safe and accessible. This is not a perfect solution, but it allows rational action to address the health consequences of unsafe abortion. It also encourages the other rational approach, urgent action to improve family planning services.

Maternal mortality

Reducing maternal mortality and morbidity has been a goal of government policies and programmes since the Safe Motherhood Initiative was launched in 1987, but there has been little or no progress. It has been hard to secure the necessary resources or policy priority, despite well-known and widely available techniques, and despite universal agreement on its importance. One study found that where maternal mortality is very high — more than one death in every 100 pregnant women — the risk could be reduced by as much as 80 per cent by providing prenatal care, information about warning signs, and services to provide emergency care.

A systematic effort to reduce the overall risk of maternity calls for a range of interventions, including skilled help during and after delivery; emergency referral and obstetric care; expanded information and education about health, pregnancy, and childbirth; pre- and post-natal care; improved nutrition and greater access by women to resources; information; and the empowerment of women to make their own decisions.

The Special Session agreed on new benchmarks for reducing maternal mortality. To stimulate action, it agreed to calculate the costs of maternal mortality to society. It called on the World Health Organization (WHO) to take leadership and on UNFPA, the United Nations Children's Fund (UNICEF), and the World Bank to intensify their role in improving maternal health.

Conclusion

The ICPD+5 review, culminating in the Special Session of the United Nations General Assembly, offered the clearest possible evidence of the strength of national commitment to the consensus reached in 1994.

Dr. Nafis Sadik
Executive Director, UNFPA
Under-Secretary-General
of the United Nations

PART I

Thirty Years of Global Population Changes

John C. Caldwell

In demographic terms, the last thirty years have been quite distinct from the period that preceded it, or, indeed, from any other period in history.[1] The global fertility level had been almost stable for at least twenty years prior to 1965-1969, with a total fertility rate just under 5 children per woman, and this stability did not hide countervailing forces in different parts of the world. The developed countries, whether they had participated or not in the post-World War II "baby boom," showed no strong trends in fertility, with a total fertility rate remaining around 2.7. The same lack of change characterized the developing countries, but there the total fertility rate was well over 6, as it may well have been for millennia.

The great demographic change in the twenty years before 1960 had been the unprecedentedly steep decline in mortality, one of the great achievements of human history and completely unpredicted. World life expectancy was probably not much over 40 years in 1945, but it was 46 years by 1950-1954, and 56 years by 1965-1969. That ten-year jump in life expectancy during those fifteen years was not to be repeated in the following fifteen years, when the increase fell back to little more than five years. Nor was the change from 1950-1954 to 1965-1969 evenly spread, for the greatest gains against mortality were in Asia, with both Africa and Latin America recording more modest gains.

The demographic instability caused by the 15-year increase in life expectancy from the early 1950s to the late 1960s was profound. The crude death rate fell by one-third, causing the annual level of population increase in the world to rise to over 2 per cent for the first (and only) time in history, whilst that of the developing countries climbed to over 2.5 per cent. Between 1950 and 1965, world population grew from 2.5 to 3.3 billion, an increase equal to that of the previous fifty years. In 1950-1954, the global increase in population had averaged 47 million people a year; by 1965-1969, this number had grown to 72 million a year.

The control of fertility, and hence of population growth, had been advocated since Malthus' *First Essay* in 1798. Controversy over the morality of practising contraception had swelled during the nineteenth century, but so had antinatal practices, with the result that French marital fertility fell after 1786.[2] In much of Northwestern Europe and in English-speaking countries of overseas European settlement, declines became general from the 1870s. In some developed countries, fertility fell below the long-term replacement level in the economic depression of the 1930s as the great majority of the population resorted to contraception or

The author acknowledges the assistance from Pat Caldwell, Wendy Cosford, Elaine Napper, and Jeff Marck in the preparation of this chapter.

abortion to limit the number of children. Even in the early 1950s, in the heart of the "baby boom," the total fertility rate for developed countries was only 2.8, and most couples attempted to control family size. Fertility in some developed countries was as low, or almost as low, as the replacement level, as exemplified by the Baltic States, Sweden, the United Kingdom, Germany, Austria, and Switzerland.

It was this achievement of fertility transition in many developed countries and the familiarity with contraception that was to provide the base for advocating worldwide fertility control and the containment of human numbers. Nevertheless, there was opposition from some religious groups and a widespread feeling that contraception was a private rather than a public matter, so that Western governments were reluctant to advocate family planning or to provide technical aid for that purpose.[3] In these circumstances, the Gordian knot was cut by Prime Minister Nehru's announcement in 1951 that India would move toward the governmental provision of family planning in its five-year plans, and this became a reality from about 1955. Although the decision was a reaction to the unexpectedly high population numbers found by the 1951 census, its antecedents had a long Anglo-Indian intellectual history and lay also in ideas and recommendations in census reports and official inquiries in the late colonial period.[4]

Asian cultures and indigenous religions were not hostile to contraception, especially in Hindu and Confucian areas. In such circumstances it was no surprise that national family planning programmes were an Asian invention, dating from 1955 in India, 1960 in Pakistan and the early 1960s in South Korea, Taiwan, and Thailand. Many of those involved in technical aid and in international organizations working in the family planning field had their first programme experiences in these countries. So it was that many of the family planning approaches and ideas that became widespread in the field came from the interaction between the experiences of these programmes and people working for foundations and international bodies. By 1965, a conference on family planning and population programmes could list large programmes, either government-run or controlled by family planning associations (FPAs) with government financial support and with contraceptives being provided by government hospitals: in Asia in India, Pakistan, South Korea, Taiwan, Thailand, Hong Kong, Malaysia, Singapore, Sri Lanka, and Turkey; in Africa in Egypt, Tunisia, and Mauritius; and in Latin America in Chile, Colombia, and Honduras.[5]

The United Nations had established a Population Division in 1945, its focus being largely demographic. In the 1950s, largely propelled by the establishment of the Asian programmes, technical aid and international assistance in the family planning field began to develop. The Population Council was founded in 1952 and became operational in 1954, at first largely focusing on training students in demography. By 1959, requests from India had brought Ford Foundation activities to that country, and soon after, the foundation began such activities in its head office in New York. The Nordic governments began giving some family planning technical aid in the early 1960s, and the United States from 1963.

The second half of the 1960s: a turning point

Following a statement by President Lyndon Johnson to the United States Congress in January 1965, large American funds were made available for Third World family planning, and in May of that year, the United States Agency for International Development (USAID) announced that it would fund the provision of contraception. During the first half of 1965, both the United Nations

3

and the World Bank sent family planning programme advisory missions to India, and initial steps to enter the field were taken by the World Health Organization (WHO), the United Nations Children's Fund (UNICEF), and the Economic and Social Council of the United Nations (ECOSOC). In August-September of that year, the United Nations Population Division joined with the International Union for the Scientific Study of Population (IUSSP) in organizing a World Population Conference (WPC) in Belgrade. In December 1966, the United Nations General Assembly called on all United Nations agencies to draw up plans for assistance in the population field in training, research, information, and advisory services. In August 1967, the Secretary-General of the United Nations, U Thant, proposed an action programme and fund that led to the establishment of the United Nations Trust Fund for Population Activities, which changed its name in 1969 to the United Nations Fund for Population Activities (UNFPA) when it really became operational.

What, then, did the population scene look like in 1969? The annual rate of population growth was at its highest point in human history, at over 2 per cent. In fact, this was the highest rate it would attain, but this would not be known for some years. The rate of increase in the developing world, also proven in retrospect to have reached its historic high, was over 2.5 per cent. The United Nations Population Division's world population estimates and projections had continued to rise as actual growth outstripped the predictions that had been based on past trends. The 1950 medium projection for the world's population in 1980 was 3.3 billion. This figure for the world's population in 1980 increased in succeeding projections: 3.6 billion in that of 1954; 4.2 billion in 1958; 4.3 billion in 1963; and 4.5 billion in 1968. In the end, the world's population reached only 4.4 billion in 1980, and it appeared that the period of reality's outstripping the informed imagination had passed. But this was not known in the late 1960s, and the rapid growth seemed inexorable. The author presented the 1974 WPC in Bucharest with a projection showing global population numbers not coming to a halt short of 14 billion; at the time this seemed only too plausible.[6]

National family planning programmes were proliferating, but there was little sign that they would succeed in substantially reducing fertility levels, let alone in reducing natural increase. However, governments certainly thought the attempt worth making. New national family planning programmes were announced in 1966 by Egypt, Morocco, Malaysia, Kenya, Chile, Tunisia, Singapore, Jamaica, and Barbados, and in 1967 by Iran, Colombia, Sri Lanka, Costa Rica, and Trinidad and Tobago. Reports of any success in reducing fertility levels came only from small countries, and they were confined to East and Southeast Asia. The contributed papers to the August 1967 Sydney Conference of the IUSSP (1967) declared that fertility was probably beginning to decline in Malaysia, Singapore, Hong Kong, North and South Korea, and Taiwan.[7] Ron Freedman told a meeting of foundation representatives in October 1967 that fertility was definitely declining as a result of interventionist family planning programmes in South Korea and Taiwan and was also falling in Singapore and Hong Kong.[8] The only country to be added to this list in the contributions to the 1969 IUSSP Conference in London was Sri Lanka, and in that country increasing postponement of female marriage appeared to be the major factor.[9]

In the mid-1960s, many social scientists were increasingly sceptical of the likelihood that fertility would soon begin to fall or that family planning programmes would do much to promote such a decline. There were four primary reasons: first, demographic transition theory did not seem to predict an early fertility decline; second, research on the relationship between family structure and fertility suggested that lower fertility might be unique to the Western European family; third, research on the socio-economic thresholds of fertility decline raised the possibility that much of the Third World might be many years away from being prosperous enough to begin fertility transition; and, fourth, sociological analysis of the Western transition appeared to provide evidence that the availability of contraception might not be enough to induce couples to limit family size.

Demographic transition theory, as put forward by Thompson (1929), Notestein (1945), and Blacker (1947),[10] certainly argued that it was a two-part process, with mortality decline preceding and leading to the fertility decline. But Notestein had pointed out that the theorists had only one historical precedent for the model — the European decline — and that in Europe, the mortality decline began three centuries before the fertility decline. Given that the onset of mortality decline in South Asia appeared to date back no further than the nineteenth century and the decline in sub-Saharan Africa to the beginning of the twentieth century, the European parallel seemed to suggest that the Third World fertility decline might occur far off into the future.

There was, however, the possibility that the precedent was not how long fertility had been falling but how far it had fallen. In this case, the situation was more hopeful. We know that fertility began to fall in both England and Sweden when life expectancy at birth was around 45 years. By the late 1960s, India and Pakistan had passed that level and Indonesia had reached it. Life expectancies were higher still in East Asia and Latin America, while parts of East and Southern Africa were reaching 45 years.

It had long been believed that the European family system might be uniquely suited to encouraging fertility decline because of the cultural insistence that the newly married couple should live apart from other family members and should not receive financial support from their extended family. This was being suggested by Davis as early as 1955. It appeared to receive strong support when Hajnal published an analysis in 1965 arguing for the uniqueness of the Western European model, an analysis admittedly focusing on marriage but easily applicable to fertility. Sklar (1974),[11] again focusing on marriage, supported the view that Western Europe was different.

In 1965, the United Nations Population Division had published a major study, "Conditions and Trends of Fertility in the World," which examined the range of socio-economic thresholds at which fertility declines had begun. It seemed to offer little prospect that decline would soon begin in the larger and poorer countries of Asia and Africa.

In sum, studies of the Western fertility decline appeared to show that the onset of fertility decline had not been prompted by breakthroughs in contraceptive technology or retailing and that the methods employed in the first decades of decline had been available earlier. Notestein had long taught that fertility control was related to reaching certain socio-economic levels and had cited a study that he and Stix had carried out in the 1930s to show that *coitus interruptus* had always been known and had always been available when control proved to be necessary.[12]

But underneath all the specific arguments, the real reason for pessimism was the feeling that mortality had been declining steeply for twenty years and that family planning had been advocated and promoted for fifteen years without any substantial decline in Third World fertility. What was overlooked was how insufficient the resources had been in the attempts to control fertility. This situation was soon to change, however.

In the 1960s, the pill and the intrauterine device (IUD) had become available, and both were suited to mass programmes. Suction abortion had also been invented. Funding became available on a scale not previously experienced. The amounts voted by the United States Congress for USAID's population work climbed. In 1969, UNFPA began work, and by 1973 its budget had reached $52 million a year. The Fund's existence was particularly important because it included the developing countries in its membership, and in this sense the move to control fertility was theirs. In its first thirty years, its two directors came from developing countries in Asia. Nevertheless, at the time of its formation, there was no certainty of a major Third World fertility transition. That was about to change.

1969-1999: The Global Demographic Transition

The mortality transition

The mortality transition is on course, as Table 1 shows. There is no sign that food or resource scarcity or poverty are presenting barriers to mortality decline.

Table 1

The Mortality Transition, as measured by life expectancies at birth: early 1950s until late 1990s

Region	Life expectancy during specified periods (years)			Average annual increase (years)		Projected year when life expectancy of 75 years is attained[b]	1996 per capita income (US$)
	1950-55	1965-70	1995-2000	1950-55 to 1965-70	1965-70 to 1995-2000		
World	46.5	56.0	65.6	0.63	0.32	2031	5,180
More developed regions	66.5	70.5	74.5	0.27	0.13	2004	20,240
Less developed regions[a]	40.9	52.2	63.6	0.75	0.38	2042	
Less developed regions[a] excluding China	41.1	49.4	61.9	0.55	0.42	2049	
China	40.8	59.6	69.9	1.25	0.34	2026	750
Least developed regions[a]	35.5	41.8	52.0	0.42	0.42	2067	
Eastern Asia	42.9	60.5	71.0	1.17	0.35	2017	4,750
Southeast Asia	40.5	49.3	65.7	0.59	0.55	2031	1,580
South Central Asia	39.2	48.0	62.2	0.59	0.47	2048	410
Western Asia	45.2	54.9	68.0	0.65	0.44	2023	3,000
Northern Africa	41.8	48.8	64.6	0.47	0.53	2031	1,280
sub-Saharan Africa	36.7	42.6	51.5	0.39	0.30	2067	510
Latin America and Caribbean	51.4	58.9	69.6	0.50	0.36	2021	3,710

Notes:
[a]The United Nations classification "Least Developed Countries" includes most countries in sub-Saharan Africa (except Southern Africa, Kenya, Senegal, Gabon); and in Asia and the Pacific, Afghanistan, Bangladesh, Bhutan, Cambodia, Kiribati, Laos, Maldives, Myanmar, Nepal, Samoa, Solomon Islands, Tuvalu, Vanuatu, and Yemen.

[b]United Nations 1998a.

Sources: United Nations 1998a; Population Reference Bureau 1998.[13]

The average annual gains in life expectancy for the world as a whole have been much less in the last thirty years than in the preceding period. This is largely explained by the fact that these gains in the developed world have nearly reached a limit as longevity has become unprecedentedly great, and a similar phenomenon is beginning to take hold in Latin America and even Western Asia. The slowdown in China occurred partly because of an inability to continue the extraordinary gains made during the first two decades of the People's Republic and partly because the country has reached a level of longevity approximating that of Latin America. Elsewhere, the fall-off in mortality was modest. However, the continued decline in mortality is surprising because the first period of such decline encompassed much of the spread of medical technology and insecticides following the Second World War, and it had been widely expected that there would be a dramatic slowdown once achieving such gains depended mostly on rising standards of living. Gwatkin[14] claimed to have discovered this "end of an era" of mortality decline, and a number of papers presented in the 1981 IUSSP General Conference in Manila came to the same conclusion.[15]

This was later disproved in the case of India by a National Academy of Science study[16] and more widely by subsequent mortality statistics (summarized in Table 1). It now appears that most poor countries can indefinitely maintain gains in life expectancy of at least one-third of a year per elapsed year. WHO may have been premature in its Alma Ata Declaration in demanding "Good Health for All" by 2000. Nevertheless, the sanguine United Nations[17] population projections anticipate the world as a whole can obtain a stricter criterion of good health than that set out by Alma Ata within 50 years; namely, a mortality level equal to that now found in only the richest countries, with a life expectancy even in the least developed countries of 72 years at birth. Even South Central Asia can get there in a quarter of a century and sub-Saharan Africa in half a century, if current trends hold.

There remains a question as to how this could possibly happen. Kenya now has a life expectancy at birth of 49 years, a level reached by the United States and the United Kingdom in 1905, at which time their real per capita incomes were four times that now found in Kenya.[18] India, with a life expectancy of 59 years, compares with the levels of the United States in 1930 and the United Kingdom in 1928, when their real per capita incomes were 50 per cent higher. Sri Lanka now has a life expectancy of 72 years, three years behind the United States, but the latter has a nominal per capita income 36 times as great and even a purchasing-power-parity income 12 times as great.[19]

The explanation for the historical comparisons is partly that medical technology is now superior to that of the earlier decades of the century. But the contemporary comparison of Sri Lanka with the United States, and the continued steep rises in life expectancy even in regions like sub-Saharan Africa where economic growth has been slow, show that neither income nor medical science is the whole answer. Part of the explanation appears to be the globalization of the economy: health services are hard to deliver to subsistence peasants accessed only by walking tracks but are much easier to provide to persons living in towns or near passable roads who earn money and buy services. Another part of the explanation lies in the globalization of society: the spread of media messages and of a common education system based on a belief in science makes even those in the poorest countries more likely to collaborate with modern medicine and public health interventions in a way that makes such services more effective. The globalization of technical aid and of the services of international institutions helps keep new knowledge and services flowing.

This field of research has become known as "health transition."[20] The evidence that parental education, especially maternal education, drives down infant and child mortality is overwhelming.[21] There are huge differentials in child survival in relation to parental education in contemporary developing countries, but these differentials were much smaller in the United States at the end of the nineteenth century. This is evidence that it is not only the export of modern medicine to developing countries that brings down mortality but also the export of Western education, which teaches belief in and collaboration with modern medicine.[22] Increased education improves not only the children's chance of surviving but that of their mother as well.[23] Studies of such societies as Sri Lanka, Kerala, and Costa Rica have shown how these factors have resulted in the marked reduction of mortality.[24]

The expenditures on health that bring the greatest results are those that are spent on democratic, easily accessible, free or cheap, simple health services that reach into the furthest rural fastnesses and the poorest parts of the urban slums. The more educated the population, the greater is the impact. Mortality is brought down furthest and fastest when gender differences are least and when societies are most democratic and egalitarian. The impact of women's education may merely be one aspect of the effect of greater women's autonomy, but it is the easiest to measure and hence prove, and is almost certainly the easiest intervention available. Education also works because it enhances the two most fundamental mechanisms in health transition: the belief that the highest priority should be given to the prevention of death, and individuals' belief that they have a personal responsibility for achieving this.[25] In addition, the continued reduction of family size has made children both more precious and easier to care for, and has played an important part in reducing infant and child mortality and hence, total mortality.

Infant and child mortality decline has played a major role in the whole mortality decline. In Sweden, where we have the longest series of data for vital events, the mortality of every age group under 15 years of age fell by at least 94 per cent between 1780 and 1965, while the decline in age groups over 60 years was less than 60 per cent.[26] Table 2 shows just how persistent infant mortality declines have been, and they show little sign of tapering off.

Table 2

Infant Mortality Decline, early 1950s to late 1990s

Region	Infant mortality rate (deaths under one year of age per 1,000 births)			Average annual percentage decline during period	
	1950-55	1965-69	1995-2000	1950-55/ 1965-69	1965-69/ 1995-2000
World	156	102	57	2.3	1.5
More developed regions	59	26	9	3.7	2.2
Less developed regions	179	115	63	2.4	1.5
Least developed regions	194	155	101	1.3	1.2

Source: United Nations 1998a.[27]

Perhaps the most impressive gains have been made in the least developed countries where the rate of decline achieved in the years immediately after the Second World War has been maintained, and where the level of infant mortality is now at the level found in Western Europe and North America at the outbreak of the First World War (forty years after birth rates began to decline). The least predicted change has been the continued lead taken by the more developed countries in reducing infant mortality, with no lower bound yet apparent. Only a few decades ago demographers taught that the infant mortality rate was not likely to decline much below 20 per 1,000 births because of biological barriers, in that perhaps 2 per cent of babies were not physically developed to a point where they were suited to survive. Advances in medical technology have overcome such barriers, and the rate is now below 4 in Finland, Sweden, and Japan.

Trend data on maternal mortality are much less secure, and it is only in recent times that we have begun to obtain reasonably accurate figures for developing countries. Until recently, such rates were not estimated from demographic surveys, partly because very large surveys would be needed and partly because not only is the person most involved, the woman, dead by the time of the survey but her household, the basic survey unit, might well have dissolved by that time. In recent times, indirect methods (such as the "sisterhood method" where the answers are supplied by women about their deceased sisters) have been employed in countries that lack cause-of-death registration.

9

WHO (1991)[28] and, subsequently, WHO and the World Bank (1997)[29] employed these estimates to secure a global picture. The latter showed maternal mortality levels of over 5 per 1,000 births in almost all of tropical Africa, most of South Asia, considerable parts of Southeast Asia, and Haiti and Bolivia in the Americas. In almost half of the countries of tropical Africa and in the mountainous countries on the northern edge of South Asia (Afghanistan, Nepal, and Bhutan), the level was over 10 per 1,000 births (compared with under 0.03 in the more developed countries). Even though 10 per 1,000 births appears low, its impact on individual women over a succession of births, especially where fertility is high, is significant. Thus, WHO and the World Bank (1997)[30] calculated that a woman's lifetime risk of maternal mortality was 1 in 7 in Guinea, Sierra Leone, and Somalia, and 1 in 8 in Afghanistan and Yemen. This is over half the lifetime risk of dying of cancer in the most developed countries, a prospect that, however, haunts their citizens.

The study also made it clear that there was a strong association between the risk of dying in childbirth and the likelihood of having no trained person to assist with the birth. There is a doctor, nurse, or trained midwife present at only 2 per cent of Somalian births and 5 to 8 per cent of those in Equatorial Guinea, Eritrea, Ethiopia, Afghanistan, and Nepal, compared with 100 per cent in most developed countries. The only way of achieving low maternal and infant mortality appears to be securing such assistance, usually in an institution. Both infant and maternal mortality plummeted in Sri Lanka and Kerala when they moved to having all births in health institutions. Everywhere, illegal abortion accounts for at least 10 per cent of maternal deaths, but in Latin America, where abortion is the most legally restricted, that proportion rises to 20 per cent.

The least predicted mortality trend is one that has characterized the more developed world over the last thirty years. That trend is that mortality levels at older ages, long believed to be fairly stable, fell significantly during that period. The cause was partly the result of advances in medical technology, but changes in lifestyle also appeared to have played a role.

Global and regional mortality declines continued in spite of an unexpected resurgence of infectious disease in the form of HIV/AIDS. In 1997, there were 2.3 million AIDS deaths,[31] which raised global deaths from all causes by about 5 per cent to almost 53 million. But half these deaths occurred among 3 per cent of the world's population stretching down the main AIDS belt from Uganda to South Africa. In some of these countries, half of future lifetime deaths are likely to be caused by AIDS. In several, particularly Zimbabwe and Botswana, a combination of unusually high levels of HIV/AIDS, their relatively advanced fertility transitions, and the probability that HIV infection reduces fecundity may lead within a few years to stationary and even declining population.[32] The more general message of AIDS for the world as a whole is that the future path of mortality is not completely certain, for it is always possible that other equally deadly but more easily transmitted infections may emerge.

The fertility transition

Unlike mortality trends, fertility change displayed a striking contrast between the period up to 1965-1970 and the period thereafter. Table 3 shows that in the developing world, the fertility transition was almost entirely a post 1965-1970 phenomenon. It occurred while UNFPA was in existence, and doubtless UNFPA helped it happen and accelerated the change. Doubtless, also, the marked mortality decline during the earlier period was an instrument of the fertility decline that occurred later.

10

Table 3

The Fertility Transition, as measured by total fertility rates: early 1950s until late 1990s

Region	Total fertility rates during specified periods			Average annual percentage decline	
	1950-55	1965-70	1995-2000	1950-55 to 1965-70	1965-70 to 1995-2000
World	5.0	4.9	2.8	0.1	1.4
More developed regions	2.8	2.4	1.6	1.0	1.1
Less developed regions	6.2	6.0	3.1	0.2	1.6
Less developed regions excluding China	6.1	6.0	3.6	0.1	1.3
China	6.2	6.1	1.8	0.1	2.4
Least developed regions	6.5	6.7	5.3	(rise) 0.2	0.7
❑ Eastern Asia	5.7	5.5	1.8	0.2	2.2
❑ Southeast Asia	6.0	5.8	2.9	0.2	1.7
❑ South Central Asia	6.1	5.9	3.4	0.2	1.5
❑ Western Asia	6.4	5.9	3.8	0.5	1.2
❑ Northern Africa	6.8	6.9	3.7	(rise) 0.1	1.5
❑ Sub-Saharan Africa	6.6	6.7	5.8	(rise) 0.1	0.4
❑ Latin America and Caribbean	5.9	5.6	2.7	0.3	1.7

Source: United Nations 1998a.[33]

In Asia and Latin America, fertility fell slowly before 1965-1970, declining mostly in the 1960s and, with one exception, in the 0.1-0.2 per cent a year range. The cause was largely the rising age of female marriage. The exception is Western Asia, which is explained by the dominating size of Turkey's population and by its early fertility transition. In Africa, fertility probably rose slowly in the early years because modernization, especially education, had proceeded far enough to reduce the duration of lactation and postpartum abstinence without increasing economic pressures on families enough to lead to a significant level of fertility control.[34]

What is extraordinary was the uniformity across wide regions in the world in the pace of the fertility decline, once it occurred. In most areas, fertility declined at about 1.5 per cent per year. There were two exceptions. One was any grouping — Eastern Asia or the less developed countries — that included China, where the pace of the decline and the enormous size of its population raised the average rates of decline. The other was sub-Saharan Africa, where substantial fertility decline anywhere has waited until recent years.

It is now possible to generalize about the global fertility decline,[35] mainly because of two bodies of work: the project on the European fertility decline carried out by Princeton University's Office of Population Research,[36] and the work of the United Nations Population Division when producing population projections in the *World Population Prospects* series[37] in reconstituting demographic measures and trends from 1950. Explanation is facilitated by the construction of real income figures from 1820[38] and by other series such as the World Bank's *World Development Reports*.[39]

Fertility transition began in France in the late eighteenth century, more generally in Europe and English-speaking countries in the last third of the nineteenth century, and in Asia and Latin America in the mid- to late-1960s. The gap between the 1920s, when all Western declines were under way, and the 1960s, when declines began in all developing regions except sub-Saharan Africa, can only partly be explained by income levels, although it is possible to argue that socio-demographic determinants were solely responsible, if one considers only the levels of schooling, especially girls' schooling, and infant and child mortality.

It is, in fact, possible that these are the major determining forces. This is why Bongaarts and Watkins[40] found the *Human Development Index* (HDI, constructed solely from education, mortality, and income figures) to be such an accurate predictor of the onset of fertility decline. That analysis showed a long succession of onsets in Asia that contrasted with Latin American rates, whose declines began at the same time, a time when Latin American countries had higher HDI levels. The explanation is probably that the Asian declines were assisted by national family planning programmes that were adopted and became efficient at earlier dates. On the other hand, the Latin American declines were retarded because of the anti-contraceptive position of the Catholic Church, until that influence was overwhelmed by media discussion of fertility control and the availability of better contraceptives in the 1960s.

It is now possible to generalize the whole global fertility transition experience.[41] It is probable that the Western fertility transition in the nineteenth century was retarded by the opposition to contraception by moral authorities and the state, by the primitive contraceptives then available, and by problems of access to them.[42] This situation still partly persisted in Latin America in the 1950s and 1960s. But it contrasted with what developed in Asia over the last half-century.[43]

Increasingly, from the time when independent India announced in 1951 that it would institute a national family planning programme (the world's first), governments and international organizations have promoted fertility restriction as a virtue rather than a vice and have facilitated access to contraception. Some have argued that family planning programmes have added little more to the situation than making it somewhat easier, for those whose circumstances and felt needs have changed, to meet those needs by preventing further pregnancies.[44] This view may underestimate the extent to which the programmes have changed parents' assessments of their circumstances and needs. It also flies in the face of research findings that most Third World rural populations feel that their parents did not restrict fertility because there was no family planning programme and hence they did not have the knowledge or the means, and that they themselves could not restrict fertility were it not for the existence of the family planning programme.[45] Pritchett's[46] parallel with nineteenth-century Europe is probably irrelevant, because there, children became slowly more of an economic burden throughout the century so that there was time to learn how to control fertility.

The opposite view — namely, that fertility decline can be achieved by an efficient family planning programme even at low levels of socio-economic development and even during periods of little socio-economic change — has been argued, particularly in the case of Bangladesh, by a World Bank Report and a preceding popular summary of it.[47] It is doubtful whether this view is tenable. Bangladesh's fertility decline began at the date on the HDI trend line where Bongaarts and Watkins[48] would have predicted it. Furthermore, the way of life in Bangladesh has changed more over the last few decades than the report had assumed.[49]

The most potent force for global fertility change over the last 30 to 40 years has probably been the revolution in education. Table 4 shows how the proportion of developing countries' girls in primary school rose steeply in the third of a century between 1960 and 1993, trebling in the least developed countries to a point where nearly all girls have some schooling. Even steeper rises occurred in secondary education. Educated adult women expected to work outside the home and found this incompatible with having a large number of children. They were also prepared to be innovative and to adopt contraception. Parents of children who were being educated found the cost of supporting too many non-working dependants to be prohibitive. There has been a striking parallel in time between the dates when mass schooling became universal and when fertility began to decline: everywhere when 90 per cent of children were in primary school, although in Africa a better indicator seems to be the point at which 30 per cent of girls are in secondary school.

Table 4

Selected Education Levels (those in school as a percentage of age group) 1960, 1993

Region	Girls in primary school		Both sexes in secondary school	
	1960	1993	1960	1993
More developed region	112	103	64	98
Less developed region	68	101	14	83
Least developed region	34	98	18	54

Source: World Bank 1994, 1997.[50]

The spread of both education and contraception were part of the globalization of the world's economy and of society. It had long been clear that fertility control was not merely a reaction to economic development's reaching some threshold but also the result of diffusion of innovation. Apart from France, the onset of fertility transition (as measured by the Princeton European Fertility Project's benchmark; i.e., the date of a 10 per cent decline) began in Northwest Europe around 1880, reached Southern Europe about 1910, and Eastern Europe in the 1920s, starting at ever-lower real per capita incomes.[51] The same patterns emerge somewhat less clearly in each major contemporary developing world region, although, as Bongaarts and Watkins[52] showed, there is a clear relation with the HDI. These relations also roughly hold in a comparison of regions, although somewhat obscured by the near-simultaneity of so many onsets in the late 1960s and early 1970s. Culture and religion play some role: in ex-Soviet Central Asia, the higher the Muslim proportion of the population, the later fertility started to decline.

There has certainly been a single global fertility transition in spite of an 80-year gap in onsets between France and the rest of the West, and a 40-year gap between the last of the West (barring Muslim Albania) and the first Third World declines. What is important to note is that none of these changes was solely the effect of material forces. All were helped by human interpretation and intervention.[53] Nineteenth and early twentieth century legitimization of birth control was achieved by lone authors and organized family planning groups. Western technical aid for family planning in the last 40 years has depended on the fact that Western voters mostly have accepted the idea of contraception and practised it. International organizations, perhaps UNFPA foremost, have played an important role in the last 30 years in legitimizing family planning at both the government and the individual levels.

The rate at which fertility control spreads from country to country has not changed much. The rate at which fertility transition began displays an interquartile range (i.e., the period between when 25 per cent of countries were in a fertility transition and when 75 per cent were) of 13 years in Europe and much the same elsewhere. The exceptional transition was the explosive one in Latin America, where the interquartile range was 2.5 years in South America and 7.5 years in Central America. In contrast, the rate at which national transitions move was slower in Europe, where, excluding France, it took countries an average of 25 years for fertility to proceed from 90 to 60 per cent of their pre-transitional levels. In contemporary transitions, that fall has usually taken only about 12 years.

Until recently, the holdout against the global fertility transition was sub-Saharan Africa. The reasons were complex. In the late 1960s and the 1970s, when many Asian fertility transitions had begun, a range of African countries had per capita incomes and schooling levels comparable with much of Southeast and South Asia.[54] But there was less demand for fertility control at both the individual and government levels than in Asia, although national family planning programmes had been set up in some countries, with Kenya and Ghana moving first. The reasons for lack of demand at the individual level were associated with the emphasis placed by traditional religion on high fertility, communal land, child fostering and extended family responsibility for children and, at the government level, by the lack of a long tradition of governments or social elites giving national political and moral leadership. By the 1980s, the region was indisputably the world's poorest, and the argument that socio-economic thresholds had not been attained could also be put forward.[55]

By the early 1990s, however, data began to be available showing that the fertility transition in sub-Saharan Africa had begun. It became clear that South Africa, alone in the region, had built up from the 1960s a national family planning programme comparable in its provision of services to the most intensive programmes in Asia.[56] New survey data also appeared to show that fertility was falling in all of South Africa's ethnic groups, and (to allow an ethnic comparison with the rest of the region) that of Black South Africans had been declining since the 1960s, probably by one-third, to a total fertility rate of 4.6 in the late 1980s. The Demographic and Health Survey (DHS) programme revealed that fertility was also falling in Zimbabwe, Botswana, and Kenya, all of which now have total fertility rates below 5. These were all countries where fewer than 11 per cent of babies born failed to survive five years, where nearly all girls were in primary school and at least 30 per cent in secondary school, and where there were efficient and comprehensive national family planning programmes.

No other countries in sub-Saharan Africa had achieved all of these criteria. Yet the same domino effect seems to be taking place in Africa as Bongaarts and Watkins[57] had revealed in Asia. Fertility appears to be falling throughout Southern Africa and in Ghana, southern Nigeria, and Senegal in West Africa. Indeed, although regional fertility is still very high, Brass and colleagues[58] concluded from their analysis of the whole region "that a transition to regimes of lower fertility through family limitation became widespread over Africa south of the Sahara in the 1980s." A major influence seems to have been economic problems and, especially, structural adjustment programmes. Governments became more serious about controlling population growth as a possible solution to their problems, and international population efforts became more focused on the region once it was seen as the world's last fertility transition frontier. Many Africans, especially in the towns and among the middle classes, began to feel the strain of large families as financial support for children became more concentrated within the nuclear family and as the "user-pays" principle began to apply to schooling and health services.

The Way to the Future

The demographic situation in 1999 was dramatically different from what it was in 1969. Global fertility had fallen by 43 per cent in thirty years, three-quarters of the way to long-term replacement fertility level. The total fertility rate is now below 4 in every world region except sub-Saharan Africa, and even there it may have fallen by almost 10 per cent to just under 6. Nevertheless, the most recent United Nations[59] medium population projection suggests that the world's population will increase by at least another half, to 9.4 billion by 2050. Two-thirds of this increase is projected to occur in two regions, which together now contain considerably less than half the world's population: sub-Saharan Africa and South Asia.

I now wish to address several questions that, although focusing on the future, have their roots in recent events and trends. The first is the role and programme of the International Conference on Population and Development (ICPD) held in Cairo in September 1994. The second is mortality; the third, below-replacement fertility; the fourth, future global population growth; and the last, the future of family planning programmes and of UNFPA in a world focusing on below-replacement fertility and AIDS.

The core of the ICPD was the emphasis on giving more attention to increasing women's autonomy and improving their situation and, aligned with that, improving and widening family planning provision until it becomes one element of a full reproductive health service. Increasing women's autonomy and moving toward a society with minimal gender differences means a great deal more than increasing female educational levels, but to date that has been our main instrument, and a remarkably effective one. In developing countries, more educated women have a higher level of contraceptive use, lower fertility, lower mortality, and lower child mortality. Furthermore, in most regions women with higher education are more likely to work outside the home, and this also tends to increase autonomy. The move to improving the position of women has a justification in itself and went far beyond the reduction of fertility, but it will doubtless have that impact, too. Exhortation, as the women's movement has shown, is a powerful instrument for improving the status and situation of females, and the ICPD stance will certainly have an impact on governments, other international institutions, and people in general. Through such exhortation, especially that originating in the women's movement, female educational levels have been catching up with male levels in most regions.[60] The largest remaining gaps are in sub-Saharan Africa and South Asia, the two regions where population growth will be greatest.

ICPD's move towards more comprehensive and higher-quality reproductive health services also has aims far beyond the containment of population growth and fits in well with the enhancement of the position of women. It was timely in the sense that family planning was by 1994 so widely practised in poor countries that greater efforts had to be made to raise standards. Some governments also had to be persuaded not to exert pressure to attain lower fertility and others to offer women a greater choice of methods. In the longer run, these changes will almost certainly help reduce fertility levels. In the immediate future, the effort to attain best practices in poor countries with vestigial health services may prove impossible and even confusing. Like all revolutions, the struggle to justify the new aims had to proceed by drawing a contrast with a darker past, which often did not do full justice to past pioneering efforts and even to UNFPA's support of these efforts.

The mortality transition will undoubtedly be aided both by increasing levels of education and by declining family size. Nevertheless, it faces challenges. The greatest is specific to one region, sub-Saharan Africa. Table 1 shows that it has had the slowest rate of mortality decline in the last thirty years. In many countries, that rate has almost certainly slowed further, especially in terms of infants and children, because troubled economies and resulting economic structural adjustment policies have brought "user-pays" principles to populations who often cannot afford

15

to pay. This is aggravated by the cultural practice in West Africa in which spouses have individual budgets, with the result that women and children are particularly likely to lack the funds to pay for services. The need for efficient and affordable services will almost certainly have to extend beyond reproductive health services to all health services. In East and Southern Africa, the whole situation is now exacerbated by the AIDS epidemic. In some countries, both overall mortality and infant and child mortality are already rising, and population growth is declining in a wholly undesirable way. Neither national governments nor international organizations have shown themselves capable of dealing adequately with the different issues of behavioural change needed to combat the epidemic.

Everywhere the reduction of maternal and infant mortality to low levels will depend on the expertise and resources available around the time of the birth and for as long thereafter as there are problems. Antenatal check-ups, while being of undoubted value, have proved less helpful than we had hoped in predicting trouble at the birth. Trained midwives are better than untrained ones, but since they are often young and alone in rural areas, they can easily face insuperable difficulties. Rapid transport in emergencies from rural areas to district hospitals does not seem to work. The Sri Lankan and Keralan experiences suggest that the best solution is to have all births in institutions, even the simple cottage hospitals of fifty years ago, as long as there is a trained doctor and senior nurses with obstetric experience on hand.

Finally, there is the problem associated with declining mortality identified by Murray and Lopez;[61] namely that, as the conquest of infectious disease proceeds and most people live to old age, then further gains, mostly against degenerative disease, will necessitate a different medical structure, far less dependant on public health measures. It might be noted that Sri Lanka has successfully passed to this stage with a pyramidal system whereby health centres (once cottage hospitals) and private medical practitioners refer patients to provincial hospitals and, if necessary, to specialist hospitals in Colombo.

Perhaps the most surprising aspect of the demographic history of the last thirty years has been its demonstration that the demographic transition does not necessarily stop at replacement-level fertility. A related point that is not often made is that the reaction in the late 1960s and early 1970s to the debate on fertility control, to better contraception, to increased educational levels, and to the march of married women into the workplace was not very different in the developed and developing worlds. Developed countries that had experienced the "baby boom" emerged from it with rising female marriage ages and consequent falling fertility.[62] But soon it became clear that marital and cohort fertility were also both declining. The steepest quinquennial falls, in the range of 19 to 29 per cent, occurred in the United States, the United Kingdom, and Germany around 1970 (i.e., 1965-1970 to 1970-1975); and, in the range of 9 to 21 per cent, in Sweden, France, Italy, Spain, Australia, New Zealand, and Japan in the mid-1970s.

Patterns were different in Eastern Europe, where the legalization of abortion brought fertility down steeply in the late 1950s, and in Canada, where the convergence of Québécois fertility with the rest of Canada resulted in a steep fertility decline in the early 1960s. Japan's fertility rate fell below long-term replacement level in the late 1950s, and Sweden's did so in the late 1960s. Fertility fell below replacement in the early 1970s in the United States, United Kingdom, and Germany; in the mid-1970s in France and Italy; in the late 1970s in Australia and New Zealand; and in the early 1980s in Spain. At present, the total fertility rate in Spain and Italy is 1.2, in Greece 1.3, and in the whole of Southern Europe 1.3. In Germany, the total fertility rate is 1.3, in Austria 1.4, and in all Western Europe 1.5. In Eastern Europe it is 1.3 and in Northern Europe 1.7. Population decline did not begin immediately, because there was still a disproportionate number of women of reproductive age, but now an actual numerical decline is occurring in Germany and much of Eastern Europe. Fertility is below long-term replacement in all of East Asia except Mongolia; in Thailand and Singapore in Southeast Asia; and in Australasia, North America and some Caribbean countries. Around 44 per cent of the world's population now live in countries with below long-term replacement fertility.

This is significant because it provides a foretaste of the way the whole world may go. Per capita income seems to be of little importance in determining the likelihood of below-replacement fertility. The major force appears to be the level of education of girls. Lengthy education itself carried an implication of subsequent female employment even when married, and the women's movement has powerfully reinforced that message. In most societies, full-time working mothers find that they have too little support from either state child-minding services or their husbands to be able to bear and raise more than one child without a great deal of stress. This reason has been advanced to explain lower fertility in Southern than Northern Europe.[63] Given that most countries will be giving at least full secondary schooling to nearly all girls by the middle of the next century and that the Southern European family and gender pattern is typical of far more of the world than is that of Northern Europe, below-replacement fertility is likely to spread to most of the world, with a real possibility that global numbers will be declining by the end of the twenty-first century.

In spite of this probability, the fact remains that the largest numerical increments ever added to the world's population are being added at the present time. According to the United Nations[64] medium projection, the world will add another 3.3 billion people to its numbers by 2050, almost as many people as the whole world contained when steps towards founding UNFPA began in 1967. Fertility transition has barely begun in sub-Saharan Africa and has probably not begun at all in a majority of its countries. Furthermore, we are only just beginning to find our way towards family planning programmes that will meet the region's needs. There is an understandable tendency to copy the Asian model.[65] Yet West African experience suggests that the demand for contraceptive access by single women and men of any marital status may make clinics and programmes established primarily for married women less than fully effective.[66] South African experience suggests that there is a need to make injectables universally available and that sterilization and IUDs may play a much smaller role than they did in the Asian fertility decline.

The international population agenda

There is going to be an urgent need for a well-defined and adequately funded international agenda in the population field. Hopefully, UNFPA will play a central role. It is an agenda that will be more complex and difficult to sell to donors than in the past.

Perhaps the major challenge will be to convince the world that, even if the end of the world's multiplication of numbers is in sight, there are still enormous challenges in the field of fertility control. The South Asian fertility decline may yet stall, and that in sub-Saharan Africa needs huge inputs of funds, experience, and ideas. This will have to be done while also showing an interest in and developing a research agenda for the low-fertility areas of the world. No one should underestimate the demand likely to come from countries with declining populations for the analysis of trends and policies.

The other challenge for the agenda will be to focus more attention on areas with continuing high fertility. This will become increasingly one of understanding the African situation and of transplanting successful approaches from one part of the region to other parts.

There will still be the need to implement the ICPD Programme of Action. The truth of its central proposition — that fertility will fall if we can move toward greater female autonomy, extended education, an expansion of women's rights, and access of all adult women to the labour market — is shown by the very low fertility of the developed world. The achievement of low fertility was completely in accord with the ICPD formula.

The move towards high levels of reproductive health services is both necessary and difficult. In many areas of the world it will almost certainly necessitate a more general improvement and extension of the health services, actions which donors may not regard as falling under the population mandate. It is still not clear what existing family planning programmes should do when working with populations lying beyond the frontiers of the general health services. This chapter has suggested that the only way of moving to satisfactory low levels of maternal and infant mortality is to have nearly all births within institutional facilities with easy access to doctors. This will also be difficult to achieve without a broad extension of the health services. The challenges are especially great in sub-Saharan Africa, where economic changes and new economic policies are discriminating against the poor. Yet the achievement of ICPD's reproductive health goals will not only be a victory for equity and human rights but will probably achieve faster fertility decline.

Finally, there are all kinds of specific or regional agendas. In many parts of the Third World, the improvements in health are now least in the cities, especially among the poor.[67] Once again, the cities, as in the industrializing nineteenth-century West, are becoming "eaters of men." There must be urban equivalents to WHO's Alma Ata Declaration, which focused mostly on rural population. Indeed, with the move towards an urban world, one where over 60 per cent of the population will be in urban areas within 30 years,[68] there will be a need for a more urban focus in many research and policy areas.

More work will be needed on changing sexual behaviour in regions with high levels of AIDS, an area the international agencies have been slow to enter. Far more effort will be needed to reconcile the AIDS epidemic with the need for fertility decline and probably in moving towards joint AIDS-family planning programmes. Finally, the achievement of overall reproductive health goals for the world will require stronger action in combating female circumcision.

Global population numbers will probably not reach the extremes that have until recently been regarded as inevitable. This is a tribute to the work of UNFPA and others. This new reality must be recognized and incorporated into thinking and planning. In spite of this, and partly because of it, the population agenda is shifting, not shrinking. It is important that funding should recognize this.

References

[1] John C. Caldwell, Pat Caldwell, "Regional Paths to Fertility Transition," *Population and Development Review*, Supplement on Global Fertility Transition (1999); Ansley J. Coale, Susan Cotts Watkins, *The Decline in Fertility in Europe* (Princeton: Princeton University Press, 1986); United Nations, *World Population Prospects: The 1994 Revision* (New York, 1995); United Nations, *World Population Prospects: The 1996 Revision* (New York, 1998a).

[2] David R. Weir, "New Estimates of Nuptiality and Marital Fertility in France," 1740-1911, *Population Studies*, 48 (2) (1994): pp. 307-331.

[3] John C. Caldwell, Pat Caldwell, *Limiting Population Growth and The Ford Foundation Contribution* (London: Frances Pinter, 1986); John C. Caldwell, "The Asian Fertility Revolution: Its Implications for Transition Theories," *The Revolution in Asian Fertility: Dimensions, Causes and Implications* (eds.), R. Leete, I. Alam (Oxford: Clarendon Press, 1993): pp. 299-316.

[4] John C. Caldwell, "The delayed Western fertility decline: an examination of English-speaking countries." Unpublished manuscript, 1999.

[5] Bernard Berelson, *et. al.* (eds.), *Family Planning and Population Programs: A Review of World Developments* (Chicago: University of Chicago Press, 1965).

[6] John C. Caldwell, "The Containment of World Population Growth," *Studies in Family Planning*, 6 (12) (1975): pp. 429-436.

[7] John C. Caldwell, "Population Forecasts and Trends in Malaysia," S*ydney Conference, Australia, 21-25 August 1967: Contributed Papers* (Canberra: Australian Government Printer, 1967): pp. 14-25 in IUSSP; P.K.C. Liu, "Differential Fertility in Taiwan," *Sydney Conference, Australia, 21-25 August 1967: Contributed Papers* (Canberra: Australian Government Printer, 1967): pp. 363-370 in IUSSP; M.V. Raman, "Levels and Trends of Fertility and Associated Factors in ECAFE Countries," S*ydney Conference, Australia, 21-25 August 1967: Contributed Papers* (Canberra: Australian Government Printer, 1967): pp. 277-286 in IUSSP.

[8] John C. Caldwell, Pat Caldwell, *Limiting Population Growth and the Ford Foundation Contribution* (London: Frances Pinter, 1986): pp. 79-80.

[9] S. Vamathevan, "Some Aspects of Recent Fertility Changes in Relation to Ceylon," *International Population Conference, London 1969: Proceedings* (Liège: IUSSP, 1971): pp. 405-418.

[10] Warren C. Thompson, Population. *American Journal of Sociology*, 34 (1929): pp. 959-975; Frank W. Notestein, "Population: The Long View," *Food for the World*, ed. T.W. Schultz (Chicago: University of Chicago Press, 1945): pp. 36-57; C.P. Blacker, "Stages in Population Growth," *Eugenics Review*, 39 (1947): pp. 88-101.

[11] Judith L. Sklar, "The Role of Marriage Behaviour in Demographic Transition: The Case of Eastern Europe around 1900," *Population Studies*, 28 (2) (1974): pp. 231-247.

[12] Regina Stix, Frank Notestein, "Effectiveness of Birth Control," *Milbank Memorial Fund Quarterly*, 12 (1) (1934): pp. 57-68.

[13] United Nations, *World Population Data Sheet 1998* (Washington, D.C.: Population Reference Bureau, 1998).

[14] Davidson R. Gwatkin, "Indications of Change in Developing Country Mortality Trends: The End of an Era?" *Population and Development Review*, 6 (4) (1980): pp. 615-644.

19

[15] M.N.A. Azefor, "Counteracting Forces in the Continuing Decline of Mortality in Africa," *International Population Conference, Manila, 1981: Solicited Papers*, Vol. 2 (Liège: IUSSP, 1981): pp. 5-20; Eduardo E. Arriaga, "The Deceleration of the Decline in Mortality in LDCs: The Case of Latin America," *International Population Conference, Manila, 1981: Solicited Papers*, Vol. 2 (Liège: IUSSP, 1981): pp. 21-50; Mathada Sivamurthy, "The Deceleration of Mortality Decline in Asian Countries," *International Population Conference, Manila, 1981: Solicited Papers*, Vol. 2 (Liège: IUSSP, 1981): pp. 51-77; Patrick Ohadike, "The Deceleration of the Decline of Mortality in LDCs," *International Population Conference, Manila, 1981: Proceedings and Selected Papers* (Liège: IUSSP, 1983): pp. 143-147.

[16] P.N. Mari Bhat, *et. al.*, "Vital Rates in India, 1961-1981," *Committee on Population and Demography*, Report No. 24 (Washington, D.C.: National Academy Press, 1984).

[17] United Nations, *World Population Prospects: The 1996 Revision* (New York, 1998a).

[18] N. Keyfitz, W. Flieger, *World Population, an Analysis of Vital Data* (Chicago: University of Chicago Press, 1968); Angus Madison, *Monitoring the World Economy 1820-1992* (Paris: Organisation for Economic Cooperation and Development, 1995).

[19] World Bank, *World Development Report: Knowledge for Development 1998/1999* (New York: Oxford University Press, 1999).

[20] John C. Caldwell, Gigi Santow (eds.), *Selected Readings in the Cultural, Social and Behavioural Determinants of Health* (Canberra: Australian National University, 1989); John C. Caldwell, *et. al.* (eds.), *What We Know about Health Transition: The Cultural, Social and Behavioural Determinants of Health* (Canberra: Australian National University, 1990).

[21] John C. Caldwell, "Education as a Factor in Mortality Decline: An Examination of Nigerian Data," *Population Studies*, 33 (3) (1979): pp. 395-413; J. Cleland, J. van Ginneken, "Maternal Education and Child Survival in Developing Countries: The Search for Pathways of Influence," *Social Science and Medicine*, 27 (12) (1988): pp. 1357-68; John Cleland, "Maternal Education and Child Survival: Further Evidence and Explanations," *What We Know about Health Transition: The Cultural, Social and Behavioural Determinants of Health* ed. John C. Caldwell, *et. al.* (Canberra: Australian National University, 1990): pp. 400-419.

[22] S. H. Preston, M. R. Haines, "Fatal Years: Child Mortality in Late Nineteenth-Century America" (Princeton: Princeton University Press, 1991); John C. Caldwell, "Major New Evidence on Health and Its Interpretation," *Health Transition Review*, 1 (2) (1991): pp. 221-229.

[23] Linda Duffy, Jane Menken, "Health, Fertility, and Socioeconomic Status as Predictors of Survival and Later Health of Women: A 20-Year Prospective Study in Rural Bangladesh." Unpublished manuscript, 1999.

[24] John C. Caldwell, "Routes to Low Mortality in Poor Countries," *Population and Development Review*, 12 (2) (1986): pp. 171-220.

[25] J. Simons, "Cultural Dimensions of the Mother's Contribution to Child Survival," *Selected Readings in the Cultural, Social and Behavioural Determinants of Health*, eds. J. Caldwell, G. Santow (Canberra: Australian National University, 1989): pp. 132-145.

[26] Pat Caldwell, "Child Survival: Physical Vulnerability and Resilience in Adversity in the European Past and the Contemporary Third World," *Social Science and Medicine*, 43 (5) (1996): pp. 609-619.

[27] United Nations, *World Population Prospects: The 1996 Revision* (New York, 1998a).

[28] World Health Organization, *Maternal Mortality: A Global Factbook* (Geneva: WHO, 1991).

[29] World Health Organization, World Bank, *Maternal Health Around the World*, Chart (Geneva, 1997).

[30] Ibid.

[31] Joint United Nations Programme on HIV/AIDS, World Health Organization, *Report on the Global HIV/AIDS Epidemic* (Geneva: UNAIDS, WHO, 1998).

[32] K. Awusabo-Asare, *et. al.* (eds.), "Evidence of the Socio-demographic Impact of AIDS in Africa," *Health Transition Review*, Supplement 2, 7 (Canberra: Australian National University, 1997).

[33] United Nations, *World Population Prospects: The 1996 Revision* (New York, 1998a).

[34] Anatole Romaniuk, "An Increase in Natural Fertility During the Early Stages of Modernization," *Population Studies*, 34 (2) (1980): pp. 293-310.

[35] John C. Caldwell, Pat Caldwell, "Regional Paths to Fertility Transition," *Population and Development Review*, Supplement on Global Fertility Transition (1999).

[36] Ansley J. Coale, Susan Cotts Watkins, *The Decline in Fertility in Europe* (Princeton: Princeton University Press, 1986).

[37] United Nations, *World Population Prospects: The 1994 Revision* (New York, 1995); United Nations, *World Population Prospects: The 1996 Revision* (New York, 1998a).

[38] Angus Maddison, *Monitoring the World Economy 1820-1992* (Paris: Organisation for Economic Cooperation and Development, 1995).

[39] World Bank, *World Development Report 1997: The State in a Changing World* (New York: Oxford University Press, 1997); World Bank, *World Development Report: Knowledge for Development 1998/1999* (New York: Oxford University Press, 1999).

[40] John Bongaarts, Susan Cotts Watkins, "Social Interactions and Contemporary Fertility Transitions," *Population and Development Review*, 22 (4) (1996): pp. 639-682.

[41] John C. Caldwell, Pat Caldwell, "Regional Paths to Fertility Transition," *Population and Development Review*, Supplement on Global Fertility Transition (1999).

[42] John C. Caldwell, The Delayed Western Fertility Decline: An Examination of English-speaking Countries. Unpublished manuscript, 1999.

[43] Richard Leete, Iqbal Alam (eds.), *The Revolution in Asian Fertility: Dimensions, Causes and Implications* (Oxford: Clarendon Press, 1993).

[44] Lant H. Pritchett, "Desired Fertility and the Impact of Population Policies," *Population and Development Review*, 20 (1) (1994): pp. 1-55.

[45] John C. Caldwell, Pat Caldwell, "The Family Planning Programmes at the Local Level: A Study of a Village Area in South India," *Demographic Transition in Asia* (ed.), G.W. Jones (Singapore: Maruzen Asia, 1984): pp. 111-124; John C. Caldwell, *et. al.*, "The Bangladesh Fertility Decline: An Interpretation," *Population and Development Review*, 25 (1) (1999): pp. 1-18.

[46] Lant H. Pritchett, "Desired Fertility and the Impact of Population Policies," *Population and Development Review*, 20 (1) (1994): p. 27.

[47] Winthrop P. Carty, Nancy V. Yinger, Alicia Rosov, *Success in a Challenging Environment: Fertility Decline in Bangladesh* (Washington, D.C.: Population Reference Bureau, 1993); John Cleland, *et. al.*, *Reproductive Change in Bangladesh: Success in a Challenging Environment* (Washington, D.C: World Bank, 1994).

[48] John Bongaarts, Susan Cotts Watkins, "Social Interactions and Contemporary Fertility Transitions," *Population and Development Review*, 22 (4) (1996): pp. 639-682.

[49] John C. Caldwell, *et. al.*, "The Bangladesh Fertility Decline: An Interpretation," *Population and Development Review*, 25 (1) (1999): pp. 1-18.

[50] World Bank, *World Development Report 1994* (New York: Oxford University Press, 1994); World Bank, *World Development Report 1997: The State in a Changing World* (New York: Oxford University Press, 1997).

[51] John C. Caldwell, Pat Caldwell, "Regional Paths to Fertility Transition," *Population and Development Review*, Supplement on Global Fertility Transition (1999).

[52] John Bongaarts, Susan Cotts Watkins, "Social Interactions and Contemporary Fertility Transitions," *Population and Development Review*, 22 (4) (1996): pp. 639-682.

[53] John C. Caldwell, "The Global Fertility Transition: The Need for Unifying Theory," *Population and Development Review*, 23 (4) (1997): pp. 803-812.

[54] John C. Caldwell, Pat Caldwell, "Is the Asian Family Planning Program Model Suited to Africa? A Comparison of Asia and Sub-Saharan Africa," *Studies in Family Planning*, 19 (1) (1988): pp. 19-28.

[55] World Bank, *Population Growth and Policies in sub-Saharan Africa* (Washington, D.C.: World Bank, 1986).

[56] John C. Caldwell, Pat Caldwell, "The South African Fertility Decline," *Population and Development Review*, 19 (2) (1993): pp. 225-262.

[57] John Bongaarts, Susan Cotts Watkins, "Social Interactions and Contemporary Fertility Transitions," *Population and Development Review*, 22 (4) (1996): pp. 639-682.

[58] William Brass, Fatima Juarez, Anne Scott, "An Analysis of Parity-Dependent Fertility Falls in Tropical Africa," *The Continuing Demographic Transition,* ed. G. W. Jones *et. al.* (Oxford: Clarendon Press, 1997): pp. 80-93.

[59] United Nations, *World Population Prospects: The 1996 Revision* (New York, 1998a).

[60] John Knodel, Gavin W. Jones, "Does Promoting Girls' Schooling Miss the Mark?" *Population and Development Review*, 22 (4) (1996): pp. 683-702.

[61] Christopher J.L. Murray, Alan D. Lopez, eds., *The Global Burden of Disease*, Vol. 1 (Boston: Harvard School of Public Health, 1996).

[62] J. Bongaarts, G. Feeney, "On the Quantum and Tempo of Fertility," *Population and Development Review*, 24 (2) (1998): pp. 271-291.

[63] M.D. Perez, M. Livi-Bacci, "Fertility in Italy and Spain: The Lowest in the World," *Family Planning Perspectives*, 24 (4) (1992): pp. 162-171; Jean-Claude Chesnais, "Fertility, Family, and Social Policy in Contemporary Western Europe," *Population and Development Review*, 22 (4) (1996): pp. 729-739; P. McDonald, "Gender Equity, Social Institutions and the Future of Fertility," *Working Papers in Demography*, No. 69 (Canberra: Demography Program, Australian National University, 1997).

[64] United Nations, *World Population Prospects: The 1996 Revision* (New York, 1998a).

[65] National Academy of Science, *Factors Affecting Contraceptive Use in Sub-Saharan Africa* (Washington, D.C: National Academy Press, 1993): pp. 128-169.

[66] John C. Caldwell, I.O. Orubuloye, Pat Caldwell, "Fertility Decline in Africa: A New Type of Transition?" *Population and Development Review*, 18 (2) (1992): pp. 211-242.

[67] Martin Brockerhoff, Ellen Brennan, "The Poverty of Cities in Developing Regions," *Population and Development Review*, 24 (1) (1998): pp. 75-114.

[68] United Nations, *World Urbanization Prospects: The 1996 Revision* (New York, 1998b).

Implementing the Reproductive Health Approach

Mahmoud F. Fathalla

The Commitment

> *"All countries should strive to make accessible through the primary health-care system, reproductive health to all individuals of appropriate ages as soon as possible and no later than the year 2015."*

Programme of Action of the United Nations
International Conference on Population and
Development, Cairo, 1994.[1]

The solemn commitment that was made in Cairo in 1994 to make reproductive health care universally available was a culmination of efforts made by the United Nations Population Fund (UNFPA) and all those concerned about a people-centred and human rights approach to population issues. The commitment posed important challenges to national governments and the international community, to policymakers, programme planners and service providers, and to the civil society at large. The role of UNFPA in building up the consensus for the reproductive health approach before Cairo had to continue after Cairo if the goals of the International Conference on Population and Development (ICPD) were to be achieved. UNFPA continues to be needed to strengthen the commitment, maintain the momentum, mobilize the required resources, and help national governments and the international community move from word to action, and from rhetoric to reality. Reproductive health, including family planning and sexual health, is now one of three major programme areas for UNFPA. During 1997, reproductive health accounted for over 60 per cent of total programme allocations by the Fund.[2]

What Reproductive Health Is About

Women are ends and not means

The basic premise of the reproductive health approach is that reproductive health needs should be met within the premise that women are ends and not means.[3]

In spite of all the benefits to the quality of life of women that they have brought, family planning programmes have left women with some genuine concerns as well as unmet needs. Women have more at stake in fertility control than anyone else. Contraceptives are meant to be used by women to empower themselves by maximizing their choices, allowing them to control their fertility, their sexuality, their health, and, thus, their lives. Family planning, however, can be and has been used by governments and others to control rather than to empower women. The family planning movement in the past has been largely demographically driven. As far as policymakers were concerned, women were often objects and not subjects. Some governments were short-sighted not to see that when women are given a real choice, and the information and the means to implement their choice, they will make the most rational decision for themselves, for their communities, and, ultimately, for the world at large.[4]

In the maternal and child health (MCH) approach that used to serve as a model, the needs of the woman were subordinated to the needs of the mother. MCH programmes and services have played and continue to play an important role in the promotion of health, and the preventive and curative health care of mothers and children. MCH services tend to focus on the healthy child as the successful outcome. Mothers obviously care very much for this successful outcome. However, this focus had the result of giving less emphasis on caring for the health risks for mothers during pregnancy and childbirth or on providing the essential obstetric care to deal with them. The concept of MCH focuses special attention on women when and if they are reproducing, to ensure that society gets a healthy child, but thereby often neglects their other reproduction-related health needs.

With women as means and not ends, important health needs in the reproductive process have been left unmet. Infertility, for example, may not be a serious hazard as far as physical health is concerned, but it can be a major cause of mental and social ill health. It is not fair that society should provide care to reproducing women but should neglect the suffering of those who are unable to conceive. Sexual intercourse exposes women to the risk of unwanted pregnancy. It exposes many women also to another serious risk; i.e., that of sexually transmitted infections, including HIV infection. Family planning programmes, with an exclusive demographic focus, did not always see the point of meeting these important needs of women.

The societal attitude of looking at women as means and not ends is even more pervasive. Services offered to women often have something of a veterinary quality about them. Proponents of the education of girls cite the advantages that such education will have for the survival and health of the children and the impact it will have on reducing birth rates. Nutrition of women is justified because of the needs of the foetus and the breastfeeding infant. Even in considerations of the tragedy of maternal mortality, a justification put forward for investment in keeping mothers alive is that their survival is critical for the survival of the children.

The concept of reproductive health puts women back at the centre of the process, as subjects and not objects, and as ends and not means. It recognizes, respects, and responds to the need of the woman behind the mother. The reproductive health concept is not limited to mothers. Nor is it limited to women of childbearing age. It recognizes that adolescents have special health needs, because they acquire the sexual and reproductive capacity before they have completed their social preparation for adult life. It recognizes that mature women, those beyond the childbearing period, still have important health needs related to the reproductive system and to the cessation of ovarian function. The concept also recognizes that the health of the adult builds on the health of the child and that this is nowhere truer than in the area of reproductive health. Finally, the concept of reproductive health is not limited to women. Men, too, have reproductive health needs, and responding to those needs is also important for the well-being of women.

The great transition in Cairo — from "counting the people" to "the people count"

At the ICPD, held in Cairo in 1994, a great transition was made.[5] Representatives of 180 countries reached a new consensus that responding to the needs of individuals is the way to address the aggregate problem of rapid population growth. Population policies should address social development beyond family planning, with particular emphasis on advancing the status and empowerment of women, and family planning should be provided in the context of reproductive health care. In the reproductive health approach, population is about people, not about numbers. Curbing rapid rates of population growth is not an objective in itself. It is a means to the objective of improving the lives and dignity of people, in present and future generations.

The Cairo ICPD should not be looked upon as an event. It is a process that has started long before Cairo and one that has gathered enough momentum to continue long after Cairo. The reproductive health concept was not invented in Cairo: it was adopted there by the consensus of the nations of the world, and an explicit commitment was made to implement it.

Reproductive health — a definition

Six years before the ICPD, the World Health Organization (WHO) constitution defined[6] health as a state of complete physical, mental, and social well-being, and not merely the absence of disease or infirmity. In the context of this positive definition, reproductive health is a condition in which the reproductive process is accomplished in a state of complete physical, mental, and social well-being, and is not merely the absence of disease or disorders of the reproductive process. "Reproductive health" implies that, apart from the absence of disease or infirmity, people ought to have the ability to reproduce, to regulate their fertility, and to practise and enjoy sexual relationships. It further implies that reproduction is carried to a successful outcome through infant and child survival, growth, and healthy development. And, finally, it means that women can go safely through pregnancy and childbirth, that fertility regulation can be achieved without health hazards, and that people are safe in having sex.

Building on the WHO definition of health, the ICPD Programme of Action explains that reproductive health is

> a state of complete physical, mental and social well-being and is not merely the absence of disease or infirmity, in all matters relating to the reproductive system and to its functions and processes. Reproductive health therefore implies that people are able to have a satisfying and safe sex life and that they have the capability to reproduce and the freedom to decide if, when and how often to do so. Implicit in this last condition are the right of men and women to be informed and to have access to safe, effective, affordable and acceptable methods of family planning of their choice, as well as other methods of their choice for regulation of fertility which are not against the law, and the right of access to appropriate health-care services that will enable women to go safely through pregnancy and childbirth and provide couples with the best chance of having a healthy infant.[7]

26

Family planning — an integral component of the reproductive health package

Fertility by choice, not by chance, is a basic requirement for women's reproductive health.[8] A woman who does not have the means or the power to regulate and control her fertility cannot be considered to be in a "state of complete physical, mental and social well-being." She cannot have the joy of a pregnancy that is wanted, avoid the distress of a pregnancy that is unwanted, plan her life, pursue her education, undertake a productive career, or plan her births to take place at optimal times for childbearing, ensuring more safety for herself and better chances for her child's survival and healthy growth and development. A woman with an unwanted pregnancy cannot be considered in good health even if the pregnancy is not going to kill her or impair her physical health and even if she delivers the unwanted child alive and with no physical disability.

Fertility regulation is also a major element in any safe-motherhood strategy.[9] It reduces the number of unwanted pregnancies, with a resulting decrease in the total exposure to the risks that pregnancy poses, as well as a decrease in the number of unsafe abortions. Proper planning of births can also decrease the number of high-risk pregnancies.

Family planning improves the quality of life not only for women but also for the family as a whole, and particularly for children. The quality of child care — including play and stimulation as well as health and education — inevitably rises as parents are able to invest more of their time, energy, and money in bringing up a smaller number of children.

In the reproductive health approach, family planning is a basic component of reproductive health care, and family planning services are not "demographic posts." Women are not "targets" for contraception, for which policymakers and administrators set "quotas" for services to accomplish. As the ICPD Programme of Action states, "family planning programmes work best when they are part of or linked to broader reproductive health programmes that address closely related health needs."[10]

Reproductive health and women

Being a woman has implications for one's health. The health needs of women can be broadly classified under four categories.[11] First, women have specific health needs related to the sexual and reproductive function. Second, women have an elaborate reproductive system that is vulnerable to dysfunction or disease even before it has begun functioning and after it no longer functions. Third, women are subject to the same diseases of other body systems that can affect men. The disease patterns, however, often differ from those of men because of genetic constitution, hormonal environment, or gender-evolved lifestyle behaviour. Diseases of other body systems or their treatments may interact with conditions of the reproductive system or function. Fourth, because women are women, they are subject to social diseases, which can impact on their physical, mental, and social health. Examples include female genital cutting, sexual abuse, and domestic violence.

There is more to women's health than reproductive health, and there is more to reproductive health than women's health. Men have reproductive health needs, too.

27

The unfair burden on women in reproductive health

Maternity is a unique privilege and a unique health burden for women. In some other aspects of reproductive health, where the responsibility is shared between men and women, the burden, for both biological and social reasons, falls heavily on women — such as the burden of sexually transmitted diseases (STDs), fertility regulation, and infertility.

According to a World Bank study quantifying the burden of disease, STDs rank as the second major cause of the disease burden in young adult women in developing countries, accounting for 8.9 per cent of the total disease burden in that age group.[12] Among males of the same age group, STDs are not among the first ten causes and account only for 1.5 per cent of the disease burden. For a mix of biological and social reasons, women are more likely to be infected, are less likely to seek care, are more difficult to diagnose, are at more risk for severe disease sequelae, and are more subject to social discrimination and consequences. The most effective method available for protection against STDs, the condom, is controlled by men. A simple and effective method of protection from STDs that a woman can use without the need or necessity of her partner's cooperation does not yet exist.

The modern contraceptive technology revolution provided women with reliable methods of birth control that they can use independently of the cooperation of the male partner. This came with a price, however. The role and responsibility of the male partner have receded, and contraception has come to be considered a "woman's business." Women now assume a disproportionate responsibility for contraception in comparison to men. Not only do women have an undue burden of responsibility in fertility regulation, but the methods available to women are associated with potential health hazards. The importance of male participation and responsibility has greatly increased, however, with the emergence of the AIDS pandemic and the increasing prevalence of sexually transmitted infections, in both of which cases the condom is the only effective means of protection other than abstinence.

Responsibility for infertility is commonly shared by the couple. Analysis of data compiled in a large WHO multinational study showed that a major factor in the female with no demonstrable cause in the male was diagnosed in only 12.8 per cent of cases, and a major factor in the male with no demonstrable cause in the female was diagnosed in only 7.5 per cent of cases.[13] However, for biological and social reasons, the burden of infertility is unequally shared. The infertility investigation of the female partner is much more elaborate and is associated with more inconvenience and risk. The burden of treatment also falls mostly on the female partner. Even for male infertility, the promise of successful management is now shifting to assisted conception technologies in which the female assumes the major burden. The psychological and social burden of infertility in most societies is therefore much heavier on the woman. A woman's status is often identified with her fertility, and her failure to have children can be seen as a social disgrace or a cause for divorce. The suffering of the infertile woman can be very real.

Implementation of the Reproductive Health Approach — Implications for Policymakers

Policymakers have to make decisions about the priority of reproductive health care in resource allocation. Reproductive health has to compete with other needs for scarce resources. Rational criteria for setting priorities include the magnitude of the problem and its impact, as well as the availability of cost-effective interventions.

The burden of disease

In a joint major exercise of WHO and the World Bank, quantitative assessments were made of the global burden of different diseases, and the results were expressed in the terms of disability-adjusted life years (DALYs) lost as a result of the disease. In infancy and early childhood, girls and boys suffer from broadly similar health problems. Striking sex differences emerge in adults. Women suffer disproportionately from their reproductive role. Although the burden of reproductive ill health is almost entirely confined to the developing regions, it is so great that even worldwide, reproductive conditions make up three out of the ten leading causes of disease burden in women aged between 15 and 44.[14] In developing countries, five out of the ten leading causes of DALYs are related to reproductive ill health, including the consequences of unsafe abortion and chlamydia infection. Almost all of this loss of healthy life is avoidable.

The impact of reproductive health

The burden of a disease is primarily a function of its prevalence and its seriousness for the individual. In the case of reproductive health, the impact is not limited to the individual directly affected. The inability of individuals and couples in developing countries to regulate and control their fertility because of lack of information and inadequacy of services not only affects their health and their families, but has implications for their societies and their countries, for global stability, for the balance between population and natural resources, and for the balance between the human species and the environment.

Communicable diseases have always been at the heart of public health concerns. Of all communicable diseases, STDs, including HIV infection, are least amenable to control. Even attempting to erect national barriers will not stop them. People with other communicable diseases are less likely to travel than people with STDs, which are sometimes described as "air-borne" diseases, to indicate the importance of air travel in their transnational spread.

Reproductive health directly contributes to socio-economic development by increasing the human capital of women. Reproductive health services provide women with the opportunity to enjoy non-reproductive as well as reproductive roles in society. Such services increase their productivity both in and outside the household. They also enhance the quality of time women spend with their children. A healthy child born and reared by a healthy mother has a better chance of becoming a healthy adult. Investment in reproductive health is an investment in the future.

Inequity in reproductive health

The Alma Ata Declaration in 1978 stated that "[t]he existing gross inequality in the health status of the people particularly between developed and developing countries, as well as within countries, is politically, socially and economically unacceptable, and is, therefore, of common concern to all countries."[15]

There is no area of health in which this inequity is as striking as in reproductive health.[16] If we look at mortality differentials in the world, we find that while the crude death rate for the population is about 10 per cent more in the less developed than in the more developed regions, the infant mortality rate is almost six times higher, the child mortality rate is seven times higher, and the maternal mortality rate is fifteen times higher.[17]

The availability of cost-effective interventions

The magnitude of the burden of disease, its impact, and these glaring inequities are not enough to provide a rational basis for allocation of resources. The availability of cost-effective interventions also has to be considered. While the total DALYs lost for the age group from 15 to 44 years old was nearly the same for men and women, the percentage that can be substantially controlled with cost-effective interventions in developing countries was estimated to be 39.5 per cent for diseases of women compared to 20.1 per cent for diseases of men.[18]

It is because of this burden of disease and its impact that transcends national boundaries, as well as a deep concern about social injustice and inequity, and the availability of cost-effective interventions that a major investment is justified in the field of reproductive health care.

Can we afford to do it? The cost of providing reproductive health services

Reliable information on the cost of reproductive health services is not readily available. A recent review found 160 publications on the subject that were issued between 1970 and June 1997, including 16 cost-effective estimates.[19] The literature review identified gaps in cost information about reproductive health interventions for the individual elements of reproductive health, within geographic regions, and by costing methods.

The ICPD Programme of Action provided cost estimates prepared by experts based on experience to date.[20] In the developing countries and countries with economies in transition, the implementation of programmes in reproductive health, including those related to family planning, maternal health, and the prevention of STDs, as well as other basic actions for collecting and analysing population data, were estimated by the ICPD to cost $17.0 billion in 2000. Of the total, the family planning component is estimated to cost $10.2 billion. It may be noted that the $17 billion bill is less than one week of the world's expenditure on armaments.

The ICPD also tentatively estimated that up to two-thirds of the costs would continue to be met by the developing countries themselves, while approximately one-third would have to come from external sources. Developing countries, apart from allocating resources, can make more effective use of existing limited resources and can mobilize untapped resources. Imbalances in the allocation of resources need to be addressed: imbalance between urban and rural services; between curative and preventive care; between building infrastructure and developing and training health-care workers; and between different roles of health professionals. Community resources should not be underestimated. The role of the private sector can also be enhanced to provide services for those who can afford to pay.

Donor input not only complements limited national resources, particularly in poor developing countries. It can also catalyse national action. There are, however, two concerns about donor inputs. On the recipient country side, it is important that donor priorities respond to national needs and do not drive national directions. On the donor side, the concern is whether programmes can be sustained when donor funds are ultimately withdrawn.

30

Can we afford not to do it? The cost of not providing reproductive health services

Although we may not know exactly how much it costs to provide reproductive health services, we have a better idea about what it will cost if we do not implement the reproductive health approach. The following are some of the costs.[21]

- 585,000 women — one every minute — will die each year from causes related to pregnancy;
- About 200,000 maternal deaths each year will result from lack or failure of contraceptive services;
- 70,000 women will die each year as a result of unsafe abortions; an unknown number will suffer from infection and other health consequences;
- 120-150 million women who want to limit or space their pregnancies will not have the means to do so effectively;
- In developed countries (where average desired family size is small), of the 28 million pregnancies occurring every year, an estimated 49 per cent will be unplanned and 36 per cent will end in abortion. In developing countries (where average desired family size is still relatively large), of the 182 million pregnancies occurring every year, an estimated 36 per cent will be unplanned and 20 per cent will end in abortion;[22]
- One million people will die each year from reproductive tract infections, including STDs other than HIV/AIDS, while there will be an estimated 333 million new cases of STDs per year;
- Six out of ten women in many countries will have a STD, and all will face a higher risk of infertility, cervical cancer, or other serious health problems;
- Based on 1998 figures, there will be nearly 6 million new cases of HIV infection this year.[23] Every minute of every day, around 11 people will become newly infected with HIV. One of ten of those who became infected during 1998 was a child under the age of 15 years. The vast majority were in sub-Saharan Africa, and most have acquired the virus from their mothers. About half of all new infections past infancy are in young people below the age of 25 years, many of them still teenagers;
- Two million young girls will be at risk of female genital cutting. Although the international community and individual governments have condemned the practice, it remains widespread in many countries and is spreading to immigrant communities;
- Rape and other forms of sexual violence will continue to increase. The stigma of rape continues to keep all but a very small percentage of cases from being reported;
- Two million girls between 5 and 15 years old will be put on the commercial sex market every year;
- An increasing number of refugees will be denied access to a basic package of reproductive health care; and
- The "Day of 6 Billion" was observed on 12 October 1999. Human numbers will certainly reach 7 billion, but whether world population then goes on to 8, 10, or 12 billion depends on policy decisions and individual actions, within the reproductive health approach, in the next decade. Whatever its size, over 90 per cent of the net addition will be in today's developing countries.[24]

Implementation of the Reproductive Health Approach — Implications for Programmes

A question of priorities

In setting priorities for reproductive health programmes, decisions should be made on the basis of a combination of three approaches: a public health, a pragmatic and a participatory approach.[25] The public health approach will define what needs to be done. The pragmatic approach will dictate what can be done. The participatory approach is the way it should be done.

There are two classic steps in using the public health approach to assess the needs in reproductive health. The first is defining the magnitude of the problems. The second is ascertaining the availability of cost-effective interventions to address those problems. However, in assessing the seriousness of reproductive health problems from a public health approach, we should take into account certain basic differences compared to other areas in the health field. First, in assessing the burden of reproductive health problems, it is not only physical morbidity and mortality figures that count: the psychological and social burden may be even more serious. Second, reproductive health problems have an impact that goes beyond the individual concerned, to the family and to the community at large, and even to the world. Third, there is a human rights dimension to which countries and the international community must respond. Examples include female genital cutting, violence against women, and, above all, women's right to life when they go through the risky process of pregnancy and childbirth.

A pitfall in the need to assess the magnitude of the problem is when research is used as an excuse for inaction. The principle should be that what cannot be known in its entirety should not therefore be ignored.

There is a need for a pragmatic approach in assessing needs and setting priorities in reproductive health. After assessing the needs from a public health standpoint, it is necessary to ascertain what is already in place and what can realistically be accomplished. An incremental approach is the most successful. A lot can be accomplished through modest investments in supplies, equipment, and maintenance, as well as by providing appropriate information, education, and communication services. The best should not be made the enemy of the good.

The participatory approach, as advocated by UNFPA, recognizes that, in order to achieve reproductive health goals, the collaborative and coordinated efforts of many actors are necessary. Each one of these actors should define the areas where they have a comparative advantage. All, collectively, have to ensure that no important area of need is ignored or left behind. UNFPA recognizes in particular the important role and potential of civil society in the implementation of the reproductive health approach.

Predictably, the outcome of any assessment of reproductive health needs will reveal a gap between the needs and the resources that can be mobilized. There will be a temptation to focus on one or two areas and to neglect the others. What is needed instead is a balanced package, compatible with the level of resources that can be mobilized. Family planning can be considered as the bread and butter of the reproductive health table, but it does not make up a complete meal.

The appropriate reproductive health package for a given country can only be designed and developed at the country level. This is the rationale for the decentralization approach adopted by UNFPA. UNFPA's programme guidelines underscore the importance of building national capacity in programme countries so that they can achieve the goals and objectives recommended in the ICPD

Programme of Action and are able to sustain those achievements even in the absence of outside assistance.

Monitoring and evaluation

Apart from the difficult exercise of defining priorities in circumstances where resources are limited, programme managers face the challenges of monitoring and evaluation. This was comparatively easy in the case of demographic-oriented family planning programmes. Under a comprehensive reproductive health approach, however, there will need to be a new set of indicators. International organizations, including UNFPA, have taken the lead in developing reproductive health indicators. UNFPA has published a document, "Indicators for Population and Reproductive Health Programmes," to provide guidance to countries and programme managers on appropriate indicators for use in reproductive health programmes in terms of assessing need, monitoring progress, and evaluating impact. These indicators were recommended to be used in groups or clusters that help in understanding a particular problem and, thus, in monitoring activities and outputs designed to resolve that same problem. Many indicators proposed in the UNFPA publication have been included in various lists compiled by international organizations and other groups.[26]

Implementation of the Reproductive Health Approach — Implications for Services

Is the reproductive health approach about *doing different things* or about *doing things differently*?

The answer is "both." Reproductive health is not simply a matter of adding new services and information to existing family planning programmes. Reproductive health is a concept, an approach, and a mindset. A service deserves the label "reproductive health," not just on the basis of the range of services it provides, but, more important, on the *way* the services are provided.

A service delivering only family planning can be reproductive health-oriented even if its range of services remains limited. Such a service would uphold the principle that family planning is a dignified behaviour based on voluntary informed choice; it would counsel clients based on listening, hearing, and follow what they say; it would offer a broad choice of contraceptive methods and would not promote methods simply for their demographic effectiveness; it would not subscribe to demographic targets or quotas, instead putting the convenience and safety of clients as the overriding consideration; it would include in its inventory only contraceptive methods that the service can deliver, that insure the safety of clients, and that are subject to their free voluntary choice; it would promote men's participation and responsibility in family planning; it would care as much about protection from reproductive tract infections as it cares about protection from unwanted pregnancy; it would offer sympathetic care and all the help that can be provided, within the law, for women with unwanted pregnancies; it would not bury its head in the sand so as not to see unsafe abortion as a major public health problem, responding in a way that is within the legal framework and within its capacity; and, finally, it would not miss an opportunity to help with other reproductive health needs or problems.[27]

33

Reproductive health is not the sum total of individual separate components

Reproductive health is more than the sum of the individual components of the reproductive health-care package. It is about how these components are proportioned and linked together to meet the needs of people. An analogy may be drawn to the human body. A head and neck, trunk, and two upper limbs and two lower limbs thrown together do not constitute a human body; if they are not well proportioned and properly linked, they may make a "monster" instead of a viable being.

The case for integration of reproductive health services

The concept of reproductive health illustrates that health in reproduction is a package.[28] People cannot be healthy if they have one element and miss another. Moreover, the various elements of reproductive health are strongly interrelated. Improvements of one element can result in potential improvements in other elements. Similarly, lack of improvement in one element can hinder progress in other elements. The different needs in reproductive health are not isolated. Therefore, reproductive health care should be an integrated package. There are, however, two levels for integration. Services can be integrated at the level of policy, management and administration, and/or at the level of service delivery.

A strong case can be made for integration of all reproductive health services at the level of policy, management, and administration to ensure that all reproductive health needs receive attention and a relatively adequate allocation of resources. This level of integration is now being implemented in many countries. Many countries have made policy and legislative changes in the area of reproductive health since the ICPD. Some countries have developed new reproductive health policies, while others have dealt only with specific aspects of reproductive health through separate policies.

At the level of service delivery, the approach should be pragmatic. The objective is to make services available, accessible, and acceptable to all people. Services should be integrated if integration makes their delivery more cost-effective. Different situations in countries should be judged individually, taking into consideration some basic principles.

In general, service delivery will be more cost-effective either through better utilization, resulting in an increase of output; or through cost savings. Better utilization of services can result when integration makes services more convenient and accessible to clients. It can also result when the demand for one service can increase or create demand for the other. Cost savings will be made when fixed costs are shared between different services. This will result if the same infrastructure can be used for these different services, if these services can be provided by the same providers, and if enough excess capacity is available to meet the demands of the new service to be added.

Integration should be distinguished from "bundling" of services. The verb "bundle" is defined as "tie in, make up into, a bundle; throw confusedly into any receptacle." When services are simply combined or joined together in one way or another, this is not necessarily integration. In such cases, it may be more appropriately labelled as bundling. When services are combined or joined together as a strategy to provide a more complete package, *this* is integration.

The need for comprehensive health care should not translate into an all-or-nothing proposition. Providing people with some elements of the service is better than providing no services. Services can be built up as resources become available, and according to the level of need and demand. Integration should not result in the dilution of available resources. Rather, it should result in more effective use of the resources that are put together.

Implications of the reproductive health approach for service providers

To implement the reproductive health approach, health-service providers need to acquire new knowledge and skills to be able to expand the range of services they can provide. But, equally important, they have some unlearning to do.[29] They have to dismantle attitudes that look upon women as targets, as objects, and as means. They should recognize and respect the right of women to make dignified, informed choices. Service providers should also move from a fragmentary response to an approach in which they respond to a totality of needs. Service providers should unlearn that they deal with "health problems" and learn that they deal with *people* who have health problems or needs. While this is applicable for the whole field of medicine, it is much more applicable in the field of reproductive health, where providers deal with healthy people and where women still suffer from injustices and lower status.

Unpacking the Reproductive Health Care Package — Handle with Care

Implementation of the reproductive health approach needs different strategies

For implementation of the reproductive health approach, we need to unpack the reproductive health package. This has to be handled with care, because some components are fragile and more sensitive than others. Different components in the package pose different challenges in implementation.

One part of the package includes traditional services we already have experience with. These include MCH/FP services. In these cases, the challenge will be discovering how to expand the coverage and improve the quality of the services. In other parts of the package, we are challenged to meet new and emerging needs. Among the new needs, it is easy to single out the new pandemic of HIV/AIDS, the dilemma of unsafe abortion, and gender-based violence and sexual abuse in all its offensive forms. The challenge is how to approach sensitive and socially divisive issues, how to overcome tradition and social barriers, and how to influence human behaviour.

In another part of the package, we are challenged to reach and serve new customers. Among these new customers are adolescents, men, and, unfortunately, the growing number of displaced persons and refugees. Services, including information and education, need to be tailored to serve the needs of these new customers.

- At 1.05 billion, today's is the biggest-ever generation of young people between the ages of 15 and 24, and this age group is rapidly expanding in many countries.[30] Since the ICPD, many countries have realized that the only way to counteract the establishment of unhealthy behavioural patterns and early childbearing is to deal with adolescent sexual and reproductive health (ASRH) concerns. This area is gaining comprehensive recognition in recent policies in many countries.

35

- Men should take responsibility for their own reproductive and sexual behaviour and health. Since the ICPD, there appears to have been some increase in men's use of condoms and vasectomy and some expansion of male STD services.
- The long-neglected reproductive health needs of refugees are now increasingly being met as a result of initiatives by UNFPA and the Office of the United Nations High Commissioner for Refugees (UNHCR), in collaboration with other organizations.

Another part of the package stands out because the services needed are more expensive, and to some countries they may seem to be unaffordable. These include treatment of HIV-positive pregnant women to prevent transmission of the infection to the foetus and the newborn, management of infertility, and the detection and management of reproductive cancers. In 1988, the Joint United Nations Programme on HIV/AIDS (UNAIDS), UNFPA, the United Nations Children's Fund (UNICEF), and WHO embarked on a new initiative to reduce HIV transmission from mother to child. The initiative offers voluntary and confidential HIV counselling and testing to pregnant women. Those who learn that they are infected are provided with anti-retroviral drugs, better birth care, safe infant feeding methods, and post-natal counselling and family planning. Mexico and Brazil, with the support of UNFPA, have embarked on a campaign for early detection and prevention of cervical cancer. The challenge is to develop and test new cost-effective interventions that can be implemented in resource-poor settings.

Meeting Old Needs and Serving Current Customers

Family planning

Contraceptives should not be looked upon as a temporary measure to ease the world population problem. Contraception will be a permanent feature of the way of life of all succeeding generations on this planet.[31] Our reproductive function is being voluntarily adapted to dramatic new realities. What we are witnessing is a major evolutionary jump that is science-mediated, rather than being brutally imposed by Nature. A major challenge is determining how to respond to the unmet needs and to the rapidly expanding demand for services and contraceptive commodities. Since the ICPD, UNFPA has been working to increase access to family planning services and to ensure availability of good quality, confidential information, counselling and services, based on free and informed choices among the full range of safe and effective contraceptive methods: including female-controlled methods such as the female condom and emergency contraception; and methods for men, such as vasectomy and condoms.

To strengthen each nation's ability to forecast its contraceptive needs and manage contraceptive supply and distribution, UNFPA launched the Global Initiative on Contraceptive Requirements and Logistics Management Need in Developing Countries. UNFPA also established the Global Contraceptive Commodity Programme (GCCP), with the immediate objective of providing essential buffer stocks of contraceptives to enable prompt response to urgent and emergency requests for contraceptives from developing countries. The long-term objective of the GCCP is to contribute, in close cooperation with the Global Initiative, to the overall strengthening of reproductive health programmes by finding ways to address unmet needs for contraceptives, to increase contraceptive choice, and to ensure quality in meeting the contraceptive needs of women and men. The GCCP provides technical training and technical advisory services and works to improve management information systems, warehousing, stock-keeping, and transportation.[32]

Maternal health

Although there is a wealth of experience on how to address traditional needs in maternal and child health, a major challenge that has not yet been adequately addressed is how to provide women with access to effective services at the first-referral level in order to manage life-threatening complications of pregnancy and childbirth. A hard lesson that we learned over the past decade is that motherhood cannot be made safe without essential and emergency obstetric care.[33] Pregnancy and childbirth are a risky business. Unfortunately, the risks are generally neither predictable nor preventable. It is a risk that unites all women and does not discriminate between the rich and the poor. While the risks are not predictable or preventable, they *are* all manageable. To make motherhood safe, both essential and emergency obstetric care should be made available and accessible to all mothers when and if the need arises. For this, there is no alternative.

The Inter-Agency Group on Safe Motherhood, of which UNFPA is an active member, organized a technical meeting in 1997 to agree on common action priorities for the next decade to improve maternal health. The meeting concluded that training traditional birth attendants (TBAs), providing antenatal screening for high-risk pregnant women, and providing simple birth kits are not enough. Women need to have ready access to well-equipped and staffed maternal health services, essential obstetric care including emergency obstetric care, effective referral and transport to higher levels of care where necessary, and postpartum care. UNFPA provided support to the International Federation of Gynaecology and Obstetrics to mobilize obstetricians worldwide to meet the challenge of organizing maternity care services and to make the best and most efficient use of available resources.

Meeting New Needs and Serving New Customers

A role for civil society

We have to find innovative ways to address these new challenges. One important way is to establish partnerships with non-governmental organizations (NGOs). NGOs can move more quickly and often "less clumsily" than governments in uncharted territory and can afford to take risks. They can explore and prepare the way for governments to step in. UNFPA's Mission Statement emphasizes that UNFPA is fully committed to working in partnership with NGOs and civil society. UNFPA established the NGO Advisory Committee in the wake of the ICPD. Its purpose is to promote and increase cooperation and collaboration between UNFPA and the NGO community and to focus on issues needing special attention, such as male responsibility and participation, quality of care, violence against women, and harmful social practices. One indication of the Fund's wide-ranging collaboration with NGOs is the fact that NGOs are implementing UNFPA-supported HIV/AIDS prevention programmes in some 80 countries. The depth such collaboration is increasing.[34]

A role for research

Two key areas of research are needed. First, we need technologies. We need to make better use of available but under-utilized technologies, and we need to support the development of new technologies that are badly needed. Second, we need health services research.

The scientific community faces a major challenge in meeting the growing and diverse demand for contraceptive methods. The scientific community once pursued the dream of coming up with the ideal contraceptive that will fit the needs of everyone, everywhere, every time. The field has now matured enough to realize that this magic bullet is a dream that cannot come true. The needs of different people have to be met by a broad choice of contraceptives. We must have a wide range of contraceptives tailored to different human needs: for people who are different, for difficult circumstances, and for the same individual at different phases of life.[35] Apart from the need to broaden contraceptive choices, three specific needs stand out as unmet in a woman-centred agenda for contraceptive research and development.[36]

For male participation and responsibility, we need, among many other things, technologies for male fertility regulation. For biological reasons, women have to carry all the burden and risks of pregnancy and childbirth. This is, however, no reason that they should also carry most of the burden of fertility regulation. A sustained research effort is needed if men are to have broader contraceptive choices than what they have today in order to enable them to share effectively in the responsibility for fertility regulation.

The ICPD Programme of Action stressed that "every attempt should be made to eliminate the need for abortion."[37] Partly because of the reality of present gender power relationships, women are often exposed to unprotected sexual intercourse. There is a need for back-up methods that women can use in such instances, before a pregnancy is established, to decrease or eliminate the need for induced abortion. This includes emergency contraception, luteal contraception (contraception to be used in the second half of the menstrual cycle) and menses-inducers to be used at the expected time of menstruation. This "retro-active contraception" would be particularly suited to the needs of adolescents, where the decision to contracept is often made post-coitally. It is also needed in refugee situations.

The need for methods that women can use to protect themselves against STDs, including HIV, has become urgent. Women need effective methods they can use and control without the necessity of obtaining the cooperation of their partner. It is possible that if such methods become available, women will do better than men in compliance, providing more hope for the control of the pandemic of STDs. We have the female condom, which is not ideal, but should be promoted. We need to push for the development of vaginal microbicides that may or may not prevent pregnancy but can provide women with a means to protect themselves against disease.

However, we should not be just looking for a technology fix. It is never enough. We also need research to test new programmes and service interventions before they are used on a large scale. We cannot put scarce resources into large-scale programmes without first confirming that it is possible to get a reasonable return. As the late Jawaharal Nehru once said: "Because we are a poor country, we cannot afford not to do research."

Implementation of the Reproductive Health Approach: The Need for Social Action

"We must be courageous in speaking out on the issues that concern us: we must not bend under the weight of spurious arguments invoking culture or traditional values. No value worth the name supports the oppression and enslavement of women. The function of culture and tradition is to provide a framework for human well-being. If they are used against us, we will reject them, and move on. We will not allow ourselves to be silenced."

Dr. Nafis Sadik, Beijing, September 1995

Implementation of the reproductive health approach needs action beyond the health sector. A woman is not different simply because of her biology but also because of the way society defines her role. Culturally-evolved gender-related differences in lifestyle behaviour are powerful determinants of women's reproductive health and account for major differences in the disease burden between males and females, probably more than genetic or hormonal factors.[38]

The noble task of reproducing our species has not brought societal awards to women. On the contrary, it has often led to their subordination and, worse, to gender discrimination practices that among other consequences, adversely impact on their health. A majority of women and girls in the world today still live under conditions that limit educational attainment, restrict economic participation, and fail to guarantee them equal rights and freedoms, as compared to men.

The subordination of women is associated with a lack of appreciation of their unpaid labour (often harder and longer than men's work) and of their contribution to the economy. A major determinant of women's health is societies' assessment of how much a woman's life is worth. In making decisions on allocation of resources for health, societies, consciously or subconsciously, make decisions on who shall live and who shall die. Where women are undervalued, and particularly where resources are scarce, societies will not allocate the necessary resources needed for women's health.

Women's health is determined not only by how society estimates a woman's worth but also by the norms that society sets for sexuality and reproduction. Women's welfare has rarely been at the centre of society-imposed norms in human reproduction.

The adolescent girl in many societies is forced into early marriage. Early motherhood can severely curtail educational and employment opportunities and is likely to have short-term and long-term effects on the health and quality of life of women and their children. In other parts of the world, the trend towards early sexual experience, combined with a lack of information and services, increases the risks of unwanted and too early pregnancy, HIV infection and other STDs, as well as unsafe abortions. Society often sets double standards for boys and girls. Educating males for sexual and reproductive responsibility, including respect for their female counterparts, is commonly lacking. Adolescent girls are both biologically and psychosocially more vulnerable than boys to sexual abuse, violence, and prostitution as well as to the consequences of unprotected and premature sexual relations.

39

Implementation of the Reproductive Health Approach: The Human Rights Dimension

The International Federation of Gynaecology and Obstetrics' 1994 World Report on Women's Health concluded that improvements in women's health need more than improved science and health care.[39] They require state action, long overdue, to correct injustices to women. Women's health is often compromised, not because of lack of medical knowledge, but because of infringements on women's human rights. The powerlessness of women constitutes a serious health hazard.

The UNFPA Mission Statement affirms its commitment to reproductive rights, gender equality, male responsibility, and to the autonomy and empowerment of women everywhere.

The Declaration and Platform for Action adopted by 187 countries in Beijing states explicitly that

> [t]he human rights of women include their right to have control over and decide freely and responsibly on matters related to their sexuality, including sexual and reproductive health, free of coercion, discrimination and violence. Equal relationships between women and men in matters of sexual relations and reproduction, including full respect for the integrity of the person, require mutual respect, consent and shared responsibility for sexual behaviour and its consequences.[40]

Women's right to decide freely and responsibly on the number and spacing of their children and when to have them has not been widely respected. It must be pointed out that as far as health and human rights are concerned, there is little to choose between coerced contraception, sterilization, or abortion, because society does not want the child, and coerced motherhood, because society wants the child.[41] In this context, unsafe abortion should be recognized for what it is, one of the great neglected problems of health care in developing countries and a serious concern to women during their reproductive lives.

Victimization as part of being female

In many societies today, the girl child is denied her right to health. Female infanticide, a practice that was prevalent in the past in many societies, has not been completely abolished. It has taken new forms. It has been made easier with the utilization of new technologies for the selective abortion of the female foetus, and it has been deferred and changed to a passive form of child death through neglect and discrimination.[42]

The clitoris has been a victim for assault, as a result of society's view of female sexuality. The practice of female genital cutting, in one form or another, continues to exist in around 40 countries, mostly in East and West Africa and parts of the Arabian Peninsula. The variation in prevalence between countries ranges from 5 per cent to almost 98 per cent. With immigration, it is now also practised in Europe and North America. Estimates of worldwide prevalence range between 85 million and 114 million girls and women who have undergone the practice, with an annual rate of increase of about 2 million per year.[43] About 6,000 girls have their genitalia cut every day. The underlying rationale is that it is supposed to attenuate sexual desire, thus "saving" the girl from temptation and preserving her fidelity. The practice of female genital cutting is a flagrant violation of human rights; it is a harmful procedure performed on a child who cannot give informed consent. Apart from the psychological trauma and the impact on sexual health, the procedure is generally performed outside the health-care system and can result in potentially serious complications, both short- and long-term. Several countries have enacted laws to forbid the procedure. However, with a deep-rooted tradition, national and community education campaigns are still needed if this harmful practice is to be eradicated.

The most pervasive form of gender violence is abuse of women by intimate male partners. Reliable data on the incidence of rape are not available because it tends to be hidden and underreported. A substantial set of victims are very young girls. In wartime, mass rapes have been documented in many countries. Rape and sexual assaults, more than other types of injuries, cause both physical and profound emotional trauma. Victims also face the risk of unwanted pregnancy and STDs, including HIV infection, and in many societies they are socially stigmatized.

Women and girls in emergency situations are at particular risk of rape. Thus UNFPA, in collaboration with other United Nations agencies and international organizations, has developed an emergency reproductive health kit that includes, among other equipment such as supplies for safe deliveries and for the prevention and treatment of STDs, emergency contraceptives for rape victims. Emergency contraception prevents unwanted pregnancies when taken early after unprotected intercourse.

Looking Back — Moving Ahead

Building up the consensus

Consensus around the principles of the Cairo agenda, including the reproductive health approach, is gaining momentum. We have moved away from demographic-driven quotas and targets towards a needs-driven, woman-centred, broadly defined reproductive health approach. It is true that acting on these principles has been uneven, as a number of studies in different countries have shown.[44]

- In 1996, the Government of India abolished the use of nationally prescribed targets for acceptors of different family planning methods throughout the country.
- In Bangladesh, the intention of moving towards a reproductive health approach is reflected in the 1997 "Health and Population Sector Strategy," which affirms the principles of the ICPD and recognizes the need for a client-centred approach and for quality in service delivery.
- Zambia has developed a Family Planning in Reproductive Health Policy Framework. The document is the result of a series of workshops with participants from all levels of the public health sector, from government to service delivery points, as well as from NGOs and other local stakeholders such as the university teaching hospital.

Breaking the silence and lifting the veil

A second signal of progress is that the silence has finally been broken on sensitive but vital issues. We have discovered that sex is a three-, not a four-letter word. Sex and sexuality are ceasing to be taboos. Sex is recognized for what it is — an important psychosocial component of the well-being of both women and men. Family planning is about sexuality. It is meant to allow women and men to enjoy mutually satisfying sexual relationships without the fear of unwanted pregnancy. Although it contradicts what some theologians may like to think, the dissociation of sex from reproduction in the human species was a purposeful evolutionary act of nature. In the evolution of our species, the temporal relationship between sex and reproduction has been completely severed.[45]

Adolescents are making their voices heard and their needs expressed. Female genital cutting is no longer kept behind soundproof walls of culture and tradition. A number of countries have passed statutes outlawing female genital cutting and have undertaken information campaigns on this and other practices injurious to the health and well-being of the girl child.

Unsafe abortion, a major public health problem, is widely discussed, and action is being taken. The public health system in Brazil has expanded support for legal abortion services from two to twelve locations.[46] A number of countries have promoted the use of the manual vacuum aspirator (MVA) for treatment of incomplete abortion and for training midwives and other providers to offer post-abortion services. Many countries have made improvements in the quality of post-abortion care. With due respect to the widely divergent views on the issue of abortion, an issue cannot be kept under the carpet when 20 million women every year are risking their health and even their life in the process.[47]

Another example of breaking the silence is that the pervasive violence against women, in all its forms, is rightly becoming a priority, both internationally and nationally. Countries such as the Philippines have included services to treat victims of violence against women as a regular component of the reproductive health package.

Partnerships

A third signal of progress is that partnerships, as called for in the Cairo agenda, are working. Governments are increasingly seeing the potential of civil society and the value added in partnerships with other actors. The five-year review of the implementation of the Programme of Action of the International Conference on Population and Development (ICPD+5), The Hague Forum, was preceded by an NGO Forum and a Youth Forum. Facilitated by UNFPA, this arrangement is sending a signal that governments want to listen before they decide and want to work with the civil society.

We Still Fall Short

Resources

Resources promised in the ICPD Programme of Action have not been forthcoming. According to the information made available at The Hague Forum, developing countries, taken as a whole, have reached 68 per cent of their share of the year 2000 goal for total spending. Grant assistance from donor nations, also taken as a whole, has so far only met 33 per cent of their ICPD commitment.[48] It is a grave concern to witness the widening gap between what UNFPA is asked by countries to do for the implementation of the reproductive health approach and the limited resources that the Fund is given. It must, however, be stated that the record of countries has been uneven. There are those who should be applauded for honouring their commitment. Let us hope that others, developed and developing countries, will soon see the light and realize that implementing the Cairo Programme of Action and the reproductive health approach is an investment that they cannot afford not to make.

It is deplorable that armed conflicts or the threat of armed conflicts are deflecting badly needed resources in poor countries, from enhancing human lives to destruction of human lives. Many are also concerned, and rightly so, about the impact of economic restructuring, and, particularly, that programmes of structural adjustment in the health sector are leaving the poor and disadvantaged, women and children, without a safety net.

Violation of women's rights

Another area of major concern is the continued violation of women's human rights, including sexual and reproductive rights, as reaffirmed in Cairo and Beijing.[49] The list of violations is becoming too long and too depressing to mention. Women are subjected to discrimination even before they are born, and as young innocent girls they begin to face the harsh reality that they are not treated as the equals of boys.

The neglected tragedy of maternal mortality

A major challenge that remains ahead, and should continue to bear heavily on our collective conscience, is the neglected tragedy of maternal mortality.[50] Maternal mortality should not be lumped with, nor ranked with, other "disease problems." Maternity is not a disease. It is the means by which the human species is propagated. Society has more of an obligation for preventing maternal deaths than for preventing deaths from diseases. The neglected tragedy of maternal mortality is basically a question of how much societies consider the life of a woman to be worth. When societies invest less in girls than in boys and underestimate the economic contribution of women, and when only a few women are in positions of decision-making, it should be no surprise, in resource-poor settings, that a low priority is given to allocating the necessary resources to save the lives of mothers.

Women, worldwide, should mobilize for the right to safe motherhood, which is basically the woman's right to life.[51] It is true that women in the North have mostly forgotten what maternal mortality is. But for their sisters in the South, the journey of pregnancy and childbirth is still dangerous and many do not return.

Towards a brighter future

Progress has been made in the implementation of the reproductive health approach. There are still some steep mountains to climb. The challenges are great. But we can take courage and pride in being the first generation of humanity to see the final emergence of the woman from behind the mother and to be a party to the process where women, all women, will be taking back their God-given rights as men's equals. We can look forward to a brighter future. For this, UNFPA, in partnerships with all who care about human welfare, can make a difference.

References

[1] United Nations, *Report of the International Conference on Population and Development,* Cairo, 5-13 September 1994. Programme of Action: para. 7.6.

[2] United Nations Population Fund, "1997 Annual Report" (New York: UNFPA, 1997): p. 10.

[3] M. F. Fathalla, "Women's Health: An Overview," *International Journal of Gynecology and Obstetrics,* 46 (1994): pp. 105-118.

[4] M. F. Fathalla, "Fertility Control Technology: A Women-Centered Approach to Research," *Population Policies Reconsidered: Health, Empowerment and Rights,* eds. G. Sen, A. Germain, L. C. Chen (Boston: Harvard University Press, 1994): pp. 223-234.

[5] W. S. Sinding, M. F. Fathalla, "The Great Transition," *Populi* (December 1995): pp. 18-21.

[6] M. F. Fathalla, "Research Needs in Human Reproduction," *Research in Human Reproduction: Biennial Report (1986-1987),* eds. E. Diczfalusy, P. D. Griffin, J. Khanna (Geneva: WHO, 1988): p. 341; M. F. Fathalla, "Reproductive Health: A Global Overview," *Frontiers in Human Reproduction. Ann. New York Academy of Science,* 626 (1991): pp. 1-10.

[7] United Nations, *Report of the International Conference on Population and Development,* Cairo, 5-13 September 1994. Programme of Action: para. 7.2.

[8] M. F. Fathalla, "Contraception and Women's Health," *British Medical Bulletin,* 49 (1993): pp. 245-251.

[9] M. F. Fathalla, "Safe Motherhood and Child Survival: The Importance of Family Planning and the Interdependence of Services," *Family Planning, Health and Family Well-being. Proceedings of the United Nations Expert Group Meeting on Family Planning, Health and Family Well-being, Bangalore, 26-30 October 1992.* (New York: United Nations, Department for Economic and Social Information and Policy Analysis — Population Division): ST/ESA.R/131.

[10] United Nations, *Report of the International Conference on Population and Development,* Cairo, 5-13 September 1994. Programme of Action: para. 7.13.

[11] M. F. Fathalla, "From Obstetrics and Gynaecology to Women's Health: The Road Ahead" (New York, London: The Parthenon Publishing Group, 1997): p. 11.

[12] World Bank, *World Development Report — Investing in Health* (New York: Oxford University Press, 1993): p. 223.

[13] T. M. M. Farley, "The WHO Standardized Investigation of the Infertile Couple," *Infertility Male and Female,* Vol. 4. (1987*);* S. S. Ratnam, E. S. Teoh, C. Anandakumar, eds., *The Proceedings of the 12th World Congress on Fertility and Sterility, Singapore, October 1986* (Carnforth, U.K.: The Parthenon Publishing Group, 1987): pp. 123-135.

[14] C. J. L. Murray, A. D. Lopez, "The Global Burden of Disease — Summary" (Boston: Harvard University Press, 1996): p. 25.

[15] World Health Organization, "Primary Health Care," *Report of the International Conference on Primary Health Care.* Alma Ata, 6-12 September 1978. WHO, "Health For All" Series, No. 1 (1978).

[16] M. F. Fathalla, "Inequity in Reproductive Health: The Challenge to Obstetricians/Gynaecologists," *Eur. J. Obstet. Gynecol. Reprod. Biol.,* 44 (1) (1992): pp. 3-8.

[17] M. F. Fathalla, "Reproductive Health in the World: Two Decades of Progress and the Challenge Ahead," *Reproductive Health: A Key to a Brighter Future,* eds. J. Khanna, P. F. A. Look, P. D. Griffin (Geneva: WHO, 1992): pp. 3-31.

[18] World Bank, *World Development Report — Investing in Health* (New York: Oxford University Press, 1993): p. 223.

[19] E. A. Mumford *et. al.,* "Reproductive Health Costs — Literature Review," *The POLICY Project Working Paper Series No. 3* (Washington, D.C.: The Futures Group International, 1998): pp. 1-76.

[20] United Nations, *Report of the International Conference on Population and Development,* Cairo, 5-13 September 1994. Programme of Action: para. 13.15.

[21] United Nations Population Fund, *The Right to Choose: Reproductive Rights and Reproductive Health* (New York: UNFPA, 1999): pp. 2-3.

[22] The Alan Guttmacher Institute, *Sharing Responsibility — Women, Society and Abortion Worldwide* (New York, Washington, D.C.: AGI, 1999): pp. 1-56.

[23] Joint United Nations Programme on HIV/AIDS, "AIDS 5 years since ICPD — Emerging Issues and Challenges for Women, Young People and Infants," *UNAIDS Discussion document* (Geneva: UNAIDS, 1999): pp. 1-4.

[24] United Nations Population Fund, "The New Generations," *The State of World Population 1998* (New York: UNFPA, 1998): p. 1.

[25] United Nations Population Fund, "Expert Consultation on Operationalizing Reproductive Health Programmes," *UNFPA Technical Report 37* (New York: UNFPA, 1996): p. 6.

[26] World Health Organization, "Reproductive Health Indicators for Global Monitoring: Report of an Interagency Technical Meeting," WHO/RHT/HRP/97.27 (Geneva: WHO, 1997): pp. 1-22.

[27] M. F. Fathalla, *From Obstetrics and Gynaecology to Women's Health: The Road Ahead* (New York, London: The Parthenon Publishing Group, 1997): p. 70.

[28] M. F. Fathalla, "Reproductive Health in the World: Two Decades of Progress and the Challenge Ahead," *Reproductive Health: A Key to a Brighter Future,* eds. J. Khanna, P. F. A. Look, P. D. Griffin (Geneva: WHO, 1992): pp. 3-31.

[29] M. F. Fathalla, *From Obstetrics and Gynaecology to Women's Health: The Road Ahead* (New York, London: The Parthenon Publishing Group, 1997): pp. 13-17.

[30] United Nations Population Fund, "The New Generations," *The State of World Population 1998* (New York: UNFPA, 1998): p. 3.

[31] M. F. Fathalla, "Family Planning and Reproductive Health — A Global Overview," *Population — The Complex Reality.* A report of the Population Summit of the world's scientific academies, ed. Sir Francis Graham-Smith (London: The Royal Society; Colorado: North American Press, 1994): pp. 251-270.

[32] United Nations Population Fund, "1997 Annual Report" (New York: UNFPA, 1997): p. 24.

[33] M. F. Fathalla, "Women Have a Right to Safe Motherhood," *Planned Parenthood Challenges,* 1 (1998): pp. 1-2.

[34] United Nations Population Fund, "1997 Annual Report" (New York: UNFPA, 1997): p. 25.

[35] M. F. Fathalla, "Tailoring Contraceptives to Human Needs," *People,* 17 (3) (1990): pp. 3-5.

45

[36] M. F. Fathalla, "Contraceptive Research and Development: The Unfinished Revolution," *Populi* (October 1993): pp. 8-10.

[37] United Nations, *Report of the International Conference on Population and Development,* Cairo, 5-13 September 1994. Programme of Action: para. 8.25.

[38] M. F. Fathalla, *From Obstetrics and Gynaecology to Women's Health: The Road Ahead* (New York, London: The Parthenon Publishing Group, 1997): pp. 195-196.

[39] M. F. Fathalla, "Women's Health: An Overview," *International Journal of Gynecology and Obstetrics,* 46 (1994): pp. 105-118.

[40] United Nations, *Report of the Fourth World Conference on Women.* Beijing, 4-15 September 1995. Platform for Action and the Beijing Declaration: para. 96.

[41] M. F. Fathalla, "The Impact of Reproductive Subordination on Women's Health — Family Planning Services," *The American University Law Review,* 44 (1995): pp. 1179-1190.

[42] M. F. Fathalla, "The Missing Millions," *People and the Planet,* 7 (3) (1998): pp. 10-11.

[43] N. Toubia, "Female Genital Mutilation and the Responsibility of Reproductive Health Professionals," *International Journal of Gynecology and Obstetrics,* 46 (1994): pp. 127-135.

[44] L. Ashford, C. Makinson, *Reproductive Health in Policy and Practice — Case Studies from Brazil, India, Morocco, and Uganda* (Washington, D.C.: Population Reference Bureau, 1999): pp. 1-32; K. Hardee *et. al.,* "Reproductive Health Policies and Programs in Eight Countries: Progress since Cairo," *International Family Planning Perspectives,* 25 (1999): pp. S2-S9.

[45] M. F. Fathalla, "Global Trends in Women's Health," *Second World Report on Women's Health,* ed. M. Seppala, Special Issue of the *International Journal of Gynecology and Obstetrics,* 58 (1997): pp. 5-12.

[46] L. Ashford, C. Makinson, *Reproductive Health in Policy and Practice — Case Studies from Brazil, India, Morocco and Uganda* (Washington, D.C.: Population Reference Bureau, 1999): pp. 1-32.

[47] S. K. Henshaw, S. Singh, T. Haas, "The Incidence of Abortion Worldwide," *International Family Planning Perspectives,* 25 (1999): pp. S30-S38.

[48] United Nations, "Report of the International Forum for the Operational Review and Appraisal of the Implementation of the Programme of Action of the International Conference on Population and Development," The Hague, 8-12 February 1999 (New York: United Nations, 1999).

[49] R. J. Cook, M. F. Fathalla, "Advancing Reproductive Rights beyond Cairo and Beijing," *International Family Planning Perspectives,* 22 (1996): pp. 115-121.

[50] M. F. Fathalla, "Safe Motherhood: The Road from Nairobi," *Afr. J Reprod Hlth,* 2 (1998): pp. 6-9.

[51] M. F. Fathalla, "The Tragedy of Maternal Mortality in Developing Countries: A Health Problem or a Human Rights Issue?" *News on Health Care in Developing Countries,* 7 (1993): pp. 4-6.

Fostering Compliance with Reproductive Rights

Rebecca J. Cook

Introduction: UNFPA at Thirty

The celebration of the United Nations Population Fund's (UNFPA's) thirtieth anniversary provides an important opportunity to review the Fund's accomplishments in protecting and promoting reproductive rights, and to assess how it might meet future challenges in fostering compliance with these rights. The realization that the protection of reproductive and sexual health is a matter of social justice and can be addressed through improved application of human rights that exist in national constitutions and regional and international human rights treaties was a significant achievement. This realization emerged during preparations for the 1994 International Conference on Population and Development (ICPD), held in Cairo, and was crystallized in the ICPD Programme of Action.[1] Recognition was expanded through the 1995 Fourth World Conference on Women (FWCW), held in Beijing, and in the Beijing Declaration and Platform for Action.[2]

The protection and promotion of rights relating to reproductive and sexual health have gained further momentum through the Cairo and Beijing monitoring processes.[3] They were further enhanced through subsequent work by the United Nations[4] and non-governmental organizations (NGOs),[5] including women's groups,[6] medical associations,[7] and academic communities.[8] Reinforcing these developments has been research into women's perspectives on the exercise of their reproductive rights[9] and research on the challenges of protecting reproductive rights in different regions.[10] For the purposes of this chapter, all of these activities will be referred to as "the Cairo process."

Human rights, whether found in national constitutions or in regional or international human rights treaties, are means through which laws and policies that foster respect for reproductive self-determination can be enhanced and norms that inhibit reproductive self-determination can be addressed.[11] The Programme of Action explains that

> reproductive rights embrace certain human rights that are already recognized in national laws, international human rights documents and other consensus documents. These rights rest on the recognition of the basic right of all couples and individuals to decide freely and responsibly the number, spacing and timing of their children and to have the information and means to do so, and the right to attain the highest standard of sexual and reproductive health. It also includes their right to make decisions concerning reproduction free of discrimination, coercion and violence, as expressed in human rights documents.[12]

This chapter explains the various mechanisms for fostering compliance with different rights relating to reproductive and sexual health, and explores programming options for fostering such compliance. The chapter is not exhaustive, but exploratory; recognizing that much more discussion is needed to address this issue adequately.

Rights Relating to Reproductive and Sexual Health

Sources of human rights

Sources of human rights are found in national constitutions and bills of rights, and in the 1948 Universal Declaration of Human Rights and the subsequent regional and international treaties that give effect to this declaration. The 1948 declaration was developed by the United Nations to add substance to its charter, dating to 1945, which observed that a purpose of the new organization was "to reaffirm faith in fundamental human rights, in the dignity and worth of the human person, [and] in the equal rights of men and women." Legal force is given to the declaration through a series of treaties.

Such treaties of legal force include the International Covenant on Civil and Political Rights (the Political Covenant),[13] the International Covenant on Economic, Social and Cultural Rights (the Economic Covenant),[14] and regional treaties such as the European Convention on Human Rights,[15] the American Convention on Human Rights,[16] and the African Charter on Human and Peoples' Rights.[17] In addition, several international treaties are directed to the relief of injustices that individuals might suffer on account of innate characteristics. These treaties include the International Convention on the Elimination of All Forms of Racial Discrimination and the Convention on the Rights of the Child.[18] These are, in part, applicable to the protection of reproductive and sexual health as well. Most directly relevant, however, is the Convention on the Elimination of All Forms of Discrimination against Women (the Women's Convention),[19] which explicitly addresses human rights regarding family planning services, nutrition during pregnancy, and information and education to decide the number and spacing of children. The table in the appendix of this chapter shows provisions of different regional and international instruments that are relevant to the protection and promotion of reproductive and sexual health.

These leading international human rights treaties established committees whose functions are to monitor states' compliance with the obligations they have accepted. The Women's Convention establishes the Committee on the Elimination of All Forms of Discrimination against Women (CEDAW) to monitor whether States Parties have brought their laws, policies, and practices into compliance with the convention. Similarly, the Political Covenant established the Human Rights Committee (HRC), the Economic Covenant established the Committee on Economic, Social and Cultural Rights (CESCR), the Children's Convention established the Committee on the Rights of the Child (CRC), and the International Convention on the Elimination of All Forms of Racial Discrimination established the Committee on the Elimination of Racial Discrimination (CERD).

48

Evolution of reproductive rights

Control of women's reproduction and sexuality has a history that reaches back into antiquity. Governments have used criminal laws over the centuries as a primary instrument to express and control morality, particularly through the prohibition of birth control or by stigmatizing forms of sexual behaviour. Gradually, however, realization of the harmful effects of punitive controls of reproduction and sexuality on the health and welfare of individuals has emerged, fostering an approach to laws and policies designed to promote individuals' interests in their health and welfare. The most recent approach challenges patriarchal laws, and requires access to reproductive and sexual health services as a matter of human rights and social justice.

These three approaches, from criminalization, through promotion of health and welfare, to an emphasis on human rights and justice, exist in all countries, and are not necessarily mutually exclusive. The tendency to use criminal law to punish and stigmatize disapproved behaviour remains, but this tendency is waning because of an increased understanding that this approach is dysfunctional. Many countries have used a health and welfare rationale to legalize and, in some cases, cover or subsidize the cost of reproductive and sexual health services. An increasing number of countries have reformed laws and policies to facilitate the provision of reproductive and sexual health services because of a growing recognition of the importance of the human rights of women in general and of reproductive and sexual rights in particular.

The Cairo process strongly endorses a new strategy for addressing population issues. This introduces a focus on meeting the reproductive health needs and preferences of individual women and men, rather than, as in the past, on achieving demographic targets. Key to this new approach is empowering women within their families and communities and protecting their human rights, particularly those relevant to reproductive and sexual health. The challenge ahead is to turn the political commitments made by governments at the Cairo and Beijing Conferences into legally enforceable duties to respect reproductive rights. That is, a major undertaking in the post-Cairo and Beijing era is to employ law as a positive force in the protection and promotion of reproductive health and self-determination. This requires states to bring their laws, policies, and practices into compliance with rights to gender equality, liberty, and security of the person; including, for example, equal rights to health care.

Significantly, the Cairo and Beijing documents set standards by which governments can show their compliance and can be held politically and legally accountable for violations. Important steps have been taken to incorporate reproductive rights into international legal norms. CEDAW uses the Cairo and Beijing standards to determine whether states are in compliance with their obligations under the Women's Convention to take all appropriate measures to eliminate discrimination in the area of reproductive and sexual health.

Compared to these significant developments in international norms, development of corresponding national norms, through, for example, national laws and constitutions, has been spotty. Attempts to enact reproductive health laws have been frustrated, and laws that are beneficial to the protection and promotion of reproductive health are often not implemented. Reproductive rights are denied, ignored, and violated in significant ways, whether it be through discrimination against adolescents by denying them reproductive health services, through coercive sterilization of minorities, or through denial of the right to impart information necessary to protect reproductive and sexual health.

Many activities that would enhance reproductive and sexual health remain thwarted by their criminal status. Many sexual practices are subject to criminal prosecution and punishment because of legislators' failure to understand the full scope of human sexuality. Resistance to reform is supported by religious concepts of sin and by moralistic attitudes that invoke concepts of social harm from human sexuality but lack an adequate understanding of the importance of sexual intimacy in people's lives and the many dimensions of sexuality.[20] Initiatives to promote the safety of sexual practices are frustrated when service providers and recipients become exposed to criminal investigation and possible prosecution. But empirical data that demonstrate the dysfunction of many doctrinally based criminal laws have contributed to the modern movement in reproductive health away from reliance on concepts of crime and punishment and towards the promotion of health and welfare.

During the decade of the 1990s, for instance, abortion law reform has been achieved in many countries.[21] It has also been frustrated by religious and moral opposition in resistant countries, however, and some attempts to restrict availability of legal abortion have been successful. In addition, some national constitutions have been amended to protect life from the moment of conception, in attempts to restrict reproductive choices. Efforts to institute sexuality education in schools have been challenged in most regions of the world, and barriers to the provision of reproductive health information and services persist.

Defending and articulating a woman's rights to quality of care, to personal choice, and to freedom in her decisions concerning her body and her reproductive options are important aspects of what has emerged as a movement to define and protect women's reproductive rights. The importance of women's self-determination to her health and well-being is more widely recognized. It is increasingly unacceptable, for instance, for a husband to force his wife into unwanted sex or unwanted pregnancy. Violence against commercial sex workers, who are vulnerable to abuse because, among other reasons, their activities are often outside the protection of the law, is no longer tolerable. Equally unacceptable is the pursuit of positive and negative population policies at the expense of individual human rights.

Religious norms continue to be an important determinant of reproductive and sexual behaviour and of the standards by which such behaviour is assessed. At the institutional level, religious doctrines create normative foundations for decisions on what is morally proper, required, and desirable in sexuality and reproduction. The influence of traditional religious doctrines and leadership is strong, and conservative and authoritarian forces within religious institutions usually remain resistant to gender equality in general and within their own institutions in particular.

The Cairo and Beijing Conferences recognized the power of religious conviction, not only in its institutional expression, but also at the level of private conscience. A democratic spirit is growing among people of religious faith that recognizes that some choices, particularly regarding reproductive and sexual well-being, are governed by individual conscience and not by doctrine revealed by hierarchical authority. A consequence of the disjunction between private conscience and religious doctrine is that private reproductive and sexual practices depart from officially approved conduct even among practising members of religious faiths. In acknowledging the significance of individual reproductive self-determination and the right of access to reproductive health services essential to self-determination, the Cairo and Beijing Conferences recognized that respect for individual religious conscience and convictions contributes to individuals' well-being.

Even though in many countries there is a constitutional separation between religious institutions and state, religious leaders often exert considerable political power and influence. They often play an important role in influencing government policy, such as in health, education, and family life, which affects the protection and promotion of reproductive and sexual health. Religious institutions exert considerable political power, by both promise of rewards and threats of condemnation, to advance their purposes. Under spiritual inspiration, they may feel obliged to employ their influence to prevent governments from acting upon commitments they made in Cairo and Beijing.

The protection of reproductive rights has evolved over time as individuals have found the courage to step forward to address and, in some cases, remedy the abuses of rights they or others have suffered. The experience of fighting for the protection of rights often varies according to context. In some situations, it will be the work to eliminate female genital mutilation (FGM) that adds meaning to the right to be free from inhuman and degrading treatment and to the right to liberty and security of the person. In other contexts, the struggle to provide adolescent reproductive health services reinforces the right to non-discrimination in health care based on age. In still other countries, framing the neglect of preventable causes of maternal mortality as an issue of social justice is adding a new dimension to the right to life. Out of these individual and collective struggles have emerged protective spheres for the advancement of reproductive rights.

Essential to these struggles has been the development of our understanding of the multiple dimensions of reproductive and sexual health — through research undertaken in a variety of different disciplines, including health and social science, and law and bioethics. This research has informed our understanding of the causes and human consequences of reproductive and sexual ill health. Once the causes, whether social or biological, are understood, the burden shifts to governments to prevent, remedy, and if appropriate, punish violations of rights relating to reproductive and sexual health. Where governments fail or refuse to act, reproductive rights activists may work with other groups to hold governments accountable for remedying the neglect and, in many cases, the violations, of these rights.

Duties to implement reproductive rights

A person's interest or need becomes a right when a duty binds another to respect that interest. That is, an "interest" is a "right" only insofar as others are bound by related duties. The binding force that creates a duty may be legal, when the right is a legal right, or moral, when the right is a moral right; and a right may be both legal and moral. Rights supersede other interests because they bind individuals or agencies to observe the rights, regardless of their personal preferences. The challenge ahead is to apply legal, moral, or other authority to create duties that require the protection and promotion of rights to reproductive and sexual health.

A CEDAW General Recommendation on Women and Health[22] explains the legal duties to respect rights by not obstructing their exercise, to protect rights by taking positive action against third-party violators, and to fulfil rights by employing governmental means to afford individuals the full benefit of their human rights. This recommendation applies human rights to women's health in the following ways:

> The obligation to *respect rights* requires States Parties to refrain from obstructing action taken by women in pursuit of their health goals. States Parties should report on how public and private health care providers meet their duties to respect women's rights to have access to health care.[23]

51

The recommendation explains that states are obliged to change laws or policies that require women to seek the authorization of their husbands, parents, or health authorities to obtain health services because such laws or policies "obstruct" women's pursuit of their health goals. This recommendation also explains that "laws that criminalize medical procedures only needed by women and that punish women who undergo those procedures"[24] may violate the Women's Convention.

The General Recommendation further explains that

[t]he obligation to *protect rights* relating to women's health requires States Parties, their agents and officials to take action to prevent and impose sanctions for violations of rights by private persons and organizations.[25]

The recommendation emphasizes the importance of this duty in the context, among others, of gender-based violence against women. The duty includes responsibility to develop health-care protocols and gender training of health-care providers and in the provision of health services in order to identify, address, prevent, and remedy violence against women and abuse of girl children. The recommendation also explains that the duty to protect requires the "enactment and effective enforcement of laws that prohibit female genital mutilation and marriage of girl children."[26]

The General Recommendation goes on to make it clear that

[t]he obligation to *fulfil rights* places an obligation on States Parties to take appropriate legislative, judicial, administrative and budgetary, economic and other measures to the maximum extent of their available resources to ensure that women realize their rights to health care.[27]

The General Recommendation explains that studies that show high rates of maternal mortality and morbidity within particular states and the presence of a large number of couples who would like to limit their family size but lack access to any form of contraception provide important indications for States Parties of their possible breaches of duties to ensure women's access to health care. The recommendation emphasizes the importance that States Parties to the Women's Convention address in their reports to CEDAW the steps they have taken to deal with preventable conditions, such as HIV/AIDS.

Applying Human Rights to Reproductive and Sexual Health

Rights relating to reproductive and sexual health may be protected through several specific, legally established human rights. Which rights are most pertinent to invoke and how they are shown to have been violated depends on the particular facts of an alleged violation and on the underlying causes of reproductive or sexual ill health. The rights addressed below are not exhaustive, but representative of rights that may be developed to advance reproductive interests.

Rights are interactive; each depends in greater or lesser degree on the observance of others. For instance, rights to information, which are central to legal principles of informed and free decision-making in health care, often depend on observance of the rights, particularly of children, to education and literacy. The following discussion shows ways that specific rights can be applied to protect interests in reproductive and sexual health.

The discussion also addresses how national law — especially court decisions, the Cairo Programme of Action, the Beijing Platform for Action, and the CEDAW General Recommendations and Concluding Comments — have been and can be used to develop standards to measure compliance with these rights.

Clustering rights

Most countries have committed themselves to respecting human dignity and physical integrity through their membership in international human rights conventions. The separate human rights that contribute to reproductive[28] and sexual health[29] can be analysed and abstracted in a variety of ways. Human rights originating in the various international and regional human rights instruments are clustered around reproductive interests in the appendix to this chapter. Interests in reproductive and sexual health may be found in the rights to:

* security, autonomy and confidentiality;
* reproductive and sexual health;
* equality and due respect of difference; and
* information, education and decision-making.

These interests can be categorized differently, depending on the issues at stake and people's perceptions of them. Security, autonomy, and confidentiality, for instance, could be expressed as subdivisions of the right to integrity of the person. The clustering of specific human rights around reproductive and sexual interests is also fluid and can be arranged differently. The right to education, for example, is relevant to the protection of both reproductive health and reproductive decision-making. Rights that are expressed separately are not insulated from others but interact dynamically with and inform other rights.

The purpose of clustering is to show how different human rights can be cumulatively and interactively applied to advance reproductive and sexual health. The purpose is not to suggest that there is any single "correct" approach to categorizing interests or to clustering human rights around them. As human rights are applied more vigorously to reproductive interests, there will in fact be a variety of ways of applying human rights in order to promote reproductive and sexual health.

Rights relating to security, autonomy and confidentiality

Rights relating to security, autonomy and confidentiality are increasingly applied to require the state to guarantee the basic conditions necessary for people's reproductive self-determination. These rights include the right to life and survival, the right to liberty and security of the person, the right to be free from torture and inhuman and degrading treatment, the right to marriage and to found a family, and the right to enjoyment of private and family life. These rights need to be more effectively applied to require governments to bring wrongdoers to account; for instance, for sterilizing men and women without their free and informed choice, or for breaching the confidence

53

of patients seeking reproductive and sexual health services.[30] They also need to be applied to require governments to take steps necessary to reduce violence against women, including FGM[31] and trafficking in women.[32]

Legal claims are slowly being brought forward under the right to life and survival, to require governments to take appropriate measures to reduce the preventable causes of maternal death. The European Commission of Human Rights took the opportunity in a case concerning a maternal death to emphasize that the right to life under the European Convention on Human Rights has to be interpreted to require states to take steps, not only to prevent intentional killing, but also to protect life against unintentional loss.[33] When statistics on high rates of maternal mortality in Peru were presented to HRC, the committee found that ". . . abortion gives rise to a criminal penalty even if a woman is pregnant as a result of rape and that clandestine abortions are the main cause of maternal mortality."[34] The committee explained that this aspect of the criminal law of Peru subjected women to inhuman treatment and was possibly incompatible with the equal entitlement of men and women to the enjoyment of the rights set forth in the Covenant, including the rights to life and to liberty and security of the person.

Autonomy interests require states to take effective measures to apply human rights in order to eliminate FGM. Its elimination involves struggles that take their direction from the various sources — cultural, religious, domestic, or economic — that contribute to perpetuation of this practice. Different combinations of human rights must be employed to advance the goal of achieving sufficient understanding of the risks of FGM, sufficient confidence that uncircumcised daughters have futures as wives, and sufficient respect for the inherent dignity of women and for the integrity of women's bodies, that will end demand for the practice.

Much work is needed to apply the right to liberty and security of the person to ensure that the legal and ethical duty of confidentiality is respected in the delivery of reproductive and sexual health services generally, and to adolescents specifically. A common reason why adolescents decline to use health services to protect their reproductive health is that they do not trust health-care professionals to maintain confidentiality. They fear that disclosures of their sexual conduct and intentions, which they have to make for appropriate health care, will be related to their parents, parents of their partners, schoolteachers, and others. Offers of reproductive health-care services may be futile unless they incorporate credible provisions against breaches of confidentiality.

Rights relating to reproductive and sexual health

The state is obligated by its membership in human rights conventions to assume an affirmative role in establishing conditions for reproductive health and to provide appropriate services. Member States of the Economic Covenant recognize "the right of everyone to the enjoyment of the highest attainable standard of physical and mental health."[35] States Parties to the Women's Convention agree to

> . . . take all appropriate measures to eliminate discrimination against women in the field of health care in order to ensure, on a basis of equality of men and women, access to health care services, including those related to family planning.[36]

Treaty-monitoring bodies build on commitments made in consequence of the Cairo and Beijing texts to develop performance standards to determine whether states have met their minimum, core obligations to respect the right of individuals to the highest attainable standard of reproductive health throughout their life cycle. The CEDAW General Recommendation on Women and Health explains that health policies need to address a variety of risk factors, including:

- biological factors that vary between women and men according to their reproductive functions, such as pregnancy and childbirth;
- socio-economic factors that can vary according to sex, race, age, and resources, such as sexual abuse of dependent young girls;
- psychosocial factors that can vary according to sex, such as postpartum depression; and
- health system factors, such as maintaining confidentiality for both men and women who seek treatment of sexually transmitted diseases (STDs).[37]

Risk factors in themselves are not necessarily causes of violations of reproductive and sexual rights. However, a state might be held accountable for its failure to pay due regard in health planning and policies to such risk factors in cases where they lead to death, serious illness, infertility, or reproductive health failure such as unwanted pregnancy. Research in medicine, public health, social science,[38] and health systems organization is instrumental in identifying risk factors and understanding state failures that result in violations of human rights regarding reproductive and sexual health. Research may also serve to hold governmental and other agencies, and perhaps individuals, accountable.

The CEDAW General Recommendation explains that reports by states under the Women's Convention "must demonstrate that health legislation, plans and policies are based on scientific and ethical research and assessment of the health status and needs of women in that country and take into account any ethnic, regional or community variations or practices based on religion, tradition or culture."[39] This recommendation also calls on states to

[p]rioritize the prevention of unwanted pregnancy through family planning and sex education and reduce maternal mortality rates through safe motherhood services and prenatal assistance. When possible, legislation criminalizing abortion could be amended to remove punitive provisions imposed on women who undergo abortion.[40]

Member States are thus obligated by the Women's Convention to systematically address in their reports to CEDAW the national experience of the practice of abortion as it affects women's right to health.

Violations of women's right to the highest attainable standard of reproductive and sexual health continue to be evidenced, not only by subtle measures of health deficits, but also by the gross measure of maternal mortality and morbidity associated with unsafe abortion. The true rate of this common national failing to respect human rights is concealed where reliable statistics are not maintained or are not available for pregnancy-related deaths and disabilities.

In its Concluding Comments on the Report submitted by the Government of Venezuela under the Women's Convention, for instance, CEDAW noted with concern:

. . . the reduction of health budgets, the rise in the maternal mortality rate, the lack of and limited access to family-planning programmes (especially for teenagers), the lack of statistics on acquired immunodeficiency syndrome and women's limited access to public health services. In addition, legislation that criminalized abortion, even in cases of incest or rape, remains in force.[41]

Similarly, when CESCR, monitoring the Economic Covenant, reviewed Poland's abortion law, it noted that:

> . . . the recent imposition of legal restrictions on abortion has excluded economic and social grounds . . . because of this restriction, women in Poland are now resorting to unscrupulous abortionists and risking their health in doing so.[42]

The Committee expressed its concern that "family planning services are not provided in the public health-care system so that women have no access to affordable contraception."[43] Legislation had been enacted in Poland to liberalize abortion law and to allow procedures for compelling social reasons, but the country's Constitutional Tribunal rejected this legislation in 1997.[44]

The right to enjoy the benefits of scientific progress and its applications has yet to be effectively applied to require governments to give high priority to conducting reproductive health research, including biomedical, social science, and legal research, or to apply its findings. The right could be invoked, for instance, where women are denied access to antiprogestin drugs that pharmaceutical science has made effective for non-surgical abortion or to emergency contraception that they want, and in cases where reproductive and sexual health services are not financially or geographically accessible to men and women who are at high risk of reproductive and sexual ill health. CEDAW has also emphasized the need to avoid discrimination against high-risk women in national strategies for the prevention and control of HIV/AIDS. In its General Recommendation, the Committee urges States Parties to the Women's Convention to implement programmes to combat HIV/AIDS that "give special attention to the rights and needs of women . . . and to the factors relating to the reproductive role of women and their subordinate position in some societies which make them especially vulnerable to HIV infection."[45]

Rights relating to equality and due respect of difference

This third cluster of rights requires the elimination of discrimination on prohibited grounds of sex, gender, marital status, age, race and ethnicity, disability, and other status, such as sexual orientation, class, caste, and rural residence. States are obligated to eliminate laws and policies that are discriminatory and laws and policies that have a disproportionately harmful impact on one group, such as adolescents or members of an ethnic minority. Moreover, states are obligated to eliminate, not only their own discriminatory practices, but also those of private individuals in all spheres. The Women's Convention, for example, identifies the need to confront the social causes of women's inequality by addressing "all forms" of discrimination that women suffer. Legal prohibitions cover discrimination on grounds both of sex, which is a biological characteristic, and of gender, which is a social, cultural, and psychological construct that identifies particular acts or functions with one sex, such as spiritual leaders' being male and nurses, female.

Equality requires that we treat the same interests without discrimination; for example, in providing access for all young people to education irrespective of race, sex, or class, but that we also treat different interests in ways that adequately respect those differences; such as women's distinct interests in access to prenatal care, care during delivery, and post-natal care. Rights to due respect for sexual differences are violated when health services fail to accommodate the fundamental biological differences in reproduction, as evidenced by the 585,000 women each year who die needlessly of pregnancy-related causes.[46]

The state is also obligated to address compounding forms of discrimination, such as intersections of sex and race. The South African Parliament recognized the contribution of a liberal abortion law to the equality of the sexes and races in the Preamble to South Africa's Choice of Termination of Pregnancy Act, 1996. The first paragraph of the Preamble states that its provisions are enacted

> [r]ecognising the values of human dignity, the achievement of equality, security of the person, non-racism and non-sexism, and the advancement of human rights and freedoms which underlie a democratic South Africa.

The elimination of sexual stereotyping requires redressing such popular assumptions as the one that holds that responsibility to guard against unwanted pregnancy rests with the couple's female partner. If she is adolescent or unmarried, barriers to access to contraceptive services on grounds of age and marital status compound the injustice. Sexual equality requires that men accept responsibility with women to take measures against unwanted pregnancy and STDs. However, in many societies, unmarried motherhood is stigmatizing in ways that unmarried fatherhood is not, and requirements of proof of virginity apply only to females eligible for marriage.

The vulnerability of intellectually mature young women to age and sex discrimination is exacerbated when reproductive health services are made available to them only on the condition of parental authorization, while it is available to adults without need for authorization.[47] Mature adolescents suffer unjust discrimination when they are not free to obtain reproductive health counselling and services with the same confidentiality as adults. The Children's Convention requires that

> States Parties shall respect the rights and duties of the parents and, when applicable, legal guardians, to provide direction to the child in the exercise of his or her rights in a manner consistent with the evolving capacities of the child.[48]

Courts favour interpretations of laws that take due account of "the evolving capacities of the child." Courts do not generally permit parents to veto their adolescent children's access to reproductive health services solely on grounds of minor age. Courts often determine that parental powers are not absolute and decline as children's decision-making capacity evolves, and parents can be overridden by the courts. A common judicial approach is to recognize that parental rights exist, not for the benefit of the parents, third parties, or society, but for the benefit of the children. Laws equip parents to discharge their legal responsibilities to protect the best health and related interests of their children, but not to be arbitrary or to pursue their own convictions by risking their children's health or well-being.

In many countries, health status varies by race and ethnicity, indicating differential access among races and ethnic groups to the health care, information, and education necessary for health protection.[49] The potential for abuse of rights is often greater among ethnic minorities, which suggests that great care and sensitivity need to be applied in the delivery of reproductive health and related services in multi-ethnic societies. This is particularly the case with the introduction of permanent or long-acting contraceptive methods, such as Norplant, which can be applied without the free and informed consent necessary for other contraceptive methods. These methods may be offered or employed in ways that exploit the powerlessness, vulnerability, and subordinate status of racial minority populations. Control of reproduction in such communities in the United States, for instance, has been attempted through suspect means, such as courts' offering minority-group, low-income women offenders early release from imprisonment on probation if they accept long-acting contraceptive implants.[50]

Where the potential for abuse or neglect of rights is high among particular racial or ethnic groups because of such factors as historical disadvantage, poverty, or lack of education, the risk of abuse needs to be reduced through appropriate approaches and procedures. Approaches that hospitals and clinics might adopt include the appointment of a person from a vulnerable racial or ethnic community as a reproductive rights advocate or ombudsman to monitor the access of community members to reproductive health services and to guard against racial discrimination in access to means of reproductive self-determination. At a governmental or public health level, similar means might be taken to ensure non-discrimination in allocating reproductive health resources among districts and regions of different racial composition.

Human rights conventions prohibit discrimination, not only on specified grounds such as sex and age, but also on general grounds such as disability due, for instance, to HIV infection or physical or mental impairment. The Cairo and Beijing texts require governments to:

*   eliminate discrimination against persons infected with HIV and their families;
*   strengthen services to detect HIV infection, making sure that they protect confidentiality; and
*   devise special programmes to provide care and necessary emotional support to men and women affected by HIV/AIDS and to counsel their families and near relations.[51]

The Cairo and Beijing texts recognize that HIV infection in women often reflects women's preconditioning disability that, *as* women, they lack the social and legal power to control whether, when, and with what protections they have sexual relations.[52] The rights of disabled persons not to suffer discrimination, which exist not only for their protection against sexual abuse but also for them to achieve sexual satisfaction and health, present new frontiers for the advancement of human rights.

Non-discrimination law increasingly includes sexual orientation as a prohibited ground of discrimination. Denying individuals in same-sex relationships the services necessary to protect their health that are provided to persons in heterosexual relationships discriminates against those individuals because of their sexual orientation, offending human rights law. Human rights agencies may develop law and practice in this area since health care must be available on a basis of non-discrimination on grounds of sexual orientation.[53]

Rights relating to information, decision-making and education

The significance of information to reproductive health is reinforced by the Women's Convention, which requires that women have access to "specific educational information to help to ensure the health and well-being of families, including information and advice on family planning."[54] Nonetheless, in a number of countries it remains a criminal offence, sometimes described as a "crime against morality," to spread information on contraceptive methods or to publicize where women can get pregnancy termination services.[55]

International human rights legal tribunals have made some progress in protecting women's rights to health information.[56] In examining whether an injunction issued against the provision of information regarding availability of abortion services violates the right to freedom of expression, the European Court of Human Rights explained that the injunction:

> . . . has created a risk to the health of those women who are now seeking abortions at a later stage in their pregnancy, due to lack of proper counseling, and who are not availing of customary medical supervision after the abortion has taken place. Moreover, the injunction may have had more adverse effects on women who were not sufficiently resourceful or had not the necessary level of education to have access to alternative sources of information.[57]

It would seem, therefore, that human rights tribunals will be especially vigilant in reviewing cases concerning infringements on the availability of information that is necessary to protect reproductive and sexual health and where such infringements disproportionately affect those who lack resources or education. This decision could be applied to require governments to provide the information necessary to ensure that individuals can protect their reproductive and sexual health.

The European Court of Human Rights has required sensitivity to parents' views, but has upheld a compulsory sex education course in a state's schools when "the curriculum is conveyed in an objective, critical and pluralistic manner [and does not] pursue an aim of indoctrination that might be considered as not respecting parents' religious and philosophical convictions."[58]

The Cairo and Beijing documents encourage educational systems that eliminate all impediments to the schooling of married and/or pregnant girls and young mothers.[59] Such a barrier was removed in 1995, for instance, when the Botswana Court of Appeal ruled a college regulation unconstitutional that discriminated against female students by requiring that they inform the college director of their pregnancy, upon which they would become liable to suspension or expulsion.[60]

Holding governments accountable for violations of reproductive rights

Remedial and preventive applications of human rights must be approached in the context of each complaint that there has been a violation of human rights or that a human rights violation is liable to occur or be repeated. A sequence of approach is to:

1. identify the injury (wrong) and its causes;
2. document alleged violations;
3. determine which rights might be violated;
4. assess what might be the remedy or remedies that would be effective in addressing the injury and its causes;
5. determine which agencies are bound by duties to provide remedies; and
6. identify procedures at domestic, regional, or international levels available to compel observance of duties to remedy, prevent, and/or punish human rights violations.

Items in this sequence are elaborated by relevant research and carried out by agencies that commit themselves to the enforcement of human rights to remedy, relieve, and prevent violations of sexual and reproductive health rights.

Identify the wrong and its causes

In many cases, an alleged injury or wrong to reproductive or sexual health will be self-evident to those who complain of it. However, allegations may not be obvious to lay people or to authorities whose routine practices have caused the injury. For instance, denying unmarried adolescent girls access to contraception may be seen as necessary to maintain girls' fear of family and social sanctions against pregnancy outside marriage. Leaders of institutions accustomed to the exercise of authority in their communities, including office holders in governmental, religious, judicial, professional, educational, and other institutions, may not recognize that their familiar practices constitute injuries or wrongs to reproductive and sexual health. They may believe that protection of these familiar practices preserves necessary social values, including family integrity, private and public morality, and social order. Accordingly, advocates of remedies for human rights violations may bear an initial burden of persuasion to show that legitimate interests in reproductive and sexual health have been violated.

Such persuasion could entail showing the injuries to peoples' lives through the denial or frustration of their human rights relevant to reproductive and sexual health, and showing that the countries and communities in which the injuries have occurred claim to respect and observe these human rights. Injuries may be explained as harms suffered by an individual or by groups of individuals at a common risk due, for example, to age, race, or poverty.

Document alleged violations

Documentation of alleged violations of human rights is a necessary step in the process of holding governments accountable for violations of reproductive rights. Data, whether events-based or standards-based,[61] can play an instrumental role in triggering the legal accountability of states for violations of internationally protected human rights of reproductive self-determination. States may be held to account before international tribunals, but evidence of abuse can also be relevant in affecting the way one state conducts diplomatic or other relations with another. States resent, but also often react to, their status as pariah states among the community of nations, and they may amend their practices, while denying the justice of their condemnation, to maintain their international reputations. It has been observed in international human rights practice that it is possible to promote change by reporting facts.[62]

The nature of the violation being investigated may define the data to be employed. For instance, sexual abuse of women detained in state prisons can be evidenced by medical reports of examinations of victims. Alternatively, data can show the failure to protect certain reproductive rights. For instance, data showing high rates of abortion in countries can be used to shift the burden to those governments to explain why they are not effectively providing contraceptive services.[63] Reports, including those developed by the United Nations and its specialized agencies[64] and by NGOs,[65] demonstrate how government action and neglect can affect rights relating to reproductive self-determination. Events-based and standards-based data can be used to evaluate how effectively the right in question has been protected by the state, and whether an alternative approach to protection would have been more effective.[66] Careful documentation of data, whatever the sources, is needed to hold states accountable for violations of the range of rights that relate to reproductive self-determination.

Meticulously documented events-based data can show that human rights abuses represent policies rather than merely individual aberrations. Cases can demonstrate the absence of government efforts to eliminate and remedy abuses and can be employed to analyse trends over time. Cases before international and national tribunals, and events that are publicized by non-governmental human rights organizations, can direct attention beyond their facts to the underlying conditions of abuse. Individual testimony can be more effective than explanations of the history and dimensions of violations of rights relating to reproductive self-determination. Testimony presented at such meetings as the Women's Tribunal at the non-governmental forum of the FWCW,[67] for example, can generate names that will come to personify victimization by abuse of basic human rights.

Standards-based data are used in international human rights monitoring where states' discharge of their programmatic obligations are the focus of analysis.[68] Standards-based data are most useful when they include accompanying references to the internationally defined standards that are at issue and that states are accused of violating.[69] Breakdown of data by sex is usually essential to prove a violation of internationally recognized standards that measure discrimination against women. Data already exist that advocates for reproductive self-determination can employ effectively to construct or support arguments. In addition, however, advocates may have to generate new standards based on available credible data or on detached investigation of suspected discrimination in order to determine whether those suspicions have demonstrable substance. Advocates can demonstrate violations of rights to reproductive self-determination by reference to standards of practice that prevail in international experience. The challenge is to apply existing credible data and to generate new data to hold governments accountable for lack of compliance with rights relating to reproductive self-determination.

NGOs concerned with reproductive self-determination may document human rights abuses with a credibility that justifies the demand for state accountability. Organizations must prepare and present their reports, however, anticipating severe scrutiny by criticized states with a view to repudiating and condemning the data. Reproductive health agencies will need to build and maintain their own international reputations for rigour and balance, which will give their reports sufficient reliability on which to base demands for state accountability.

Determine the rights violated

Domestic, regional, and international judicial tribunals are increasingly willing to treat human rights as interdependent and to recognize that infringement of one right frequently implicates another. Nevertheless, advocates must specify which right or rights they claim have been violated in a particular injury and complaint. Specification is necessary because the domestic, regional, and international legal instruments containing rights may have differential applications, allowing agencies to defend and escape liability by making technical claims; such as, for example, that the instrument or provision alleged to have been violated is not binding on the agency, or was not binding at the time of incidents alleged to constitute or to have caused injuries.

Rights are rarely expressed in language that is directly applicable to reproductive and sexual health. The advocate must show the relevance of a particular right to .an alleged failure of reproductive or sexual health by drawing on legal literature: including judicial decisions; documents of international authority, such as the Cairo and Beijing documents; and those of treaty-monitoring bodies, such as CEDAW. This is frequently challenging, because human rights have been applied only infrequently to reproductive health problems. The challenge is to achieve collaboration among colleagues who can bring their individual knowledge of medicine, local culture and practice, law, health system organization, and governmental structure to the task.

Assess how to pursue effective remedies

Advocates must know what outcome they want to achieve, since not every initiative may be effective. For example: if the aim is to achieve future government services, it may be necessary to consult with government; if the aim is to achieve compensatory or even punitive remedies, it may require proceedings in law courts. If, on the other hand, the aim is to hold governments to their international commitments, it may require action before international treaty-monitoring agencies that can determine governments' failures and call for improved performance.

Desired outcomes must be determined by the causes of injuries to reproductive or sexual health. The effectiveness of remedies, even when successfully pursued, depends on the proper identification of the causes of the injuries. Nevertheless, for political, procedural, or other reasons, it may not be possible to pursue the best remedies, and root causes of reproductive ill health may be too complex or culturally ingrained to be changed by anything other than fundamental social change. Therefore, within the limits of resources, personnel, time, and other practical constraints, outcomes may have to be targeted and remedies pursued that are less than perfect but that will achieve significant advances in reproductive health.

For example, a study in the state of Washington in the United States showed that two-thirds of a sample of 535 young women became pregnant as a result of some form of sexual abuse by older men.[70] These findings showed that the government needed to address the problem of sexual abuse of adolescent girls. Providing contraceptive services to reduce the incidence of pregnancy does not remedy such abuse. Criminal law enforcement and parental and other protection of vulnerable adolescents, reinforced by judicial and welfare agency initiatives, are required for effective remedy of this sexual abuse and exploitation of young girls. Pregnancy rates due to sexual behaviour among age-related peers may be addressed through promotion of sexuality education. However, management of their voluntary sexual behaviour and of their victimization by predatory older men, who may perhaps be in positions of authority over them, are two different things that present different challenges, requiring different remedies for effectiveness.

Determination of agencies bound to provide remedies

As discussed above, remedies may be found by referring to accessible agencies or tribunals that can be obliged to address and rectify a failure of reproductive or sexual health. It is a matter of strategy, opportunity, and circumstance whether it is preferable to determine a goal and then seek agencies to act through to achieve that goal, or to identify accessible agencies that can be motivated or compelled to act.

Accessible agencies may be bound by different obligations. Obligations may originate by force of law, established at domestic, regional, or international levels. Obligations may also originate through political pressure, which may be brought to bear by legal action; political persuasive power wielded by political, religious, and other institutions, including news media; and, at times, the force of public opinion. The advantage of domestic laws is that they may be enforceable by courts or administrative bodies with the power to compel parties to attend proceedings initiated there and to defend accusations of misconduct made against them and with the power to enforce their judgements. Some regional human rights agencies are developing comparable authority, such as the Inter-American Commission and Court of Human Rights. However, the higher the level at which remedies are pursued, through domestic, regional, and international agencies, the weaker the compulsory powers are to enforce compliance. The bodies that monitor regional and international human rights conventions often depend on the power of moral condemnation, political embarrassment, and national pride to induce reform.

Governmental officers sensitive to their reputations for humane, effective, and just management of the concerns of the populations they claim to serve, and proud to act within the framework of the rule of law, may be persuaded by advocacy and the findings of judicial and other inquiries that their administrations are failing to protect human rights in general and reproductive rights in particular. Governments widely recognize that the greatest assets of their countries are the people themselves, especially their children. Demonstration that the interests of the people, families, and children are compromised through political policies or neglect that harm reproductive health may inspire, or oblige, incentives for reform. The task of advocates remains, however, to direct reform towards specified goals, otherwise reform initiatives may turn out to be inadequate, misguided, or counterproductive.

Identify procedures at domestic, regional, or international levels

Procedures available at the domestic, regional, and international levels to compel observance of duties to remedy, prevent, and punish violations of reproductive rights may be undertaken by a spectrum of means, ranging from more consensual, non-confrontational discussions and inquiries to sharply adversarial political and legal action. Which means are used will be a matter of political and social judgement and of how comfortable activists feel in initiating procedures to compel compliance with human rights standards before particular tribunals.

The least invasive, most collegial approaches are to inquire of the agencies that control reproductive and sexual health services or service funding levels if they are satisfied that the results of their practices meet human rights standards. They may be presented with data from other agencies or countries on levels of performance that meet such standards, and asked if they are performing at this level or have programmes in place to do so. If public data exist indicating that they are not meeting such standards, they can be asked how they propose to raise their performance to these standards of achievement. This approach supposes that questioners and agencies share common purposes, and questioners may offer assistance or advice on developments towards meeting standards.

Responsible agencies may claim that their performance is satisfactory or that they have no obligation, or means, to satisfy higher standards than they claim to be achieving. A response may be to call for an inquiry into the prevailing standards of agency performance, into methods of determining the level and adequacy of standards, and into the source and extent of the obligations they are required to discharge. Such inquiries may be investigative, in which an appointed investigator asks questions and seeks evidence, or adversarial, in which opposing interests present their evidence and question the evidence presented by others.

In some circumstances, officers may already exist who are equipped to conduct their own inquiries and perhaps receive representations on behalf of agencies and interests in dispute about facts and standards that should be met. Derived from the Swedish ombudsman, the model of "ombudspersons" has been widely adopted. It is a mechanism through which institutions such as hospitals, government departments, and private organizations appoint independent officers to conduct inquiries into their procedures at the request of, for example, patients, service recipients, or staff members.[71] Ombudspersons usually follow predetermined procedures to hear questions or complaints, to determine facts by their own inquiries and receipt of evidence from interested parties, and to present their conclusions. Often, they may make recommendations for reform and for correcting improprieties that investigations have disclosed. For example, the Women's Ombud in Costa Rica has reported significant lapses in gynaecological and obstetric care, including lack of attention to privacy, and failure to follow through on tests for detecting cervical cancer.[72]

The model of the ombudsperson is a systematic example of what is generically described as alternative dispute resolution (ADR) through an officer established in advance of any particular dispute. Commonly, however, disputes arise before informal mechanisms for resolution are put into place. ADR may be approached through agreement among the parties in dispute to appoint an agreed person to proceed in agreed ways to propose means by which the dispute can be resolved to parties' mutual satisfaction. However, ADR cannot be employed when an agency complained against refuses to recognize the capacity of the complainant to question its performance or to call it to account. ADR is consensual, depending upon mutual recognition, respect, and collaboration among parties.

Where it is claimed that those bound by professional codes of ethics regarding reproductive and sexual health services are failing to comply, professional licensing and informal professional associations may be asked to conduct inquiries into professional conduct. Licensing authorities appointed by law, whose mandate is usually to protect the public against unqualified health-care practice and unethical practice by those who are qualified, usually have power to compel licensed practitioners' attendance before disciplinary tribunals that conduct hearings on allegations of professional misconduct. In addition, voluntary professional associations may also be entitled under terms of members' contracts of membership to ensure that members maintain conditions of membership, particularly that they act in accordance with an association's ethical requirements.

Courts of law may conduct hearings according to civil law, administrative law, or criminal law processes. In some countries, separate constitutional courts exist. All courts of law conduct proceedings according to publicly available rules of practice and are usually open to the public and reportable in news media. According to their traditions, they may conduct their hearings by adversarial or inquisitorial procedures, but they will usually accommodate the arguments and evidence of parties to which they award standing to be heard. It is usually expected that they give reasons for their decisions and that their decisions are issued publicly and are enforceable by the authority of the tribunals themselves.

The transcending problem of courts of law is that the justice they offer is frequently practically inaccessible to many people and interests. Access depends on the purchase of expensive legal skills, knowledge of detailed procedures, drafting and interpretation of complex documents, and the willingness to be patient for many months or years for completion of sequential procedural steps leading to a judgement. Trial judgements are often open to appeal, which further prolongs the process to resolution, and increases complexities and costs. Important initiatives are under way to educate judges of domestic courts in domestic application of the Convention on the Rights of the Child.[73] Similar work could usefully be initiated to train judges about the application of national, regional, and international human rights concerning reproductive and sexual health.

Procedures to foster regional and international compliance among members of treaty regimes include procedures for undertaking reports, complaints, and inquiries. A careful reading of each convention is required to determine which mechanisms are available under the convention to achieve compliance and the conditions required to apply them.

Reporting procedures. Countries that are members of different international and regional human rights conventions are obligated to report national performance of their duties on a periodic basis to each appropriate treaty-monitoring body. For instance, through the Women's Convention, 163 states have committed themselves to report regularly to CEDAW on what they have done to

> . . . take all appropriate measures to eliminate discrimination against women in the field of health care in order to ensure . . . access to health-care services, including those related to family planning . . . pregnancy, confinement and the post-natal period, granting free services where necessary, as well as adequate nutrition during pregnancy and lactation.[74]

To assist countries in their reporting obligations, treaty-monitoring bodies have developed a series of General Recommendations.[75] These recommendations explain the content and meaning of treaty articles and outline the kind of information that treaty bodies find useful in reviewing the compliance records of reporting countries. For example, the CEDAW General Recommendation on Women and Health requires that:

> . . . in order to enable the Committee to evaluate whether *measures to eliminate discrimination against women in the field of health care are appropriate*, States Parties must report on their health legislation, plans and policies for women with reliable data disaggregated by sex on the incidence and severity of diseases and conditions hazardous to women's health and nutrition and on the availability and cost-effectiveness of preventive and curative measures.[76]

This recommendation stresses that:

> . . . reports to the Committee must demonstrate that health legislation, plans and policies are based on scientific and ethical research and assessment of the health status and needs of women in that country and take into account any ethnic, regional or community variations or practices based on religion, tradition or culture.[77]

In addition to developing General Recommendations, CEDAW agreed to use the ICPD Programme of Action in developing performance standards[78] to determine whether states are in compliance with their obligations under the Women's Convention.

Monitoring committees are mandated to be vigilant in their scrutiny of states' reports regarding evidence of defaults on responsibilities. For this purpose, most treaty-monitoring committees, including CEDAW, receive alternative reports or comments on state performance submitted by NGOs,[79] which may incorporate significant findings of states' failures to protect and promote reproductive and sexual health. Such findings may result from medical, public health, or social science research.

Once a treaty-monitoring committee has considered a country report and any additional information on treaty compliance, it issues Concluding Observations noting the achievements of the reporting state to take steps to bring its laws, policies, and practices into compliance with its treaty obligations and the concerns the committee has with lack of compliance.[80] For example, CEDAW's Concluding Observations on the Report of the Government of Hungary included the following points with regard to reproductive health and related matters:

> . . . the state of health of the female population was unsatisfactory when judged by international standards. In particular, the high cost of contraceptives prevented women from freely planning when to have children. The very high increase in the rate of abortions was of concern to the Committee.[81]

As a result, CEDAW requested the government to offer sex education programmes to all young people and to subsidize contraceptives in order to promote family planning and reduce the number of abortions.[82] CEDAW also requested the government to take urgent legislative and concrete measures to provide female victims of violence with protection and appropriate services.[83] CEDAW further noted with concern the scale of the problem of prostitution, which affected girls and women of ethnic minorities in particular,[84] and urgently requested the government to take all necessary measures to rehabilitate and reintegrate prostitutes into society.[85]

Complaint procedures. Procedures exist under some conventions, such as the American Convention on Human Rights, the European Convention on Human Rights, and the International Covenant on Civil and Political Rights, which enable individuals or groups of individuals from consenting states to bring international complaints against their own states for violations. Accommodation of a complaints procedure under the Optional Protocol to the Women's Convention has recently been approved by the United Nations Commission on the Status of Women.[86]

A normal condition of regional and international tribunals receiving individuals' petitions is that such individuals must have exhausted all reasonable possibilities of achieving remedies before national tribunals of the state against which the petition is brought. This condition respects the legal duties and rights of states to afford remedies for wrongs through their own procedures. Once complainants have exhausted domestic procedures available to them, they can then proceed to either regional or international tribunals to claim remedies for alleged violations. While complaints are brought by individuals or a group of individuals, their successful complaints can have the effect of requiring governments to change laws to the benefit of their entire societies.

Inquiry and communications procedures. The Optional Protocol to the Women's Convention[87] allows for a procedure of inquiry, which may include a visit to a territory if reliable information is received indicating grave or systematic violations by a State Party. This procedure would allow, for example, for visits to appropriate sites to investigate governmental neglect of high rates of preventable maternal mortality or preventable cervical cancers.

Outside the treaty regimes is the United Nations Special Rapporteur on Violence Against Women, who has facilitated clarifications of both international and domestic standards of protection. The United Nations Commission on Human Rights appointed the Special Rapporteur on Violence Against Women with a broad mandate to eliminate such violence and its causes, and to remedy its consequences by recommending ways and means at national, regional, and international levels to eliminate gender violence.[88] The Special Rapporteur receives communications about alleged incidents of gender-specific violence against women that have not been effectively addressed through national legal systems. In ways that are similar to those of an ombudsman working at the domestic level, the Rapporteur uses this information to conduct dialogue with governments about finding resolutions to complaints.[89] Reports of the Special Rapporteur[90] show that such violence may be an offence by a state itself against a broad range of accepted rights expressed in international human rights treaties already binding on the state in question.[91]

UNFPA's Next Thirty Years: Programming to Foster Compliance

In order to ensure improvements in reproductive and sexual health in the next phase of its work, UNFPA will need to devote a major part of its programming to fostering compliance with rights relating to reproductive and sexual health. Programming might begin by reviewing the work that has been undertaken at the domestic, regional, and international levels to address why certain rules of law "exert more pull towards compliance than others."[92] Some analysts explain that nations obey rules of international law because of considerations of legitimacy and distributive justice.[93] While much work is needed to understand how best to promote compliance, three steps might be useful starting points for UNFPA to devise programming strategies to promote compliance with reproductive rights.[94]

Actors

If it is true that actors — whether they be national governments, international governmental or NGOs, or (for example) national health professional associations — obey human rights law as a result of repeated interactions with other actors in the transnational legal process, a first step is to empower more actors to participate in these interactions.[95]

The Cairo process has in fact empowered more actors to participate in the transnational legal process. Moreover, the process helped a new generation of people engage in interactions that induce state compliance with reproductive rights. If the momentum is to be maintained, more and different voices have to be brought into the debate. Particularly important are participants who are at risk of poor reproductive and sexual health and whose reproductive rights are not adequately respected. They include adolescents, marginalized or minority groups, and those at high risk of unwanted pregnancy and of contracting STDs, including HIV/AIDS. Programming needs to focus on empowering those groups and developing their capacity to make use of the human rights systems at the domestic, regional, and international levels.

Forums

If the goal of interaction is to foster compliance through improved interpretation and application of reproductive rights, programming strategies need to focus on the identification and use of all available forums and mechanisms for interaction at the domestic, regional, and international levels and in and outside existing human rights regimes.[96] The primary forums for advancing protection and promotion of human rights are at the national level. National authorities are obligated to prevent violations of human rights and to provide remedies for violations. When national authorities fail in these obligations, regional or international systems are often called upon to enforce observance of such obligations. That is, the regional[97] and international[98] systems supplement national systems.[99]

The application of human rights to remedy reproductive and sexual ill health at any of these levels has been infrequent and mixed. Effective programming will have to begin with diagnosing the causes of the failures of application of reproductive rights. Causes are many, and vary according to each country and context. They include societies' reluctance to address matters of reproduction and sexuality, a lack of understanding of the human rights discourse, and a lack of literacy about reproductive rights.

Human rights treaty bodies constitute increasingly important forums for interpreting and applying human rights norms on reproductive and sexual health in specific countries. The Cairo process increased the understanding of reproductive rights among members of human rights treaty bodies. If treaty bodies are to continue to be effective in the development and application of reproductive rights, there needs to be an ongoing process of training their members, particularly since new individuals are elected by Member Governments on a periodic basis, usually every two years.

Integration

Effective strategies must be sought for integrating or internalizing reproductive rights into domestic laws, policies, and practices, and for sharing norms conducive to the protection of reproductive and sexual health across national and regional boundaries.[100] It might be useful to distinguish among social, political, and legal integration. Social integration occurs when a norm acquires so much public legitimacy that there is widespread general obedience to it. Political integration occurs when political leaders accept an international norm and adopt it as a matter of government policy. Legal integration occurs when regional[101] and international[102] norms are incorporated into the domestic legal system through executive action, judicial interpretation, legislative action, or some combination of the three.

Another way to achieve integration is by pulling down norms from international and regional levels into domestic systems in order to develop domestic norms that are conducive to reproductive and sexual health. Countries might also pull norms across from other national systems, particularly from countries that share common cultural traditions, such as among Hispanic, Francophone, or Islamic countries. Another option might be to explore the enhancement of norms that exist within a country, such as those found in local laws and customs.

Effective programming to foster compliance with sexual and reproductive rights requires a review of the understanding of such rights, the capacity to implement them, and the motivation to do so.[103] A review has to determine the extent to which these rights are understood and enjoyed. It needs to identify whether standards of compliance are sufficiently developed to bind those responsible for the implementation of those rights. A review also needs to determine whether the exercise of rights varies according to groups of persons, distinguished for instance by sex, race, or age.

A review must identify the administrative, technical or financial capacity of a population to exercise rights to advance their sexual and reproductive health interests, including legal services to enforce the observation of rights.[104] An assessment might usefully be made of progress achieved and potential created for future progress to remedy deficiencies in capacities to implement sexual and reproductive health.

Finally, effective programming requires UNFPA to determine whether governments intend to apply sexual and reproductive rights. Intent might be objectively assessed by the actual measures governments take to improve women's status and the proportion of their available financial resources that they allocate for this purpose. The requisite intent might exist in some ministries, such as the health ministry, but not in others, such as the budget office. The intent of governments to devote their resources and time to advance sexual and reproductive rights will limit how much they can devote to governmental commitments in other sectors. Therefore, a rights agenda will always face competition within a government from advocates of other causes that the government wants to support.

Programming strategies to foster compliance with sexual and reproductive rights can be grouped into three categories: "negative incentives in the form of penalties, sanctions and withdrawal of membership privileges; sunshine methods, such as monitoring, reporting, transparency and NGO participation; and positive methods, such as special funds for financial or technical assistance, access to technology or training programs . . . The question then becomes, which methods work best under what set of circumstances?"[105]

"Negative incentives" are usually invoked through the judicial system and require a high degree of legal capacity. "Sunshine methods" refers to methods that bring unseen, oppressive practices to light. The choice between sunshine methods on one hand and positive methods on the other, or adopting a mix of the two, will depend on the capacity and the intent of governments to comply.[106] For example, where a country has a genuine intent to comply but limited capacity, positive methods might be more appropriate. Where there is capacity to comply but the requisite political intent is lacking, sunshine methods might be more effective, particularly to engage NGOs in promoting the priority of sexual and reproductive rights. Where both capacity and intent are limited, a mixture of both methods might be appropriate.

Appendix

Table: Human Rights Regarding Reproductive and Sexual Health

(The numbers show the relevant provisions of the international instruments [top line] that relate to the named right [left column].)

International/Regional Instruments → Rights	Universal Declaration of Human Rights	Int'l Covenant on Civil and Political Rights	Int'l Covenant on Economic, Social and Cultural Rights	Int'l Convention on Elimination of All Forms of Racial Discrimination	Convention on Elimination of All Forms of Discrimination against Women	Convention on the Rights of the Child	European Convention on Human Rights and Its Five Protocols and Social Charter	American Convention on Human Rights and Its Protocol	African Charter on Human and Peoples' Rights	Cairo Programme of Action	Beijing Declaration and Platform for Action
Rights Relating to Security, Autonomy and Confidentiality											
Right to Life and Survival	3	6				6	2	4	4	Principle 1 8.21 8.25	97 106(I)-(1)
Right to Liberty and Security	1 3	9		5(b)		37(b)-(d)	5	7	6	4.10 4.22, 5.5 7.12, 7.40	97 106(g)(h) 106(k) 107(e)(q) 124(l) 135 269 277(d) 283(d)
Right to Be Free from Inhuman and Degrading Treatment						8 9					
Right to Marry and Found a Family	16	23	10	5(d)(iv)	16		12	17	18	4.21	93 274(c) 275(l)

Table: Human Rights Regarding Reproductive and Sexual Health

(The numbers show the relevant provisions of the international instruments [top line] that relate to the named right [left column].)

International/Regional Instruments → Rights	Universal Declaration of Human Rights	Int'l Covenant on Civil and Political Rights	Int'l Covenant on Economic, Social and Cultural Rights	Int'l Convention on Elimination of All Forms of Racial Discrimination	Convention on Elimination of All Forms of Discrimination against Women	Convention on the Rights of the Child	European Convention on Human Rights and Its Five Protocols and Social Charter	American Convention on Human Rights and Its Protocol	African Charter on Human and Peoples' Rights	Cairo Programme of Action	Beijing Declaration and Platform for Action
Right to Private and Family Life	12	17	10		16	16	8	11	4 5	7.3 7.12 7.17-7.20	103 107(e) 108(m) 267
Rights Relating to Reproductive and Sexual Health											
Right to Highest Standard of Health	25		12	5(e)(iv)	11(1)(f) 12 14(2)(b)	24	Charter: 13	26 Protocol: 9, 10	16	7.2, 7.3 7.5, 7.6 7.16 7.23 7.27-7.33 8.28-8.35	92, 94 95, 98 103 106(c)(e) 106(g) 108
Right to Benefits of Scientific Progress	27(2)		15(1)(b) 15(3)					26	22	2.10 12.10-12.26	104 106(g)(h) 108(o)(p)

Table: Human Rights Regarding Reproductive and Sexual Health

(The numbers show the relevant provisions of the international instruments [top line] that relate to the named right [left column].)

International/Regional Instruments → Rights	Universal Declaration of Human Rights	Int'l Covenant on Civil and Political Rights	Int'l Covenant on Economic, Social and Cultural Rights	Int'l Convention on Elimination of All Forms of Racial Discrimination	Convention on Elimination of All Forms of Discrimination against Women	Convention on the Rights of the Child	European Convention on Human Rights and Its Five Protocols and Social Charter	American Convention on Human Rights and Its Protocol	African Charter on Human and Peoples' Rights	Cairo Programme of Action	Beijing Declaration and Platform for Action
Rights Relating to Equality and Due Respect of Difference											
Right to Non-Discrimination on Grounds of Sex and Gender	1, 2, 6	2(1), 3	2(2), 3		1, 2, 3, 4, 5	2(1)	14	1, 24	2, 3, 18(3), 28 (duty)	4.16 4.25	97 277(l)
Right to Non-Discrimination on Grounds of Marital Status	1, 2, 6	2(1)	2(2)		1		14	1, 24	2, 3, 18(3), 28	7.3, 7.7, 7.8, 7.12, 7.14	93, 95, 106(g), (h)
Right to Non-Discrimination on Grounds of Age	1, 2, 6	2(1)	2(2)			2(2)	14	1, 24	2, 3, 18(3), 28	7.41 7.45 7.46	83(k)(l) 106-108 281
Right to Non-Discrimination on Grounds of Race and Ethnicity	1, 2, 6	2(1)	2(2)	1, 2, 3		2(1)	14	1, 24	2, 3, 18(3), 28	7.3, 7.7, 7.8, 7.12, 7.14	106(b) and (h), 107(e)
Right to Non-Discrimination on Grounds of Disability (e.g., HIV positivity)	1, 2, 6	2(1)	2(2)			2(2)	14	1, 24	2, 3 18(4), 28	7.34-7.40 8.34	99 108
Right to Non-Discrimination on Grounds of Sexual Orientation	1, 2, 6	2(1)	2(2)			2(2)	14	1, 24	2, 3 18(4), 28	7.34-7.40 8.34	99 108

Table: Human Rights Regarding Reproductive and Sexual Health

(The numbers show the relevant provisions of the international instruments [top line] that relate to the named right [left column].)

International/Regional Instruments → Rights	Universal Declaration of Human Rights	Int'l Covenant on Civil and Political Rights	Int'l Covenant on Economic, Social and Cultural Rights	Int'l Convention on Elimination of All Forms of Racial Discrimination	Convention on Elimination of All Forms of Discrimination against Women	Convention on the Rights of the Child	European Convention on Human Rights and Its Five Protocols and Social Charter	American Convention on Human Rights and Its Protocol	African Charter on Human and Peoples' Rights	Cairo Programme of Action	Beijing Declaration and Platform for Action
Rights Relating to Information, Decision-Making and Education											
Right to Receive and Impart Information	19	19			10(e) 14(b) 16(e)	12 13 17	10	13	9	7.3 7.20 7.23	95 103 106(m) 107(e) 108(i) 223
Right to Education	26		13, 14	5(e)(v) 7	10 14(d)	28 29	Protocol 1:2 Charter: 13	26	17	4.18 7.47 11.8	74 80 81 83 (k)(l) 267 277(a)

References

[1] United Nations, *Report of the International Conference on Population and Development*, Cairo, 5-13 September 1994. Programme of Action.

[2] United Nations, *Report of the Fourth World Conference on Women*. Beijing, 4-5 September 1995 (New York: United Nations, 1995); see generally, United Nations Population Fund, *Compendium of Social Issues from the United Nations Global Conferences in the 1990s* (New York: UNFPA, 1997).

[3] Development Alternatives with Women for a New Era, *Implementing ICPD: Moving Forward in the Eye of the Storm, Suva, Fiji* (DAWN, 1999); Health, Empowerment, Rights & Accountability, *Confounding the Critics: Cairo, Five Years On* (New York: HERA, 1998); Women's Environment and Development Organization, *Risks, Rights and Reforms: A Fifty Country Survey Assessing Government Actions Five Years After the International Conference on Population and Development* (New York: WEDO, 1999).

[4] United Nations Population Fund, *The State of World Population: 1997 — The Right to Choose: Reproductive Rights and Reproductive Health* (New York: UNFPA, 1997); United Nations Division for the Advancement of Women, United Nations Population Fund, United Nations High Commissioner for Human Rights, Round Table of Human Rights Treaty Bodies on Human Rights Approaches to Women's Health, with a Focus on Sexual and Reproductive Health and Rights: "Summary of Proceedings and Recommendations" (New York: UNFPA, 1998); United Nations Population Fund, *Ensuring Reproductive Rights and Implementing Sexual and Reproductive Health Programmes Including Women's Empowerment, Male Involvement and Human Rights* (New York: UNFPA, 1998).

[5] International Planned Parenthood Federation, *Charter on Sexual and Reproductive Rights and Guidelines* (London: IPPF, 1996).

[6] See for instance, Women's Health Project, *From Words to Action: Sexual and Reproductive Rights, Health Policies and Programming in South Africa 1994-1997* (Johannesburg: Women's Health Project, 1998).

[7] See for instance, Commonwealth Medical Association, *A Women's Right to Health, Including Sexual and Reproductive Health* (London: CMA, 1996).

[8] See for instance, "Conference on the International Protection of Reproductive Rights," *American University Law Review*, Vol. 44, No. 4 (1995); "Symposium on Sexual and Reproductive Rights," *International Nordic Journal of International Law*, Vol. 67, No. 1 (1998).

[9] Rosalind P. Petchesky, Karen Judd (eds.), *Negotiating Reproductive Rights: Women's Perspectives Across Countries and Cultures* (London, New York: Zed Books, 1998).

[10] Center for Reproductive Law and Policy, Estudo para la Defensa de los Derechos de la Mujer, *Women of the World: Laws and Policies Affecting their Reproductive Lives: Latin America and the Caribbean* (New York: CRLP, 1997); Center for Reproductive Law and Policy, International Federation of Women Lawyers — Kenya Chapter, *Women of the World: Laws and Policies Affecting their Reproductive Lives: Anglophone Africa* (New York: CRLP, 1997); See also references at Women's Human Rights Resources web site at: http://www.law-lib.utoronto.ca/Diana/index.htm. Last accessed April 12, 1999.

[11] For legal developments on reproductive rights, see *Annual Review of Population Law* web site: http://www.law.harvard.edu/programs/annualreview. Last accessed April 12, 1999.

[12] United Nations, *Report of the International Conference on Population and Development*, Cairo, 5-13 September 1994. Programme of Action: *supra* note 1, para. 7.3.

¹³ United Nations, General Assembly resolution 2200 (XXI), 21 UN GAOR Supp. (No. 16) at 52, UN Doc. A/6316 (1996).

¹⁴ Ibid.: at 49.

¹⁵ 213 U.N.T.S. 221 (1959).

¹⁶ OASTS at 1 (1969).

¹⁷ OAU Doc. CAB/Leg/67/3/Rev. 5 (1981).

¹⁸ United Nations, General Assembly resolution 25 (XLIV), UN Doc. A/Res/44/25 (1989), reprinted in 28 I.L.M. 1448 (1989).

¹⁹ United Nations, 34 UN GAOR Supp. (No. 21) (A/34/46) at 193, UN Doc. A/Res/34/180, 18 December 1979.

²⁰ See generally, *Reproductive Health Matters*, Vol. 6, No. 12, "Thematic Issue on Sexuality" (1998).

²¹ Rebecca J. Cook, Bernard M. Dickens, Laura E. Bliss, "International Developments in Abortion Law from 1988 to 1998," *American Journal of Public Health*, 89 (1999): pp. 579-586.

²² Convention on the Elimination of All Forms of Discrimination against Women, General Recommendation 24 on Women and Health, CEDAW/C/1999/I/WG.II/WP 2/Rev.1, 1 February 1999.

²³ Ibid.: para. 14.

²⁴ Ibid.

²⁵ Ibid.: para. 15.

²⁶ Ibid.

²⁷ Ibid.: para. 17.

²⁸ See for example, Reed Boland *et. al.*, "Honoring Human Rights in Population Policies: From Declaration to Action," *Population Policies Reconsidered: Health, Empowerment, and Rights*, eds. Gita Sen, Adrienne Germain, Lincoln Chen (Boston: Harvard University Press, 1994): p. 89; Rebecca J. Cook, "International Protection of Women's Reproductive Rights," 24, *N.Y.U. J. Int'l. L. & Pol.*, 645 (New York: New York University, 1992); Rebecca J. Cook, "International Human Rights and Women's Reproductive Health," *24 Studies in Family Planning*, 73 (1993); Sonia Correa, Rosalind Petchesky, "Reproductive and Sexual Rights: A Feminist Perspective," in *Population Policies Reconsidered*, eds. Sen, Germain, Chen, p. 107; Ruth Dixon-Mueller, *Population Policy and Women's Rights: Transforming Reproductive Choice*, 12-15 (1993); Lynn P. Freedman, "Reflections on Emerging Frameworks of Health and Human Rights," *Health and Human Rights*, eds. Jonathan M. Mann, Sofia Gruskin, Michael A. Grodin, George Annas (New York: Routledge, 1998): pp. 227-252; Lynn P. Freedman, Stephen L . Isaacs, "Human Rights and Reproductive Choices," *24 Studies in Family Planning*, 18 (1993); Berta E. Hernandez, "To Bear or Not to Bear: Reproductive Freedom as an International Human Right," 17, *Brooklyn J. of Int'l. L.* (Brooklyn, NY: Brooklyn Law School, 1991): p. 309; Corinne A. A. Packer, *The Right to Reproductive Choice* (Turku, Finland: Abo Akademi University, Institute for Human Rights, 1996); Anika Rahman, Rachel Pine, "An International Human Right to Reproductive Health Care: Toward Definition and Accountability," *Health and Human Rights*, 1 (1995): pp. 400-427; Katarina Tomasevski, *Human Rights in Population Policies* (Stockholm: Swedish International Development Agency, 1994); Noel Whitty, "The Mind, Body, and Reproductive Health Information," *Human Rights Quarterly*, 18 (1996): pp. 224-239.

[29] Larry O. Gostin, Zita Lazzarini, *Human Rights and Public Health in the AIDS Pandemic* (New York: Oxford University Press, 1997); Dayanath C. Jayasuriya, ed., *HIV Law, Ethics and Human Rights* (New Delhi: UNDP, 1995); Jonathan Mann, "Human Rights and AIDS: The Future of the Pandemic," *Health and Human Rights,* eds. Jonathan M. Mann, Sofia Gruskin, Michael A. Grodin, George Annas (New York: Routledge, 1998): pp. 216-226.

[30] Mirta T. Insurralde, 148 PS. 3757/428, Corte Suprema de la Provincia de Sante Fe, Argentina, August 2, 1998 (Court found that a doctor incurred no legal liability for breaching patient confidentiality by reporting an adolescent girl to the authorities for seeking treatment for complications resulting from an allegedly illegal abortion).

[31] Anita Rahman, Nahid Toubia, eds., *Female Genital Mutilation: A Human Rights Analysis — A Practical Guide to Worldwide Laws and Policies* (London: Zed Books, forthcoming 1999).

[32] Proceedings of the 1998 Regional Conference on Trafficking in Women, (Tokyo: Asian Women's Fund, 1999).

[33] *Tavares v. France*, Application No. 16593/90, decision on admissibility (European Commission of Human Rights, 12 September 1991).

[34] United Nations, Concluding Observations of the Human Rights Committee, CCPRC/79/Add.72 (18 November 1996): para. 15.

[35] Article 12.

[36] Ibid.

[37] Convention on the Elimination of All Forms of Discrimination against Women, General Recommendation 24 on Women and Health, CEDAW/C/1999/I/WG.II/WP 2/Rev.1, 1 February 1999: para. 9.

[38] Shireen J. Jejeebhoy, "The Importance of Social Science Research in the Promotion of Sexual and Reproductive Choice of Adolescents," *Medicine and Law,* Vol. 18, symposium edition on "Legal and Ethical Aspects of Reproductive and Sexual Health in Central and Eastern Europe" (1999).

[39] Convention on the Elimination of All Forms of Discrimination against Women, General Recommendation 24 on Women and Health, CEDAW/C/1999/I/WG.II/WP 2/Rev.1, 1 February 1999: para. 9.

[40] Para. 31(c).

[41] United Nations, Report of the Committee on the Elimination of Discrimination Against Women (Sixteenth Session), Doc A/52/38 (Part I) 24 June 1997: para. 236.

[42] Committee on Economic, Social and Cultural Rights, Concluding Observations on Poland, Doc. E/C.12/1998/28: paras. 11-12.

[43] Ibid.

[44] Polish Constitutional Court Tribunal *Ruling K 26/96*, 28 May 1997.

[45] United Nations, Report of the Committee on the Elimination of Discrimination Against Women (Ninth Session) Doc. A/45/38 (1992).

[46] World Health Organization, Maternal Mortality Rates: A Tabulation of Available Data at 2 WHO Doc. FHE/86.3, (2ed), (Geneva: WHO, 1986).

[47] Corinne A.A. Packer, "Preventing Adolescent Pregnancy: The Protection Offered by International Human Rights Law," *Int'l. J. of Children's Rights*, 5 (1997): pp. 47-76.

[48] Article 14(2).

[49] Taunya Banks, "Women and AIDS: Racism, Sexism and Classicism" *N.Y.U. Rev. of Law and Social Change*, 17 (New York: New York University, 1988-1989): p. 351; Dorothy E. Roberts, *Killing the Black Body: Race, Reproduction and the Meaning of Liberty* (New York: Vintage, 1997).

[50] Tamara Lewin, "Implanted Birth Control Device Renews Debate Over Forced Contraception," *New York Times*, January 10, 1991.

[51] United Nations, *Report of the International Conference on Population and Development*, Cairo, 5-13 September 1994. Programme of Action: para. 8.34; United Nations, *Report of the Fourth World Conference on Women*. Beijing, 4-15 September 1995. Platform for Action: para. 108.

[52] Ibid.: paras. 7.34-7.40; *Ibid.*: para. 99.

[53] *Korn v. Potter*, 134 D.L.R. (4th), (British Columbia Supreme Court, 1996): p. 437.

[54] Article 10(h).

[55] Sandra Coliver, ed., *The Right to Know: Human Rights and Access to Reproductive Health Information, Article 19* (London, U.K., 1995, Philadelphia, Pa., U.S.A.: University of Pennsylvania Press, 1995).

[56] *Open Door Counselling and Dublin Well Women Centre v. Ireland*, 15 Eur. H.R. Rep. 244 (1992).

[57] Ibid.: para. 77.

[58] *Kjeldsen v. Denmark*, 1 Eur. H.R. Rep. 711 (1976): para. 53.

[59] United Nations, *Report of the International Conference on Population and Development*, Cairo, 5-13 September 1994. Programme of Action: para. 11.8; United Nations, *Report of the Fourth World Conference on Women*. Beijing, 4-15 September 1995. Platform for Action: para. 277(a).

[60] *Student Representative Council, Molepolole College of Education v. Attorney General of Botswana* (for and on behalf of the Principal of Molepolole College of Education and Permanent Secretary of Ministry of Education). Unreported, Civil Appeal No. 13 of 1994, Misca No. 396 of 1993. Judgement delivered on 31 January 1995, reported in E. K. Quansah, "Is the Right to Get Pregnant a Fundamental Human Right in Botswana?" *Journal of African Law*, 39 (1995): pp. 97-102.

[61] Thomas B. Jabine, Richard P. Claude, eds., *Human Rights and Statistics: Getting the Record Straight* (Philadelphia: University of Pennsylvania Press, 1992).

[62] Diane F. Orentlicher, "Bearing Witness: The Art and Science of Human Rights Fact Finding," *3 Harv. Hum. Rts. J.* (Boston: Harvard University, 1990): p. 83.

[63] World Health Organization, *Unsafe Abortion: Global and Regional Estimates of Incidence of and Mortality Due to Unsafe Abortion with a Listing of Available Country Data* (Geneva: WHO, 1998).

[64] See, for example, United Nations, *Too Young to Die: Genes or Gender?* (New York: United Nations, 1998); United Nations, *The World's Women 1970-1990* (New York: United Nations, 1991); United Nations, *Reproductive Health in*

Refugee Situations: An Inter-Agency Field Manual UN High Commissioner for Refugees (New York: United Nations, 1996); United Nations, Violence Against Women in the Family (New York: United Nations, 1989).

[65] See for example, Latin American and Caribbean Committee for the Defense of Women's Rights, Center for Reproductive Law and Policy, Silence and Complicity: Violence Against Women in Peruvian Public Health Facilities (New York: CLADEM, CRLP, 1999): also available in Spanish; The Women's Rights Project of Human Rights Watch, Criminal Injustice: Violence Against Women in Brazil (New York: Human Rights Watch, 1991): also available in Portuguese.

[66] Thomas B. Jabine, Richard P. Claude, eds., Human Rights and Statistics: Getting the Record Straight (Philadelphia: University of Pennsylvania Press, 1992): supra note 61.

[67] Niamh Reilly, Without Reservation: The Beijing Tribunal on Accountability for Women's Human Rights (New Brunswick, N.J.: Center for Women's Global Leadership, Rutgers University, 1996).

[68] Thomas B. Jabine, Richard P. Claude, eds., Human Rights and Statistics: Getting the Record Straight (Philadelphia: University of Pennsylvania Press, 1992): supra note 61.

[69] Ibid.: pp. 9-10.

[70] D. Boyer, D. Fine, "Sexual Abuse as a Factor in Adolescent Pregnancy and Child Maltreatment," Family Planning Perspectives, 24 (1992): pp. 4-11.

[71] Ester Kismodi, "The Ombudsman Approach to the Protection of Reproductive Rights in Hungary," Medicine and Law, Vol. 18, symposium edition on Legal and Ethical Aspects of Reproductive and Sexual Health in Central and Eastern Europe (forthcoming 1999).

[72] International Women's Rights Action Watch, The Women's Watch, Vol. 12 (2 & 3) 7 (1998).

[73] Vanessa Yolles, The United Nations Convention on the Rights of the Child: A Practical Guide to Its Use in Canadian Courts (Toronto: UNICEF Canada, 1998).

[74] Article 12.

[75] United Nations, International Human Rights Instruments, Compilation of General Comments and General Recommendations Adopted by Human Rights Treaty Bodies, HRI/Gen/1/Rev.2, 29 March 1996.

[76] Para. 9.

[77] Ibid.

[78] United Nations, Report of the Committee on the Elimination of Discrimination Against Women (Fourteenth Session) A/50/38, 31 May 1995.

[79] See for instance, CEDAW, Alternative Report by Indian NGOs: Article 12, Health Care, CHETNA, Litavatiben Lalbhai's Bungalow, Civil Camp Rd. Shahibaug, Ahmedabad, 380 004 Gujarat, India, cited in Women's International News Network 23 (3) (1997): pp. 23-24; Latin American and Caribbean Committee for the Defense of Women's Rights, the Center for Reproductive Law and Policy, Estudio para la Defensa de los Derechos de la Mujer, Women's Sexual and Reproductive Rights in Peru: A Shadow Report, (CLADEM, CRLP, 1998); Center for Reproductive Law and Policy, Women's Legal Aid Centre, Women's Reproductive Rights in Tanzania: A Shadow Report (CRLP, 1998).

[80] See for instance, Inked Boerefijn, Brigit Toebes, "Health and Human Rights, Health Issues Discussed by the United Nations Treaty Monitoring Bodies," Netherlands Institute for Human Rights, SIM Special Issue, 21 (1998): pp. 25-53;

Julie Stanchierei, Isfahan Merali, Rebecca J. Cook, *The Application of Human Rights to Reproductive and Sexual Health: A Compilation of The Work of UN Treaty Bodies* (Toronto: Programme on Reproductive and Sexual Health Law, Faculty of Law, University of Toronto, 1999).

[81] Para. 254.

[82] Para. 260.

[83] Para. 259.

[84] Para. 255.

[85] Para. 261.

[86] E/CN.6/1999/WG/L.2, 10 March 1999.

[87] Ibid.

[88] United Nations, Doc. E/CN.4/1995/42, 22 November 1994.

[89] United Nations, Doc. E/CN.4/1997/47/Add.4, 30 January 1997.

[90] See particularly, country missions reports of the Special Rapporteur: "Report on the Mission to Democratic People's Republic of Korea, the Republic of Korea, and Japan," on the issue of military sexual slavery in wartime, E/CN.4/1996/53/Add.1, 4 January 1996; "Report on the Mission to Poland," on the issue of trafficking and forced prostitution of women, E/CN.4/1997/Add.1, 10 December 1996; "Report on the Mission to Brazil," on the issue of domestic violence, E/CN.4/1997/Add.2, 21 January 1997; "Report on the Mission to South Africa," on the issue of rape in the community, E/CN.4/1997/47/Add.3, 24 February 1997.

[91] See for example, *Velasquez Rodriquez v. Honduras*, Inter-American Court of Human Rights, OAS/Ser.L/V/III.19, Doc. 13 (1988); *X & Y v. The Netherlands*, 91 Eur. Ct. H.R. (ser. A) (1985).

[92] Thomas M. Franck, "Legitimacy in the International System," *American Journal of International Law*, 82 (1988): pp. 705 and 708.

[93] Thomas M. Franck, *Fairness in International Law and Institutions* (1995).

[94] Harold H. Koh, "Why Do Nations Obey International Law?" *Yale L. J.* 106: 2599 (New Haven: Yale University, 1997): at 2634.

[95] Ibid.: at 2656.

[96] Ibid.

[97] Further information is available for the following regional treaty systems at the following web sites:
Inter-American system: http://www.iachr.org;
European system: http://www.coe.fr;
African system: http://www.oau-oua.org.

[98] Further information is available for the following international treaty-monitoring bodies at the following web sites:
Committee on the Elimination of All Forms of Discrimination against Women (CEDAW):
http://www.unhchr.ch/html/menu2/6/scedaw.htm;

Committee on Economic, Social and Cultural Rights (CESCR):
http://www.unhchr.ch/html/menu2/6/scescr.htm;
Committee on the Elimination of Racial Discrimination (CERD):
http://www.unhchr.ch/html/menu2/6/scerd.htm;
Committee on the Rights of the Child (CRC):
http://www.unhchr.ch/html/menu2/6/scrc.htm;
Human Rights Committee (HRC):
http://www.unhchr.ch/html/menu2/6/shrc.htm.

[99] Andrew Byrnes, *Toward a More Effective Enforcement of Women's Human Rights through the Use of International Human Rights Law and Procedures, in Human Rights of Women: National and International Perspectives* (Philadelphia: University of Pennsylvania Press, 1994); Julie Mertus, Nancy Flowers, Malika Dutt, *Local Action, Global Change: Learning about the Human Rights of Women and Girls* (New York: UNIFEM, the Center for Women's Global Leadership, 1999); Women, Law, and Development, International and Human Rights Watch, Women's Rights Project, *Women's Human Rights Step by Step: A Practical Guide to Using International Human Rights Law and Mechanisms to Defend Women's Human Rights* (Washington, D.C.: Women, Law and Development, 1997).

[100] Ibid.

[101] Chaloka Beyani, "Toward a More Effective Guarantee of the Enjoyment of Human Rights by Women in the African System"; Cecilia Medina, "Toward a More Effective Guarantee of the Enjoyment of Human Rights by Women in the Inter-American System," both in *Human Rights of Woman: National and International Perspectives,* ed. R. J. Cook (Philadelphia: University of Pennsylvania Press, 1994), translated into Spanish and available from PROFAMILIA, Bogota, Colombia; Frans Viljoen, "Application of the African Charter on Human and Peoples' Rights by Domestic Courts in Africa," *Journal of African Law,* 43 (1999) : pp. 1-17.

[102] Andrew Byrnes, Jane Connors, Lum Bik, *Advancing the Human Rights of Women: Using International Human Rights Standards in Domestic Litigation* (London: Commonwealth Secretariat, 1997).

[103] United Nations Children's Fund, *A Human Rights Approach to UNICEF Programming for Children and Women: What It Is, And Some Changes It Will Bring* (New York: UNICEF, 1998).

[104] Maria Isabel Plata, "Reproductive Rights as Human Rights: The Colombian Case," *Human Rights of Woman: National and International Perspectives,* ed. R. J. Cook (Philadelphia: University of Pennsylvania Press, 1994), translated into Spanish and available from PROFAMILIA, Bogota, Colombia.

[105] Oran Young, "Two Models of Effectiveness," 91 *Proc. Am. Soc'y Int'l Law* 51, 57 (1997).

[106] Abram Chayes, Antonia Handler Chayes, *The New Sovereignty: Compliance with International Regulatory Agreements* 5 (1995).

Women Are the Key to Development

Noeleen Heyzer

Gender, Population and Development: Overview

Over the last thirty years since the United Nations Population Fund (UNFPA) was established, there have been fundamental changes in policies on and approaches to population and gender equality. These are best exemplified in the Programme of Action of the International Conference on Population and Development (ICPD) and the Platform for Action of the Fourth World Conference on Women (FWCW) in Beijing.

The ICPD recognized that population is basically a development issue and must be addressed in relation to the larger developmental processes. It emphasized intersectoral linkages between consumption and production patterns; social and gender inequities; and population growth, structure and distribution. It moved the focus from a narrow preoccupation with rates of population growth and the provisions of contraceptive services alone, to a broader concern for problems caused by the deepening of poverty and inequality within and across societies. These problems were seen as a result of inappropriate economic and development policies, and not just of population pressures. The ICPD also put more emphasis on investments in people and on quality-of-life issues. For the first time, the reproductive and sexual health rights of women and their empowerment became essential to an international agreement on population and development.

This redefinition of the population and development agenda had been earlier aided by the emergence of a strong women's movement following the Nairobi World Conference on Women in 1985. By the time of the FWCW in 1995, several countries reported a narrowing of gender inequality as measured by increases in life expectancy, literacy, labour force participation rates, higher age at marriage, and lower fertility rates. In fact, governments throughout the world have had to recognize and address gender inequalities and reconcile substantively different views on human rights.

Nevertheless, gender inequality remains significant in many areas of life. Women have fewer social and economic rights, including rights over basic necessities such as food, health care, and education; less access to labour markets, and lower economic returns for their labour. They also have fewer legal and customary rights over land, property, credit, and other productive resources such as energy, technology, and information. This is despite their multiple burdens, including financial contributions through their work, resource management, and household responsibilities, as well as the care of children and the elderly. In many countries of the world, women still fall far short of men as beneficiaries of development. Their full contribution is still not acknowledged, nor their potential realized, ultimately to the detriment of development itself.

Gender Equality: Progress and Obstacles

Efforts are being made to measure such gender gaps more accurately, since this information is vital for advocacy, for developing policies, for achieving gender equality, and for implementing an empowerment agenda.

The 1995 edition of the United Nations publication *World's Women: Trends and Statistics*,[1] launched at the Beijing Conference, reported progress in education, health, economic opportunities, and political participation in varying degrees in much of the world, but it also underlined the often, enormous gender gaps that persist. Some of the information on gender gaps from this publication is summarized below.

Ratio of women to men. There are fewer women in the world than men: 98.6 women per 100 men. The sex ratio at birth is biologically stable, with about 93 to 96 female births for every 100 male births. However, in a few Asian countries, sex ratios deviate from the norm in favour of male children, which may reflect very strong son preference and active discrimination against females at birth. The sex ratio in Western Asia is estimated at 92 women per 100 males, in East Asia at 97, and in South Asia at 95. Imbalances may be explained by female infanticides, underreporting of female births, and the increased availability of technologies that enable sex-selective abortion.

UNFPA supported a study, conducted by Harvard University, "Gender Bias in China, South Korea and India: Causes and Policy Implications,"[2] which also indicates strong son preference in these Asian countries.

Life expectancy. Life expectancy for women is longer than for men almost everywhere, but in Africa, the difference is small, and in South Asia, women's and men's life expectancies are still about equal. There are different causes of death for women and men, different patterns of mortality and morbidity, and different needs and uses of health services. But data collection and research to explore these differences are only beginning.

Literacy. Through widespread promotion of universal primary education, literacy rates for women have increased over the past few decades — to at least 75 per cent in most countries of Latin America and the Caribbean and in Eastern and Southeastern Asia. But high rates of female illiteracy persist in much of Africa and in South Asia. Moreover, progress, especially in secondary and higher education, in Africa, Latin America and the Caribbean was reversed in the 1980s as a result of war, economic adjustment, and declining international assistance.

Health. Likewise, there has been progress in achieving gender equality in health, including reproductive health. The total fertility rates for Latin America and in most parts of Asia have dropped significantly, but in Africa women still have an average of six children. Pregnancy and childbirth have become safer for women in most of Asia and Latin America; however, in most of sub-Saharan Africa there is little progress, and in some parts it is worsening. *The World's Women, 1995,* says, "Too many women lack access to reproductive health services. In developing countries maternal mortality is a leading cause of death for women of reproductive age." The number of women contracting HIV is growing faster than the number of men. In Africa, it is estimated that among over 10 million cumulative infections, more than 50 per cent are women. Young women are the most susceptible. A United Nations Development Programme (UNDP) review of AIDS studies in three African and two Asian countries estimated that those aged 15 to 25 account for 70 per cent of the 3,000 women who contract HIV every day.

Economic activity. The invisibility of women's work remains a serious problem since much of it continues to be unmeasured by the System of National Accounts. But time-use data for many developed countries show that almost everywhere women work at least as many hours as men, and in a large number of countries they work at least two hours more than men daily. In developing countries, their work as unpaid family labourers in subsistence agriculture, household enterprises, and in the household and family care are unreported or at best inadequately reported. Labour force participation rates should be higher than reported. This deficiency in data subverts the development of policies for credit, income, and security of women and their families. Some efforts have been made to correct the underreporting in labour force participation rates by changes in the statistical methods used. The estimated increase in the participation rates in South Asia from 25 per cent in 1990 may be due to just this reason.

Power and influence. Women in decision-making are underrepresented nearly everywhere: there are few women in ministerial and senior levels of governments and in parliaments, and most are in less powerful positions than men. In the world of business, women at the top are very few — rarely more than 1 or 2 per cent of senior management positions. In the media, which can be another indicator of power and influence, women are increasingly more visible, but even in that field they are found more often as presenters and reporters than in decision-making positions.

Excluded from most political offices, women have nevertheless made remarkable advances in less traditional paths to power and influence. Taking advantage of the round of global conferences in the past two decades, especially those for women, women have found a voice in non-governmental organizations (NGOs) at all levels and have helped shape the agenda of all the global conferences that took place in the 1990s. The ICPD is one clear example.

UNDP's *Human Development Reports* (HDR), particularly since 1995, when UNDP developed the Gender Development Index (GDI) and the Gender Empowerment Measure (GEM), are an attempt at ranking countries by achievements in gender equality and empowerment of women.

GDI. The HDR of 1995 introduced the GDI,[3] which measures, as does the Human Development Index (HDI), life expectancy, educational attainment, and income, but adjusts the HDI for gender inequality. The HDR of 1997 draws several conclusions from the GDI rankings of countries.

First, no society treats its women as well as men. This is evident from the fact that the GDI value for every country is lower than its HDI value. Second, human poverty is strongly associated with gender inequality. The four countries ranking lowest in the GDI — Sierra Leone, Niger, Burkina Faso, and Mali — also rate lowest in the human poverty index. Third, gender inequality is not always associated with income poverty. Countries such as Ecuador do relatively well in GDI rankings but have quite high rates of income poverty. Fourth, and perhaps most interestingly, countries showing a marked improvement in GDI relative to HDI are fairly diverse. They include such industrial countries as Norway and Sweden and such developing countries as Barbados and Viet Nam.

GEM. The GEM[4] measures gender inequality in key areas of economic and political participation and decision-making. The HDR of 1997 estimated the GEM for 94 countries. Four countries at the top were Nordic. The interesting finding is that some developing countries outperform much richer industrial countries in gender equality in political, economic, and

83

professional activities. Thus, Barbados is ahead of Belgium and Italy, while France lags behind Suriname, Colombia, and Botswana.

Gender Differences in Development

It has also been recognized, especially during the last decade of United Nations conferences, that because of the different roles that societies assign to women and men and the value placed on these roles, men and women can experience development in very different ways. On one hand, economic growth can generate very different consequences for women and men. What benefits men does not automatically benefit women. Gender inequalities, even during periods of economic growth, can curtail women's access to jobs, property, and credit skills acquisition. Even when they enter the work force, they may find that due to their relative lack of autonomy, the economic benefits of their work accrue not to themselves but to other family members. Furthermore, even in many industrialized countries, women do not get the same pay as men for equal work.

On the other hand, women are likely to suffer disproportionately as a result of imbalances in development. For example, the globalization process has the potential to exacerbate existing imbalances and inequalities. Women have suffered more than men from the results of structural adjustment programmes. These programmes have often led to in cutbacks in health budgets. Meanwhile, the privatization of health care as a market commodity has opened the door to a transnational health industry, dominated by transnational pharmaceuticals and the high technology hospitals of the North and, increasingly, the newly industrialized countries of Asia. Structural adjustment programmes in many countries focus on reducing social investments, including health. The recent trend toward the large-scale privatization of health services has increasingly made health care the preserve of the small upper and middle classes while the poor have decreasing access to health services. This disparity between rich and poor translates into reduced access and availability of primary health services. Women are especially marginalized due to the feminization of poverty — a poverty that is deepened by the increasing privatization of health care.

The report of The Hague Forum held in February 1999 for the review and appraisal of the implementation of the ICPD Programme of Action in its first five years, reinforces these findings. "Globalization of the economy has contributed to deepening the feminization of poverty, while privatization of social and health sectors has increased the proportion of women without access to adequate social services and health care."[5]

The Asian economic crisis. The late-1990s economic crisis in some Asian countries bears out the validity of the argument that, not only do women and men experience development in different ways, but women tend to suffer more in times of economic crisis. In 1998,UNFPA published a report with the Australian National University (ANU), "Southeast Asian Populations in Crisis: Challenges to the Implementation of the ICPD Programme of Action."[6] The report, which is based on rapid assessment techniques, looked at the effect of the economic crisis on reproductive health, education, and employment, particularly in relation to women in Indonesia, Thailand, Malaysia, and the Philippines. It finds that the crisis is disproportionately affecting the lives of girls and women in these areas.

Thus, the report finds that increasing unemployment and poverty mean that women are turning to the commercial sex industry in order to find work and support their families. In Indonesia, women who lost jobs in factories and turned to commercial sex reported that their earnings as sex workers were lower than as factory workers, because their clients could not afford to pay much for their services. These new recruits to the sex trade, many of whom have had a limited education, are likely to be poorly equipped to protect themselves from sexually transmitted diseases (STDs) and HIV/AIDS. A number of STD clinics surveyed cited increases in the numbers of sex workers attending the clinics and a corresponding increase in cases of diseases. One clinic in Lentera Yogyakarta, Indonesia, reported a doubling of its clients in a nine-month period.

The economic crisis has led to budget cuts, which have reduced available reproductive health services; including cutbacks in STDs and HIV/AIDS prevention and treatment programmes. The report notes, for example, that the Thailand Ministry of Public Health cut its AIDS budget by 24.7 per cent in 1998, compared to a 5.5 per cent cut for the non-AIDS budget. The report says that the recession has particularly affected the lives of women who are single parents or have heavy financial commitments. The crisis has reduced access to reproductive health services for adolescents and youth at a time when school dropouts are increasing and youth unemployment rates are rising. This reduced access appears to lead more young women to resort to unsafe abortion to terminate unwanted pregnancies in the countries surveyed. The cutbacks are also having immediate and tangible effects on the quality and safety of lives of individuals in the countries in question.

In education, the crisis has led to significantly increased school dropouts, with the adverse effects rising with the age of the child and their level of education. Girls appear to be most disadvantaged. Tertiary level students are also affected.

It only needs to be added here that these are not just challenges to the implementation of the ICPD Programme of Action, which is the focus of the report. They are obstacles to the implementation of the Beijing Platform for Action in these countries as well, and indeed to the overall goal of gender equality and the empowerment of women.

Religious fundamentalism. Women can also suffer disproportionately compared to men in having their rights curtailed through another phenomenon that is becoming more apparent in many countries; namely, religious fundamentalism. There are many complex reasons for religions fundamentalism, but the imbalance between community and global forces can have serious consequences for women. In a globalized economy, public policies are increasingly shaped to accord with external interests, such as those of international organizations and foreign investors. As vulnerable communities and families are increasingly stressed, religious fundamentalism becomes an appealing alternative because, among other things, it offers an explanation and a proposed solution to the increase in suffering. It reinforces the idea that the state is inadequate to respond to community needs and that there must be a return to old ways. The curtailing of the economic, political, and personal autonomy of women, including their reproductive rights, thus comes to be institutionalized.

The ICPD in historical perspective, and UNFPA's evolving role

The extent of the changes in the last few decades that have brought gender equality to the fore are best appreciated when we consider them in light of the historic perspective of international conferences since the Bucharest (1974) and Mexico City (1984) Conferences on population. The agenda has been moved from advancing women's status to promoting their human rights and to mainstreaming gender concerns into population and development. As a result of this evolution, gender issues are now seen as being global and universal. The rights approach, advanced by women's groups, has added to the core objectives of development policy and the movement for women's equality. The gender approach places the roles of women and men in the context of the power relations between them.

At the Bucharest Conference, female delegates had to point out that the World Population Plan of Action (WPPA) had paid no attention to "women's issues." As a result, such issues did get somewhat perfunctory mention in the WPPA; it urged governments to "ensure full participation of women in the educational, social, economic and political life of their countries on an equal basis" and to "make a sustained effort to ensure that legislation regarding the status of women complies with the principles spelled out in the Declaration on the Elimination of All Forms of Discrimination against Women and other United Nations declarations, conventions and international instruments, to reduce the gap between law and practice through effective implementation, and to inform women at all socio-economic levels of their legal rights and responsibilities."[7]

The Mexico City Conference in 1984 went further in asking governments to "pursue more aggressively action programmes aimed at improving and protecting the legal rights and status of women through efforts to identify and to remove institutional and cultural barriers to women's education, training, employment and access to health care."[8]

Between these two conferences, two United Nations World Conferences on Women (Mexico City, 1975, and Copenhagen, 1980) were instrumental in generating enormous global attention to "women's issues," as they were still called. Many of these issues were directly related to the population issues that were the subject of the 1974 and 1984 conferences and contributed to advancing steadily the ideas on women, population and development.

Thus, at the 1984 Mexico City Conference, an *ad hoc* caucus working on family planning and women's rights succeeded in getting government delegations to accept major recommendations related to women and population. The conference accepted the proposition that "demographic policy or cultural tradition," or "the biological role of women in the reproductive process," should not be used in any way to limit women's rights to work.[9]

Another recommendation (7) from the same conference says: "[G]overnments should provide women, through education, training and employment, with opportunities for personal fulfillment in familial and non-familial roles, as well as for full participation in economic, social and cultural life, while continuing to give due support to their important social role as mothers. To this end, in those countries where child-bearing occurs when the mother is too young, Government policies should encourage delay in the commencement of child-bearing."[10]

At the Third United Nations Conference on Women in Nairobi in 1985, lobbyists for population, as well as women's NGOs, succeeded in ensuring the integration of population and family planning issues into the conference recommendations to a much greater extent than the previous women's conferences. The language too was forthright and plain. Thus, the Nairobi Conference declared that, "the ability of women to control their own fertility . . . forms an important basis for the enjoyment of other rights."[11]

During the United Nations Decade for Women (1976-1985), at the international level the United Nations was able to give substance to its institutional commitment to the advancement of women. Three entities specifically devoted to the advancement of women were established. The

United Nations Development Fund for Women (UNIFEM) was one of them, along with the International Research and Training Institute for the Advancement of Women (INSTRAW) and the Division for the Advancement of Women (DAW) in the United Nations. The 1995 Beijing Platform for Action, paragraph 335, states: "UNIFEM has the mandate to increase options and opportunities for women's economic and social development in developing countries by providing technical and financial assistance to incorporate the women's dimension into development at all levels. Therefore, UNIFEM should review and strengthen, as appropriate, its work programme in the light of the Platform for Action, focusing on women's political and economic empowerment. Its advocacy role should concentrate on fostering a multilateral policy dialogue on women's empowerment. Adequate resources for carrying out its functions should be made available."[12]

Any discussion on the progress made globally on gender issues would be incomplete without mention of the Committee and Convention on the Elimination of All Forms of Discrimination against Women (CEDAW), the international bill of rights for women, which, since its adoption by the General Assembly in December 1979, has been successfully used to advance women's equality and empowerment in all major international conferences. As of 31 December 1998, 163 countries — more than two-thirds of the Members of the United Nations — are parties to the convention, and an additional four have signed the treaty, binding themselves to do nothing in contravention of its terms. A recent publication by UNIFEM, "Bringing Equality Home," demonstrates how the convention has been used by women in all regions to bring about real change at national levels. The publication contains stories about new and changed constitutions, court decisions giving women the legal right to own land and to protection from sexual harassment, new laws that prohibit gender-based discrimination, and about changes in government policies or adoption of new policies that respect women's right to health. Thus, for example, the Colombian constitution, largely as a result of women's networking, includes provisions that reflect CEDAW's substantive vision of equality. Article 42 of the constitution states that "family relations are based in the equality of rights and duties of couples and in reciprocal respect among all its members."[13] Article 42 also guarantees the right of couples to "freely and responsibly decide the number of their children."[14]

Another development merits mention. On 12 March 1999, the forty-third session of the United Nations Commission on the Status of Women adopted an Optional Protocol to CEDAW. The protocol contains two procedures: a communications procedure allowing individual women, or groups of women, to submit claims of violations of their rights to the Committee on the Elimination of All Forms of Discrimination against Women, and an inquiry procedure enabling the committee to initiate inquiries into situations of grave or systematic violations of women's rights. In either case, states must be party to the protocol for it to be applied.

Thus, a global consensus has finally been reached that advancing gender equality and women's empowerment are central to the notion of sustainable human development, including population and development. Today, this consensus is best embodied in the ICPD Programme of Action and the Platform for Action of the FWCW. As one of its key principles, the ICPD Programme of Action emphasizes that advancing gender equality and the empowerment of women, eliminating all kinds of violence against women, and ensuring women's ability to control their own fertility are cornerstones of population and development-related programmes.[15] The Programme of Action is unprecedented in setting out as an important objective to encourage and enable men to take responsibility for their sexual and reproductive behaviour and their social and family roles.[16]

The rationale for the promotion of gender equality and the empowerment of women in population and development programmes is underscored by the fact that women's disadvantaged social position, which is often related to the economic value placed on familial roles, helps perpetuate poor health, inadequate diet, early and frequent pregnancy, and a continued cycle of poverty.

Women's low socio-economic status also exposes them to physical and sexual abuse and mental depression. Unequal power in sexual relationships exposes women to unwanted pregnancy and STDs, including HIV/AIDS. With changing social values and economic pressures, girls are engaging in sexual relationships at earlier ages. Additional health risks for women also arise from the general level of underdevelopment that is reflected, for example, in poor roads and lack of transport. This may hinder women from receiving timely medical treatment for pregnancy-related complications. Inadequate water supply, lack of electricity and poor sanitation impose extra burdens on women because of their household responsibilities, such as fetching water and fuelwood.

The Beijing Platform for Action brought together in one document the cumulative understanding achieved as a result of previous women's conferences; along with others, the ICPD. The Platform reaffirmed and strengthened the Cairo consensus. The advances made in Beijing over Cairo include: (a) the affirmation that the human rights of women include their sexual rights; (b) the commitment to "consider reviewing laws containing punitive measures against women who have undergone illegal abortions"; (c) the balancing of parental rights and duties with the right of adolescent girls to privacy and counselling, with primary consideration being given to the best interests of the child; (d) the agreement that girls should have equal rights over inheritance; and (e) the valuing of women's unpaid work.

It was also left to the FWCW to elaborate on the issue of violence against women as one of the twelve critical areas of concern of the Platform for Action. The issue is also addressed explicitly in other critical areas, including "women and armed conflict" and human rights of women.

The recognition of violence against women as a human rights violation, and the implementation of legal and policy measures to further enforce this recognition, have been pivotal goals of the international movement for women's human rights for many years. Since the World Conference on Human Rights in Vienna (1993), women have successfully used major world conferences including ICPD and FWCW as arenas to gain visibility for abuses of women's human rights. Many concrete gains were secured, which paved the way for the Platform for Action. These included the acknowledgement in the Vienna Declaration that violence against women is a violation of human rights, whether perpetrated by public or private actors (June 1993); the adoption of a United Nations Declaration on the Elimination of Violence Against Women (December 1993); the appointment of a Special Rapporteur on Violence Against Women by the Commission on Human Rights (March 1994); the appointment of a Focal Point on Women's Human Rights at the United Nations Centre for Human Rights, who is to initiate the task of integrating gender perspectives into the United Nations human rights machinery; and the recognition in the Beijing Declaration and Platform for Action of the obligation of governments to pursue and punish perpetrators of rape and sexual violence against women and girls in situations of armed conflict as war crimes.

The Beijing Platform for Action states unequivocally that violence against women is an obstacle to the achievement of the objectives of equality, development, and peace. It both violates and impairs or nullifies the enjoyment by women of their human rights and fundamental freedoms. Under its detailed definition of acts that constitute violence against women, it includes many areas that are directly relevant to the work of most United Nations agencies, including UNIFEM and UNFPA, such as physical, sexual, or psychological violence inflicted on victims within the family, in the community, or by the state.

UNFPA's evolving role in the area of gender

As the principal United Nations agency in population and development as well as the largest multilateral source of funding assistance for population programmes, UNFPA's own mandate, policies, and programmes in women, population, and development have continued to evolve over the years. Thus, immediately after the 1975 Mexico City World Conference of the International Women's Year, UNFPA issued a set of guidelines, "Policies and Support to Special Programmes in the Field of Women, Population and Development." In recognition of continuing developments in this area, it has been revised several times since. By 1978, UNFPA had established an institutional framework for addressing women's issues through the creation of a Women and Youth Section at its headquarters to ensure adequate attention to women's issues, including their participation in UNFPA programmes, and to serve as liaison with the United Nations specialized agencies, NGOs, and women's organizations. In 1986, the Special Unit for Women, Population and Development was established in the Office of the Executive Director and then reorganized in 1991 as the Women, Population, and Development Branch in the Technical and Evaluation Division (TED) in the interest of mainstreaming women's concerns into the work of the Fund. Later, in response to progress from "women, population and development" to "gender, population and development" (GPD), the branch was renamed. After the ICPD (UNFPA's key role is discussed elsewhere in this book), a further reorganization took place with the establishment of the Gender, Population and Development Theme Group, drawing its support from a wider range of the units at headquarters that are charged with technical responsibilities in this area.

At the field level, there has been a corresponding strengthening in the technical area of GPD. Thus, all eight Country Support Teams (CSTs) that provide backing to UNFPA-assisted country programmes have at least one GPD adviser. In the field, UNFPA Representatives and their staff regularly participate in inter-agency activities related to GPD.

The wider perspective that the ICPD Programme of Action has on both gender and population has meant that it has considerably broadened UNFPA's mandate in gender issues, especially in the advocacy area, by including the empowerment and autonomy of women and the improvement of their political, social, economic, and health status as a highly important end in itself, in addition to being essential for achieving sustainable development. The Fund's post-Cairo Mission Statement states: "UNFPA affirms its commitment to reproductive rights, gender equality and male responsibility and to the autonomy and empowerment of women everywhere." GPD is now a cross-cutting issue in all of UNFPA's work, and the Fund has ventured into sometimes-new areas, often with innovative approaches.

One area that UNFPA is committed to strengthening in response to the conceptual shift from "women, population and development" to "gender, population and development" is that of the roles and responsibilities of males. Enhancing the involvement of men and male adolescents in reproductive health and family life issues is an important component of UNFPA's GPD strategy post-Cairo. With support provided by the Government of Denmark, UNFPA is working with an NGO, the Population Council, to examine the social behaviour of adolescent boys with respect to their future roles and relationships, and the expectations, attitudes, and behaviour of men and their effects on male/female decision-making about sexuality and reproduction. This research is focusing on such areas as sexual relations, fertility regulation, reproductive health, family size, and investment in children.

Post-ICPD, UNFPA is taking a leading role in implementing the rights-based approach to women's health with a focus on reproductive and sexual health. Thus, in December 1996, a meeting was held in Glen Cove, New York, titled "Human Rights Approaches to Women's Health, with a Focus on Reproductive and Sexual Health and Rights," organized by UNFPA in collaboration with the Office of the United Nations High Commissioner for Human Rights (OHCHR), the United Nations Centre for Human Rights, and DAW. This meeting was historic: it was the first time that experts from all six treaty bodies, representatives of the United Nations system entities, and NGOs had met to discuss a substantive area. A major outcome of the round table was a call for treaty bodies, United Nations agencies, and NGOs to work together to integrate a gender-sensitive reproductive rights/human rights perspective into their respective programmes.

Another outcome of the ICPD was a renewed focus on encouraging partnerships with civil society in implementing the Programme of Action. Although NGOs and other civil society organizations (CSOs) were already involved in sexual and reproductive health efforts, the ICPD clearly legitimized them as full partners in the implementation of the Programme of Action. Indeed, the agenda for both Cairo and Beijing, as well as for other major United Nations conferences, was shaped by CSOs to an impressive and unprecedented degree. Since then, UNFPA has been able to increase its support to partner organizations, including NGOs, in support of women's empowerment. It is strengthening women's NGOs in networking and technical abilities to advocate and monitor progress in implementing the Cairo and Beijing agreements at global, regional, and national levels.

Cairo and Beijing: integrated follow-up

The global goals set out in the United Nations conferences in the 1990s, including the ICPD and FWCW, are aspirations for the entire development process. Coordinated follow-up is focusing the cooperative efforts of the whole United Nations system to help countries achieve priority goals and objectives, including those of gender equality and the empowerment of women. Many mechanisms have been put into place for this purpose at global, regional, and country levels as part of the United Nations reform process.

One of these, the United Nations Development Group (UNDG) has a gender subgroup chaired by UNIFEM. Another example is a task force set up in 1995, the Basic Social Services for All (BSSA), chaired by UNFPA. BSSA was one of three task forces established to galvanize the United Nations system to meet priority goals emerging from the world conferences and to strengthen the system's follow-up mechanisms for delivering, at country and regional levels, coordinated assistance aimed at meeting the overall goal of poverty eradication. UNFPA called upon UNIFEM to be the lead agency for a Working Group on Women's Empowerment. One concrete result of this working group was the establishment of guidelines identifying key components of women's empowerment:

- Women's sense of self-worth;
- Their right to have and to determine choices;
- Their right to have access to opportunities and resources;
- Their right to have the power to control their own lives, both within and outside the home; and

- Their ability to influence the direction of social change to create a more just social and economic order, nationally and internationally.

In the context of the Programme of Action, special mention should be made of the UNFPA/UNIFEM partnership. In 1997 UNFPA and UNIFEM established a close working relationship whereby UNIFEM provides technical backstopping to the UNFPA Country Support Teams in the area of GPD. This is facilitating and maximizing the efforts of both agencies to implement the goals of Cairo and Beijing within their respective mandates. At the operational level, many linkages are being strengthened, such as in the human rights area, including eradication of violence against women and support for implementation of the CEDAW.

A number of endeavours have been undertaken to publicize the campaigns countering violence against women, many of them involving cooperation between UNIFEM and UNFPA. The year 1998 marked the commemoration of the fiftieth anniversary of the Universal Declaration of Human Rights and the five-year review of the World Conference on Human Rights with its historic recognition of women's human rights. During the year, UNIFEM initiated three inter-agency United Nations regional campaigns to eliminate violence against women — in Latin America and the Caribbean, Asia, and Africa. The following year, a spectacular inter-agency global videoconference was held on 8 March, International Women's Day, called "A World Free of Violence Against Women." This unprecedented event, organized by UNIFEM and held in the United Nations General Assembly Hall in New York, linked five sites: Strasbourg, Mexico City, Nairobi, New Delhi, and New York, and represented ground-breaking collaboration among United Nations agencies in their commitment to ending violence against women. It featured women whose personal experiences of violence have inspired grass-roots initiatives or policy changes. Participation was at the highest level and included, among others, the United Nations Secretary-General Kofi Annan, the Executive Directors of UNIFEM and UNFPA, and the United Nations Special Rapporteur on Violence Against Women, Radhika Coomaraswamy. The videoconference focused on domestic violence, trafficking in women and girls, harmful traditional practices (female genital mutilation (FGM), honour killings), and wartime violence against women (rape, forced prostitution). Experts and activists shared their innovative and effective approaches to eliminating violence against women for possible replication in other geographic regions. They challenged governments to enact and support initiatives that prevent or eradicate gender-based violence.

Meanwhile, United Nations agencies are supporting initiatives at the country level even as they continue global and regional advocacy and awareness-creation work in an area where, too often, silence still prevails. UNFPA has helped establish women's health centres that provide integrated packages of critical services and social support in areas where abuse is widespread. In Gaza, the Fund is assisting Palestinian refugee women, in collaboration with local and international NGOs, by supporting a centre set up to combat violence against women within and outside the family. In almost all twenty-eight African countries where FGM takes place, UNFPA has programmes to reduce and eliminate the practice. Striking success has been achieved in Uganda, where the REACH campaign has demonstrated that FGM can be reduced by as much as one-third in just one year by working with traditional community elders and by instituting new rites of passage into womanhood, such as celebrating and gift-giving.

UNFPA also supports reproductive health care for women in crisis situations in collaboration with the Office of the United Nations High Commissioner for Refugees (UNHCR) and the International Federation of Red Cross and Red Crescent Societies. Thus, it has helped provide refugees from Africa's Great Lakes region with a package of reproductive health services that includes care and post-coital contraception for sexually violated women. Emergency reproductive health kits were provided to Kosovo refugees in Albania and Macedonia during the recent crisis.

An empowerment agenda with women as key

At The Hague Forum in February 1999, in an echo of all United Nations conferences before and after the ICPD, the international community remained steadfast in its conviction that gender equality and the empowerment of women are key to the conceptual shift to human-centred development, to promoting social justice, and to eradicating poverty. The issue is no longer whether women's empowerment is the key to sustainable development but, rather, what kind of agenda is needed to achieve that goal.

A basic requirement would be that the agenda be grounded in the realities of women's lives. At the global level, poverty and inequality have been the most urgent realities for women and men and also a major challenge for population and development. Therefore, empowerment of the poor, especially empowerment of poor women, in the context of economic globalization and trade liberalization, is urgent. The reproductive choices of the poor are made, not only to meet labour needs, but also to compensate for high infant and child mortality. Reproductive choices can be changed only if the context of those choices is changed first. Poverty has to be tackled directly. The HDR for 1996, which focused on human poverty, identified specific actions for eradicating poverty. Among these are sustained investments in human capabilities, which includes, at a minimum, the capability to be well nourished and healthy, the capability for healthy reproduction, and the capability to be educated and knowledgeable. In the foregoing discussion on gender gaps, we have already seen that women are often at a great disadvantage in this respect.

The empowerment of rural communities, including women, is another urgent priority for developing countries whose population problems are very much rooted in the rural and agricultural sector of society. Since rural women are important resource managers in providing food security and overall family welfare, they hold the key to changes in reproductive behaviour and fertility levels and, ultimately, to population structures, growth, size, and distribution.

We have said earlier that the Beijing Platform for Action reinforced the Cairo Programme of Action in many ways, including the area of reproductive health and rights. Hence it follows that any agenda for empowerment must make operational linkages between the Programme of Action and the Platform for Action. Indeed, from the point of view of GPD, this (a recommendation of The Hague Forum) is perhaps the basis that should underlie all strategies for the empowerment of women. These linkages should be made in all four areas where The Hague Forum recommends action:

- Incorporating a gender perspective into policy, programmes and activities;
- Promoting gender equality;
- Addressing violence against women; and
- Promoting male responsibility and partnership with women.

Some of the necessary linkages are set out in the very detailed actions that The Hague Forum recommended in its findings and conclusions on gender equality and the empowerment of women. One of the recommended actions is to further develop and strengthen the ICPD reproductive rights approach, which "should include mechanisms for consultations with women's organizations and other equity seeking groups." Likewise, "the gender-differentiated impact of globalization of the economy and of the privatization of social and health sectors must be closely monitored and specific mitigating measures adopted, especially for the poor." And, finally, "every action should be taken to remove all gender gaps and inequalities pertaining to women's participating in the labour market both by governments and the private sector. . . ."[17]

An empowerment agenda must be based on a framework of rights, with equal weight given to economic, political, and reproductive rights. The women's movement is now a broad, coherent movement that takes on all issues related to the human condition. It remains unified by a gender perspective that views equality and the eradication of violence and poverty as a core ethic of development. This is in the spirit of the rights-based approach advocated by both the Cairo and Beijing conferences. Such an approach means commitment to the pursuit of sustainable human development as a fundamental right, nationally and internationally. Ultimately, the most fundamental of the rights we have is the universal right to social justice, without which there can be neither balanced development nor sustainability.

References

[1] United Nations, *World's Women: Trends and Statistics*, 1991 (New York: United Nations, 1995).

[2] Monica Das Gupta, Chief Researcher, *Gender Bias in China, South Korea and India: Cause and Policy Implications* (Boston: Harvard University, Center for Population and Development Studies).

[3] United Nations Development Programme, *Human Development Report. Gender Development Index* (New York: UNDP, 1995).

[4] United Nations Development Programme, *Human Development Report. Gender Empowerment Measure* (New York: UNDP, 1997).

[5] United Nations, *Report of the International Forum for the Operational Review and Appraisal of the Implementation of the Programme of Action of the International Conference on Population and Development.* The Hague, 8-12 February 1999. *Enhancing Gender Equality, Equity and the Empowerment of Women: Findings and Conclusions* (New York: United Nations, 1999): constraints and issues, para. 56.

[6] United Nations Population Fund, *Southeast Asian Populations in Crisis: Challenges to the Implementation of the ICPD Programme of Action* (New York: UNFPA, in collaboration with The Australian National University, 1998).

[7] United Nations, *Report of the United Nations World Population Conference.* Bucharest, 19-30 August 1975. World Population Plan of Action: recommendation 41(d).

[8] United Nations, *Report of the International Conference on Population,* Mexico City, 6-14 August 1984: recommendation 5.

[9] Ibid.: recommendation 6.

[10] Ibid.: recommendation 7.

[11] United Nations, *Third United Nations Conference on Women*, Nairobi, 1985 (New York: United Nations, 1986): para. 156.

[12] United Nations, *Report of the Fourth World Conference on Women,* Beijing, 4-15 September 1995. Platform for Action: para. 335.

[13] United Nations Development Fund for Women. *Bringing Equality Home.* (CEDAW: 1998): article 16.

[14] Ibid.: articles 12 and 16.

[15] United Nations, *Report of the International Conference on Population and Development,* Cairo, 5-13 September 1994. Programme of Action: principle 4.

[16] Ibid.: para. 4.25.

[17] United Nations, *Report of the International Forum for the Operational Review and Appraisal of the Implementation of the Programme of Action of the International Conference on Population and Development.* The Hague, 8-12 February 1999. *Enhancing Gender Equality, Equity and the Empowerment of Women: Findings and Conclusions* (New York: United Nations, 1999): proposed actions, para. 58.

Broadening Partnerships

Bradman Weerakoon

There is no doubt that the success that has attended the initiatives of the United Nations Population Fund (UNFPA) in population activities during the thirty years of its existence owes much to its ability to work at global, national, and local levels in close partnership with governments, non-governmental organizations (NGOs), representatives of civil society including the private sector, development banks, bilateral aid donors, and agencies of the United Nations system. By any objective standard, the record of achievement of UNFPA over the last three decades in meeting its objectives has indeed been impressive. As other chapters of this book chronicle, major progress has been achieved in slowing down global population growth; reducing infant and maternal mortality and morbidity; improving reproductive health care, including family planning (FP) and sexual health; progressively empowering women and improving their status and role in society; and promoting sustainable development.

These significant gains in human development, many of them specific objectives of the Fund, have been achieved with great effort and considerable cost in most parts of the world. The Fund would be the first to acknowledge that the successes achieved so far have much to do with the painstaking and sustained work done by developing country governments, international and local NGOs with a long history of voluntary endeavour in related fields, and the steadfast material support of the international donor community.

But in a similar vein, it needs to be acknowledged that the catalytic role played by the Fund in raising issues, mobilizing resources and energizing the movement has contributed significantly to the total achievement. It is this cooperation and collaboration — or "partnership" as it was called at the International Conference on Population and Development (ICPD) in Cairo in 1994 — between the Fund and its several partners that has brought us, at the end of the twentieth century, to this present stage of achievement. But, as also documented in these pages, there continue to be several formidable obstacles, foremost among them the widespread poverty that haunts around half the population of the developing world, and emerging challenges such as ageing, increasing violence against women, mass refugee movements, and the HIV/AIDS pandemic, which tell us that our work is far from completed. Broadening, deepening and strengthening the promising partnerships that have been developed will remain crucial to the overall agenda of improving the human condition in the new millennium.

The global consensus reached at the ICPD, as synthesized in its comprehensive Programme of Action, represents humankind's collective response to several of the critical population and development challenges that face us today. As the Programme reiterates, one of the imperative preconditions for reaching the goals of the ICPD will be the ability to broaden and deepen the many partnerships that have been nurtured by the Fund. One of the most important of these, which will be discussed at length later, is the relationship between governments and civil society as represented generally by NGOs.

As the Programme of Action, devoting an entire chapter (Chap. XV) to this vital area, puts it:

> To address the challenges of population and development effectively, broad and effective partnership is essential between governments and non-governmental organizations (comprising not for profit groups and organizations at the local, national and international levels) to assist in the formulation, implementation, monitoring and evaluation of population and development objectives and activities.[1]

While this recommendation is addressed directly to the Member States that participated in the ICPD, there is a corresponding invitation to NGOs as well to collaborate with each other at local, national, regional, and international levels, as well as with local and national governments; namely,

> in recognition of the importance of effective partnership, non-governmental organizations are invited to foster coordination, cooperation and communication at the local, national regional, and international levels and with local and national governments, to reinforce their effectiveness as key participants in the implementation of population and development programmes and policies.[2]

Similarly, other provisions of the Programme of Action underline the need for governments and NGOs to develop partnerships with the private sector, and they highlight the value and responsibilities of development partners, of the United Nations system and outside, in cooperating internationally to achieve population and development goals. So what is envisaged is a multiplicity of partnerships, building alliances with the widest possible range of constituencies and with all of the actors engaged in population and development in the expectation that dialogue and working together will develop synergies that would be helpful in promoting and implementing the consensus reached at Cairo.

This chapter will seek to review and assess, both globally and nationally, UNFPA's experience thus far in encouraging and building partnerships, analysing and reflecting on some of the successes as well as on the constraints and challenges that exist in broadening partnerships. It will also attempt to explore some specific measures that may be taken to nurture and protect effective partnerships that will endure over time.

Creating an enabling environment for partnership-building

It is perhaps a truism that the foundation for a stable and effective partnership among organizations is a common ideology or vision that unites the members, and shared interests and purposes whose achievement can be realized by working together. The concept of partnership also seems to imply a relationship of equality and complementarity. In the case of NGOs in relationship to governments, the earlier ideal position was that they would "complement and supplement" the work of government. However, this would seem to imply a secondary role for the NGO, placing the government in a dominant position. True partnership would entail a recognition of the strengths of the NGO and more fully reflect equality of status. Clearly, such a partnership in an ideal sense does not prevail in the real world; the reason for this will be a subject we will return to later in this discussion. But in the context of changes over the last thirty years, it would be fair to assume that the environment for partnership-building, for a variety of reasons, has been facilitating rather than restricting. Some of these are political, like the ending of the Cold War; some economic, like the increase in trade relations and the effects of globalization; and some social, like the intercountry movements of people and the rapidity of communication.

Moreover, two broad conceptual shifts can be identified during the last three decades that have provided the ideological bonding necessary for the building of partnerships. One was the growing perception of "population" and "development" as being, not antithetical or opposing concepts — which had guided the polemics and rhetoric of Bucharest (1974) and had led to statements such as "development is the best contraceptive" — but, rather, to the evolving acceptance that there were complex, cross-cutting and intersecting relationships between population and sustained economic growth and sustainable development. The Cairo Conference marked the climax of this evolution in rethinking the relationship by such unambiguous statements as: ". . . persistent widespread poverty as well as serious social and gender iniquities have significant influences on, and are in turn influenced by, demographic parameters such as population growth, structure and distribution,"[3] and: "explicitly integrating population into economic and development strategies will both speed up the pace of sustainable development and poverty alleviation and contribute to the achievement of population objectives and an improved quality of life of the population."[4]

Such statements emphasize the integral relationship between population and development and endorse a holistic view of social development, in which health care, education, and gender equality were recognized as cross-cutting rights. They provided a ready foundation for activists and supporters of varied causes — developmental, environmental, human rights, women's concerns, and so on — to dialogue, find common cause, and build coalitions for action that were durable.

The other conceptual underpinning for partnership, achieved at Cairo, was the negotiation and approval of a comprehensive definition of "reproductive health" by as many as 179 Member States of the United Nations system. Paralleling the change from a somewhat narrowly defined demographic approach to population to a developmental, rights-based approach, Cairo crystallized a paradigm shift in thinking from the centrality of family planning to the more relevant, broader, and inclusive concept of reproductive rights and reproductive health. The revised definition of reproductive health not only recognized the "right of men and women to be informed and have access to safe, effective, affordable and acceptable methods of family planning of their choice," but also allowed men and women access to "other methods of their choice for regulation of fertility which are not against the law." So access to abortion in countries in which it is legal was included. By including under "reproductive health" services that were to be provided via primary health care such areas as the diagnosis and treatment of sexually transmitted diseases (STDs), including HIV/AIDS, and the active discouragement of harmful practices such as female genital mutilation (FGM), the definition of reproductive health was broadened to accommodate a wider range of human rights and women's concerns.

The broad ideological platform finally achieved at Cairo was the culmination of a long and sustained campaign in which many actors combined. The Fund facilitated and acted as a catalyst in moving the process forward. Indeed, the process itself, which has been dramatically captured in Jyoti Shankar Singh's[5] outstanding insider commentary on the ICPD, served as a modality for bringing on board a very large number of governments and representatives of civil society in effective partnership.

The role that NGOs would play in the ICPD process was something the ICPD secretariat had to contend with right from the beginning. Given the importance of the issues that would be articulated, there was no doubt that NGOs would want to play a significant role. The Economic and Social Council of the United Nations (ECOSOC), on the 12th of February 1993, decided on a procedure that greatly facilitated this role. It recognized "the importance of non-governmental participation in the preparatory process and the Conference itself" and encouraged "all support to enable representatives of non-governmental organizations from developing countries to participate fully." Utilizing this mandate, the secretariat proceeded to obtain support from several bilateral agencies and foundations to enable NGOs from developing countries to be represented at the preparatory meetings leading up to the conference and at the conference itself. The success that attended this initiative is evident from the following figures. The Preparatory Committee (PrepCom) accredited 396 NGOs at its second session and another 538 at the third session. At the ICPD itself, many more NGOs were admitted, bringing the total number accredited to 1,254 representing 138 countries and territories.

Since the ICPD was to be an intergovernmental conference, there was some concern that NGOs might seek to get involved in the actual negotiating process. Responding to this, the ECOSOC resolution said that "non-governmental organizations shall have no negotiating role in the work of the Conference and its preparatory process." However, in view of the fact that representatives of NGOs participated actively as members of government delegations, this prohibition did not prevent NGO views and opinions from being forcefully manifested in the ensuing discourse, both at the preparatory meetings and at the ICPD itself. They also had every opportunity to lobby delegates in the corridors as issues of concern to them were being taken up. The following extracts from Jyoti Shankar Singh's account of NGOs in the ICPD process succinctly portray the crucial part NGOs played in influencing the final consensus that emerged at Cairo.

> NGOs played an extremely important role at PrepCom II. They organized themselves into thematic and regional causes, and formulated their positions on PrepCom issues on a day-to-day basis. One of the most effective of these caucuses was the Women's Caucus. . . . The Women's Caucus had an estimated membership of 132 women from 41 countries . . . and included environmental, population and development activists as well as those devoted to feminist causes. At PrepCom III, the Women's Caucus was again among the most active lobbying groups. Its meetings were attended by more than 300 women and men from 44 countries. The Caucus organized itself into five task forces, which prepared and circulated priority amendments for each Chapter.[6]

Several international NGOs used the opportunity provided by Cairo to energize their worldwide networks by convening meetings at regional level, in addition to encouraging national affiliates to raise awareness of and engage in discussion of ICPD issues at the local level, both in the run-up to the conference and thereafter. Organizations such as the International Planned Parenthood Federation (IPPF), the Centre for Development and Population Activities (CEDPA), and the Commonwealth Medical Association (CMA) brought together their own members and affiliates for briefings and discussions during the meetings of the PrepCom and the main Cairo meeting. These sustained engagements among NGOs around a common cause; namely, the adoption and inclusion of the most forward-looking recommendations in the final Programme of Action, strengthened and broadened alliances and laid the foundation for durable partnerships in the future. In a very real sense, the conference process itself was taking forward the message and creating an environment in which new partnerships could emerge and flourish.

It has also become customary for the United Nations system when organizing global intergovernmental meetings to run parallel NGO events, which have brought together literally thousands of NGO representatives. The conferences held in Rio de Janeiro, Vienna, Copenhagen, and Beijing were immensely successful in contributing a user or people's perspective on a range of critical issues: the environment, human rights, women, and social development. Similarly, three major NGO events took place around the Cairo Conference. The NGO Forum brought together 4,200 participants, representatives of more than 1,500 NGOs from 133 countries. The International NGO Youth Consultation on Population and Development gave the opportunity for more than 100 youth representatives from all parts of the world to discuss issues such as youth and reproductive health, teenage pregnancy, safe sexual behaviour, and environmental protection. And the International Conference of Parliamentarians on Population and Development brought together 300 parliamentarians from 107 countries.

While participation at these seminal occasions undoubtedly strengthened and further motivated NGO representatives, there is an important caveat that needs to be entered as to the nature of the overall impact of the NGO endeavour on the final product of the ICPD. Some commentators in discussing the context and characteristics of the conference have referred to certain problems, not always sufficiently recognized, that presented themselves. NGOs, they assert, usually originate to address specific issues about which people have strong feelings. Three possible dangers can follow from this. First is that an NGO driven by such particular concerns may lack a broad understanding of the full range of issues. The second is that sometimes NGOs, in their desire to push a point of view, may promote views that are not sufficiently corroborated by scientific analysis. And third, the vocal opinions presented at the meeting may not represent the majority view of the NGO itself.

Clearly the dangers referred to above exist, but the fact is that NGOs at intergovernmental meetings are indeed a subordinate grouping and, although vocal and articulate, often find themselves unable to persuade the conference to accept their views. The benefits of participation certainly seem to outweigh any of the negative influences. In the case of the ICPD, it was patently clear that NGOs had become very much a part of the decision-making process and were largely responsible for the Programme of Action, which was accepted by the world's governments and which moved all of the actors decisively forward in many areas of policy and programme.

Experiences in partnership building at international, national and local level

UNFPA has played a leading role since its inception in 1969 in promoting the active involvement of civil society at both the national and international levels in population and development activities. It has done this both directly, through facilitating the engagement of civil society actors in policy discourse at the international level, and indirectly, through its country programmes, which encourage the mobilization of civil society in the form of NGOs, the academic community, the private sector, and the media; in particular in policy formulation, policy dissemination, and programme implementation.

A worldwide field inquiry that UNFPA conducted in 1998 indicated the great extent to which the Fund's efforts at promoting the involvement of civil society had succeeded in bringing about legislative and administrative changes to strengthen the capacity of civil society, to energize civil society itself to be a more effective partner, and to stimulate the private sector to become more engaged and involved. The inquiry revealed that since the ICPD, several countries in Latin America, Africa, and Asia had strengthened partnerships with civil society by including civil society representatives in the national bodies responsible for addressing issues of population and development. Moreover, many NGOs and parliamentary groups in many countries were seen to be playing a much more effective role in promoting the population and development agendas. While NGOs had undertaken major initiatives in coalition building, strengthening their institutional sustainability, and mobilizing resources, parliamentarians had formed special committees to exert pressure on governments to push population issues forward. The inquiry also disclosed that the private sector in several countries had begun playing a more active role in the implementation of reproductive health-care services through operating clinics, undertaking social marketing schemes, and providing relevant information through the mass media. The efforts of UNFPA through its national offices and Country Support Teams in these multifarious, sustained, catalytic initiatives remain an unpublicized but much appreciated endeavour and achievement in which the Fund could take pride.

A look at three examples, in all of which the Fund was deeply involved, may be of value in understanding the modalities that need to be employed in building partnerships and in identifying the challenges that may have to be confronted and addressed.

South-South collaboration. South-South collaboration among countries in the Southern Hemisphere, particularly in the areas of population and development in which several developing countries — notably Indonesia, India, China, Zimbabwe, Kenya, Colombia and Mexico — had acquired valuable experience that could be shared and, indeed, was being shared on an *ad hoc* basis, was a concept in which many countries, both North and South, had been interested in for a considerable time. The idea had been advanced in a sporadic fashion through a mechanism known as "technical cooperation among developing countries" (TCDC) in the 1970s and 1980s. However, this was generally limited to short-term training and study tours.

In the run-up to Cairo, a meeting was convened by the Rockefeller Foundation at Bellagio, Italy, in October 1993, at which UNFPA played a seminal role. Several key donors and developing country ministers responsible for ICPD planning were present at the meeting, at which the idea emerged of establishing a formal partnership of developing countries to put South-South collaboration in family planning and reproductive health on a more durable basis. The environment was ripe for such an initiative. The meeting recognized that considerable progress had already been made in achieving population goals in the developing world. They saw the need to deal with emerging issues — such as the threat of HIV/AIDS, the continuing high levels of unwanted pregnancies in some countries, the recourse to voluntary abortion where abortion was yet illegal, and teenage pregnancy — at the same time that official development assistance (ODA) was stagnant or declining. Yet there was also a renewed sense of confidence in several developing countries in the efficacy of their own policy and programmatic innovations, which encouraged all concerned to bring the collaboration concept to fruition. The ICPD Programme of Action itself endorsed the idea:

> In devising the appropriate balance between funding sources, more attention should be given to South-South cooperation as well as to new ways of mobilizing private contributions, particularly in partnership with non-governmental organizations. The international community should urge donor agencies to improve and modify their funding procedures to facilitate and give higher priority to supporting direct South-South collaborative arrangements.[7]

The ICPD was therefore not only giving a strong signal to donors to support South-South collaboration but was also suggesting government partnership with NGOs and a search for innovative ways to mobilize private sector contributions in cash or kind.

Today, the resulting organization, Partners in Population and Development, is an intergovernmental organization of 14 developing countries with a permanent secretariat in Dhaka, bylaws, policies, a governing mechanism and a mission statement. The mission statement enjoins the Partners to "expand and improve South-South collaboration in the fields of family planning and reproductive health" through helping member countries and other developing countries learn more about each others' programmes, by facilitating the development of project proposals for South-South activity, and by helping member countries find funding, either from traditional donors or from new sources. Partners in Population and Development as an institution owes much to the initial and continuing assistance given to it by both the Rockefeller Foundation and UNFPA.

The Fund's support to Partners extends to handling administrative functions and the management of trust funds through which donor contributions are channelled for projects in the field. Indeed, now that the initial phase is coming to an end, the very close involvement of the Fund in the operational management of Partners may itself prove to be a problem, and the relationship may require some readjustment. Sustainability of the partnership is, at the basic level, ensured by membership fees, which are available as general support funds, and by specified funding by the Hewlett and Gates foundations and the World Bank. However, partnerships are by their very nature delicate, and flexibility in accommodating to changing situations is crucial to their survival and success. While Partners has already accomplished much, the ongoing evaluation of its work thus far, which has been agreed to by its governing body, is a clear indication that the organization is prepared to learn from past experience and to adapt and renew itself.

International Planned Parenthood Federation. The second example comes from the international NGO sector. The IPPF, which has been active in the field of sexual and reproductive health, including family planning, for five decades now links almost 160 voluntary national associations worldwide in a unique partnership. Literally hundreds of thousands of voluntary workers — women and men, young and old, rural and urban — are linked, not only with each other but with myriad networks that join them to other volunteers working at the community level, in both developed and developing countries. IPPF has had a Memorandum of Understanding with UNFPA since 1987, at a time when the Federation had to face a 25 per cent cut in funding because of its refusal to knuckle under to the iniquitous "Mexico City Policy" imposed by some bilateral donors. The Memorandum of Understanding serves as a guide to relations between UNFPA and IPPF in their field operations.

One of the more recent initiatives broadening the partnership between these two institutions was an international advocacy campaign, *Face to Face*, which aimed to create awareness about the unmet needs of women around the world and to provide support to reproductive health programmes addressing such needs. At the NGO Forum that was held at The Hague as part of the ICPD+5 process, IPPF's European network (which now includes several countries of Eastern Europe) sponsored a *Face to Face* encounter that provided an opportunity for individuals to share experiences in obtaining reproductive health, information and services at national and local levels from countries as different as Albania, Algeria, Mali, and Pakistan.

Local-level projects. The third example, reminiscent of many other community-level projects in several countries of the developing world, is part of a typical ongoing UNFPA-funded country programme. A project in Sri Lanka involves three national-level NGOs with deep outreach into the local community. At no time in the past had they had institutional or programmatic links with reproductive health or family planning, but in this project they have been closely linked to four conventional family planning NGOs in an effort to take reproductive health information and services to individual men and women at the periphery, especially to vulnerable groups such as displaced persons, refugees, and under-served, isolated communities. The rationale behind the partnership was that the non-family planning NGOs, who had established an enviable reputation for service in their chosen fields (rural income-generation, nutrition, health, and women's development) could become new and credible agents who would extend reproductive health information and services to new clienteles beyond the limits of those reached by traditional family planning NGOs. The three non-family planning NGOs had earlier been firm opponents, in philosophy and action, of the ideology and practices of the family planning NGOs. However, the inclusive nature of the concept of reproductive health, its relevance to the life-cycle health needs of men, women, and adolescents, and its availability and relative ease of access through primary health-care services broke down the barriers that had earlier prevented collaboration between these NGOs in the provision of services to the community.

A mid-term evaluation of the project by UNFPA, which had provided the resources, technical advice, and initial impulse for the initiative, observed that the enthusiasm of the volunteer workers in the non-family planning NGOs for acquiring and extending knowledge of reproductive health and rights was remarkable, and the overall progress in achieving programme goals was extremely satisfactory. The major constraint had been the initial bureaucratic delays in passing down funds from government sources to the NGOs for capacity-building. Contrary to expectations, the rapport and support extended to the volunteer workers at community level by government cadres, such as medical officers in peripheral institutions and public health nurses, had been commendable.

A similar local-level project whose overall goal was to support the efforts of the Government of Bangladesh in providing high-quality, sustainable family planning and maternal and child health (MCH) services at the community level is LIP — the Local Initiatives Program. LIP's premise is that effective, sustainable service delivery of MCH/FP services needed to be based on local government officials, service providers, community leaders, and citizens managing and participating in the design and implementation of their programmes. LIP uses four main programme strategies:

- Forming partnerships between family planning programme staff, local leaders, and administrators of government health and development programmes through the formation of subdistrict teams;
- Involving community members actively in managing their MCH/FP and reproductive health programme through their service in local-level management committees that oversee service delivery at the community level;
- Mobilizing local women participants in service delivery activities as community volunteers providing family planning and other health services directly to eligible couples; and
- Encouraging the community to finance the implementation of the action plan by matching LIP small grants with at least a 10 per cent cash contribution from local resources.

Recent evaluations of LIP have indicated that it has resulted in more-focused client services, better training of volunteers, and a higher coverage of modern contraceptive acceptors. What is also interesting about LIP is that it represents a successful implant in Bangladesh of South-South technology and community development methods that were first developed in Indonesia. This successful example of broadening partnerships at the local level has also been successfully adopted in Kenya and Nepal.

Partnership with the private sector — the under-utilized factor

One of the important objectives identified for the ICPD Programme of Action was to strengthen the partnership between governments, international organizations, and the private sector. Although a prominent element of civil society, for a long time the private sector was not sufficiently included and utilized as a factor in social development, perhaps because of unfavourable attitudes attached to profit-making.

In recent times, two notable trends within and outside the private sector have helped delineate its role more clearly and increase its acceptance as a partner in interventions that could materially contribute to human welfare. The first has been the growing realization within the private sector in general, and industry in particular, that it has a social responsibility that must manifest itself in service of some kind to its community. Numerous examples of this now exist worldwide. The other trend, external to the sector but one that has an impact on the culture and behaviour of individual firms, is that governments see the private sector as an effective and efficient producer and distributor of goods and services. This has been reflected in the drive for privatization of formerly state-owned assets and the assertion in government policy statements, especially in the developing countries, that the private sector is the engine of growth in these economies.

Accordingly, and in light of these developments, the consensus at ICPD was that the role of the private sector should be promoted in service delivery and in the production and distribution of high-quality reproductive health and family planning commodities and contraceptives in order to make them more accessible and affordable. Specifically, the Programme of Action called for the following actions:

> Governments and non-governmental and international organizations should intensify their cooperation with the private, for-profit sector in matters pertaining to population and sustainable development in order to strengthen the contribution of that sector in the implementation of population and development programmes, including the production and delivery of quality contraceptive commodities and services with appropriate information and education, in a socially responsible, culturally sensitive, acceptable and cost-effective manner.[8]

Also important, in terms of how the partnership with the not-for-profit private sector (the NGO) could be assisted in its quest to mobilize resources, the Programme of Action suggested that

> [t]he profit-oriented sector should consider how it might better assist non-profit non-governmental organizations to play a wider role in society through the enhancement or creation of suitable mechanisms to channel financial and other appropriate support to non-governmental organizations and their associations.[9]

Although this admonition to the profit-oriented sector to support the not-for-profit NGO sector has been publicly made, and there has been some attempt by the NGO community to look for resources, either material or financial, from the business community in developing countries, the picture has not been promising. Undoubtedly, the somewhat bleak financial prospects for business after the financial crisis hit Southeast Asia and East Asia in the late 1990s could be one of the major reasons for the inability of the private sector in Asia to live up to the expectations engendered in Cairo. Similarly, the domino effects of economic recession in one part of the world on other areas, the fall in oil prices affecting the Middle East, and economic turbulence in Latin America may all have hindered the private sector from cementing what could be a mutually productive partnership. The relative lack of success here underlines the need to be creative in devising ways and means by which the nascent partnership could be strengthened.

Not everywhere has the story been discouraging. The section below on the international partnership's response to HIV/AIDS indicates how, in favourable circumstances, the partnership between governments, the NGOs and the for-profit private sector can be extremely successful and productive.

Dealing with HIV/AIDS — responding globally in partnership

Many of the modalities implicit in the broadening of the partnership between governments, NGOs, other elements of civil society, and the international community may be observed in the global campaign to contain and reverse the spread of the HIV/AIDS pandemic. The alarm bells were rung loud and clear at the ICPD, where it was indicated that while AIDS was a major concern in both developed and developing countries, about four-fifths of all persons ever infected with HIV lived in developing countries. In those countries, the infection was being transmitted mainly through heterosexual intercourse, and the number of new cases was rising most rapidly among women. Three clear objectives were presented in the ICPD Programme of Action:

- To prevent, reduce the spread of and minimize the impact of HIV infection;
- To ensure that HIV-infected individuals have adequate medical care and are not discriminated against; and
- To intensify research on methods to control the HIV/AIDS pandemic and to find an effective treatment for the disease.

In mid-1993, as reported in the Programme of Action, the World Health Organization (WHO) had estimated that the cumulative number of AIDS cases in the world amounted to 2.5 million persons, and that more than 14 million people had been infected with HIV since the pandemic began. The 1998 estimate of WHO and the Joint United Nations Programme on HIV/AIDS (UNAIDS) was that more than 33 million were infected with HIV and that 16,000 new infections are acquired every day. It was estimated that worldwide 13.9 million had lost their lives to the disease, 2.5 million in 1998 alone. These figures show that the rate of infection has increased even more rapidly than assumed five years earlier, and that the death toll from HIV/AIDS will increase exponentially in future years.

Inter-agency response to HIV/AIDS

The seriousness of the pandemic and its implications for the social, economic, and political stability of the countries most severely affected demanded that a collective multipartite response be launched if the emerging crisis were to be arrested. Broadening and strengthening existing partnerships has become imperative if AIDS is to be contained. In the ongoing attempt to do so, the roles of the different partners — the international organizations, the non-governmental sector, and the private sector — have become more clearly delineated. It is well known that individual governments, the United States being a notable example, have assumed leading roles in helping to mitigate the devastating effects of the pandemic.

The instrumentality through which the international organizations have become involved is UNAIDS, which came into being as an independent United Nations agency on 1 January 1996. UNAIDS has brought together the work of five United Nations agencies; namely, UNFPA, WHO, the United Nations Children's Fund (UNICEF), the United Nations Development Programme (UNDP), and the United Nations Educational, Scientific and Cultural Organization (UNESCO), in addition to the World Bank. The chief focus of UNAIDS is to strengthen capacity in national governments to respond effectively to the HIV/AIDS threat. Its work at international, regional, and national levels is in the four mutually reinforcing areas of policy development and research, technical support, advocacy, and coordination.

Role of the NGOs

NGOs that generally work in close relationship with target communities and have experience with community-based civic groups have demonstrated that they are able to mobilize people for HIV/AIDS prevention and care. NGO prevention programmes have not only targeted the population as a whole but also groups who are most vulnerable to HIV, like adolescents, women, refugees and displaced persons, commercial sex workers, and intravenous drug users. Some of the communication materials produced by NGOs have been outstandingly successful, dealing with the subject in a culturally sensitive manner. Targeting young adults to promote safer sexual behaviour, providing counselling, encouraging abstinence as a viable alternative, making condoms the choice for protection, have all been part of campaigns in countries such as Bolivia, Haiti, South Africa, Uganda, and Zambia. Two further initiatives in which NGOs have shown much ingenuity in AIDS prevention have been in workplace interventions with the cooperation of labour unions, and in social marketing, in which they have acquired much experience and expertise.

It has been found that in developing countries people can be best reached where they work. This is especially true of workers like truckers, transit workers, miners, and others whose jobs require them to travel. These professions are also the ones most often associated with the spread of HIV. Recent evidence suggests that peer education in a workplace setting is a low-cost preventive strategy especially suited to developing countries.

Making condoms easily accessible at affordable prices for low-income clients through social marketing is a methodology in which family planning NGOs have had considerable experience. This well-known technique has been adapted to prevent HIV/AIDS through effective communication using a mix of channels, such as mass media, interpersonal contact, and generic educational efforts, to reach selected audiences and help them understand why changing their behaviour is necessary.

Role of the private sector

In relation to the control of HIV/AIDS, there is a general role for an important part of the private sector; specifically, the pharmaceutical industry. Its role will be to find long-term solutions that will improve the health of those infected with AIDS. As far as the research-based pharmaceutical industry is concerned (and this applies particularly to U.S.-based concerns), the role would be to continue to utilize their capacity in biomedical research and drug development to discover more effective treatments, and in the longer-term to develop an effective HIV vaccine. In other parts of the world, too, both public and private members of the world health-care community are using their expertise in partnership to achieve a breakthrough. The research-based pharmaceutical industry, with its contacts with government and health agencies throughout the world, is particularly well positioned to provide a major input, not only in the production and distribution of effective treatments, but in the broader areas of health education and policy as well. The development of an HIV vaccine, a major breakthrough that could save millions of lives, would be a signal, practical demonstration of the value of partnership.

Achievements, constraints and challenges in broadening partnerships

While there is widespread agreement on the value of partnership between governments; civil society, generally represented by NGOs; and the international community in achieving developmental goals and particularly the objectives of the ICPD, it would be naïve to assume that this partnership would happen in the natural course of events merely because governments or the international community or civil society wished it to be so. In reality, there is considerable tension between these three dynamic components in most situations. A great deal of skill and patience must be exerted in accommodating the doubts and mistrust that are ever present in human relationships and in identifying and stabilizing the working arrangements that allow for harmonious, mutually satisfying, and productive partnerships.

UNFPA's pre-eminent contribution

UNFPA has had a wealth of experience in working with civil society groups over the more than thirty years of its existence. The Fund has used many hundreds of NGOs as executing agencies for the projects it supports in the field through material resources and technical advice. In fact, more than 15 per cent of its current allocations are for projects directly executed by NGOs. In some country programmes, the proportions are much higher. In Egypt, for example, it reaches 32 per cent; South Africa, 40 per cent; and in Haiti as much as 53 per cent. In absolute terms, the records show that expenditures for NGO-executed programmes have nearly doubled since 1990. However, the overall average of 15 per cent, while commendable, is indicative of the constraints that even the Fund may at times encounter in accessing and accepting NGOs as executing agencies in some situations.

In some countries, governments have appreciated the contribution that NGOs can make in furthering goals to which they are committed. However, in most countries — except in the so-called failed states — the government of the day is the repository of all power and the final arbiter of resource allocation, especially where resources come into the country from abroad. Resources from the agencies of the United Nations system, in which Member States play a governing role, are particularly subject to careful monitoring by governments. At most times, governments would wish that the "lion's share," as it were, of potential resources would be available to fund programmes and projects to which the government is committed. The priority attributed to a project and its timeframe are nearly always determined by the government, and the portion available to the NGOs in a typical UNFPA country programme could accordingly be limited, depending on the attitude of the government of the day toward the NGO community. Dr. Nafis Sadik, at a round table meeting in Dhaka, Bangladesh, in July 1998, reflected on this almost natural mistrust and the need to overcome it when she said: "Governments are sometimes leery of activist groups because of their potential for opposition and disruption. Such groups, on the other hand, are sometimes strident in their criticism, alienating potential partners. What we need are dialogue, cooperation and synergy."

Since good and harmonious relations are essential between governments and civil society for partnerships to work, it will be useful to examine in some detail what the basic difficulties seem to be between governments and civil society. The UNFPA-sponsored round table in Dhaka was devoted to the topic "Partnership with Civil Society." It explored this important issue in depth, and the following observations reflect several of the valuable insights that came out of the discussions.

One of the concepts about which there was uncertainty was that of "civil society" itself. The term was, and is, used freely, even though it may mean different things to different people. At Dhaka, for example, while a generally accepted working definition was that civil society "included NGOs and other private associations, community institutions, religious leaders, business associations, professional groups, trade unions, the media, and various activist groups and individuals, among others," some participants questioned why government should be excluded from civil society — "was government uncivil?" Others seemed to imply that the term should encompass the entire population. Perhaps the best definition of civil society, for our purposes, may be what was agreed at The Hague in February 1999 at the forum on the five-year review of the ICPD, which saw "civil society" as non-state institutions: including NGOs, community groups, professional associations, religious communities, the private sector, labour and trade unions, political parties, foundations, academic and research institutions, the media, and women, men and youth groups, as well as individuals. Parliamentarians were referred to in this context as "bridges between civil society and the government apparatus."

In the discussions about civil society, it was not universally agreed that NGOs are driven by the highest considerations of service and commitment to the cause. This viewpoint was expressed not only by members of government bureaucracies. These sources would argue that NGOs by themselves do not constitute civil society, which is, in fact, "citizens engaged in civic mobilization to improve their own communities." Accordingly, to such proponents, civil society should be seen as the "spontaneous efforts of citizens who are infected with a sense of public purpose to improve the society around them."

At Dhaka, there were, as always, conflicting views about what the role of the government has been and should be. One view expressed by quite a few academics and intellectuals in South Asia — and perhaps echoed in Africa and Latin America as well — can be stated as follows. Governments no longer have the resources to shoulder their basic responsibilities of ensuring basic social services to their populations. The reasons for this are various and can range from misallocation of resources for "defence," to spectacular but inefficient structures, to meeting the costs of unsustainable "welfare" programmes that have been promised in order to gain office. As a result, governments in some countries have been reduced to being mere "coordinating agencies" for aid donors, who have "appropriated the development policy agenda." The consequence of external sources acquiring such a position is assumed to be the lack of "ownership" of programmes by governments and the inability to mobilize and generate resources locally once the external assistance is gone. This school of thought even avers that the area that has been most affected by this process has been that of family planning and reproductive health, because donors with a variety of perspectives have provided resources that have resulted in projects with competing aims, leading to a waste of resources.

Similar reasoning about the role of government sees them as being downsized, with many of their functions being privatized or handed over to NGOs. The question is then raised as to whether the NGOs who take over such functions have the transparency, accountability, and capacity to handle the job. On the other hand, it is argued that, being reduced in power and authority, civil servants in the government are demoralized and react by withholding cooperation, especially at the higher rungs of the administration. This depressing scenario may be overdrawn, but it contains some elements that have indeed been experienced in real-life situations and therefore merits consideration in planning for healthier relationships.

There are therefore varying perceptions about the value and efficacy of NGOs in meeting programmatic goals, both among others in civil society in general and in government circles. Some of the most critical comments have come from civil society activists themselves who have contended that the increased reliance on NGOs to carry out programmes "has weakened and disempowered civil society in many societies." It has been urged that the use of NGOs as alternative delivery agents for aid in place of the government channels that are regarded as inefficient and often prone to corruption will in fact perpetuate the problems. Those who say this point out that the real problem, over the years, has been "misuse, inefficiency, and malfeasance" in the way resources have been used. Transparency and accountability in resource use has been lacking. While that did happen at times when governments handled the resources, there was also the danger of this happening in the case of NGOs as they grew and changed from being spontaneous groups of dedicated volunteers, driven by loyalty to a cause, to becoming large bureaucracies employing thousands of people with a consequent lack of transparency and accountability.

While such things do happen, as the several documented cases of mismanagement and fraud in large NGOs demonstrate, they do not tell the whole story. Clearly, the magnitude and complexity of the work NGOs do has increased exponentially. Where a handful of volunteers might have successfully managed a small urban-based project in the past, the multifaceted programmes that the modern NGO is expected to handle require a new type of volunteer, one who is more professional, with less time but more focused on policy and strategic decisions, and a new type of executive staff, one that is professionally trained and has competency in law, accountancy, public relations, and most of all, the management skills to work with and inspire large numbers of technical staff members.

While the criticisms above have come largely from other civil society groups, there are questions pertaining to NGOs that governments ask as well, underlining some of the potential tensions that exist in the relationship. Some of these relate to the more liberal funding, higher remuneration, and greater resource availability of NGOs; other questions relate to lifestyles, visibility, and the tendency to claim "government successes as their own." Finally, there are questions about conformity to government policy and direction, monitoring of government operations (the watchdog function), and straightforward opposition to the government. The emergence of internal conflict, terrorism, organized crime with international ramifications, and other threats to civil order has also engendered in governments a more cautious attitude towards NGOs — one that has resulted, in a number of countries, in the establishment of mechanisms to regulate and monitor the work of NGOs. These tendencies of governments, under severe strain themselves, have to be understood, accommodated, and managed, and taken as part of the reality in which, increasingly, current and future partnerships will have to be formed and sustained.

Nurturing and protecting effective and durable partnerships

In spite of the dynamic and at times antagonistic tensions that exist between the essential components in the partnership we are seeking, there is no doubt that overall there has been more collaboration between governments and NGOs in the years since the ICPD. This has been demonstrated by governments' willingness to allocate more funding to NGOs directly or (as is more often the case) by permitting NGOs to access donor funds. There has also been a noticeable readiness by governments to involve NGO and civil society activists in public policy development and programme design. Several developing countries have embarked on radical shifts in policy on population and development and in the formulation of changed policies to reflect the consensus generated at Cairo; in many of these policies, the NGO component has been very prominent. A feature of this improved collaboration has been that it has not been confined to any particular part of the world but has been virtually uniform globally. For example, in the countries of Central and Eastern Europe and the former Soviet Union, where NGO activity was minimal or non-existent before Cairo, active NGOs have now emerged. With the help of international NGOs like IPPF, country-level affiliates have played a leading role in placing reproductive and sexual health on policy-making agendas.

Parliamentarians have proven to be a potent source of advocacy and social mobilization on population and development issues. UNFPA, thirty years ago, saw the critical value of parliamentarians in influencing policy change and effecting legislative reforms of policies and laws that impeded progress in moving forward on population and development goals. In addition, networks of parliamentary groups, transcending local political bounds and territorial borders, like the Global Committee of Parliamentarians, the Asian Forum, and the Latin American grouping, with the support of UNFPA, have been invaluable in helping to forge the global consensus. Today, most countries of the world have become sensitized to the Cairo Programme of Action and to ICPD issues, and parliamentary advocacy has significantly assisted in keeping levels of funding of some donor countries (Japan and Australia, for example) at consistently high levels.

Five years after Cairo, the International Forum for the Review and Appraisal of the Implementation of the Programme of Action of the ICPD, held at The Hague in February 1999, provided an excellent opportunity for an intensive review of what stood in the way of broadening and strengthening partnerships and what more needed to be done. Some major constraints were identified.

Notwithstanding new policy development and legislation, the enabling environment for civil society participation needs to be improved in most countries. Clear guidelines to facilitate partnerships with NGOs often do not exist. Only limited progress has been made in strengthening the human resource, institutional, and financial capacities of civil society organizations (CSOs). Mobilizing additional public and financial support through CSOs is still problematic owing to weaknesses in transparency, accountability, and responsiveness to constituencies. Networking among CSOs at the country level has remained weak. Constraints on government resources, in addition to other local reasons, has limited provision by governments of technical and financial support for NGOs. Sometimes, the dependence on external sources of funding has limited NGOs' options in strategic planning. Although special initiatives for youth have been supported in many countries, youth involvement in programme design, implementation, monitoring, and evaluation remains insufficient.

What, then, are the specific actions we need to take in the future to improve relationships between the major components of the partnership we have been exploring? The Hague Forum suggested an agenda for all three components — governments, civil society, and the international community — that would, if carried out, work towards the objective of the broader partnership that is critical for the achievement of the ICPD goals. The guiding principle must be that partnerships involving governments, donors, and civil society need to be based on negotiation and agreed intentions and explicit outcomes that bring benefits for all people.

As far as governments are concerned, they should ensure the legitimacy and autonomy of NGOs by providing an appropriate legal framework. However, this should not be used to regulate them to the extent that their freedom to act and to be autonomous in their decision-making is affected. Policies should be adopted and legal and bureaucratic obstacles removed to facilitate the involvement of civil society, especially NGOs, more fully in the formulation and implementation of strategies and programmes. In seeking common objectives on which to build partnerships with civil society, it is important that governments carry on a dialogue with the broadest spectrum of society, including women's organizations, traditional community leadership structures, religious groups, indigenous peoples, children, youth, the elderly, and people with disabilities.

As far as NGOs are concerned, their priorities should be to promote and strengthen their human resources and institutional capacities. They should give increased attention to coalition building and to networking at local, national, and regional levels to promote the replicability, complementarity, and synergy of their programmes.

There are also actions that governments, civil society, and the international community can do together. These include:

- Continually looking at innovative and creative ways of enhancing civil society participation;
- Adopting innovative financial and technical assistance approaches to NGOs, including direct funding; and
- Supporting and strengthening South-South cooperation to share relevant experiences and to mobilize technical expertise and other resources among developing countries.

In all of these initiatives and endeavours, UNFPA will have a major role to play. As the custodian of the Programme of Action of the ICPD and the keeper of its conscience, the Fund has a key contribution to make in keeping alive and brightening the sometimes-flickering flame of partnership. As we have seen, there is a great deal to be gained by broadening and strengthening the partnerships so carefully and painstakingly constructed. There is, conversely, a great deal to be lost by its erosion. UNFPA should therefore continue, as it has done during the last thirty years, to focus on including civil society in partnerships as far as possible, helping to develop among all constituents a clearer understanding of the roles and responsibilities of all partners in population and development, and should strongly support governments in their work with civil society.

References

[1] United Nations, *Report of the International Conference on Population and Development,* Cairo, 5-13 September 1994. Programme of Action: Chapter XV, para. 15.1.

[2] Ibid.: para. 15.6.

[3] Ibid.: para. 3.1.

[4] Ibid.: para. 3.3.

[5] Jyoti Shankar Singh, *Creating a New Consensus on Population* (London: Earthscan, 1998).

[6] Ibid.: pp. 129-133.

[7] United Nations, *Report of the International Conference on Population and Development,* Cairo, 5-13 September 1994. Programme of Action: para. 14.16.

[8] Ibid.: para. 15.16.

[9] Ibid.: para. 15.19.

The Cairo Imperative: How ICPD Forged a New Population Agenda for the Coming Decades

Fred T. Sai

Introduction

The remarkable originality and achievements of the International Conference on Population and Development (ICPD), held in Cairo in September 1994, have sometimes been disregarded in the years since. Most fair-minded people acknowledge that ICPD succeeded in its main aims. But for those of us who participated in earlier population conferences and in the preparations for Cairo, it can be said to have succeeded beyond our wildest dreams — in terms of its intent and programmatic content at least. In addition, it helped mobilize the population, health, women's rights and allied communities to shape a broad agenda for the population and related development fields for the next two decades.

Of the three international conferences organized by the United Nations to help build world consensus on the need to address population issues, ICPD was by far the most successful, measured by numbers attending, levels and quality of delegates, international media attention, and the quality of the final consensus — and an important watershed. After long preparation and vigorous debate, more than 180 countries agreed to adopt the 16-chapter ICPD Programme of Action. The 115-page document outlines a 20-year plan to promote sustainable, human-centred development and a stable population, framing the issues with broad principles and specific actions. The Cairo Programme of Action was not simply an updating of the World Population Plan of Action (WPPA), agreed to at Bucharest and revised at Mexico City, but an entirely fresh and original programme, calling for a major shift in strategies away from demographic goals and towards more individual human welfare and development ones.

ICPD was the largest intergovernmental conference on population ever held: 11,000 representatives from governments, non-governmental organizations (NGOs), United Nations agencies and intergovernmental agencies participated, 4,000 NGOs held a parallel forum, and there was unprecedented media attention.

ICPD was not just a single event, but an entire process culminating in the Cairo meeting. There were six expert group meetings, and regional conferences in Bali, Dakar, Geneva, Amman and Mexico City. There were many formal and informal NGO meetings and three official Preparatory Committee (PrepCom) meetings. Other crucial influences came from the 1987 Safe Motherhood Conference, the 1990 World Summit for Children, the 1990 Jomtien World Conference on Education for All, and the 1993 Vienna Conference on Human Rights.[1]

Climate of the Times

It is best to begin by recalling the context and the climate of the times when preparations for ICPD were beginning. On several occasions during the previous five or more years, and notably at the Earth Summit in Rio in 1992, voices had been raised in alarm at the prospect of what was feared to be a new "population control" mentality fuelled by economic development and environmentalist arguments. Certainly the polarization displayed at Rio of conflicting concerns about population growth did not augur well for the 1994 conference.

Stated briefly, many delegates from the industrialized countries appeared to blame the world's environmental problems on overly rapid increase of population in the less advanced countries. Developing country delegates, on the other hand, emphasized excessive consumption, production of toxic and other wastes, and poor industrialization policies of the advanced nations as the major causes of the problems. The impasse could not be resolved when even the Rio Conference Secretary-General, Maurice Strong, commented bluntly: "Population must be stabilised, and rapidly. If we do not do it, nature will, and more brutally." This was the language of twenty years earlier of *Limits To Growth* and *The Population Bomb*.

The Earth Summit should have made population, environment and development as inextricably linked in people's minds, in the future formulation of every development strategy and policy formulation, as they are in reality. But before the conference there was a marked reluctance to grasp the population nettle, and at the conference the Vatican and others were able to remove the much misunderstood word "population," which many of them believed to be an euphemism for family planning and population control, from parts of the final Earth Summit texts. They even succeeded in watering down the long-established definition of "family planning" in Agenda 21 by referring instead to the "responsible planning of family size." This again harks back to the language of the 1970s and the denigration of the value of family planning that was much in evidence at the Bucharest Population Conference.

Some people feared — quite logically — that environmental arguments, calling for the rapid stabilization of world population, would likewise turn the clock back in time to 20 or 30 years ago. They recalled when some governments, alarmed by dire predictions of the consequences of rapid population growth, employed heavy-handed and occasionally coercive measures to induce women to use contraception and men and women to be sterilized, often against their best interests and occasionally against their will.

Targets versus Needs

How do such situations arise? More often than not, a government's decision to introduce family planning — often a politically risky step — is based on the social and economic considerations arising from rapid population growth. Planners point out the disharmony between the population growth rates and the projected increase in resources and services. They may state that in ten years' time, so many more schools, so many more jobs, so many more hospitals will be required for a population growing at such and such a rate. Politicians, from donor and recipient countries alike, are likely to find these arguments a far more cogent justification for introducing family planning services than human rights or maternal health considerations. Similarly, they may be swayed by arguments about soil exhaustion and erosion caused by land shortage, water shortage, and the influx of "environmental refugees" into their already overcrowded cities.

Obviously such considerations may be justified, and there may be perfectly legitimate global, regional and national demographic goals. As Dr. Nafis Sadik pointed out at the International Conference on Population Education in Istanbul in 1993: "The fact is that many developing countries simply cannot meet the needs of rapidly growing populations. They cannot provide adequate access to safe water and sanitation, nor can they provide food, shelter, education or employment for expanding numbers of people. Their attempts to do so draw off resources from productive investment." This is not considered enough justification for policies and programmes that ignore other more basic issues, such as freedom of choice, quality of care, individual autonomy and others, in their implementation.

Experience in many countries suggests that setting demographic *targets* in family planning programmes, especially at the local level, is not only offensive and likely to lead to inhumane service systems, it is simply unnecessary. At the International Planned Parenthood Federation (IPPF) Family Planning Congress in New Delhi in October 1992, one of the most important NGO meetings to provide an input to the ICPD process, Steven Sinding summarized the findings of an important piece of research as follows: "In terms of demographic outcomes there is no significant difference between programmes designed to achieve demographic targets and those designed to respond to the individual reproductive needs and aspirations of women and couples." The demographic goals that governments set can, in most cases, be achieved — or even exceeded — simply by responding to existing unmet needs. If women could have only the number of children they desired, he found, the effect on total fertility rates would, in 13 out of 17 countries where the government had quantitative targets to reduce fertility, more than exceed those targets. If the same procedure were to be applied globally, and the contraceptive needs of the 17 per cent of women of reproductive age in developing countries outside China who were not achieving their family size preference were met, there would result a fall in the total fertility rate that more than matched that required to meet the United Nations medium projection for 2000.[2]

Articulated demographic targets were a feature of many family planning programmes, especially in Asia, in the 1960s and 1970s. Expressed in terms of contraceptive prevalence, crude birth rates, "births averted," total fertility rates and population growth rates, these target numbers were frequently found in national development plans and sometimes in the strategy documents of family planning programmes. Critics argued that they led to insensitive delivery programmes, because rather than being motivated by a desire to help individuals and improve family health, target-driven programmes militated against caring service, with field workers and clinic staff being more concerned with meeting their quotas.

Steven Sinding proposed abandoning the use of demographic targets and instead expressing the objectives of family planning programmes solely in terms of achieving a fully satisfactory response to the stated desires of women and couples. "Family planning programmes still need quantitative objectives by which to assess their performance. But these objectives can and should be expressed in terms of satisfying people's stated needs rather than planners' notions of what a society's birth rate should be."[3] The position of many women's rights and health advocates had been scientifically supported and validated with this thesis, especially when it is expanded to include concepts of quality of care and several ethical principles on control of programmes and services.

Bucharest and Mexico City

As has been pointed out in another chapter of this book, ICPD differed radically from its two major predecessors in Bucharest (1974) and Mexico City (1984). Cairo marked a major step forward in humankind's approach to solving the problems caused by rapidly increasing numbers. The central achievement is that the programmes and strategies for solving these "population problems" were to be moved from the target-oriented solutions promoted at Bucharest and Mexico City. As Nafis Sadik put it, the Cairo Programme of Action "represents a quantum leap to a higher state of energy."

Let me spell out the major differences, based on my recollections of those earlier meetings. Bucharest in 1974, the first truly international population meeting organized under United Nations auspices, was an exciting meeting. It had a relatively small attendance of some 1,400 people, many of whom felt they had a unique chance to set about solving the problem of too-rapid population growth. They soon discovered that many developing countries were more interested in a new economic order than in population issues. The Marxist states, notably China, as well as the Vatican, were equally uninterested in promoting family planning as a means of reducing family size and controlling population growth. China's opposition was most baffling since it had previously released figures of the success of its family planning efforts. It chose rather to blame what it termed "hegemonism" for the population and development problems of the less developed countries. African countries, in particular, were almost all united in voicing the jargon of the time, "development is the best contraceptive."

At Mexico City ten years later, a major step forward was taken when the majority agreed that population and development are two sides of the same coin. The United States, a long-standing supporter of family planning, had changed horses, with a change of government from Democrat to Republican, and now saw population as a "neutral issue." Siding with the Vatican and a few countries, the U.S. was opposing all discussion of abortion and playing down the importance of family planning. The U.S. delegation, led by the conservative James Buckley, took positions that were often diametrically opposed to those it had taken at Bucharest. The U.S. government enunciated a policy on abortion that came to be known (unfairly to the Mexican hosts of the conference) as the "Mexico City Policy." Basically, the policy considered population as a neutral factor in development, it accepted family planning as a health issue but was against abortion, which many behind the policy equated to murder of unborn children and called for its proscription. The U.S. announced that it was cutting off all funding to IPPF and other NGOs that would not support the new U.S. policy on abortion, irrespective of whether they used U.S. funds in supporting programmes that performed or promoted abortions or not. Subsequently, UNFPA was also stripped of funding by the U.S. because of their support for family planning in China, claiming the China programmes were coercive.

However, China also reversed the position it had taken at Bucharest and now supported measures to slow rapid population growth. There were other positive developments — largely overlooked by the media because of the dramatic positions taken by the United States. These included the near-universal acceptance of the importance of family planning in development programmes and the reaffirmation of the Bucharest principle that "all families and individuals have the right to decide freely and responsibly the number and spacing of their children and to have the education, information and means to do so."[4] This recommendation had been one of the most contentious in Bucharest, and it withstood a well-organized effort to alter it in Mexico.

The PrepComs

Ten years on, the Cairo Conference was different in several ways. For the first time, "development" became part of the official title at the first PrepCom meeting in 1991. The demographic basics, such as growth rates, were all taken for granted, and for the first time the draft Programme of Action contained no demographic targets. While few still seriously questioned the problems associated with rapidly growing human populations, these were now seen as part of a broader human development agenda. Women's education, equality, and empowerment were recognized as paramount, and the importance of providing family planning within the context of full sexual and reproductive health care was stressed. The United States delegation, which had been led with real distinction at the PrepComs by Timothy Wirth, was led in Cairo by Vice-President Al Gore. The delegation was totally supportive of the Cairo agenda and provided much-needed leadership in moving the consensus forward. The "Mexico City Policy" had been overturned by President Clinton during his first days in office.

PrepCom meetings II and III, which I chaired, were, I believe, instrumental to the success of the Cairo Conference itself. The main objective of PrepCom II was to reach agreement on the form and substance of the final document. The committee was guided by a secretariat draft document on the issues to be considered. It then made extensive proposals on the subject matter and the organization of the final document. Many of the major positions taken at Cairo, such as the centrality of women to all development issues, reproductive rights, sexual health, and adolescents' sexual and reproductive rights, were first debated extensively at PrepCom II. Additional round-table discussions were convened to focus on the impact of HIV/AIDS, women's perspective on family planning and reproductive health, and the ethical dimensions of family planning and reproductive health.

PrepCom III, the most important of the three meetings, attempted to reach consensus on the wording of the final ICPD document, the result of the input from experts, governments, and the series of regional United Nations meetings. The document was discussed paragraph by paragraph by representatives of more than 170 Member States. In the end, while the vast majority supported and approved the document, a few countries led by the Holy See failed to agree on certain definitions, which were then bracketed for resolution in Cairo. The Vatican delegation and a handful of countries were still opposed to important areas in family planning; they were extremely suspicious of "sexual rights," and completely opposed to the phrase "unsafe abortion." Their position was that no abortion was safe, since the foetus always died. The Vatican representative, in particular, questioned why the document had no regard for ethical concerns. This called for a remark from the chair that there was no single set of ethics for all humankind and that developing countries had their own ethical concerns in these fields.

The Cairo consensus process had worked to build a bridge between advocates for women and family planning organizations, who in the past had sometimes found themselves opposing each other. Family planners had believed in providing services in several different ways and settings — some services be single-purpose for family planning only, others polyvalent including elements of health care — believing that the provision of family planning helped meet the circumstances of all being served and thereby empowered women. Feminists, on the other hand, believed that the ability to make responsible and informed choices about sexual and reproductive health is both a condition and a vehicle for improving the status of women. In their view, programmes and services that were not under the complete control of women and were not holistic should not be tolerated; some family planning methods, particularly injectables and implants (to some extent), were to be condemned. These disagreements required a great deal of bridge-building before and during Cairo. This bridge-building process was revisited and reinforced at the Fourth World Conference on Women (FWCW) at Beijing the following year (*see Box*).

Partly because of the spread of HIV/AIDS, which had largely occurred since the Mexico City Conference, service providers had increasingly begun offering diagnosis and counselling on sexually transmitted diseases (STDs), and so for the first time the prevention of STDs became an important feature of a population conference.

ICPD applied basic human rights principles to population and family planning programmes, and rejected coercion, violence and discrimination in any form in reproductive health services. It recognized the central role of sexuality and gender relations in women's health and rights; asserted that men must be fully involved in decisions involving fertility, sexual behaviour, STD and the welfare of their partners and children; and recognized unsafe abortion as a major public health issue. For the first time, it achieved an international consensus on such controversial topics as adolescent sexuality and female genital mutilation (FGM). Its programme was more nuanced, less confrontational, and more broadly focused than both Bucharest and Mexico City.

NGO Participation

One of the most positive developments to come out of the ICPD process has been a new relationship between the government and non-governmental sectors, based on a growing awareness of the need to work together and to find common ground on the issues. At Mexico City, only a handful of NGOs had had the opportunity to address the conference, and there had not even been an NGO forum. In Cairo, by comparison, the extent of NGO participation at the conference and in the planning process was unprecedented. At the PrepCom meetings, hundreds of NGOs with representatives from all regions of the world attended. At the conference itself, many representatives of NGOs were members of their governments' delegations. IPPF Family Planning Associations (FPAs) sat on a total of 80 national government delegations. Altogether, over 1,250 NGOs from over 130 countries were accredited to ICPD, and no fewer than 1,500 took part in the Cairo NGO Forum. The role and contributions made by women's NGOs to the final recommendations of the conference were outstanding.

As a direct result of the NGO community's influence, the Programme of Action reflects concerns that emanated from the NGO sector as well as the governmental sector. Traditionally, NGOs have played an important role in providing information and services to groups in society not well served by government programmes — the poor, ethnic minorities, adolescents, and others. They have also addressed issues considered too sensitive for many governments to address, such as abortion, violence against women and FGM. All of these areas were emphasized at the Cairo Conference, and governments have turned to NGOs to help them implement the Programme of Action.

Cairo signalled an understanding that population concerns and programmes are at last seen as part of the necessary investment in people, without which none of our development or environmental problems will be solved. Educating girls and making women truly equal partners in development, reducing infant and child mortality, promoting safe motherhood, giving access to quality family planning, tackling the problems of STDs and providing clean water, are all connected with improving family health and reducing family size. Slowing population growth, in turn, will feed back its social, economic and environmental benefits.

Vatican Opposition

For the first time, too, the Vatican found itself out on a limb, shorn of its former allies in the Communist world and the United States. Yet the biggest threat to the Cairo Conference came from the Roman Catholic Church, which called the conference a "serious setback for humanity." The Vatican appealed to the participants to avoid "legitimising abortion on demand, sexual promiscuity and distorted notions of the family." Before PrepCom III, the Pope had actually written to many, if not all, heads of state and government, condemning the draft and calling for support for rejecting or radically changing it. At the start of the Cairo Conference much of the wording on important issues in the draft Programme of Action was in square brackets, indicating that consensus could not be reached on its inclusion during the PrepCom meetings. For example, the term "reproductive and/or sexual health" appeared in brackets 79 times. The term "family planning" appeared in brackets 32 times.

As a result of high-profile lobbying and systematic opposition during the preparatory stages of the ICPD, the Vatican was able to influence the positions of a handful of Member States including Guatemala, Ecuador, Argentina, Malta, Honduras, and Benin. The Holy See also, perhaps out of desperation, attempted an alliance with some Muslim states. Church officials consistently misrepresented the draft plan as encouraging abortion, and then tried to claim it as a victory when the final text included the statement that "abortion should never be promoted as a method of family planning." The fact is that no one ever wanted to promote abortion — on the contrary, the aim has always been to minimize the incidence of abortion through better family planning. The Programme of Action only ever mentioned abortion in the context of the women's health, because all agreed that something must be done to curb the appalling extent of unsafe abortions and the damage they cause to women's lives and health.

In the view of many distinguished participants, the Vatican delegation wasted everybody's time by opposing such benign expressions as "safe motherhood" and "reproductive health care". In her forthright statement to the conference, Gro Harlem Brundtland, Prime Minister of Norway, expressed the exasperation of many: "I have tried, in vain, to understand how that term [reproductive health care] can possibly be read as promoting abortion or qualifying abortion as a means of family planning. Rarely, if ever, have so many misrepresentations been used to imply meaning that was never there in the first place."[5]

It is my view and that of many that the Vatican's obstinate stance on many issues gained the conference much free publicity and in the end perhaps even helped to gain it recognition within the highest circles of many governments. Of course, it took away time that might have been devoted to issues of implementation and perhaps more detailed debating of the resources problem. In the end, though, the Vatican attracted the opprobrium of the media and the international community by its obstructive tactics, and perhaps this helped make it announce its endorsement of several parts of the document, including the Principles — something it had never done before at any previous population conference.

Muslim Opposition

Some Muslim countries opposed the discussion of adolescent sexuality and sex education and the provision of contraceptives to the unmarried, and were suspicious of the talk of "empowering" women; a few even boycotted the conference in the wake of fundamentalist outbursts. This was partly due to a poor understanding of parts of the text, which they interpreted as an endorsement of total sexual freedom, although they were not. The question of "equality for women" was claimed by some to be impossible of accommodation within Sharia Law. The final text of the Principles, which were only fully discussed and agreed to in Cairo, put an end to the concerns of many individuals and countries whose opposition to parts of the text were not simply ideological. In particular, the introductory paragraph to the Principles states: "The implementation of the recommendations contained in the Programme of Action is the sovereign right of each country, consistent with national laws and development priorities, with full respect for the various religious and ethical values and cultural backgrounds of its people, and in conformity with universally recognized international human rights."

But I believe that it was good that these subjects were aired at Cairo, because the status of women and the needs of adolescents have been ignored for far too long at international meetings. Like the fuss over abortion, their heated discussion, and even threats to participants from some quarters prior to the conference, helped to raise the profile of the conference for the world's media and forced people to discuss these issues, however sensitive they are supposed to be.

Essential Points in the Imperative

As the Preamble to the Programme of Action rightly points out, ICPD occurred "at a defining moment in the history of international co-operation." What is the background to this revolutionary Programme of Action? And why has our approach to family planning and reproductive health changed?

I was surprised that some of the rich countries and some developing countries were so hesitant about making the financial commitments necessary for improved reproductive health services. But on the whole I was very pleased with the outcome. We certainly succeeded in getting the expansion we wanted in the Programme of Action: the inclusion of the improvement of the status of women, and the need for human resource development in its widest sense, as part of the population dimension. And in programme terms, for us to agree that reproductive health is the main basis from which to proceed on fertility management or family planning was in my opinion a major advance.

There were four essential points that emerged from the ICPD process. First, it is now accepted that population and development problems are not simply a relationship between numbers and development needs, such as school places, health care, and low savings and investment — but also between numbers and development attainments (by which I mean lifestyles and consumption patterns). The Programme of Action clearly recognizes that excessive consumption in the wealthier Northern countries and rapid population growth in the poorer South both contribute to global environmental and development problems.

The second point is the need for poverty alleviation programmes between and within countries — and this was taken forward at the Copenhagen World Summit for Social Development (WSSD) in March 1995 — which is an essential plank to all attempts to lower fertility and human numbers. These two points were instrumental in reducing significantly some of the North-South conflicts that were apparent at the two previous population conferences.

Third, and most important, it is now definitively accepted that population problems cannot be tackled through a macro numbers approach: solutions must be found at the micro level. So much of what needs to be done turns on a proper understanding of people as individuals and communities, on the status of women and their education, and the provision of proper health and particularly appropriate, good-quality reproductive health care.

Fourth, population and development are issues of concern to many sectors. They should therefore be shared issues to be handled by many stakeholders, severally and in coalitions.

In the 20-year programme approved at Cairo, the world's nations also agreed to:

- Ensure universal access to quality and affordable reproductive health services, including family planning and sexual health. Reproductive health services, including family planning, can save the lives and improve the health of women and children. A 1996 report by the United Nations Children's Fund (UNICEF) concluded that "the first and most obvious step towards reducing the toll of maternal mortality and morbidity is to make high-quality family planning services available to all who need them."[6] These services are also a key component of efforts to slow population growth.
- Enable couples to make real choices about family size through a series of social investments.
- Improve rates of child survival. No country in the developing world has experienced a sustained reduction in family size without first reducing infant and child mortality. Couples must feel confident that their children will survive before they are willing to have fewer children.
- Expand educational opportunities, close the "gender gap" in education, and provide universal access to primary education. Educated women tend to want smaller families, and are better at looking after the children they do have. The World Bank has for some years been proclaiming the importance of educating girls: "As shown in China, Costa Rica, and Sri Lanka, basic education of girls and women is also good for health. Educated individuals tend to adopt healthier lifestyles, make more efficient use of scarce resources such as food and health care, and avoid risks caused by the abuse of tobacco, alcohol, and illicit drugs."[7] Educated parents rely less on children for income and support, particularly in old age.
- Invest in women's development. When women can exercise their full legal and social rights, they often have both the desire and the ability to choose smaller families. Where women are valued as full human beings, there is less societal preference for sons. Efforts

to increase women's self-determination have been shown to improve the health and well-being of women and their children, and to slow the pace of population growth.[8]

- Expand opportunities for young women. In the year 2000, some 400 million adolescent girls stood on the brink of adulthood. If many choose to delay childbearing, even for a few years, they will enhance their health, education and employment prospects. In the year 2100, the developing countries' population will be smaller by 1.2 billion if the average age at bearing the first child is delayed by five years.[9]

A further remarkable development at Cairo was the inclusion of certain definitions in the final document, which condemned any form of coercion and were grounded in the human rights perspective. Thus governments defined "reproductive rights" as embracing certain human rights, including:

- The right of couples and individuals to decide freely and responsibly the number and spacing of their children and to have the information and means to do so;
- The right to attain the highest standard of sexual and reproductive health; and
- The right to make decisions free of discrimination, coercion or violence.[10]

The conference adopted the World Health Organization (WHO) definition of "reproductive health" as a "state of complete physical, mental and social well being and not merely the absence of disease or infirmity, in all matters relating to the reproductive system . . ."[11] And delegates committed themselves to promoting the reproductive rights of all individuals and couples, and to ensuring universal access to reproductive health-care services, including family planning and sexual health, by the year 2015.[12]

First, the high-quality data that became available from the World Fertility Survey (WFS) in the 1970s and more recently from the Demographic and Health Surveys (DHSs) have shown a high level of unwanted fertility in almost all countries covered. These surveys confirmed the universal desire of people to have smaller families, to control the timing of births, and to have access to the means to do so. The unmet need and the demand for family planning were shown still to be vast.

Information coming from the new DHS allowed the demand for family planning to be quantified with a higher degree of accuracy than before. The most conservative estimates of unmet need were based on the proportions of women who expressed a wish to delay or avoid pregnancy but who had not obtained contraceptive protection. These calculations yielded a range of figures from 12 to 21 per cent of women in the developing world who had an unmet need for contraception. These were based on the early DHS, which, in the main, omitted single women, as well as couples who were using an unsuitable, unsafe or unreliable method, and those who were dissatisfied with the method they were currently using. Including such couples and individuals would obviously greatly increase the estimates of unmet need for family planning.

It became clear, as people began to look at why there was so much unmet need, that the lack of availability or the inaccessibility of services was only one reason. There would be much more uptake of family planning if services were planned with community involvement, and orientated towards clients, offering them real choices and paying more attention to them as individuals. This expansion is at the heart of the Cairo agenda.

An important development was the unanimous adoption, at the IPPF Fortieth Anniversary Members' Assembly in New Delhi in October 1992, of *Vision 2000*, a bold strategic plan for the Federation and its member associations, which set out six challenges for the future:

- The demand and unmet need for family planning;
- The promotion of sexual and reproductive health for all;
- The elimination of unsafe abortion;
- The empowerment of women;
- Helping young people realize their sexuality in a positive and responsible manner; and
- The need for quality of care.

These challenges broadly overlap with many of the concerns addressed by the ICPD, and helped "prime" the family planning community for what was going to be asked of them at Cairo.

The Life-Cycle Approach

By the time of ICPD, there was a clear consensus on the need for a more comprehensive, client-centred view of services and for family planning to be part of a wider reproductive health approach. In this approach, the whole life cycle of people's health needs in relation to sexuality and reproduction is taken into account. The unfinished agenda to increase access to and improve the quality of existing services still remains, but the range of services is expanded according to the particular needs of communities.

Under this holistic approach, these added services may include providing care for women during pregnancy, delivery, and post-partum; providing counselling and help to menopausal women; providing gender-sensitive information, education and counselling on sexuality; taking care of people's concerns about STDs and infertility; HIV/AIDS prevention; the prevention and management of unsafe abortion, and the provision of safe abortion services where legal.

All these different elements of sexual and reproductive health are connected, and gains in one area will more than probably have beneficial repercussions in other areas. People are much more likely to take advantage of family planning when they find their other needs and concerns are being recognized as well. One example is of a family planning client who is screened for risk of STD before being fitted with an intrauterine device (IUD). A good family planning provider will, of course, make sure that a client who is found to be at risk is offered an alternative method. But under the holistic approach, the client will be given the chance to express and realize her needs for guidance, treatment, or referral for her other sexual and reproductive health concerns.

Beijing Box

How Beijing and ICPD+5 reiterated and strengthened the ICPD agenda

The key to the Cairo consensus, and perhaps its chief achievement, was recognition that the empowerment of women is not only essential for the success of population policies and programmes, but is also an important end in itself. Women must be provided with more choices through expanded access to education and health services, skill development and employment, and full involvement in policy and decision-making at all levels. The ICPD process worked to build bridges between advocates for women and family planning organizations, and most women's organizations were much more supportive of the Cairo Programme of Action than of the results of earlier population conferences. This is because the Programme of Action put women's equality, empowerment, reproductive rights, and sexual health at the center of population and development policies.

A year later, the Fourth World Conference on Women (FWCW) in Beijing endorsed and strengthened many of the recommendations of ICPD, and notably affirmed the far-reaching and comprehensive Cairo definition of reproductive health, which was reiterated in the Beijing Platform for Action. In fact, Beijing went further: whereas the ICPD Programme of Action refers to culture specificity and national sovereignty in reproductive health and rights, no such equivocation exists in the Beijing Platform for Action. The Platform for Action reaffirms the human rights of women, including their reproductive rights and the right to control matters related to their sexuality. In Beijing, governments agreed to take action to ensure that these rights were treated as human rights.

Beijing repeated the Cairo targets to reduce maternal mortality rates by one-half of their 1990 levels by the year 2000, and to cut levels by a further half by 2015. And it reinforced the call made at Cairo (for the first time at a United Nations population conference) for governments to recognize unsafe abortion as a leading cause of maternal mortality and a major public health concern. Included in the Platform for Action is a call for all countries to review laws containing punitive measures against women who have undergone illegal abortions. This directive is a step towards decriminalizing abortion. It also keeps the focus, first recognized internationally in Cairo, on the number of women worldwide who die or are seriously injured as a result of unsafe abortions.

Beijing reinforced Cairo's emphasis on adolescent sexuality. Despite vociferous opposition, the final agreement recognized the primacy of adolescent rights over the duties, rights and responsibilities of parents, thereby taking into account the evolving capacity of the child, and remaining true to the basic premise that the needs of the child come first, as expressed by the international community in the 1990 Convention on the Rights of the Child.

Finally, Beijing established that the rights of women include the right to control their sexuality, free from coercion, discrimination or violence, which gives women the basis to be free from multiple abuses of their sexual rights, including trafficking, rape, battering, and female genital mutilation (FGM).

Implementation and Results

What changes have taken place as a direct result of the Cairo consensus? Following ICPD, many governments have introduced policy and programme changes. For example, in Mexico, post-Cairo, the Ministry of Health began by merging the maternal/child care and family planning directorates into one new directorate of reproductive health. The national reproductive health programme includes family planning, adolescents, safe motherhood, women's health, and STDs, with an overall gender perspective. The new, more inclusive, thinking in the family planning sector includes strengthening women's roles, highlighting men's responsibility in the reproductive process, and the prevention and management of infertility. Advocacy, education and communication efforts are used to spread the message — mass media are used to educate and inform health workers, clients and the general population about reproductive health.

Mexico's efforts are among the good practices being disseminated through the Partners in Population and Development Initiative, established during ICPD, to support South to South transfer of experience among countries of the Southern Hemisphere. Other experiences being used as good examples are those of Indonesia; a Muslim country with good training and service experiences.

India, for a long time noted for its insistence on demographic and individual programme targets such as births averted and number of sterilizations performed, removed these after ICPD and is now using more total health and welfare-oriented goals. The national programme is now totally integrated with other family welfare elements and is more community-oriented. Results of these changes are very encouraging so far. Recently, the Philippines has announced similar changes in policy.

Benin is one of the African countries where some of the most remarkable policy changes have taken place since Cairo. In 1996, the government adopted a very comprehensive population policy and is establishing a framework for the provision of reproductive health services through local health centres. The new constitution of South Africa prohibits discrimination based on gender, sex, pregnancy, marital status or sexual orientation, and guarantees the right of individuals to make reproductive decisions and to have access to reproductive health services.

In Latin America, Peru has introduced a new policy that supports the provision of a wide range of reproductive health services within its health-care system. And Bolivia has established a new Maternity and Child Insurance Programme, which gives women free access to reproductive health care, including antenatal care, delivery and post-natal care, family planning and PAP tests. The management of the complications of abortion is also included in its health service.

My own country, Ghana, has formulated a national reproductive health policy based on ICPD definitions, and is taking steps to improve the delivery of services, especially in the marginal communities. We have also set up a national coordinating body for adolescent reproductive health, which has received great impetus since Cairo. Kenya has developed a new health framework with four major components: family planning, STD and HIV/AIDS control, the early detection of reproductive cancers, and counselling on sexuality.

In Indonesia, whose family planning programmes have shown remarkable success, the government is now paying greater attention to the prevention and treatment of STDs and HIV/AIDS, and to reducing maternal mortality, where Indonesia lags behind other countries of the region.

Policy Commitments

In Britain, the new Labour Government's White Paper on International Development, "Eliminating World Poverty — A Challenge for the 21st Century," published in November 1997, put the goals of Cairo and other landmark United Nations conferences at the centre of UK international development policy for the first time. It included this policy statement:

> Britain supports countries implementing the Programme of Action agreed at the International Conference on Population and Development in Cairo in 1994. Through multilateral and bilateral action Britain will do what it can to enable more people, particularly the poor, to have choices about the number and timing of their children. We will help women to go through pregnancy and childbirth more safely, and help women and men, whether adolescent or older, avoid sexually transmitted infections and sexual violence.
>
> This means improving the quality and accessibility of reproductive health information, services and commodities. Our goal is to contribute to meeting by 2015 internationally agreed targets of reproductive health for all and a three-quarters reduction in maternal mortality.[13]

The United States government played a major role in constructing the Cairo agenda and achieving the Cairo consensus. Not surprisingly, they have strongly backed the implementation of the Programme of Action. Speaking shortly after the Cairo Conference, the United States Agency for International Development (USAID) Administrator, the Honourable J. Brian Atwood, made this policy statement:

> The one-dimensional, top-down programmes of the last several decades are no longer appropriate. Peoples of the developing world want to have a say in what happens to them and we must listen to what they have to tell us. This is a fact of life for development in general, not just population issues. We recognise it and we are acting accordingly. In that same vein, we have established that choice and responsiveness to needs are the basic operating principles of our population and health programmes.
>
> Following these basic principles, we have determined that our programmes in population and health need to be strategically unified, and directed toward the best use of our limited resources in pursuit of clearly defined goals. Broadly speaking, our goals can be defined as follows:
>
> - First, no woman should become pregnant if she does not wish to bear a child.
> - Second, no one should be subjected to the risk of disease or harm because of sexual activity, and that activity should always be voluntary.
> - Third, no woman should be subject to the risk of death or illness because of pregnancy.
> - And fourth, no family should suffer the death of a child.
>
> These are expansive goals. They incorporate our view that the quality of care is as important as our global goal of stabilising population growth. They call for a core emphasis on family planning services — high quality, responsive to choice, and widely accessible. They call for a new concentration on women's reproductive health, including HIV/AIDS prevention. And they call for a continued focus on Child Survival.

And he went on to stress the importance of two other priority areas for USAID: adolescent sexual and reproductive health (ASRH), and post-abortion care.[14]

The United Nations and Its Agencies

Progress made with implementing the ICPD Programme of Action demonstrates the importance and role of a permanent United Nations organ that assumes responsibility for the actions mandated by a United Nations conference. In this case UNFPA, which was the conference secretariat, assumed leadership for the implementation of the Programme of Action. By mainlining the Programme of Action and providing stimulant meetings and financial help, as needed, the Programme has received the widest possible dissemination, discussion, and translation into action at all levels within the United Nations system, by regional intergovernmental organizations, within countries, and among international, national, and even local NGOs, including parliamentarians. The major United Nations organs with a role to play have identified such roles.

The General Assembly has provided the fora for debate and for assessing progress. The Population Commission has been mandated to carry out a periodic review of the progress. WHO and UNICEF, in particular, deserve mention as agencies that responded actively to the Programme.

WHO carried out an extensive reorganization and brought together its divisions for Family Health, including Adolescent Health, Child Health, and the Programme for Research and Research Training in Human Reproduction, into one group, termed "Family and Reproductive Health." The Director's position was elevated to that of Executive Director, and within a short time a document was developed on what the new ICPD Programme of Action should mean to all levels of WHO. The document defines the health problems and services to be considered in the reproductive health approach.[15]

UNICEF, which had been considered by many as unable or unwilling to develop a strong policy and assist family planning programmes, began speaking out more forcefully. The needs of the girl child, of adolescents, and "Safe Motherhood" have featured prominently in their activities. In fact, UNICEF's publication *The Progress of Nations, 1996* featuring Safe Motherhood perhaps helped people and countries all over the world to understand and wake up to the problem more than did all of the previous efforts.[16]

Foundations

Many international foundations support research and programme activities in advocacy, communication, HIV/AIDS prevention, and other issues emphasized at ICPD. In 1996, the top foundation donors were the Ford Foundation, the Rockefeller Foundation, the MacArthur Foundation, the Hewlett Foundation, and the Mellon Foundation. In November 1998, the Packard Foundation announced that it would be allocating more than $300 million to international population and reproductive health programmes over the next five years (1999 to 2003).

The newly created United Nations Foundation (a subsidiary of the Turner Foundation) has given specifically targeted grants focusing on population and women, with special emphasis on adolescents. In May 1998, the Foundation provided UNFPA with $8 million for six projects, and in its second round of grants, some $4.3 million for the advancement of ASRH. The William H. Gates Foundation has given UNFPA $1.7 million to support collaboration in reproductive health among developing countries.

Non-Governmental Organizations

Perhaps not surprisingly, there are even more examples of initiatives by NGOs, who are usually quicker off the mark than bureaucratic governments:

- In Russia, the abortion rate is one of the highest in the world. IPPF and the Russian FPA have had a direct and positive influence on reducing the reliance on abortion, with the provision of information, model services, and pioneering service provision for young people. As a result of access to modern and reliable contraception and the promotion of women's health needs, the high abortion rate has been cut in half and the contraceptive prevalence rate has increased dramatically. The FPA is also working with UNFPA to develop an appropriate sex education programme for teenagers in and out of school.
- In Eastern Europe generally, the transition from centralized economic systems has been difficult, and public services have deteriorated. In Latvia, the FPA is working with the private sector in a social marketing project to reduce unwanted pregnancy and the spread of STDs. In Romania, the Youth for Youth Foundation is producing videos with UNFPA support, to provide information and raise awareness about STDs and HIV. UNFPA is also supporting youth summer camps run by the Romanian FPA, SECS, which include reproductive health and family planning issues.
- The FPA of Nepal is playing a leading role by involving itself in the movement to legalize abortion. It is a bold first step in a country where women are currently jailed for undergoing abortion. The President of the Nepal FPA has put forward to Parliament a private members bill called "The Protection of Pregnancy Bill 1996."
- The Caribbean associations of Belize, Guyana, and St. Lucia are continuing their pioneering efforts to change from a clinic-centred, medical focus on family planning to a community-oriented sexual health approach. The FPAs have trained lay facilitators to handle group and individual discussions on sexual and reproductive rights in their own neighbourhoods and have trained clinic staff and outreach workers to respond to the newly identified needs related to sexual and reproductive health.
- In Kenya, the FPA's Women Empowerment Centre serves as a model for other countries wishing to set up projects at the grass-roots level that offer women's rights and reproductive rights services. The centre is run in the peri-urban community of Kangemi by a coalition of five organizations, and offers legal advice, counselling, and referrals to reproductive health services.

- Safe motherhood is a serious concern in sub-Saharan Africa, where more than half of women aged 15 to 19 are sexually experienced and where the highest levels of adolescent childbearing worldwide occur. In Ghana, the FPA's Teenage Mothers Project provides education and employment opportunities through skills training as a means of encouraging teenagers to delay first births beyond adolescence.
- In some areas of Brazil, where pregnancy rates and rates of HIV/AIDS among young people were extremely high, the FPA BEMFAM launched a school-based sex education programme that incorporated sexual and reproductive health information into every aspect of the curriculum.
- The FPAs in the Dominican Republic, Brazil, Jamaica, Venezuela, El Salvador, and Ecuador have demonstrated significant interest in learning how to integrate early identification of gender-based violence into family planning service delivery. The associations are training the staff and health-care providers to learn when and how to raise the topic of violence — whether past sexual abuse or current coercion or battering. To support this initiative the region is creating necessary materials, ranging from training curricula to patient handouts.
- Several FPAs have stepped up their efforts to eliminate the harmful procedure of FGM. Among them, the FPA in Kenya began a campaign to educate parents, young people, and the community. The campaign received the support of the Roman Catholic Church and the Kenyan President and there is strong evidence that public attitudes toward FGM are changing. The FPA of France runs an active campaign to protect the rights of young migrant women who may be subjected to FGM in France or on return to their country of origin. And in the community of Kapchorwa, the Uganda FPA is working to eliminate the practice of FGM in a UNFPA-funded project called REACH. The FPA provides back-up support by using the Community Based Distribution Network to do advocacy in the community, and uses its clinics to provide care for the girls who have been circumcised.
- Young people have been involved in the provision of information and services to their peers in the Indonesia FPA's Lentera Project, which also provides counselling to transvestite prostitutes.
- Algeria's Kamikaze youth project, designed by the FPA and young volunteers, brought much-needed information about unsafe abortion, unwanted pregnancies, and STDs to the young people of the country.
- In the FPA of India, young people are playing a major role in sexual and reproductive health education. One example is the use of folk media in the Youth Inspirers' peer education programme, in which a group of young people went on a ten-day rail journey through three districts, stopping at railway stations to put on puppet shows and drama sketches and sing songs about various aspects of sexual and reproductive health.[17]

Other NGO Initiatives

- In Bangladesh and Honduras, advisory networks of NGOs have been set up to work with the government in implementing ICPD recommendations.
- In India, NGOs including the network Health Watch are working to ensure that women are given a strong role in planning, monitoring and evaluating the new "target-free"

family welfare programme. And in the red-light district of Sonagachi, West Bengal, an NGO supported by the British Government is providing condoms and treatment for sexual infection to 800,000 people, which has been successful in keeping HIV prevalence below 5 per cent.

- In Russia, women's organizations have helped shape a draft law criminalizing violence against women in the family, and another to guarantee women's reproductive rights.
- In Chile, the Corporación de Salud y Politicas Sociales is helping parliamentarians draft legislation to reduce unwanted pregnancies; and the health NGO Educación Popular en Salud organized a seminar for poor women on the ways in which violence makes women more vulnerable to HIV infection, and on how to communicate better with their partners and defend themselves against violent behaviour.
- In Egypt, several NGOs collaborated in a project to train youth leaders to conduct peer counselling on reproductive health and gender issues. The trainees, aged 18 to 25, advocate adolescents' rights to reproductive health service providers and help young people make informed decisions about responsible sexual behaviour.
- In Cambodia, NGOs are promoting awareness of domestic violence, conducting training and counselling, and have opened the country's first shelters for battered women.
- "One Year after Cairo," a country-by-country survey of ICPD implementation that includes NGO projects in 65 countries, was published in 1996 by Earth Summit Watch, a project set up by the Natural Resources Defense Council and the Women's Environment and Development Organization (WEDO).

Generally, there is no shortage of examples of projects and programmes that would have been unthinkable — or at least very rare — before Cairo. The holistic approach advocated by ICPD is in harmony with all modern thinking on development, and should not be taken as de-emphasizing the importance of fertility reduction activities. The fact that there are "add-ons" and new approaches in the ICPD Programme of Action was not intended to imply that family planning was considered less important: it is just as important — but it is now seen in a wider context.

Several organizations, including UNFPA, the Population Reference Bureau (PRB), Family Care International (FCI), and Population Action International (PAI) have attempted an assessment of progress with implementing the ICPD Programme of Action. The results on the whole are very encouraging. Several governments have now created functioning ministries for women or gender. Others have strengthened the mandates of existing ones. International and national women's organizations are increasingly being involved in reproductive health programmes. Legislative changes have occurred in many countries aimed at removing the barriers to women's involvement or progress and to eliminate discrimination against women. Laws against violence to women have been enacted or strengthened; and training for law enforcement officers on gender violence is becoming widespread.

The reproductive health approach has been widely adopted by countries and organizations. As stated elsewhere, progress has not been as rapid as might be expected, for technical as well as financial reasons. Legal and policy changes have been made by many countries to ensure implementation of the ICPD recommendations. Many national agencies and organizations are still confused about what the phrase "reproductive and sexual health" means in programme terms. Even where such confusion does not exist, organizational problems within ministries of health and other relevant ministries and agencies have often blocked action. The inclusion of STD is still problematic in some cultures. Extensive discussion and debate of these issues took place in The Hague in 1999.

Critics and Criticisms

It would be amazing if Cairo did not have its critics. During the PrepComs and the Cairo Conference there were two types of criticism. One was that "development" was not given enough attention despite the title of the conference. The other was that the population conference had capitulated to the women's advocates and the critics of family planning by removing demographic targets and de-emphasizing the importance of fertility reduction in programmes. More tellingly, some objected that to expand family planning to embrace all sexual and reproductive health services will inevitably lead to a dilution of basic services and that FPAs will be unable to cope or afford the extra services they are expected to provide.[18] Most argue that the reproductive health approach will be far more expensive and less efficient than vertical or single-purpose family planning programmes, and that population resources, small to begin with, certainly should not be stretched to cover the kind of "social engineering" — health, empowerment, rights — mandated by ICPD.

The first criticism has not been extensively addressed because it appears to be based on the concept that once the word "development" appears, there should be an extensive and in-depth discussion of all aspects of socio-economic development, whether directly relevant to population programmes or not. The plain fact is that selected areas of development, those most relevant to population issues, were discussed extensively during the PrepComs and at Cairo. These included, in particular, education, especially of the girl child; health in general; improvement in the status and roles of women; and equity and equality between the sexes. It must be stressed that the majority of delegates representing countries in Cairo were drawn from health, population and diplomatic backgrounds and not from that of economic development. Many other United Nations fora, including the General Assembly, discuss general development all of the time, and discussion of such issues at Cairo could have been both superficial and a fruitless diversion.

In a thorough discussion of the second criticism, Adrienne Germain, then Vice-President and Programme Director, now President, of the International Women's Health Coalition (IWHC), points out that the Cairo approach will be more cost-effective in meeting demographic goals in at least two ways: "first by reducing contraceptive dropout and failure rates, and second by appealing to the younger individuals and couples who, in demographic terms, need to delay sexual initiation and marriage, and contracept earlier and longer."[19]

She then examines the case of Bangladesh, where twenty years of an intensive, vertical family planning programme has been pronounced a success story. However, the quality of family planning services is poor, discontinuation and failure rates are high, and maternal mortality has hardly fallen and remains among the world's highest, partly because of botched abortions. Adolescent marriage is common, and HIV/AIDS has arrived. Faced with this situation, the Government of Bangladesh has now framed the first national health and population sector strategy, taking the Cairo agenda as its starting point.

This leads her to call for a "new research agenda for a post-Cairo demography," pointing out that "the DHS in Bangladesh as elsewhere, for example, does not survey the young and unmarried, nor have they analysed the published data on abortion, safe or unsafe . . . most demographic research in Bangladesh . . . has been narrowly focused on contraceptive acceptance and use, and on fertility reduction."

To support implementation of the Cairo agenda, not only in Bangladesh but also worldwide, research is needed in several new areas:

- The situation of young people and their life choices;
- The significance of both sex and gender, which underlie reproductive and health-seeking behaviour;
- The decision-making environment;
- Applied demographic research to estimate the costs and benefits of reproductive health services, including family planning; and
- Assessing and promoting changes in broader national development policies.

And she concludes, "the Cairo agenda is a demographic agenda. It offers demographers, and all other population professionals, unprecedented opportunities to expand our vision, to revitalise and strengthen our field, and to broaden the base of popular and political support for our work."[20]

A further answer to the "dilution" criticism is that the social investments called for by Cairo — to create socio-economic conditions in which it makes sense for individuals to have fewer children — are to be made from broader development agencies and budgets, not from family planning budgets. And as for the "overstretched" criticism: it is true that some will be unable to cope — but the proof that it is possible is that some FPAs were already providing much fuller services before Cairo, and others have started doing so since. And part of the spirit of Cairo is to encourage all family health organizations to cooperate more closely with each other and other agencies.

The question about the cost of reproductive health services and counselling is, however, a very real one. Of course it costs more money to provide extra services — and this was recognized in the ICPD funding targets. ICPD realized that just to maintain the levels of contraceptive use that had led to global fertility declines, about 100 million more couples would need access to reproductive health and family planning services by 2000. The financial targets set in the ICPD Programme of Action carefully laid out the costs and how they were to be raised.

While there was a good start in the first year after ICPD, when a global total of $9.5 billion was earmarked for population programmes, a substantial rise from 1994 spending, since then most donor nations have been reducing their support, rather than increasing it as they had promised. If this trend is not soon reversed, implementation will naturally be difficult. But this difficulty should surely not be turned into a criticism of the Cairo concept of extending sexual and reproductive health care to all.

132

ICPD+5

In 1999, the international community was engaged in a five-year review of the ICPD Programme of Action (ICPD+5) to assess the progress made to date, examine the obstacles remaining, reaffirm the commitments made at Cairo, and produce practical recommendations aimed at making ICPD's twenty-year goals a reality.

The ICPD+5 process had several aims:

- To move the debate forward, not reopen it;
- To reinvigorate international political will;
- To consolidate progress;
- To focus attention on priorities where more intensive support is needed; and
- To position reproductive health as a central priority for international action and to clarify the roles of the various international organizations.

An international forum was convened by UNFPA at The Hague, The Netherlands, in February 1999, following an NGO Forum, a Parliamentarians' Forum, and a Youth Forum. At The Hague Forum, governments, NGOs and other elements of civil society took stock. Several research organizations, including PRB, Columbia University, PAI, and some national groups had been commissioned to research progress made.

Evidence of the considerable progress made in implementing key areas of the ICPD Programme of Action was presented to delegates, and the consequences of shortfalls in funding levels were spelt out. A report was agreed. In March, the United Nations Commission on Population and Development (CPD) prepared the way for a three-day special session of the United Nations General Assembly in June, the culmination of Cairo+5, which reviewed and finalized key future steps and recommendations for further implementation of the Programme of Action. This meeting of the CPD was enlarged to become a PrepCom for the June General Assembly discussions.

Conclusion

The consensus is that the Cairo Programme of Action did in fact alter world thinking on population and development issues. It gave rise to a new way of approaching population programmes. Together with the Beijing Conference, it helped raise the profile of the women in development debate and helped shape approaches that could yield progress. It raised the lid over issues that hardly ever receive public discussion, such as human sexuality and adolescent reproductive health. It helped start coalitions for action. Implementation has not been uniform, and there are areas in which progress has been slow.

All in all, however, all involved should be satisfied with the extent to which the new Programme of Action developed in Cairo has been generally accepted for implementation the world over. The rhetoric has been mostly positive. With the exception of a very few countries, programmes are being advocated with greater courage and conviction. NGOs are increasingly

133

accepted as legitimate partners of governments in the field of sexual and reproductive health. The participation of communities is either being actively promoted or tentatively examined. Gender equity and equality are increasingly being promoted.

The developing countries generally are meeting or even increasing their budgetary inputs into the sexual and reproductive health fields. Unfortunately, with the laudable exception of a few, the majority of donor contributions have stagnated or even decreased. The United States, in particular, has proved a disappointing partner for development in this field. Not only has its contribution not increased, but it is nowhere near the expected level in terms of its vast gross domestic product (GDP). Furthermore, the U.S. Congress has tried, mostly successfully, to continue the defunding of UNFPA and IPPF. Efforts to get the "Mexico City Policy" repealed have not been successful. Instead, the internally divisive issue of abortion has become an obstacle to many development inputs from the U.S. Even the United States' willingness to pay its outstanding debt to the United Nations is held hostage to abortion.

The general feeling after five years is that much progress has been made, while a great deal still remains to be done in all of the areas covered by the Programme of Action. The area of women and development, in particular, needs constant pressure and attention. Reproductive health, especially safer motherhood, requires more inputs, as does adolescent reproductive health. Resources are sorely deficient for a field to which the world is now so well committed on paper. It would be a shame if the enthusiasm, commitment and dedication generated by the ICPD were to wane in the next few years because some donor countries are unwilling to share to the extent of their capability.

References

[1] Jyoti Shankar Singh, *Creating a New Consensus on Population* (London: Earthscan, 1998).

[2] S. Sinding, *Family Planning: Meeting Challenges, Promoting Choices*, "Getting to Replacement: Bridging the Gap Between Individual Rights and Demographic Goals," eds. P. Senanayake, R. L. Kleinman (UK: The Parthenon Publishing Group/IPPF, 1993).

[3] Ibid.

[4] United Nations, *Report of the United Nations World Population Conference 1974*, Bucharest, 19-30 August 1974. World Population Plan of Action: Chapter II, article 14f.

[5] United Nations, *Report of the International Conference on Population and Development*, Cairo, 5-13 September 1994. Programme of Action.

[6] United Nations Children's Fund, *The Progress of Nations, 1996* (New York: UNICEF, 1996).

[7] World Bank, *Health, Nutrition and Population Sector Strategy Paper* (Washington, D.C.: World Bank, 1997).

[8] Population Council, "The Unfinished Transition," *Population Council Issues Papers No. 3* (New York: Population Council, 1996).

[9] J. Bongaarts, "Population Policy Options in the Developing World," *Science*, 263, No. 5148 (1994).

[10] United Nations, *Report of the International Conference on Population and Development*, Cairo, 5-13 September 1994. Programme of Action: para.7.3.

[11] Ibid.: para. 7.2.

[12] Ibid.: paras. 7.3 and 7.6.

[13] Her Majesty's Stationary Office, "Eliminating World Poverty — A Challenge for the 21st Century," British Government White Paper on International Development (London, 1997).

[14] United States Agency for International Development, "International Family Planning," remarks of J. Brian Atwood at Columbia University, New York, 6 February 1997 (Washington, D.C.: USAID, 1997).

[15] World Health Organization, *Maternal and Child Health and Family Planning: Quality of Care. Reproductive Health: WHO's Role in the Global Strategy.* Report by the Director-General. Document A48/10 (Geneva: WHO, 1995): unpublished.

[16] United Nations Children's Fund, *The Progress of Nations, 1996* (New York: UNICEF, 1996).

[17] International Planned Parenthood Federation, *Position Paper on the Five-Year Review of the 1994 International Conference on Population and Development* (London: IPPF, 1998).

[18] M. Potts, Julia Walsh, "Making Cairo Work," *The Lancet* 353 (23 January 1999): pp. 315-318.

[19] A. Germain, "Addressing the Demographic Imperative Through Health, Empowerment and Rights: ICPD Implementation in Bangladesh," *Health Transition Review*, Supplement to Volume 7 (1997).

[20] Ibid.

Challenges Remain But Will Be Different

Steven Sinding and Sara Seims

This volume chronicles the remarkable success — indeed, the reproductive revolution — that has taken place over the last thirty years, in which the United Nations Population Fund (UNFPA) has played such a major role. Our purpose in this chapter is to contrast the situation at the century's end with the one that existed at the time of UNFPA's creation thirty years ago, and to project from the current situation to the new challenges that lie ahead. In many respects, the successful completion of the fertility transition that is now so far advanced will bring an entirely new set of challenges, and these will require a fundamental rethinking about the future mandate, structure, staffing and programme of UNFPA in the twenty-first century. Our purpose here is to identify those challenges and speculate about their implications.

Yesterday and Today: Thirty Years of Demographic Transformation

Thirty years ago, the term "population explosion" was on the lips of most educated people. It was taken as given that population growth on the planet was careering out of control, and that the cause was both a desire for large families and a substantial unmet need for family planning services in the face of rapidly declining mortality rates. Demographers and other social scientists furiously debated in the 1960s and early 1970s whether the best strategy was to meet existing demand for family planning services or to bring about more fundamental social transformations that would reduce desired family size. However, they all agreed that the combination of unmet need for services and high desired fertility combined to form the crux of the population challenge. Indeed, to a very considerable degree, UNFPA's mandate at its founding was to deal directly with these two causes of high population growth rates, and the history of the last thirty years represents the successful efforts of both developing countries and their supporters to respond to this challenge. Thus, as we cross the threshold into a new century and millennium, the demographic picture has changed dramatically.

Today, average family size in the developed world has declined from six to three or fewer children; contraceptive use has increased from under 10 per cent to well over 50 per cent of couples; and desired fertility has declined from five or more children to slightly over two. Satisfying unmet need remains an important challenge and large desired family size remains an issue in a few regions (e.g., sub-Saharan Africa and much of South Asia), but the central challenge has shifted to the third important component of population growth: population momentum.

High fertility vs. population momentum

Our current population momentum is a consequence neither of contemporary unmet need nor of high desired fertility. Rather, it is the result of high fertility in the past. As long as more people enter the reproductive age group than leave it, population growth will continue. As we shall discuss below, the high fertility of the entire post-World War II era has produced enormous momentum, which has resulted in 800 million adolescents, the largest such group in history, who are soon to enter their peak reproductive years. Even if each young woman in the developing world who is now reaching the age of 14 or 15 has only two children throughout her reproductive lifetime, the developing world's population would still increase from 4.5 billion in 1995 to about 6.5 billion by the year 2050 because the base of reproductive-aged young people is so enormous.

While unmet need can be satisfied by good-quality reproductive health services, including family planning, and while high desired fertility can be influenced by social and economic development policies that relate to the status of women and general well-being, population momentum can only be dealt with by two interventions: delaying the onset of childbearing and spacing births relatively widely. It appears that the best way of achieving both these objectives is by closing the gender gap in education in order to achieve universal primary education for both girls and boys, and by ensuring that women as well as men have subsequent employment opportunities. The longer girls stay in school, the later they begin bearing children; and the more educated they become, the better their employment opportunities. Employed women are much more likely to space births and are also more likely to delay the onset of childbearing than unemployed women. Investments in human capital (health, education, livelihoods) that affect demographic momentum are likely to promote lower desired fertility, setting in motion a virtuous cycle.

Some governments have mandated delayed age of marriage as another means of slowing population momentum, but such policies vary in their effectiveness; in only a very few cases are they as effective as the female-education approach. Furthermore, of course, there are many other important social benefits associated with the education of girls, including better health and nutrition of children, higher family incomes, and stronger and stabler marriages. So, over the past thirty years the fertility challenge has clearly shifted from reducing wanted and unwanted fertility to addressing the issue of population momentum.

"Two worlds" of fertility vs. many worlds

In 1969, it was relatively easy to divide the world into two distinct demographic regimes: The high-fertility (and still relatively high-mortality) countries of "the South," and the low fertility (and low mortality) countries of "the North." Included in the latter category were the countries of Eastern Europe and the former Soviet Union — what used to be called "Second World." So, the First and Second Worlds of the 1960s were in one demographic category, while the Third World was in another. The First and Second Worlds were characterized by average family sizes of around two children, with virtual stability in population growth rates. The Third World was characterized by uniformly high fertility, rapidly declining mortality, and explosive population growth.

In 1969, there were not very many differences among the countries that were then called the Third World. While fertility decline had begun in East Asia and was just beginning in parts of

Southeast Asia, the countries of South Asia, Africa, and Latin America still had fertility rates of around six children per woman, and there were relatively small differences among these countries.

**Table 1. Total fertility rates, by major areas and region,
late 1960s to late 1990s**

	1965-1970	1995-2000
World	4.90	2.79
More developed regions	2.36	1.59
Less developed regions	6.00	3.08
Least developed regions	6.66	5.25
Africa	6.69	5.31
Asia	5.69	2.65
Eastern Europe	2.35	1.41
Northern Europe	2.45	1.73
Western Europe	2.45	1.46
Latin America & Caribbean	5.56	2.65
North America	2.54	1.93
Oceania	3.55	2.46

Source: United Nations, 1996.[1]

In other words, in most of the countries of the Third World the fertility transition had not yet begun. Today, the situation is highly variegated. While some developing countries, particularly in sub-Saharan Africa, still have fertility rates as high as five or six children per mother, other countries, such as Brazil, Colombia, and Sri Lanka have achieved replacement-level fertility. Generally, East and Southeast Asian fertility levels have now dropped to virtual replacement level, and Latin American countries are rapidly approaching that level as well. Some countries in the Arab world have experienced rapid fertility declines, while others are barely beginning the demographic transition. And even in Africa there is wide variation, with countries like South Africa, Kenya, Zimbabwe, and Botswana now well into the demographic transition, while others, particularly among Francophone countries, do not yet show even early signs that the transition has begun.

Shifting dependency ratios

In 1969, in the developing world more than 75 per cent of the entire dependent population was under the age of 15, and only 7 per cent was over 65.

Table 2. Dependency ratios of children and the elderly (per 100 population aged 15-64), by major areas and region, 1970-2000

	1970	2000
World		
0-14	65.7	47.4
65+	9.6	10.8
More developed regions		
0-14	40.6	27.1
65+	15.4	21.0
Less developed regions		
0-14	76.8	52.7
65+	7.0	8.1
Least developed regions		
0-14	84.1	78.3
65+	5.7	5.6

Source: United Nations, 1996.[2]

By "dependency," demographers and economists mean the proportion of the population that is not in the labour force. The dependency ratio thus is the number of people outside the working-age range over the number within it. The least developed regions of the world in 1969 had a dependency ratio of almost 1, in which just under half the population was under the age of 15 while only a very small proportion lived to the age of 60 or 65. In contrast, in 1969 the dependency ratio in a highly industrialized, modern country like Sweden was not only far lower (almost two people of working age for every member of the population who was in school or elderly) but its composition was very different — about two-thirds were represented by those under 15 while one-third were over 64. However, by 1990, this ratio had shifted so that the young and the old populations were almost equal in size.

Fertility declines in Asia and Latin America have changed their situation dramatically. Dependency ratios in these regions have been greatly reduced for the under-15 group and have increased slightly for the 65 and over. However, overall dependency ratios still remain about double those in the industrialized countries. By contrast, the reduction in under-15 dependency has shifted hardly at all in the least developed regions, especially in sub-Saharan Africa. Indeed, as we will see in the last part of this chapter, the drastically reduced under-15 populations in countries where fertility decline has been recent and rapid pose unprecedented challenges in the years immediately ahead.

At the same time, the situation has also changed in the industrialized countries. While the demographers' assumption of long-term population stability at the end of the demographic transition seemed appropriate fifteen years ago, the decline of fertility in Europe to levels well below replacement and the fact that these have remained at below-replacement levels for some time, portends the possibility of significant fertility decline in many parts of the erstwhile First World. European countries are struggling with the implications that this exceptionally, and historically unprecedented, low level of fertility will have for the size of their labour force and its productivity.

Many have responded, at least temporarily, by permitting heretofore-unknown levels of immigration, but the social consequences of such population movements have produced political tensions and uncertainties throughout both Eastern and Western Europe.

An urbanizng world

In 1969, just under 25 per cent of the developing world was urban, with the vast majority of people in the developing countries engaged in agriculture and living in rural areas. Today, the Latin America and Caribbean region is 70 per cent urbanized, and Asia and sub-Saharan Africa have over one-third of their populations living in urban areas. While the first region of the developing world to experience a majority urban population was Latin America, much of Asia and the Middle East are now also following this pattern, and one sees signs throughout Africa of exploding urban populations as well.

Table 3. Proportion of the world living in urban areas, by major areas and regions, 1970-2000

	1970	2000
World	36.6%	47.5%
More developed regions	67.5	76.3
Less developed regions	25.1	40.7
Least developed regions	23.0	25.3
Africa	23.0	37.3
Asia	23.4	37.7
Eastern Europe	55.8	75.1
Northern Europe	80.4	84.5
Western Europe	76.1	81.4
Latin America & Caribbean	57.4	69.6
North America	70.5	76.6
Oceania	70.8	70.2

Source: United Nations, 1995.[3]

A combination of rural population pressures and the communications-driven lure of the cities has resulted in massive internal migrations toward the cities of the Third World. Such cities as today's Mexico City, Sao Paulo, Bangkok, and New Delhi would be unrecognizable to anyone who left one of them in the 1950s. Some developing world cities have grown more than tenfold in just the last thirty years. Urbanization has grown far faster than natural population increase and represents more than just the migration of excess rural population. A world that is rapidly changing in economic terms, and in which technology-fuelled opportunities are primarily found in urban centres, has significantly accelerated rural-to-urban migration.

141

The significance of national boundaries

In 1969, most population movement occurred within nations, not between them. This is still true today, but there has also been massive international migration in the intervening years, much of it economic, some of it political. We are seeing not only the previously mentioned large-scale migrations from high fertility, low-income countries to low fertility, high-income countries, but also large-scale migrations within the developing world. National boundaries no longer have the significance they once did, as modern transportation systems and mass communications break down the barriers to travel and knowledge about other places that made movement a much less common social phenomenon before World War II. There is no industrialized country that is not grappling with the economic, social, and political dilemmas posed by large-scale migration pressures. And there are very few developing countries that are not struggling with the negative consequences of out-migration, particularly the loss of the most talented, skilled, and entrepreneurial of its younger people (the famous "brain drain"). The international movement of people has become one of the great economic issues of our time and has the potential to become one of the most political as well.

An end to mortality decline?

The perceived population explosion of the 1960s was driven by the extraordinary declines in mortality that followed the end of World War II. In 1969, nearly every country in the developing world was experiencing declining mortality, some with exceptional rapidity, as public health systems were expanded and living standards rose. Widespread famine ended in the early 1970s; smallpox was eradicated during the same period; vaccines for other infectious diseases and major killers were developed; and water supplies were dramatically improved. Public health education massively informed people throughout the globe of good hygiene and the simple benefits of washing hands, cleaning food, and so on. It was inevitable that the rapid decline in mortality would eventually level off. By the 1980s many countries in the developing world had reached mortality levels that were actually lower than those in the industrialized world because of their very young populations and their very low incidence of endemic diseases. Life expectancy, of course, grew rapidly as mortality declined, while areas of high mortality remained (and indeed remain today). The 1980s probably represented the historical low point of global mortality.

The reason for this is that populations are ageing as a result of the end of the fertility transition. Because of the very large numbers of people now entering the over-65 age category, mortality levels will slowly rise, even though life expectancy will continue to increase. In most of the developing world, the plateau in mortality and the subsequent very gradual rise is a natural phenomenon and a measure of their success in completing the demographic transition. However, in some regions mortality is rising for other, more sobering reasons. In Africa in particular, the AIDS pandemic is resulting in very significant increases in the mortality of relatively young adults and children, the latter because of so-called vertical transmission from mother to baby. The significant mortality effect of AIDS is only being felt in a relatively small number of countries today, but there is concern that this may become a more generalized problem, at least in Africa, with the passage of time. In the absence of known cures, only behavioural changes can be expected in the near term to arrest the progression of the pandemic.

In other words, rapidly declining mortality has probably run its course in most of the developing world. It is to be hoped, however, that a reversal of the economic downturn, accelerating fertility decline, and effective AIDS control strategies will enable Africa to complete the demographic transition. At century's end, we see a global regime of stable mortality but with ominous signs of an increase. The significant ageing of the populations of most industrialized countries only contributes further to the general likelihood of very slow increase in mortality rates in the years ahead.

The communications revolution and attitudinal change

When UNFPA was created, there was enormous ignorance about family planning and modern contraception in the developing world. Not only were services not available, as we mentioned earlier, but information and knowledge about the opportunity and means to control one's own reproduction was largely unknown, particularly in Africa and South Asia. Furthermore, only a few modern methods of contraception existed.

Thanks to concerted efforts to spread the word about contraception and family planning, as well as an explosion of mass media that spread throughout the world, a new, largely Western-influenced idea of the small family has emerged practically everywhere. Knowledge about family planning and attitudes about family size have undergone a revolution since UNFPA was born. These changes occurred far more rapidly than the overall pace of social change and development, suggesting that the notion that family-size preferences change only in response to structural changes in family economics and the economic value of children was an oversimplification. It turns out that knowledge of the opportunity and means to control one's own fertility exerted an independent effect on reproductive behaviour, above and beyond what "development" itself would have produced. This is one of the reasons that the demographic transition has proceeded so much more rapidly in today's developing countries than it did in the now-industrialized countries a century and more ago.

Furthermore, in addition to the condom, the high-dose oral contraceptive, and the early generation of intrauterine devices (IUDs), we now have available such widely adopted innovations as injectable contraception, low-dose orals that significantly reduce side effects, a modern generation of IUDs that similarly diminish many of the early side effects, and such new-generation contraceptives as long-acting subdermal implants, the female condom, the contraceptive sponge and vaginal spermicidal preparations. The range of choices available to couples in developing countries through both governmental and commercial channels has expanded exponentially, along with awareness about modern methods of contraception and changing attitudes about family size.

A diminishing sense of urgency

A final, very significant change that has altered the landscape since the formation of UNFPA is a shift in public perceptions about the "population crisis" that has accompanied changes in demographic behaviour. In 1969, as was mentioned earlier, there was virtual unanimity among intellectuals and many persons influential in policymaking that rapid population growth represented one of the most important global issues of our time. Indeed, it was in the late 1960s that

Robert McNamara, then president of the World Bank, issued his famous dictum that after thermonuclear war, population growth represented the greatest threat to mankind.

Such a sense of urgency is largely gone today. In part, this is the consequence of the very success of the programmes that the early crisis mentality generated. But it is also the consequence of a shift in opinion among scholars and intellectuals about how significant a problem population growth is, at least in terms of economic development. A generation of economists in the 1970s and 1980s grew highly sceptical in the face of data that appeared unable to confirm a linear relationship between rapid population growth and economic stagnation. Their findings, most widely heralded by Julian Simon[4] and his followers, called into question the priority that should be given to efforts to reduce population growth around the world. Ironically, just as fertility was entering the period of its most rapid decline, questions were being raised about how compelling a problem high fertility really was. At century's end, the population crisis mentality that existed at the time of UNFPA's formation has given way to a more sanguine view. However, economists have once again begun to reverse field and now generally argue that slower population growth is in most countries highly beneficial to economic growth. But the very success of population policies and fertility control efforts over the last thirty years has significantly diminished the sense of urgency with which the world confronts population growth in the twenty-first century.

One significant exception

There is one area in which, sadly, not much has changed at all. This is in the rate of maternal mortality, almost all of it preventable. While most maternal mortality is the result of complications arising from pregnancy, especially obstructed labour, some of it is the result of unsafe and dangerous abortions. Even as contraceptive use has risen dramatically, it has not yet displaced abortion as a very widespread means of fertility control. Without taking a moral position on the question of abortion *per se*, we do regret that so many women still need to resort to abortion to avert unwanted births. Unsafe abortion has contributed to the fact that there has been little if any improvement in the number of maternal mortalities that occur each year. Notwithstanding the Safe Motherhood Initiative, which was launched in 1987, the number of maternal deaths each year has remained constant, at around half a million. In this area, the situation looks today much as it did for millions of women in 1969, a sobering reminder of failure in the midst of so much positive change.

New Challenges: Implications of the Changing Global Situation for UNFPA Activities

The challenges facing UNFPA over the next thirty years stem from the major paradox now facing the world — dramatic convergence among regions in many areas as a result of advances in information technologies and transportation, heightened environmental concerns, and economic globalization; coinciding with increased divergence between the "haves" in the industrialized countries and the "have nots" in the rest of the world. This paradox has implications for what UNFPA should focus on over the next thirty years, how it should work, and the ways it will need to gather support.

2000-2030 — Priorities for UNFPA

UNFPA is going to need to target its resources (human, financial and policy) even more than at present on regions with the greatest need, particularly sub-Saharan Africa and the poorest countries of South Asia and Indochina. It is in these areas that poverty is greatest, fertility is highest, the least amount of progress has been made in reducing infant and maternal mortality, and where HIV/AIDS mortality threatens years of progress in increasing life expectancy.

Just as the virtuous cycle discussed earlier in this chapter illustrates how positive change becomes mutually reinforcing, the reverse is also unfortunately true. The reinforcing links among poverty, large family size, and infant, child and maternal morbidity and death are well documented. In our view, UNFPA should focus on what it knows and does best — reproductive health, including family planning — while finding new ways to support the efforts of those involved in addressing the other major needs.

Over the next thirty years, UNFPA will need to pursue new partnerships, including cooperation with individuals and groups that the Fund may not have worked with before. Case studies presented at the 1999 forum in The Hague, as part of a five-year review of the International Conference on Population and Development (ICPD) Programme of Action, document that progress since Cairo has been significant, but uneven. Policy changes at the national level consistent with the ICPD Programme of Action have occurred in many countries. However, at the grass-roots level more needs to be done to provide women, particularly those in rural areas and urban slums, with a full range of good-quality family planning services and an essential minimum of reproductive health care. Much less progress has been made in the other elements of the Cairo Programme of Action, such as combating domestic violence, reducing unsafe abortion, enhancing the legal status of women, involving men and boys in sexual and reproductive health in meaningful ways, and providing a full range of information and services to sexually active, unmarried adolescents.

Although at both Cairo and The Hague these priorities were acknowledged, progress at the country level, with some significant exceptions, remains elusive. UNFPA is limited in its ability to become too directly involved in the politics of the individual countries where these problems reside. However, there may be ways in which the Fund can empower local groups, perhaps more activist than traditional partners, whereby these "controversial" issues can be addressed head on.

It is also important that UNFPA expand the mechanisms by which it receives information concerning progress and problems at the country level. While it is clear that UNFPA country representatives are the key contacts for the Fund, their data sources may not be broad or deep enough to gather the richness of data and the nuances that are so necessary, given the daunting needs of the next thirty years. It is often the grass-roots organizations, think tanks, research communities (national and international) that possess the data and insights to complement those of the UNFPA local office.

Over the next thirty years, the problems facing UNFPA's work in the poorest countries will be compounded by the HIV/AIDS epidemic. Since the epidemic began, 34 million Africans have been infected, and almost 12 million of them have already died from the disease. Four countries in sub-Saharan Africa now estimate that 20 per cent to 26 per cent of their adult populations are living with HIV, and South Africa alone accounts for one out of every seven new infections on the continent. In the city of Mutare, Zimbabwe, surveillance data indicate that close to 40 per cent of pregnant women are HIV-infected and that probably 30,000 adults are living with HIV. Even as new drug regimens are being developed, all the major international agencies (the Joint United Nations

145

Programme on HIV/AIDS (UNAIDS) and the World Health Organization (WHO), as well as UNFPA) will have to devise cost-effective delivery systems to prevent sexually transmitted infections, particularly among the young, which are implicated in HIV and exacerbate the transmission of HIV from mothers to newborns. With its extensive field staff, including Country Support Teams (CSTs), UNFPA can play a vital role in coordination, in policy dialogue about potentially promising results of research efforts, and in fundraising for policy, research and service agencies.

The energies of both UNFPA and UNAIDS will be increasingly directed toward sub-Saharan Africa. UNFPA also will have to play a major role in creating support for services aimed at the diagnosis and treatment of other sexually transmitted diseases (STDs) and in encouraging and assisting the growing use of condoms; so far the only known and available defence against HIV transmission.

Epidemiologists the world over recognize the role played by STDs in reducing immunity levels and in increasing the likelihood of HIV infection among sexually active young people and adults — particularly girls and women. Studies from countries like Thailand and Uganda show that increased condom use is associated with quite rapid declines in primary HIV infection rates among members of the military and prostitutes. A major responsibility for making both STD services and condom supplies widely available in Africa (particularly in rural areas) will often rest with reproductive health and family planning clinics. What is more, in some of the hardest-hit African countries, the existing network of family planning/reproductive health facilities has been in place long enough to have gained the confidence of the population, which is especially important in an area of human behaviour in which people are often likely to react with embarrassment, shame, and denial.

The example of HIV/AIDS illustrates the importance of national political leadership and commitment. It is largely because of the understanding and political commitment of the leaders of Thailand, Uganda, and Senegal that such progress has been made in these countries. UNFPA must, over the next thirty years, promote positive policy change more aggressively.

Another profound change facing the developing world over the next thirty years is growing urbanization. As discussed earlier in this chapter, the world looks quite different today than it did thirty years ago, when only one in four people in all developing regions were city dwellers (see Table 3). Now, almost four in ten Asians and Africans and almost seven in ten people in Latin America live in urban areas. But despite this process of rapid urbanization, one-half of the developing world's population today still live in rural areas. For example, over two billion Asians (mostly in China and India) and half a billion Africans still live in rural areas of the world. UNFPA, therefore, will not be able to abandon its policy and programme emphasis on strategies to take reproductive health services to these rural populations even though it shifts some emphasis to serving urban needs. Indeed, it is going to have to strengthen and diversify these services.

Urban life exerts profound influences on the family, on family-size aspirations, on the roles of women. It also introduces the young to more secular and more consumerist values, which in turn are likelier to encourage the desire for and recognition of the need for better education, better-paying jobs, delayed marriage and fewer children. UNFPA therefore no longer needs to give as high priority as in the past to urban campaigns to foster contraceptive use and smaller families. Life in big cities provides this education compellingly and effectively in its own right. However, UNFPA should increasingly experiment with programmes to reduce levels of ignorance about reproduction and sexuality (especially the risks) often prevalent among young people in cities. Collaboration with a much wider group of representatives from civil society (churches, professional groups, unions, employers, schools, youth clubs, micro-credit organizations, private-sector health professionals) is probably the best way to achieve this end.

2000-2030 — UNFPA and the "D" in ICPD

Two major factors will make it necessary for UNFPA to broaden its scope of interests into the non-core areas of the ICPD Programme of Action, while improving its focus on its major mandate of reproductive health. The more important factor, as demonstrated by evidence from both the virtuous and vicious cycles discussed above, is the inextricable interdependence that exists among all areas of human development; the second factor is the reality of health sector reform, which is dramatically changing the landscape in which the ICPD must be implemented.

To promote the virtuous cycle, UNFPA should join with other groups that support the "20/20 Initiative." It is only through the achievement of 20/20 goals (20 per cent of aid and 20 per cent of developing country budgets earmarked for the social sectors) that poverty can be truly alleviated.

Foremost among the disparities between rich and poor is the quality or even the existence of sanitation and disposal systems, indoor plumbing and toilets, clean water — indeed, the basic living conditions required for the maintenance of good health. Probably next in importance is universal education, at least through primary school and ideally through several years of secondary schooling. Next is the ability to get people and goods moved from one part of the country to another — roads and transportation, and communications networks of all kinds.

It perhaps bears repeating that the beneficial impact of fulfilling the 20/20 Initiative would be felt on many fronts. Improved health systems and services would, among other desirable outcomes, bring down infant and maternal mortality levels — two important goals highlighted in the ICPD Programme of Action. And improved educational levels, especially for girls, are strongly associated with the desire for and achievement of smaller families. Both improved health in general and increased schooling for girls are prerequisites for women to achieve the equality with men that is also a key element of the Programme of Action.

Health sector reform incorporates four major initiatives:

1. New modes of payment for health services (e.g., private insurance; cost-recovery mechanisms such as fee-for-service; and cross-subsidization);
2. The decentralization of authority (including the organization and management of health services) from the national to the district levels, and devolution — government turning over hospitals and other health sites to the private sector;
3. Strengthening accountability to ensure that health resources are spent properly; i.e., where they will do the most good; and
4. Clarifying the role of the public sector, with emphasis on its role in establishing and regulating health-care norms and standards, rather than government's being the universal direct provider of services.

The rationale for health sector reform is clear. Governments cannot afford to, and are often unable to, meet the health needs of the people; populations have shown that they are willing to pay

147

for better health care; and decision-makers who live locally are likely to know more about local conditions and be better able to match resources and needs more precisely. Local decision-makers, at least in theory, should be more accountable to the people they live among, and there will be more opportunities for communities to participate in planning the health services they need and want. The jury is still out on whether health sector reform will succeed, but for now it is an all-encompassing reality for the implementation of the ICPD.

A key component of health sector reform is to replace vertical programmes with more integrated services offering comprehensive care. To many of the economists involved in planning the reforms, reproductive health is yet another vertical programme. Several case studies of health sector reform in sub-Saharan Africa have shown that to the district health establishment, many of whose officials have little international training or exposure, the ICPD is not well known, and its importance *vis à vis* other priorities is often not clear.

UNFPA staff at headquarters and in the field need to become familiar with health sector reform and become involved in health reform policy dialogues. This will require providing special training to programme staff and the recruitment of economists sympathetic to ICPD goals and able to explain these to their peers at the World Bank and in ministries of finance. The virtuous cycle and poverty alleviation arguments are critical here and should become a standard part of UNFPA's policy dialogue armamentarium.

UNFPA should also pay increasing attention to the training and information needs of district-level health personnel. This might mean moving some of its offices outside of the centre, encouraging officers to travel more widely in the hinterlands, and encouraging them to learn to deal with stakeholders who may not operate from the same set of class or caste assumptions or share the same level of knowledge or policy awareness as high-level Ministry of Health or Ministry of Planning officials in the capital.

2000-2030 — The Changing Environment for Advocacy

UNFPA will need to nurture new stakeholders. Within the developing world, these will include the district-level health personnel and decision-makers within ministries of finance discussed above. Within the industrialized world, UNFPA will have to mobilize financial support from countries facing problems of their own: rapidly ageing populations increasingly worried about their own old-age social security system and confusion about whether high and unwanted fertility still exists anywhere in the world. Major questions arise as a result: Will an increasingly elderly population be less inclined to provide funding for international development cooperation? Will people see spending for development as threatening to their own social security benefits? Will the very-low-fertility countries in Europe and East Asia develop internal pro-natalist policies and then worry that promoting births at home and birth control abroad would seem hypocritical?

Over the next thirty years, UNFPA should pay more attention to the industrialized world and should support activities that keep the principles and strategies of the ICPD foremost in policymakers' minds. Surveys and focus group interviews from many developed countries indicate that citizens strongly support voluntary, culturally sensitive population and reproductive health funding. The reasons for this support are several — altruism, environmental concerns, and self-interest (including fear of migration and the potential valuable markets for goods produced in the

North). UNFPA should capitalize on the strong reservoir of support within the industrialized world but should not become complacent about it. The Fund should expand its support to donor-country groups dedicated to implementation of the ICPD in order to keep that commitment alive and fresh.

Conclusion

While many take great satisfaction from the fact that fertility rates are declining nearly everywhere — and in some places very rapidly — the fact remains that unless the reproductive health needs of this largest-ever cohort are effectively met, there is a potential for enormous population growth still ahead. Indeed, depending on the reproductive choices of people entering the reproductive age groups in the next decade, there could be as many as 15 billion or as few as 9 billion people in the world by the end of the next century. Future population size is enormously sensitive to very small changes in fertility rates over the next few years. Thus, the most compelling challenge of the immediate future is to effectively implement the remarkable consensus that emerged from the ICPD in Cairo in 1994, a consensus that called for high-quality reproductive health services, including family planning, to be made available to every woman and man of reproductive age in the world by the year 2000 and continuing through 2015 — and particularly those just entering their childbearing years in that period.

The ICPD Programme of Action was a comprehensive, farsighted and eminently achievable plan, whose effective implementation will largely determine whether the global population stabilizes at the lower or the higher end of the aforementioned range. At Cairo, the community of nations agreed that by 2000 some $17 billion would need to be spent annually by individuals, non-governmental organizations (NGOs), developing country governments, and donors to achieve the objectives outlined in the plan. Unfortunately, by 1999, we were less than halfway toward the realization of that spending level. Of course, many countries experienced especially severe economic hardships in the 1990s, especially those hit by the economic crisis in Asia. We can certainly hope that economic recovery will occur and that spending levels will consequently increase over the next decade. While spending does not automatically translate into accomplishments, a 50 per cent shortfall clearly represents insufficient commitment to the goal of meeting the reproductive health needs of this largest generation.

The impressive work that began with the formation of UNFPA in 1969 and that has characterized so much of the past thirty years stands in jeopardy of not being completed because the resources that are required for its completion may not be forthcoming. The greatest immediate challenge, therefore, is to mobilize the resources and to deploy them in the most efficient possible ways to ensure that all children who are wanted are born, that all children who are born survive and are healthy, to ensure that their mothers enjoy good health, and to ensure that all parents are able to have only the number of children they want when they want them.

References

[1] United Nations, Department for Economic and Social Information and Policy Analysis, Population Division, *World Population Prospects: The 1996 Revisions, Annex I* (1996): Tables A18, A19, pp. 120-129.

[2] Ibid.: Tables A30, A31, pp. 214-253.

[3] United Nations, *World Urbanization Prospects: The 1994 Revisions* (New York: United Nations, 1995): Table A2, pp. 78-85.

[4] Julian L. Simon, *The Ultimate Resource* (Princeton: Princeton University Press, 1981).

PART II

UNFPA and the Global Conferences

Jyoti Shankar Singh

The United Nations Fund for Population Activities (UNFPA), later to be known as the United Nations Populations Fund, was established in July 1967 as a trust fund of the United Nations by an administrative decision of Secretary-General U Thant. In many ways, his decision was inspired by a General Assembly resolution titled "Population Growth and Economic Development" that called upon the United Nations system "to assist, when requested, in further developing and strengthening national and regional facilities for training, research, information and advisory services in the field of population, bearing in mind the different character of the population problem in each country and region and the needs arising therefrom."[1]

The resolution did not propose any specific mechanism for this purpose, however, and at that time many people still considered population to be a rather controversial topic. It was left to the Secretary-General to determine how the United Nations could provide assistance in the field of population. Mr. U Thant decided that a trust fund would be the most practical channel for obtaining and disbursing funds for this purpose. No fanfare attended his decision. As Stanley Johnson, who has chronicled the history of United Nations involvement in population in several books, put it, "[w]hen UNFPA was born, no trumpets had sounded from the steep."[2] In May 1969, the trust fund was transferred to the United Nations Development Programme (UNDP), and its first director, Rafael M. Salas, who had been selected by UNDP Administrator Paul Hoffman, came on board in late 1969.

UNFPA's origins are thus different from those of the United Nations Children's Fund (UNICEF) and UNDP. Both of these organizations were created by the General Assembly, and they started with fairly well-defined structures and functions. On the other hand, UNFPA's policies and programmes were shaped in its early years almost entirely by Mr. Salas, the Executive Director, with some help from an Advisory Board made up of eminent individuals. UNFPA was brought to the attention of the General Assembly for the first time in 1971 when its resolution 2815 (XXVI) of 14 December 1971 recognized that the Fund had "become a viable entity in the United Nations system." The following year, the General Assembly placed UNFPA under its direct authority, thus ending its status as a trust fund and giving it recognition as a subsidiary organ of the General Assembly.[3] The same resolution made the Governing Council of UNDP the governing body of UNFPA as well.

In the years that followed, UNFPA's structure, functions and operations have been shaped in stages by the General Assembly, which considers UNFPA, as well as UNICEF, UNDP and several other funds and programmes its subsidiary organs; by the Economic and Social Council of the United

Nations (ECOSOC), which defined the aims and objectives of UNFPA in 1973[4] and continues to provide general policy guidance to UNFPA; and, most of all, by the Governing Council of UNDP (now the Executive Board of UNDP and UNFPA), which oversees its administration, finances and programmes. Concurrently, the work of UNFPA has also been influenced by the global population conferences that took place in Bucharest in 1974, Mexico City in 1984, and Cairo in 1994, and UNFPA has in turn influenced them. Indeed, this interaction became stronger with each succeeding conference. It is clear that the conclusions of the most recent conference, the International Conference on Population and Development (ICPD), held in Cairo in 1994, have had and will continue to have a profound and lasting influence on UNFPA.

UNFPA's interaction with global conferences organized by the United Nations outside of the population field has been more limited. Among these conferences, UNFPA has given the greatest technical and financial support to the conferences on women (Mexico City, 1975; Copenhagen, 1980; Nairobi, 1985; and Beijing, 1995). The evolution of the position of the international community on issues relating to family planning (FP), reproductive health and reproductive rights first reflected in the recommendations of the global population conferences has regularly found an echo in the conferences on women that followed them. In that regard, the Beijing Conference in 1995 is seen by most observers as being part of a continuum that began in Cairo the previous year.

The World Population Conference, 1974

When I came to UNFPA towards the end of 1972, the major decisions regarding the organization of the 1974 World Population Conference (WPC) were taken by the General Assembly and by ECOSOC. The World Population Conference secretariat, headed by Antonio Carrillo Flores, former Minister of Foreign Affairs of Mexico, who served as the Secretary-General of the conference, was located at United Nations Headquarters and was expected to work through the Population Division on the substantive aspects of the preparations. He was assisted by Ralph Townley and Leon Tabah of the United Nations. Parallel to this, the secretariat of the World Population Year (WPY) was established at UNFPA by Mr. Salas in his capacity as the overall WPY Coordinator. The ECOSOC resolution that gave Mr. Salas the responsibility for WPY urged the Secretary-General of the conference and the Executive Director of UNFPA "to cooperate to the extent necessary to ensure that preparations for the World Population Conference and World Population Year proceed smoothly, bearing in mind the complementary nature of the activities of the Year and the Conference."[5]

Mr. Salas saw the World Population Year as a wonderful opportunity to focus global attention on population issues and, simultaneously, to raise UNFPA's profile. He therefore decided to find an experienced and well-known writer and media personality to head the WPY secretariat. Tarzie Vittachi, a noted Asian journalist who was then the editor of a tabloid named *The Asian*, was approached and agreed to head the secretariat. I joined the secretariat towards the end of 1972, and became Mr. Vittachi's deputy in 1973. Several other journalists and writers were appointed to the WPY secretariat in 1973, and it soon had a complement of twelve to fourteen professionals.

In the context of the WPY, UNFPA supported numerous activities by non-governmental organizations (NGOs), academic institutions, and media groups around the world that were aimed at promoting and building up awareness of population and related development issues. Though most of these activities ended with the conclusion of the WPY, the invaluable experience acquired by

UNFPA during 1972-1974 helped it later in building up strong alliances and partnerships with individuals and institutions throughout the world in pursuit of common programme objectives. As Stanley Johnson points out, "[t]he knowledge and experience gained by UNFPA during World Population Year was to stand it in good stead. More than many other United Nations agencies, the Fund has realized that 'outreach' is all-important. Preaching to the converted is easy and always has been. What the Fund recognized in the build-up to 1974 was that the *non-committed* were the primary targets and that both sides of the fence — developed and developing, donors and recipients, rich and poor — had to be worked with equal energy."[6]

The WPY also encouraged and promoted the formation or designation of national WPY committees charged with organizing national conferences and carrying out media and information activities. By the time of the Bucharest Conference in 1974, such committees were functioning in 64 countries. Some of these committees were specially set up for the WPY; in other cases, existing institutions were given the responsibility of organizing and coordinating WPY-World Population Conference-related activities. The WPY secretariat organized a meeting attended by forty of these committees in Brussels from 10-12 July 1974, prior to the World Population Conference. The meeting recommended that these national population commissions or similar bodies be continued after the conclusion of the WPY.[7] In an increasing number of developing countries, national population committees of one kind or the other have indeed taken on the responsibility of promoting and coordinating population inputs into development plans and programmes. This has been one lasting result of the World Population Conference.

UNFPA gave a major grant to the United Nations to cover approximately half the costs of the World Population Conference. It also supported the organization of an NGO Tribune and a Youth Forum as parallel activities at the conference. UNFPA was represented at the conference by its senior and middle-level management as well by its field representatives (who were called "coordinators" in those days). But overall it would be true to say that UNFPA was not greatly involved in the running of the conference.

As it turned out, the World Population Plan of Action (WPPA) that emerged from the conference gave only cursory attention to operational activities, and UNFPA itself did not figure much in the Plan of Action, though the Fund was mentioned by many of the country delegations in their plenary statements who expressed appreciation for the Fund's support to country programmes. The WPPA mentions UNFPA only once, in paragraph 105, where UNFPA was asked to produce a periodical guide for international assistance in population matters. UNFPA produced the first *Guide to Sources of International Population Assistance* in 1976 and has issued it every three years since.

The WPPA was essentially a political document and, as such, was criticized for accommodating many inconsistencies and compromises. It is, however, undeniable that the plan as adopted helped lessen the abrasiveness of public discussion of population issues. It established a clear link between population factors and development planning, encouraging even the governments that had been exclusively preoccupied with economic development to take action on population questions.[8]

What did the WPPA mean for UNFPA at the operational level? The principles and objectives of the plan include the recognition of an integral relationship between population and development[9] and the sovereign right of each country to formulate and implement population policies,[10] with the understanding that these should be consistent with "basic human rights and national goals and values."[11] These were the cornerstones of UNFPA's programming process even before 1974. The results of the conference thus vindicated UNFPA's basic approach to the implementation of its programmes.

But perhaps the most important contribution of the conference was an elaboration of certain rights of couples and individuals that provided UNFPA with a solid rationale and justification for its support for voluntary family planning programmes:

> [A]ll couples and individuals have the basic right to decide freely and responsibly the number and spacing of their children and to have the information, education and means to do so; the responsibility of couples and individuals in the exercise of this right takes into account the needs of their living and future children, and their responsibilities towards the community.[12]

Most of this language came from the International Conference on Human Rights (Tehran, 1968), which had declared that "parents have a basic human right to determine freely and responsibly the number and spacing of their children."[13] But the Bucharest Conference made a highly significant change, substituting "parents" with "couples and individuals."

The language on the rights of "couples and individuals" was not in the original draft that had been prepared by the Population Division with the help of a group of experts. It was first introduced as an additional, new principle in the working group of the conference that was discussing the draft WPPA. Many delegations spoke in favour of the proposal; but there were others who indicated that they were against including the reference to "individuals," as this might imply endorsement of the availability and provision of contraceptives to the unmarried. The chairman of the working group decided to hold a straw vote on whether to include the term "couples and individuals" in the text: there were 48 votes in favour, compared with 41 that favoured only "couples," and 6 abstentions. Although the term "couples and individuals" had been adopted in the working group with a rather narrow majority; it was subsequently adopted in the plenary without further discussion and thus became part of the WPPA. Though attempts were later made at both the Mexico City and Cairo Conferences to delete "individuals," they did not succeed; similar attempts at other United Nations conferences have also failed. As a matter of fact, the Bucharest language provided the foundation for the definition of reproductive rights that was extensively discussed during the ICPD process and that was finally included in the ICPD Programme of Action.

UNFPA in the Post-Bucharest Era

In the period following the 1974 Bucharest Conference, UNFPA promoted family planning as a basic human right as well as a health measure. Many of the statements made by the Executive Director and other senior officials and the documents submitted to its governing bodies referred to these dual concepts. At the same time, in the programming exercises known as the "needs assessments," UNFPA sought to highlight the specific needs and requirements of each country. In many countries, UNFPA supported "vertical" family planning programmes outside of regular primary health-care services, largely because the health infrastructures were not strong enough to sustain the inclusion of any additional service. "Also, it was felt that the creation of a family planning programme as a distinct entity called attention to the importance of the endeavor. Gradually, however, increased emphasis has been put on establishing community-oriented family planning delivery systems within the context of primary health care and ongoing local development efforts. Most of the action programmes UNFPA supports are of such an integrated nature. The integrated approach not only facilitates the provision of closely related services — for example, pre- and post-natal care, nutrition and immunizations — but also helps to blunt some of the sensitivity still attached to family planning."[14]

That the Executive Director's statement quoted above was made in a UNFPA publication issued prior to the 1984 International Conference on Population (ICP) is significant because it underlined UNFPA's increasing support over the years for an integrated approach to family planning and to related maternal and child health (MCH) services. UNFPA's guidelines, while emphasizing family planning as a priority also underscored the relationship between family planning programmes and those designed to promote MCH

In 1975, the year following the World Population Conference, the United Nations organized the first World Conference on Women in Mexico City. The Plan of Action adopted at the Mexico City Conference on Women reiterated the right of "couples and individuals" as outlined in the WPPA but went beyond the WPPA by stating that "the exercise of this right is basic to the attainment of any real equality between the sexes and without its achievement, women are disadvantaged in their attempt to benefit from other reforms."[15] In a separate resolution, "Family Planning and the Full Integration of Women in Development," the Mexico City Conference on Women proposed a range of actions that would need to be taken by national governments to fulfil family planning needs.[16]

UNFPA formulated its first guidelines on "Women, Population and Development," immediately following the Mexico City Conference on Women. Issued in 1976, these guidelines (subsequently updated in 1980) recommended UNFPA support for the following types of activities:

(a)   Formal as well as informal education programmes for women, including functional literacy, family life education, and programmes to promote the educational and vocational aspirations of women;

(b)   Employment programmes, including pilot projects aimed at increasing the access of women to employment, career guidance and training;

(c)   Programmes aimed at promoting the participation of women in decision-making in family and public life;

(d)   Support of institutional development at the grassroots as well as at government levels to ensure attention to the status and role of women in population and development activities; and

(e)   Efforts to improve the health of women and children as part of an integrated approach to MCH/FP in health, with special attention to the employment of women as providers of health care.

To institutionalize these guidelines, a chapter on women, population, and development was included in the *UNFPA Manual for Needs Assessment and Programme Development*, and a UNFPA unit on women and youth was established in 1978.[17] The unit later became a unit on women, population and development within the Office of the Executive Director and was later transferred to the Technical and Evaluation Division (TED). It has been replaced now by a theme group on gender issues.

UNFPA has also worked closely with other like-minded United Nations agencies and organizations in this area. In particular, it has provided substantial institutional and financial support to all the World Conferences on Women — 1975 (Mexico City), 1980 (Copenhagen), 1985 (Nairobi) and 1995 (Beijing) and to their preparatory and follow-up activities. The evolution of UNFPA policies on gender issues has also been influenced by the outcomes of these conferences.

It is interesting to note that over the last two decades there has been a continuous debate within UNFPA on two questions: (a) how much emphasis should be placed on efforts and activities aimed especially at women; and (b) how far should UNFPA go in supporting projects that go beyond MCH/FP, and related population activities. On the first question, those who support "mainstreaming" gender concerns have taken issue with those who believe that special attention must be given to specific activities aimed at improving the role and status of women. The debate on the second question has focused on such issues as the nature and extent of UNFPA support for general literacy and education programmes and for income-generating activities. My own assessment is that in the end, UNFPA has leaned towards a broader and more flexible interpretation of its mandate in response to both of these questions. UNFPA's review of two decades of experience (1969-1989) stated in unequivocal terms that "[i]mproving the role and status of women is, by itself, an important goal of population policies and programmes."[18] This view was reaffirmed by the ICPD in 1994.

Another set of guidelines was formulated by UNFPA to delineate its relationship with NGOs and support for projects carried out by such organizations. During the World Population Year process, UNFPA had given a series of grants to international and regional NGOs, and the idea behind formulating NGO guidelines was to institutionalize this process and to encourage the increasing involvement of NGOs at the national level in population policy and programming processes. These guidelines have been updated and revised every few years, most recently after the ICPD. UNFPA established a regular process of consultation with NGOs starting in 1975, and in recent years it has received advice on UNFPA/NGO collaboration through annual meetings of an advisory committee of NGOs constituted by the Executive Director.

The International Conference on Population, 1984

The proposal to organize another world conference on population ten years after Bucharest came from the Population Commission, which had also been the originator of the idea for the Bucharest Conference. In 1979, ECOSOC requested that the Population Commission, in consultation with appropriate United Nations bodies, consider the possibility of holding an international conference to review developments in the first decade following the World Population Conference.

In November 1981, ECOSOC decided to "convene in 1984, under the auspices of the United Nations, an International Conference on Population open to all States as full members and to the specialized agencies."[19] It designated the Population Commission, meeting in an open-ended session open to participation by all countries, to serve as the Preparatory Committee (PrepCom) for the conference. At the same time, it asked the United Nations Secretary-General to name the Executive Director of UNFPA as the Secretary-General of the conference and the Director of the United Nations Population Division as the Deputy Secretary-General. The appointment of Mr. Salas as Secretary-General of the conference was announced by Javier Perez de Cuellar, the United Nations Secretary-General, in January 1982.

157

This appointment recognized the emergence of UNFPA as the major actor in the area of population within the United Nations system. There was also the hope that the Executive Director of UNFPA would be in a position to raise most of the money needed for the conference. The substantive responsibility for the preparation of the conference was left, as in the case of Bucharest, with the Population Division of the Department of International Economic and Social Affairs (DIESA). Leon Tabah, Director of the Population Division, concurrently served as Deputy Secretary-General until his retirement in February 1984. In March 1984, P. Shankar Menon replaced him as Acting Director of the Division and as Deputy Secretary-General of the conference. I was appointed as the Executive Coordinator of the conference in 1981, while I also continued to serve as Director of the UNFPA Information and External Relations Division (IERD). My assignment was to coordinate the conference arrangements, including those in the preparatory phase.

The substantive preparations, entrusted to the Population Division, included the holding of four expert group meetings in the first half of 1983. These meetings were convened to review the major developments in each of the four thematic areas identified by the Population Commission as being of the highest priority: fertility and family (New Delhi, 5-11 January 1983); population distribution, migration and development (Hammamet, Tunisia, 21-25 March 1983); population, resources, environment and development (Geneva, 25-29 April 1983); and mortality and health policy (Rome, 30 May-3 June 1983). Although the expert group meetings were substantively prepared by the Population Division, UNFPA contributed a paper on operational perspectives to each of the meetings.

Preparatory activities at the regional levels included meetings in Asia, Europe, Latin America, Africa and the Arab States region. For each of these meetings, UNFPA provided financial support as well as support by its field offices to ensure adequate country representation. UNFPA was represented at the conferences both by headquarters and field staff, and in most cases they collaborated with the staff of the United Nations regional commissions in preparing the drafts of the final outcomes.

UNFPA also supported the organization of a major consultation among NGOs in Geneva from 13 to 15 September 1983. Almost 200 participants from 62 international and 30 national NGOs took part in the meeting. Although the consultation itself did not issue recommendations, a document containing a series of specific recommendations was prepared at this meeting and signed individually by most of the participants.

The reports and recommendations of the expert group meetings, the regional conferences, and the NGO consultation served as inputs for the preparation of the review and appraisal of the implementation of the WPPA and the draft recommendations for further implementation of the Plan of Action that were prepared for the consideration of the PrepCom.

Mexico City Recommendations and UNFPA

The Mexico City Conference reaffirmed the three main principles adopted at Bucharest.[20] Beyond that, however, it was much more forthcoming than the Bucharest Conference had been on ways that the provision of family planning would, in practice, ensure "the right of couples and individuals" to information and services. Reflecting the increasing experience gained by governments and NGOs in the 1970s and early 1980s in providing family planning services, it suggested that

. . . family planning services should be made available through appropriate and practicable channels, including . . . community-based distribution. . . . Governments should bear in mind the innovative role which non-governmental organizations, in particular women's organizations, can play in improving the availability and effectiveness of family planning services.[21]

Recommendation 27 stated that

[g]overnments and intergovernmental and non-governmental organizations are urged to allocate, in accordance with national policies and priorities, the necessary resources to family planning services, where these services are inadequate and are not meeting the needs of a rapidly growing population of reproductive age.[22]

Two other recommendations bring up the themes of information and services for adolescents and the role of men in family planning. Recommendation 29 suggests that "suitable family planning information and services should be made available to adolescents within the changing socio-cultural framework of each country." Recommendation 9 says:

[g]overnments should promote and encourage, through information, education and communication, as well as through employment legislation and institutional support, where appropriate, the active involvement of men in all areas of family responsibility, including family planning, child-rearing and housework, so that family responsibilities can be fully shared by both partners.[23]

On the issue of abortion, which was not a topic for discussion at Bucharest, the Mexico City Conference adopted a recommendation urging governments "to take appropriate steps to help women avoid abortion, which in no case should be promoted as a method of family planning, and whenever possible, provide for the humane treatment and counselling of women who have had recourse to abortion."[24] The draft proposed by the PrepCom had the word "illegal" before abortion, but it was deleted at the conference. Although the final consensus on the abortion issue came close to the position taken by the Holy See, its representative did not join the consensus, on the grounds that the conference had agreed to support family planning services for adolescents and that insufficient attention had been paid to the concept of the family.[25]

In addition to family planning, the role and status of women and the role of NGOs were two other areas where the Mexico City Conference represented major advances over what had been agreed upon at Bucharest. Two world conferences on women had taken place since Bucharest — Mexico City in 1975 and Copenhagen in 1980. The results of these conferences, and the follow-up actions that had taken place at both national and international levels, had made the international community strongly conscious of the need to give increasing attention to women's rights issues. Furthermore, many more women's NGOs had emerged since 1974 to expand public awareness and understanding of a whole range of issues relating to the rights and status of women.

An *ad hoc* caucus of women at Mexico City pushed for and succeeded in adopting a separate chapter devoted to women's rights, covering such diverse issues as legal, economic, and social equality; access to education and family planning; and delay of marriage. The conference recognized that achieving the full integration of women in society on an equal basis with men and removing all forms of discrimination against women were "integral to achieving development goals, including

159

those related to population policy."[26] It also accepted the proposition that "the broadening of the role and the improvement of the status of women remain important goals that should be pursued as ends in themselves."[27]

The Mexico City Conference also recognized the increasingly important role of NGOs in the area of population. Although NGOs did not organize a separate meeting of their own in Mexico City, as they had in Bucharest, they were represented in large numbers at the official conference, and many of them addressed the conference. The Mexico City Conference called on governments to encourage NGO activities and to draw upon NGO expertise, experience and resources in implementing national programmes;[28] supported the full participation of community groups and NGOs, including women's organizations, in all population and development activities;[29] and invited donors to increase their support to NGOs.[30]

The outcome of the Mexico City Conference therefore reaffirmed and strengthened three emerging trends in UNFPA-supported programmes at both country and inter-country levels: the need to increase the outreach and quality of family planning programmes, the need for greater emphasis on gender-equality issues, and a clearer recognition of the role of NGOs in formulating and implementing population policies and programmes. UNFPA policies and guidelines in all three of these areas were revised and updated after the Mexico City Conference. At Mexico City, various governments in Africa demonstrated their growing acceptance of population as an urgent and important issue, and as a result UNFPA clearly saw a need to strengthen its role in Africa by giving greater support to country programmes and by strengthening its field presence in the region. UNFPA was asked by its Governing Council in June 1986 to give increased attention to the countries in the sub-Saharan Africa region.

UNFPA also got an institutional boost from the Mexico City Conference through its Recommendation 83:

> In view of the leading role of the United Nations Fund for Population Activities in population matters, the Conference urges that the Fund should be strengthened further, so as to ensure the more effective delivery of population assistance, taking into account the growing needs in this field. The Secretary-General of the United Nations is invited to examine this recommendation, and submit a report to the General Assembly on its implementation as soon as possible but not later than 1986.[31]

In its resolution dealing with the outcome of the Mexico City Conference, the General Assembly recognized the growing role of UNFPA:

> [The General Assembly] emphasises that international cooperation in the field of population is essential for the implementation of recommendations adopted at the Conference, and, in this context calls upon the international community to provide adequate and substantial international support and assistance for population activities, particularly through the United Nations Fund for Population Activities, in order to ensure more effective delivery of population assistance in the light of growing needs in the field and the increasing efforts being made by developing countries.[32]

The General Assembly resolution further requested the Secretary-General

to take, without delay, appropriate steps regarding the relevant recommendations, in particular recommendation 83, for further implementation of the World Population Plan of Action concerning the role of international cooperation, taking note also of the suggestions offered by various delegations and benefitting in the process, from the deliberations of the Economic and Social Council, and to report to the General Assembly, through the Economic and Social Council, on their implementation as soon as possible but not later than 1986.[33]

In response to these requests, ECOSOC discussed in 1986 how the role of UNFPA could be strengthened further. There was general agreement on its leading role in providing multilateral population assistance, but there were divergent views on how its role could be strengthened within the United Nations itself, and how the United Nations Population Division, which was supervised by the Population Commission, and UNFPA, which was supervised by its Governing Council, could work more closely together. The outcome of the discussion was, not surprisingly, a call for strengthening of the existing institutions within their respective mandates, and a plea for greater exchange of information among them. Through its Resolution 1986/7 of 21 May 1986, ECOSOC agreed that in the future it would consider the report of the Population Commission and the UNFPA portion of the report of the Governing Council under one single agenda item called "Population Questions." At the same time, it invited the Governing Council to "use reports of the Population Commission for greater exchange of information on population questions." The idea was that these measures would promote greater exchange of information between the Population Commission and the Governing Council as well as between the Population Division and UNFPA. In subsequent years, UNFPA was invited to submit a written report for information to the Population Commission, and DIESA was invited to address the Governing Council.

The Amsterdam Forum

Five years after the Mexico City Conference, UNFPA decided to organize an international meeting to coincide with its twentieth anniversary to review the operational experience that had been gained in formulating and implementing population programmes. In February 1989, the Government of the Netherlands offered to host the meeting in Amsterdam. The meeting, called the "International Forum on Population in the Twenty-First Century," took place in Amsterdam from 5 to 9 November 1989, with the participation of senior ministers and government officials from 79 countries, as well as representatives of a large number of United Nations agencies, NGOs, and academic and research institutions.

The main product of the forum was the Amsterdam Declaration, entitled "A Better Life for Future Generations." The declaration was noteworthy for outlining a blueprint for how the world could achieve the medium-variant population projection of the United Nations, and for proposing, in this context, a number of quantitative goals and targets — an increase in contraceptive prevalence in developing countries so as to reach at least 56 per cent of women of reproductive age by the year 2000, a reduction in the average number of children born per woman commensurate with achieving, as a minimum, the medium-variant population projection of the United Nations, and a doubling of investment in population programmes in developing countries from around $4.5 billion to $9 billion by the year 2000.[34]

Even though the forum was not an official United Nations event, its declaration was noted with appreciation by the General Assembly at the urging of the Netherlands and a number of developing countries.[35] The global funding estimate of $9 billion became the benchmark for fundraising efforts in the population field until more comprehensive estimates were developed by the secretariat of the ICPD in 1993.

The International Conference on Population and Development

The process of organizing the ICPD began in 1989, when the Population Commission discussed several options for a follow-up to the Bucharest and Mexico City Conferences and opted for what was then foreseen as a rather modest international meeting on population. The proposal for such a meeting was formally endorsed by ECOSOC through its Resolution 1989/91.

Following the formula adopted for Mexico City, Dr. Nafis Sadik, who had succeeded Mr. Salas as the Executive Director of UNFPA after his untimely death in March 1987, was designated by the Secretary-General Perez de Cuellar as the Secretary-General of the proposed international meeting, with the Director of the Population Division serving as the Deputy Secretary-General. Through a letter dated 29 June 1990 addressed to Member States of the United Nations on the subject of the international meeting on population, the Secretary-General announced these appointments and, at the same time, appealed for extra-budgetary contributions to support the event. At the time of the announcement, Shunichi Inoue was Director of the Population Division and was therefore designated as Deputy Secretary-General of the 1994 event. He was involved in the first session of the PrepCom (1991) and the expert group meetings that took place during 1992 and early 1993. He was succeeded by Joseph Chamie in January 1993.

Soon after her designation as Secretary-General of the 1994 event, Dr. Sadik began discussing with the Department of Economic and Social Information and Policy Analysis (DESIPA, the former DIESA) how the conference secretariat should be organized. These discussions led to the understanding that DESIPA, through its Population Division, and UNFPA would constitute a joint secretariat for the conference. The joint secretariat would be responsible for initiating and coordinating the overall organizational and substantive preparations for the ICPD, including preparation of major conference documents; promotion of international, regional, and national activities; fundraising; and activities designed to raise awareness of ICPD-related issues.

I was named by Dr. Sadik as Executive Coordinator for the conference, while German Bravo-Casas of the Population Division was nominated to serve as Deputy Executive Coordinator. As in the case of Dr. Sadik and Mr. Inoue, our conference assignments were to run concurrently with those relating to our regular posts. As I was then also the Director of the UNFPA Technical and Evaluation Division (TED), we were able to make use of the technical expertise of the TED staff on a continuing basis and to seek the involvement and cooperation of other UNFPA divisions as needed. With extra-budgetary funding and secondments from a number of United Nations organizations, we were also able to obtain additional staff fully dedicated to conference-related tasks.

There was a division of responsibilities between UNFPA and the Population Division, and frequent consultations and meetings, chaired on many occasions by Dr. Sadik herself, enabled the two organizations to work together very closely and harmoniously throughout 1990-1994. Mr. Chamie, who succeeded Mr. Inoue in January 1993, handled, with great distinction, substantive and technical responsibilities at the second and third sessions of the PrepCom, as well as at the Cairo Conference itself. At each of these events, the Population Division and UNFPA staff members were paired for drafting and reporting of each of the proposed chapters in the Programme of Action, and this arrangement worked extremely well.

An interdepartmental steering committee consisting of senior departmental heads and, under its authority, a working group consisting of officials directly involved in day-to-day activities were set up at an early stage to coordinate inputs from various United Nations departments involved in the ICPD process. The steering committee met only a few times, but the working group met regularly to receive progress reports and to chart the future course of action on conference-related matters. Many members of the working group participated in the planning missions sent to Egypt and also played highly significant roles at the conference itself.

An inter-agency task force under the chairmanship of Dr. Sadik sought to actively involve all the United Nations agencies concerned in the conference preparations. This task force met three times between 1992 and 1994. In addition, representatives of specialized agencies such as the World Health Organization (WHO), the International Labour Organization (ILO), the United Nations Educational, Scientific and Cultural Organization (UNESCO), and the Food and Agriculture Organization of the United Nations (FAO) participated actively in all the PrepCom meetings and in a large number of *ad hoc* consultations on thematic issues.

The first session of the PrepCom (PrepCom I), which took place from 4-8 March 1991 (following a regular session of the Population Commission), proposed that the international meeting on population be called the International Conference on Population and Development (ICPD) and further defined its objectives and themes. On 26 July 1991, ECOSOC, through its resolution 1991/93, decided to accept these proposals. The PrepCom, which was open to participation of all Member States of the United Nations, first served as a subsidiary body of ECOSOC, which had taken the formal decision to convene the ICPD. In 1993, under pressure from the bloc of developing countries, informally known in the United Nations as the Group of 77 or "G-77," the PrepCom was made subsidiary to the General Assembly in order to make its status comparable to that of another subsidiary body of the General Assembly, the United Nations Conference on Environment and Development (UNCED), and to give it a higher profile and greater visibility.

Subsequent to PrepCom I, six expert group meetings were organized by the Population Division in consultation with UNFPA on the themes identified by ECOSOC as requiring the greatest attention in the forthcoming decade. These were: population, environment, and development (New York, 20-24 January 1992); population policies and programmes (Cairo, 12-16 April 1992); population and women (Gaborone, Botswana, 22-26 June 1992); family planning, health, and family well-being (Bangalore, India, 26-29 October 1992); population growth and demographic structure (Paris, 16-20 November 1992); and population distribution and migration (Santa Cruz, Bolivia, 18-23 January 1993). In contrast with the two previous conferences, UNFPA was fully involved in the planning of all these events, helped secure their sites and local funding, and fully participated in formulating their recommendations.

Also during 1992-1993, the five United Nations regional commissions in cooperation with UNFPA organized regional intergovernmental conferences, with a view to reviewing regional experiences and perspectives on population. UNFPA in collaboration with the regional commissions concerned played an active role in preparing for and organizing all of these conferences.

163

After three years of intense preparations, the ICPD took place in Cairo from 5 to 13 September 1994, with 179 countries in attendance. Although its preparatory process had been marked by a number of highly publicized controversies on such issues as reproductive health, including adolescent sexual and reproductive health (ASRH); reproductive rights, and abortion, the conference managed to arrive at a consensus on these and all other issues. Commentators agree that the conference radically transformed the views and perceptions of thousands of policymakers and programme managers on how population policies and programmes should be formulated and implemented in the future — moving away from top-down approaches and centrally formulated demographic goals to those that would seek to respond to the needs of "couples and individuals." It established a broadly based definition of reproductive health, including family planning and sexual health, that has since been accepted by an increasing number of countries around the world.

The ICPD also set clear benchmarks to measure progress over a period of two decades (1995-2015) towards reaching goals in the reduction of infant, child, and maternal mortality; ensuring availability of reproductive health services to all those who need them; education, particularly of young girls and women; and empowerment of women. It brought to the fore the critical role of the non-governmental sector in population activities, firmly establishing the concept of "partnership" between governments, international organizations, and NGOs. Finally, it approved specific estimates for mobilization of the financial resources at both domestic and international levels that would be needed to achieve the ICPD goals over the twenty-year period from 1995 to 2015.

Follow-up by UNFPA

As Dr. Sadik saw it, with the Programme of Action that emerged from the Cairo Conference, a new threshold in population had clearly been crossed. In a UNFPA anniversary volume published just after the conference, she said, "The Programme of Action has considerable ramifications for the work of UNFPA. The Fund's policies and operational work for the coming years will be guided by the principles, goals and recommendations contained in the Cairo document. UNFPA will redouble activities to secure the resource allocations necessary for the implementation of the Programme of Action."[36]

UNFPA, along with UNICEF and WHO, is one of the three United Nations organizations most directly concerned with the implementation of the ICPD recommendations on reproductive health issues. Each of the three organizations has undertaken a series of actions in the context of their respective mandates. The initial turf battles on who does what seem to have been sorted out, and the three organizations are working together on several critical issues: including adolescent health, HIV/AIDS, reduction of maternal mortality, and female genital mutilation (FGM).

UNFPA received the approval of its Executive Board in 1995 to reorient its programme priorities to focus on three main areas: reproductive health, including family planning and sexual health; population and development strategies (PDS); and advocacy. As a United Nations report pointed out:

> UNFPA support for reproductive health is based on a public-health, pragmatic and participatory approach. UNFPA will support all aspects of family planning at the primary, secondary and tertiary levels. Support for other components of reproductive health will be

concentrated at the primary health-care level. Recognizing the need for strengthening referral services for the evaluation and treatment of reproductive health problems that cannot be managed at the primary health-care level, UNFPA will promote the appropriate strengthening of reproductive health services at the secondary and tertiary levels.[37]

The report further notes that:

[i]n order to position itself better to play a lead role in the follow-up to ICPD, UNFPA has reviewed and adjusted all its operational guidelines to align them with the recommendations of the ICPD Programme of Action. In 1995, UNFPA also held a series of regional follow-up consultations that yielded valuable insights into the differing needs of various countries and regions. As a result, country programmes are being designed or reoriented to reflect the priorities and commitments emerging from ICPD. Thus increased emphasis is being placed on the following themes and issues: adopting a reproductive health approach; increasing the role and responsibility of men in reproductive health and family life; expanding reproductive health services and information for youth and adolescents; ensuring women's empowerment and the gender perspective; and expanding partnerships with non-governmental organizations.[38]

Subsequent to the adoption of its post-ICPD programme priorities, UNFPA has revised its technical and programme guidelines to bring them into line with the ICPD Programme of Action. The revised guidelines take into account UNFPA's "comparative advantage, key elements of the Programme of Action that are within its mandate, and the need to maximize the impact and effectiveness of its assistance, within individual countries as well as within and between regions."[39] The guidelines suggest that in the area of reproductive health, including family planning and sexual health, UNFPA assistance is intended to help programme countries achieve universal access to reproductive health and address unmet needs for quality family planning services as soon as possible. In the area of PDS, UNFPA assistance is aimed at institutionalizing the inclusion of population issues and concerns in development policy dialogues among policymakers, and at integrating population factors into development strategies that are people-centred and that recognize the interrelationship among demographic, social, economic, and environmental factors. In the area of advocacy, UNFPA assistance is aimed at securing the necessary commitment and resources and catalysing the consensus and support needed to transform the principles and objectives of the ICPD into practical reality.

Most of the technical and programme guidelines for achieving these goals were issued during 1997 and 1998, but as UNFPA officials themselves are quick to point out, they will have to be revised and updated regularly on the basis of operational experience. They should thus be considered works in progress.

In line with its revised programme strategies, UNFPA has also updated its strategy for resource allocation. The revised strategy, which was approved by the Fund's Executive Board in 1996, seeks to concentrate on the countries that, judging by several economic and social indicators, need the most help in implementing ICPD goals and objectives. These countries (most of which are in sub-Saharan Africa and South Asia) will receive support in all major programme areas; whereas the countries that have already achieved significant success in reaching some of the ICPD goals will receive support in the specific programme areas where it is still needed. A third group of countries will receive mainly technical assistance. Countries of Eastern and Central Europe will receive special attention on a temporary basis.

Governance of UNFPA

The governing body of UNFPA was not part of the three-tiered structure (General Assembly, ECOSOC, and the newly expanded Commission on Population and Development (CPD)) envisaged in General Assembly resolution 49/128 for monitoring and follow-up of the ICPD Programme of Action. However, as UNFPA was expected to play a major role in the follow-up to the ICPD, particularly at the country level, its governing body was invited by the General Assembly in the same resolution

> to oversee, on a regular basis, the response of the Fund to the needs of countries regarding activities to strengthen national population and development programmes, including the specific requests from developing countries for assistance in the preparation of national reports, within its area of competence, and to report to the Economic and Social Council on this matter.[40]

The ICPD Programme of Action had also asked the General Assembly to give further consideration to the idea of a separate Executive Board for UNFPA. This had already been discussed at the General Assembly's forty-eighth session in 1993; following the ICPD, it was considered again at the forty-ninth session. Since 1973, the governing body of UNDP has also served as the governing body of UNFPA, although the Administrator of UNDP and the Executive Director of UNFPA report to it separately. Among many members of the G-77, there was a great deal of sentiment in favour of giving UNFPA greater recognition and visibility after the ICPD by providing it with a governing body separate from that of UNDP. On the other hand, most of the donor countries wanted the existing arrangements to continue, while ensuring that more time and attention would be devoted to UNFPA matters. Some of them also felt that as the reforms on governance of United Nations funds and programmes, which envisaged revised arrangements for the joint oversight of UNDP and UNFPA, had been initiated quite recently, any major changes in this regard ought to be considered later, in light of experience with these reforms.

The negotiations between the two groups ended rather inconclusively. The General Assembly, therefore, chose not to act on this issue, but requested ECOSOC, at its 1995 substantive session, to consider "[t]he establishment of a separate executive board of the United Nations Population Fund."[41] In the meantime, they indicated that the newly constituted UNDP/UNFPA Executive Board (which had replaced the Governing Council of UNDP) should devote more time to consideration of UNFPA matters at its regular sessions.[42]

In order to take care of some of the concerns voiced during the General Assembly, the UNDP/UNFPA Executive Board agreed in early 1995 on a set of practical measures that would provide UNFPA with a direct role in organizing and administering the sessions devoted to its items. Several changes were made in the procedure to allocate agenda items and time slots at the regular sessions of the Executive Board to ensure that both UNDP and UNFPA would get adequate time and attention, and UNFPA was encouraged to play a more direct role in organizing the Executive Board meetings.

On a separate track, the UNFPA Executive Director's proposal to give UNFPA Country Directors a clear profile and adequate visibility by designating them as UNFPA Representatives won the approval of the Executive Board, ECOSOC and the General Assembly. These developments seemed to generally satisfy many of the delegates who were interested in giving UNFPA greater attention than in the past. ECOSOC did not take any specific action in response to the General

Assembly request on the question of a separate executive board for UNFPA, and the entire matter has been put aside for the foreseeable future.

Institutional Arrangements

Another matter under discussion at the forty-ninth session of the General Assembly was how the responsibilities and functions of the follow-up to ICPD should be assigned within the United Nations system. In the ICPD process, UNFPA and the Population Division had worked together well under the direction of the conference Secretary-General (who was also the Executive Director of UNFPA). In the post-ICPD phase, would it be possible to envisage a similar arrangement? The idea was given a good deal of thought, but ultimately it did not move forward. Whereas UNFPA was responsible to its own Executive Board on programme matters, the Population Division's work programme was considered and approved by the Population Commission. Those who did not favour a joint secretariat for ICPD follow-up made up of the Population Division and UNFPA took the position that such an arrangement would create considerable confusion in the formulation of work programmes and reporting procedures.[43]

The report of the United Nations Secretariat on the implementation of General Assembly resolution 49/128 emphasized the role that DESIPA, in particular the Population Division, has played as the focal point for the provision of integrated secretariat support to the commission:

> In the past, this role has consisted of the provision of substantive support, the preparation of documentation and the coordination of relevant inputs. Effective substantive support for the work programme of the Commission has required the involvement of many organizations of the United Nations system, in particular UNFPA, and could only have been carried out on the basis of cooperative and coordinated relationships. At the same time, UNFPA has taken the lead in coordinating and implementing operational activities in the field. It is proposed this basic pattern of work should continue with respect to provision of support for the Commission and implementation of the Programme of Action.[44]

Under the arrangements proposed by the CPD in 1995, the Population Division remains the secretariat of the commission, while it shares with UNFPA the responsibility for preparing the documentation on ICPD follow-up. The Population Division prepares the report on world population monitoring, whereas UNFPA is responsible for several other reports: the monitoring of population programmes, the report of the inter-agency task force for the implementation of the Programme of Action, the report on the activities of intergovernmental bodies and NGOs, and the report on the flow of financial resources. A decision taken by the commission in 1997 eliminated the separate report on the activities of intergovernmental organizations and NGOs, with the understanding that information on these activities would be included in other reports.

Inter-Agency Collaboration

UNFPA also serves as the lead agency in the United Nations on promoting and coordinating inter-agency cooperation on the follow-up to the ICPD. An inter-agency task force, under the chairmanship of the Executive Director of UNFPA, was established towards the end of 1994. It set up four working groups to develop proposals for inter-agency collaboration at the country level: (a) a common data system in the field of health at the national level, notably in the areas of infant, child and maternal mortality, led by UNICEF; (b) basic education, with special attention to gender disparities, led by UNESCO; (c) policy-related issues, including the drafting of a common advocacy statement on social development issues, led by UNFPA; and (d) women's empowerment, led by the United Nations Development Fund for Women (UNIFEM).

Two other working groups were established in early 1995 on: (a) reproductive health, led by WHO; and (b) international migration, led by ILO. Five of these working groups produced guidelines for Resident Coordinators, who head up United Nations operational teams in developing countries, to enable them to implement the ICPD Programme of Action and to promote and strengthen inter-agency collaboration at the country level. The sixth working group developed a common advocacy statement that emphasized the importance of population as an integral component of development strategies. The statement was endorsed in late 1996 by the United Nations Administrative Committee on Coordination (ACC), which groups together executive heads of specialized agencies and major operational funds and programmes under the chairmanship of the Secretary-General.

In October of 1995, following the Social Development Summit in Copenhagen, the Inter-Agency Task Force (IATF) was expanded and reconstituted as the ACC Task Force on Basic Social Services for All (BSSA), with UNFPA continuing to serve as the lead agency. The ACC established, at the same time, two other task forces to focus on major goals emerging from global United Nations conferences that had taken place in the 1990s (Rio de Janeiro, Cairo, Copenhagen, Beijing, and Istanbul in particular) and to promote more effective and better coordinated delivery of United Nations assistance at the country level. The two task forces that were established were the ACC Task Force on Employment and Sustainable Livelihoods, chaired by ILO, and the ACC Task Force on an Enabling Environment for Economic and Social Development, chaired by the World Bank. All three ACC task forces were expected to coordinate, on a regular basis, with an Inter-Agency Committee on Women and Gender Equality.

The ACC Task Force on Basic Social Services was asked to focus on six major topics under the general theme of poverty eradication: (a) population, with an emphasis on reproductive health and family planning services; (b) basic education; (c) primary health care; (d) drinking water and sanitation; (e) shelter; and (f) social services in post-crisis situations. At its first meeting, on 23 February 1996, the task force decided to continue three of the previous working groups; i.e., those on reproductive health, international migration, and a common approach to building national capacity to track child and maternal mortality. It also decided to establish a working group on primary health care and another one on basic education.

The output of the ACC Task Force on Basic Social Services (which completed its work in 1997) included updated and revised guidelines for United Nations Resident Coordinators on primary health care, reproductive health, basic education, women's empowerment, international migration, and national capacity-building in measuring infant and maternal mortality. These were prepared on the basis of the comments received from the Resident Coordinators on earlier guidelines, while taking into account six "cross-cutting dimensions": selection and use of performance indicators; financing and resource mobilization; the gender perspective; targeting of specific groups, including those in post-crisis and/or emergency situations; policy; and the involvement of civil society. In addition, issues concerning nutrition, the environment and shelter were taken into consideration, as appropriate.[45] Other end products produced by the task force included a wall chart on social indicators, a publication on lessons learned and best practices in social sector assistance, the selection and use of indicators, a pocket card on advocacy, and a compendium of international commitments on poverty alleviation and social integration.

Various inter-agency groups, including the ACC Task Force on Basic Social Services, have emphasized the need for reliable indicators to measure progress towards reaching the goals of the ICPD and other global conferences. This was further emphasized by the General Assembly in a resolution adopted at its fifty-first session in 1996.[46] The wall chart mentioned above, which provides country data in six key areas (population, primary health care, nutrition, basic education, drinking water and sanitation, and shelter) is one step in that direction. It brings together currently available data and estimates, but it is clear that further work is needed to revise and update them.

One of the areas that requires further work is the methodology for monitoring reproductive health programmes. In 1997, the working group on reproductive health, led by WHO, produced a list of 15 indicators that provide an overview of the reproductive health situation in different settings.[47] These were later incorporated in a WHO publication titled "Monitoring Reproductive Health: Selecting a Short List of National and Global Indicators."[48]

For its part, UNFPA has issued an updated and revised list of indicators that are meant to be used by programme managers for programme monitoring and evaluation.[49] In 1998, the Organisation for Economic Cooperation and Development's Development Assistance Committee (OECD/DAC), in cooperation with experts from the World Bank and other parts of the United Nations system, produced a set of core indicators for monitoring the goals of major global conferences.[50] The result has been that there are several lists of indicators currently in use or in preparation, with a good deal of commonality among them. Ultimately, a system-wide agreement on common indicators will be essential to developing common follow-ups to the ICPD and other major United Nations conferences at both the country and inter-country levels.

Mobilization of adequate resources to implement the ICPD Programme of Action remains a priority of UNFPA's post-Cairo agenda. Through its publication entitled *Global Population Assistance*, an annual report that it submits to the CPD based on regular consultation with multilateral and bilateral donors, UNFPA has continued to update the information on availability of resources. As the reports show, international funding for population did go up in 1994 and 1995, at the time of the ICPD and immediately following, but it has remained stagnant since. UNFPA's own funding, after going up for several years, declined in 1998 and 1999.

If present trends continue, the goals agreed upon at Cairo for resource mobilization are unlikely to be met. The five-year review of the implementation of the Cairo agenda, known as ICPD+5, which took place in 1999, was expected to provide fresh impetus towards greater mobilization of financial resources from both public and private sectors. The special session of the General Assembly on ICPD+5 (New York, 30 June-2 July 1999) noted that translation of commitment to the ICPD goals into commensurate levels assistance of donor countries had not been forthcoming, and therefore there was an urgent need for donor countries to renew and intensify efforts to meet the needs for complementary external funding required to implement the costed elements of the ICPD Programme of Action.[51]

In the post ICPD+5 period, substantially more funds for population are indeed being provided by several large private foundations (e.g., Bill and Melinda Gates Foundation, Packard Foundation, and Ted Turner's United Nations Foundation); and it would seem also that the private sector in many developing countries is willing to provide funding for activities in this area. However, there are no clear prospects for notable increases in the funding provided through bilateral and multilateral channels. A vigorous advocacy campaign aimed at persuading donors to provide greater funding for population will, therefore, continue to be a major element of UNFPA's ICPD follow-up agenda.

Conclusion

The conclusion from this overview of UNFPA and the major global conferences in the last thirty years is that UNFPA's involvement in the global population conferences has grown incrementally. UNFPA provided half the budget of the Bucharest Conference and its preparatory activities, but it was not greatly involved in the substantive preparations for the conference or in its actual operation. The World Population Year activities during 1972 through 1974, which were coordinated by the Executive Director of UNFPA, were, however, of enormous help to UNFPA in defining its long-term information and awareness-creation strategies and in helping it to establish wide-ranging contacts with NGOs, academic institutions, parliamentary groups, and the media. UNFPA's successful advocacy programmes owe much of their basic philosophy and character to the WPY. The conference itself validated UNFPA's approach on the relationship between population and development and its focus on country programmes, while giving the Fund a definition of the rights of couples and individuals that continues to serve as the basis for legitimizing and expanding its support for voluntary family planning programmes.

UNFPA was more fully involved in the Mexico City Conference, primarily because its Executive Director served as the Secretary-General of the conference. The preparatory process, however, still maintained a distinction between technical activities and organizational and political arrangements. Among the results of the conference, its unequivocal support for family planning, its emphasis on the equal role of women in population and development activities, and its recognition of the increasing role of NGOs were three of the major clusters of recommendations that helped shape the further development of UNFPA policies and programmes.

Following the precedent of Mexico City, the Cairo Conference was, again, headed by the Executive Director of UNFPA. At that conference, however, the involvement of UNFPA in the preparatory process went much further than was the case with the Mexico City preparations. The United Nations Population Division and UNFPA worked together as the joint secretariat for the conference, and the UNFPA Executive Director, as Secretary-General of the conference, provided clear leadership and direction on both substantive and practical issues. The actions taken by UNFPA, including its Executive Board, subsequent to the ICPD show a total commitment to the objectives and principles of the Cairo Conference. UNFPA played an active role in the ICPD+5 process and remains the focal point within the United Nations for system-wide follow-up on ICPD. UNFPA has also continued to play an active role, within its areas of interest and concern, in the follow-up to other United Nations conferences, in particular the Fourth World Conference on Women (FWCW) in Beijing.

While UNFPA's involvement, particularly in the Mexico City and Cairo Conferences, has helped shape its policies and programmes in many ways, these conferences, in my view, have not had a major or significant impact on UNFPA's institutional development. The only noteworthy result of the call in Mexico City for further strengthening UNFPA was the development of an arrangement for exchanging information between the Population Commission and the UNFPA Governing Council. The ICPD was somewhat more specific in its recommendations concerning UNFPA. But it is worth noting that when they came to the General Assembly, ECOSOC, and UNFPA's own governing body, these recommendations were reviewed within the broader political context of the ongoing efforts for United Nations reform and the evolving patterns of donor-recipient relationships. The actions taken reflect these two major considerations. The result: support for closer cooperation and coordination among major United Nations funds and programmes, including UNFPA; giving UNFPA a distinct and separate role at the UNDP/UNFPA Executive Board; and leaving aside the question of a separate Executive Board for UNFPA.

References

[1] United Nations, General Assembly Resolution 2211 (XXI), 17 December 1966.

[2] Stanley P. Johnson, *World Population and the United Nations: Challenge and Response* (Cambridge: Cambridge University Press, 1987): p. 80.

[3] United Nations, General Assembly Resolution 3019 (XXVII), 18 December 1972.

[4] United Nations, Economic and Social Council (ECOSOC) Resolution 1763 (LIV), 18 May 1973.

[5] United Nations, Economic and Social Council (ECOSOC) Resolution 1672 (LII), 2 June 1972.

[6] Stanley P. Johnson, *World Population and the United Nations: Challenge and Response* (Cambridge: Cambridge University Press, 1987): p. 129.

[7] United Nations Population Fund, *Report on National Population Commissions* (New York: UNFPA, 1974).

[8] Jyoti Shankar Singh, *World Population Policies* (New York: Praeger, 1979).

[9] United Nations, *Report of the United Nations World Population Conference*, Bucharest, 19-30 August 1974 (New York: United Nations, 1975): para. 14(c).

[10] Ibid.: para. 14.

[11] Ibid.: Recommendation 17.

[12] Ibid.: para. 14(f).

[13] United Nations, International Conference on Human Rights, Tehran, 22 April-13 May 1968: para. 16.

[14] Nafis Sadik, ed., *Population: The UNFPA Experience* (New York: New York University Press, 1984): p. 101.

[15] United Nations, World Conference of the International Women's Year, Mexico City, 19 June-2 July 1975. *World Plan of Action for the Implementation of the Objectives of the International Women's Year* (New York: United Nations, 1976): p. 8.

[16] Ibid.: Resolution 15.

[17] Nafis Sadik, ed., *Population: The UNFPA Experience* (New York: New York University Press, 1984).

[18] Nafis Sadik, ed., *Population Policies and Programmes: Lessons Learned from Two Decades of Experience* (New York: New York University Press, 1991): p. 247.

[19] United Nations, Economic and Social Council (ECOSOC) Resolution 1981/87, 15 November 1981.

[20] Jyoti Shankar Singh, *Creating a New Consensus on Population* (London: Earthscan, 1998).

[21] United Nations, *Report of the International Conference on Population*, Mexico City, 6-14 August 1984: Recommendation 28.

[22] Ibid.: Recommendation 27.

[23] Ibid.: Recommendation 9.

[24] Ibid.: Recommendation 18(e).

[25] Leon Tabah, "A Turning Point," *Populi* 11(4) (1984): pp. 13-20.

[26] United Nations, *Report of the International Conference on Population,* Mexico City, 6-14 August 1984: para. 7.

[27] Ibid.: para. 16.

[28] Ibid.: Recommendation 84.

[29] Ibid.: Recommendation 12.

[30] Ibid.: Recommendation 84.

[31] Ibid.: Recommendation 83.

[32] United Nations, General Assembly Resolution 39/228, 18 December 1984.

[33] Ibid.

[34] United Nations Population Fund, *Report of the International Forum on Population in the Twenty-first Century,* Amsterdam, 6-9 November 1989 (New York: UNFPA, 1989).

[35] United Nations, General Assembly Resolution 44/210, 22 December 1989.

[36] Nafis Sadik, ed., *Making a Difference: Twenty-five Years of UNFPA Experience* (London: Banson, 1994): p. 136.

[37] United Nations, Implementation of the Programme of Action of the International Conference on Population and Development, 25 September 1996: para. 30.

[38] Ibid.

[39] United Nations Population Fund, *Policies and Procedures Manual* (New York: UNFPA, 1997): p. 1.

[40] United Nations, General Assembly Resolution 49/128, 20 June 1995.

[41] Ibid.

[42] United Nations, Implementation of General Assembly Resolution 49/128 on the Report of the International Conference on Population and Development (New York: United Nations, 1995).

[43] Jyoti Shankar Singh, *Creating a New Consensus on Population* (London: Earthscan, 1998).

[44] United Nations, Implementation of General Assembly Resolution 49/128 on the Report of the International Conference on Population and Development (New York: United Nations, 1995): para. 28.

[45] United Nations, Implementation of the Programme of Action of the International Conference on Population and Development, 25 September 1996: para. 9.

[46] United Nations, General Assembly Resolution 51/176 (New York: United Nations, 1996).

[47] United Nations, Implementation of the Programme of Action of the International Conference on Population and Development (New York: United Nations, 24 June 1997).

[48] World Health Organization, *Monitoring Reproductive Health: Selecting a Short List of National and Global Indicators* (Geneva: WHO, 1997).

[49] United Nations Population Fund, *Indicators for Population and Reproductive Health Programmes* (New York: UNFPA, October 1998, reprint July 1999).

[50] Organisation for Economic Cooperation and Development, *Measuring Development Progress: A Working Set of Core Indicators* (OECD website: http://www.oecd.org/dac/indicators/ftm/slides.htm, 1999).

[51] United Nations, Review and Appraisal of the Progress Made in Achieving the Goals and Objectives of the Programme of Action of the International Conference on Population and Development (New York: United Nations, 1999): para. 95, key actions.

Population, Resources and the Environment: Struggling Towards Sustainability

Don Hinrichsen

Introduction

According to United Nations estimates, on October 12, 1999, the population of the Earth reached 6 billion, another milestone in the upward rush of human numbers, which are expected to top eight billion by 2025. If, as is most likely, "Baby 6 Billion" was born in the developing world, where three-quarters of humanity is concentrated, he or she stands a good chance of being thrown into a life of misery and deprivation. The statistics of poverty are numbing:

- One-third of humanity, 2 billion people, subsist on two dollars a day or less, in conditions most Americans and Europeans would find abominable;
- 1.5 billion do not have access to clean water;
- Three billion, half of the global population, live without proper sanitation facilities;
- Two billion are living in substandard housing, many in tin-roofed shacks with dirt floors;
- Up to half a billion women are forced to give birth without trained assistance from qualified medical staff or access to a clinic or hospital;
- Half a million deaths occur annually from pregnancy-related causes;
- Just under one billion adults are illiterate; two-thirds of them women; and
- Nearly one billion people — 30 per cent of the global workforce — do not have adequate employment opportunities.

If, on the other hand, Baby 6 Billion was fortunate enough to be born in a developed country, say the United States, she or he will automatically be in the top 20 per cent of the human race in terms of quality-of-life indicators — good housing, potable water, proper sanitation, a high school or college education, sound medical care (including reproductive health and family planning), jobs, disposable income, and leisure time.

Regardless of where Baby 6 Billion was born, he or she will contribute to the relentless population consumption machine that continues to devour global resources at non-sustainable rates, while generating enormous quantities of waste in the process. Of course, the scale of consumption, and therefore, the environmental and resource impact — each person's "environmental footprint," so to speak — varies dramatically between the rich and poor worlds. The average American, for instance, consumes 37 metric tons of resources a year — fuels, metals, minerals, food, and forest products — and generates an equal quantity of waste. In all, 270 million Americans consume nearly

10 billion metric tons of materials a year, 30 per cent of the world's total.[1] By contrast, the average Indian consumes less than one metric ton of the Earth's resources each year and generates much less waste than an American or European. According to the United Nations, if the entire population of the Earth were to have the same standard of living as the average American or West European, it would take three Planet Earths to supply the necessary resources at current rates of consumption.[2]

The concept of an environmental footprint was first researched by a group from the University of British Columbia seeking to calculate the amount of land needed to sustain national populations (including "land" in the form of imported resources). Although there are clear connections between population growth, level of income, consumption, and resource destruction, the data are hotly contested. Depending on whether you are a Malthus or a Julian Simon, Lester Brown or the United States Chamber of Commerce, you will have far different views on the subject of the Earth's capacity to absorb more people and their ever-growing needs.

Technocrats like Julian Simon have argued that the Earth's greatest resource is the innate capacity of human beings to invent or engineer our way out of population and resource crises. In their view, "the more the merrier," since more people mean potentially more solutions to problems. The flip side of this argument, propounded by experts like Lester Brown, President of the Worldwatch Institute, and Stanford University professor Paul Ehrlich, is that with the poorest third of humanity effectively barred from the solutions part of the equation, they continue to contribute to the problems. Additionally, we have the knock-on effects of 1 billion rich people consuming 80 per cent of the Earth's resources while 5 billion make do with the 20 per cent that is left over.

This has given rise to the study of the population, poverty, environment, and resource connections that contribute to non-sustainable patterns of development. Often referred to as the "PP&E" nexus, these linkages have both synergistic and antagonistic feedbacks. One such linkage has been substantially documented: efforts to slow population growth and reduce poverty in order to achieve economic progress, improve environmental protection, and reduce unsustainable consumption patterns tend to be "mutually reinforcing."[3]

Meanwhile, as the debate intensifies, so do the impacts of population growth and consumption on the Earth's resource base. When all is said and done, human activities are already taking a heavy toll of our planet's life-support systems as each new human being leaves a larger ecological footprint.

This analysis looks at the United Nations Population Fund's (UNFPA's) work in the area of population-environment-development linkages. It then analyses the collective effects of 6 billion people, their consumption patterns, and resource use trends, in six different critical resource areas.

UNFPA's Involvement in Environment: Its Mandate, Activities and Accomplishments

Legal basis for UNFPA involvement

Since its founding in 1969, UNFPA has had a critical and strategic role in: (a) helping to analyse the relations between population, environment, resource management, and development; (b) promoting appropriate policies at the national level in developing countries; and (c) creating awareness of these issues in both developed and developing countries. UNFPA has helped United Nations organizations and non-governmental organizations (NGOs) to work across disciplines and sectoral institutions on action-oriented research, data collection, and advocacy activities that show the

176

linkages between population, environment, and the Earth's limited resource base. No other United Nations organization has a similar role. In this way, the Fund has fostered a holistic approach that is widely recognized as being essential if success in environmental management is to be achieved.

UNFPA guidelines on population and development, which were first drawn up in 1987, gave priority to activities related to policy-oriented research and advocacy in the areas of poverty alleviation, environmental stewardship, and sustainable resource use, all as part of an integrated approach to development. According to UNFPA's policies and procedures, the Fund may support "socio-cultural and economic research on population and development policies and programmes, especially interlinkages with poverty, the environment, the economy, food security and so on. UNFPA may also support work on how development projects and programmes influence demographic trends, and vice versa, including migration, poor women, rural populations, indigenous groups, adolescents, youth and ageing. Support may also be given to research on areas affected by population pressures, poverty, destruction of ecosystems and degradation of resources."

According to UNFPA's "Guidance Note on Population and the Environment" (1998),[4] the Fund can support, within its three thematic areas, the following types of population and environment projects:

- Under "reproductive health": synergistic interventions in cases where environmental degradation, poverty, and population pressures are interacting with each other to exacerbate environmental problems. Included in this area are the reproductive health problems of women and girls, who often act as *de facto* resource managers.
- Under "population and development strategies": the integration of population and environmental linkages in policies and plans, policy-oriented research, analysis, and rapid assessment of linkages between population factors and the environment, and capacity-building of developing countries through data collection, analysis, and training.
- Under "advocacy": awareness creation and disseminating information about the links and synergies between population and the environment.

More specifically, under the area of reproductive health, the cornerstones of population and development-related programmes include advancing gender equality and equity, the empowerment of women, and ensuring women's ability to control their own fertility. UNFPA support is given to synergistic interventions in this regard, by, for example, targeting unsustainable enclaves or geographical areas where environmental degradation, poverty, and population pressures collide.

Under population and development strategies, UNFPA supports the integration of population and environmental dimensions into the planning process at all levels of government. Under this sector, UNFPA has supported a wide array of research and analysis in the following areas:

- The relationship between population pressures, poverty, and environmental degradation;
- The population dimension of the food supply system, including the causes of food insecurity and imbalances in supply and distribution;
- The population dimension of desertification (desert creation);
- The population factors related to water-scarce and water-short regions, including effective strategies to conserve and utilize water resources sustainably;
- The causes and consequences of environmental refugees; and
- The roles of women and men as resource stewards.

Under advocacy, UNFPA supports activities designed to inform, educate, and communicate the nature of these interlinked issues to policymakers, NGOs, the media, and the public, including community efforts to produce and disseminate relevant information.

The ICPD reinforced UNFPA's work in this area, devoting one chapter of its Programme of Action to the "Interrelationships Between Population, Sustained Economic Growth and Sustainable Development" (chapter 3, paragraphs 3.1-3.32). Subsection C deals exclusively with "Population and Environment."

The ICPD Programme of Action includes the following key statements:

- Sustainable development implies, *inter alia*, long-term sustainability in production and consumption relating to all economic activities, including industry, energy, agriculture, forestry, fisheries, transport, tourism and infrastructure, in order to optimize ecologically sound resource use and minimize waste. . . . Explicitly integrating population into economic and development strategies will both speed up the pace of sustainable development and poverty alleviation and contribute to the achievement of population objectives and an improved quality of life of the population. (paragraph 3.3)
- Governments, international agencies, NGOs and other concerned parties should undertake timely and periodic reviews of their development strategies, with the aim of assessing progress towards integrating population into development and environment programmes that take into account patterns of production and consumption and seek to bring about population trends consistent with the achievement of sustainable development and the improvement of the quality of life. (paragraph 3.6)
- Poverty is also closely related to inappropriate spatial distribution of population, to unsustainable use and inequitable distribution of such natural resources as land and water, and to serious environmental degradation. (paragraph 3.13)
- Meeting the basic human needs of growing populations is dependent on a healthy environment. These human dimensions need to be given attention in developing comprehensive policies for sustainable development in the context of population growth. (paragraph 3.24)

Following on the heels of the ICPD Programme of Action came General Assembly resolution 49/128, which was adopted in December of 1994. Among other things, it "fully acknowledges that the factors of population, health, education, poverty, patterns of production and consumption, empowerment of women and the environment are closely interconnected and should be considered through an integrated approach."

Furthermore, the ICPD Programme of Action recommended actions to ensure population and environmental integration, including integrating environmental factors into planning and decision-making, modifying unsustainable consumption and production patterns in order to foster sustainable resource use and prevent environmental degradation, and the implementation of policies to address the ecological implications of demographic dynamics. It also called for measures to enhance the full participation of relevant groups, especially women, at all levels of population and environmental decision-making to achieve sustainable management of natural resources (paragraphs 3.29-3.30).

The Hague Forum, held in February of 1999, underscored these linkages. The report of the Forum called for governments to initiate legislative and administrative measures designed to promote balanced patterns of consumption and production, foster sustainable resource use, and prevent environmental degradation. In particular, the Forum report called for more research on the impact of environmental degradation on health, "especially women's reproductive health."[5]

Making the Connections: Links with Other Major Initiatives

From its inception, UNFPA has entered into productive partnerships with other United Nations agencies and with NGOs that are concerned about the interconnections between population and the environment. In fact, UNFPA has played a catalytic role in furthering policy-relevant research on the links between population variables and the state of key natural resources.

For example, a UNFPA grant financed a major study by the Food and Agriculture Organization of the United Nations (FAO) in the early 1980s to assess, globally, the carrying capacity of agricultural lands to support their then-current and projected populations. An oft-referenced summary of that project was published under the title "Land, Food and People" in 1984. Again, UNFPA financed a multi-country study carried out by the International Institute for Applied Systems Analysis (IIASA) in Vienna on the linkages between population pressures and ecosystem degradation. In 1996, UNFPA published an advocacy booklet, "Food for the Future: Women, Population and Food Security," as input to the World Food Summit, held in Rome. UNFPA also participated in the inter-agency response to the mass displacement of people in Central America, mostly poor, affected by Hurricane Mitch. More recently, in 1999, UNFPA signed a memorandum of understanding with the United Nations Environment Programme (UNEP) to foster enhanced cooperation and activities dealing with population and the environment.

The UNCED Process

The Rio Conference of 1992 (the United Nations Conference on Environment and Development, or UNCED) devoted a small section of its report to the links between population and the environment. Agenda 21, the action plan of UNCED, did contain some references to the need to link population and environment with consumption patterns and sustainable development. The following are some of the key statements in Agenda 21:

- The growth of world population and production combined with unsustainable consumption patterns places increasingly severe stress on the life-supporting capacities of our planet. (paragraph 5.3)
- Policies should be designed to address the consequences of population growth built into population momentum, while at the same time incorporating measures to bring about demographic transition. They should combine environmental concerns and population issues within a holistic view of development whose primary goals include the alleviation of poverty; secure livelihoods; good health; quality of life; improvement of the status and income of women and their access to schooling and professional training, as well as fulfilment of their personal aspirations; and empowerment of individuals and communities. (paragraph 5.16)
- Special attention should be given to the critical role of women in population-environment programmes and in achieving sustainable development. . . . Population-environment programmes must enable women to mobilize themselves to alleviate their burden and

179

improve their capacity to participate in and benefit from socio-economic development. (paragraph 5.48)

Recognizing the critical importance of the connections between population and environment, Chapter 5 of Agenda 21 identified three main programme areas as a basis for action:

- Developing and disseminating knowledge concerning the links between demographic trends and factors and sustainable development;
- Formulating integrated national policies for environment and development, taking into account demographic trends and factors; and
- Implementing integrated environment and development programmes at the local level, taking into account demographic trends and factors.

In light of these connections, the following section of this chapter looks at six specific resource areas and the population interactions that impinge upon them.

Population and Resources — The Ultimate Determinators

Water — the planet's lifeblood

Water is the liquid of life. Without it, the blue planet would be a dead and barren wasteland. Fresh water is also the most finite of the Earth's resources. There is no more water on Earth now than there was 2,000 years ago, when the population was less than 3 per cent of its current size.[6] Population growth and rising demand have put the squeeze on available water resources. Today, 31 countries with a collective population of half a billion people are experiencing chronic water shortages for all or part of the year. But within just 25 years, that figure could explode to 3 billion people in 50 countries, or 35 per cent of the global population in 2025.[7] There are two main reasons for this drastic increase in the number of countries and people suffering from water scarcity: population growth and rising consumption. During this century, the world's population has tripled, while water withdrawals have increased by over six times.[8] Since 1940, the annual demand for water has grown twice as fast as the global population.

While population growth and escalating consumption patterns mean there is less water available per person, water resources are increasingly fouled with all manner of wastes — raw sewage and garbage from urban areas, toxic industrial effluents, and runoff from agriculture. FAO estimates that each year roughly 450 cubic kilometres of wastewater are discharged into rivers, streams, and lakes. To dilute and transport this dirty water, another 6,000 cubic kilometres of clean water are required. If current trends continue, argues FAO, the world's entire stable river flow would be needed just for pollution transport and dilution by the middle of the twenty-first century.[9]

As a global average, agriculture accounts for the lion's share of water withdrawn for human use (70 per cent), and for the largest amount of pollution to surface and ground waters (70 per cent in the United States and Europe, 50-60 per cent in developing countries). Dirty water kills over 12 million people a year, mostly women and children.[10] Nearly all these deaths take place in the developing world.

180

There is another sinister side to the water crisis. As of 1996, the world's human population was expropriating 54 per cent of all the accessible freshwater contained in rivers, lakes, and underground aquifers. By 2025, population growth alone will push this figure to 70 per cent.[11] As humankind withdraws more and more water to satisfy its unquenchable thirst, less is available to maintain vital wetland ecosystems, like the Everglades in Florida.

The wholesale loss and degradation of life-giving riverine, lake, and wetland habitats has translated into a species holocaust. Globally, close to one-quarter of all freshwater fish species are either endangered, vulnerable, or on their way to extinction. Southeast Asia's Mekong River reports a two-thirds drop since 1970 in fisheries production due to dams, deforestation, and the conversion of 1,000 square kilometres of mangrove swamps into rice paddies and fish ponds.

Caught between finite and increasingly polluted water supplies on one hand and rapidly rising demand from population growth and development on the other, many countries face uneasy choices. The World Bank warns that the lack of freshwater is likely to be one of the major factors limiting economic development in the decades to come. It is also likely to spawn outright conflict among water-short regions and states as they compete for shrinking supplies.[12]

Forests — the Earth's lungs

The Earth's green mantle of forests provides humanity with multiple benefits — they absorb carbon dioxide and produce oxygen, anchor soils and prevent erosion, regulate water flow and protect watersheds, modify climate, and provide habitat for countless species of plants and animals. Yet over the course of the past half-century, this green mantle has been reduced to tattered remnants. Currently, about 16 million hectares of forest, an area roughly the size of Nepal, are cut, bulldozed, or burned each year. According to the World Resources Institute (WRI), an environmental think-tank based in Washington, D.C., half of the world's original forest cover — some 3 billion hectares — has been lost, with most of the destruction taking place during the last four decades.[13] WRI reports that only one-fifth of the world's remaining forests are classified as "frontier forests" — pristine areas that have not been disturbed or degraded by human activities.

Trees do not necessarily a forest make. Despite Europe's greenbelts, only a tiny patch of the continent's original forest remains, cloistered away in Bialowieza National Park in southeast Poland, hard against the border with Belarus. Here 1,000 year-old lindens, oaks, and hornbeams stand cathedral-like, silent reminders of what has been lost irrevocably. Old-growth forests in the United States have been decimated, too: in the lower 48 states, 99 per cent of the frontier forests are gone.[14]

As with water, there is a clear connection between forest loss and population growth. Lester Brown, President of the Worldwatch Institute, reckons that 75 per cent of the historical growth of population and 75 per cent of the loss in global forest cover has taken place in the twentieth century. "The correlation makes sense," reasons Brown, "given the additional need for farmland, pastureland, and forest products as human numbers expand. But since 1950, the advent of mass consumption of forest products has quickened the pace of deforestation."[15]

Dirk Bryant, a senior researcher at WRI, estimates that fuelwood collection and overgrazing by domestic animals are now responsible for degrading about 14 per cent of the world's remaining frontier forests, nearly all of which — disregarding northern Canada and Russia — are found in developing countries.[16]

The relentless and rapidly escalating consumption of forest products by the rich world is responsible for whittling away much of the world's remaining old-growth, or frontier, forests. The use of paper and paperboard per person has nearly tripled since 1960, with the developed countries of North America, Europe, and Asia accounting for most of it. North America, Europe, and Japan, with just 16 per cent of the global population, consume two-thirds of the world's paper and paperboard and half its industrial wood.

Researchers at Friends of the Earth, UK, have determined that humanity's demand for forest products is already 25 per cent beyond the point of sustainable consumption. What this means is that, given population growth in the developing world and continued demand for forest products in the industrialized world, the future of the world's frontier forests and all of the free ecosystem benefits they provide to humankind are in jeopardy.[17]

Down to Bare Earth — soils and food production

The world's topsoils, the "bottom line" in food production, are increasingly eroded and degraded by the demands of large-scale mechanized agriculture and the desperate needs of subsistence farmers. We could be entering what some experts call the "century of scarcity," as rising demand for food is paralleled by a corresponding drop in supply, due mainly to widespread land degradation and inappropriate agricultural policies, including $228 billion worth of subsidies spent on price supports and outright payments to farmers.

Food shortages may seem incredible to those who subscribe to the "horn of plenty" scenario of agricultural productivity. Sceptics argue that since the end of World War II, the world's population has doubled, while food production has tripled. Moreover, the daily calories available per person in the developing world increased from an average of 1,925 in 1961 to 2,540 by 1992. World food production has expanded since the early 1960s due mainly to the Green Revolution — adoption of crop rotation, the mass production and use of petroleum-based fertilizers and chemical pesticides, expanded irrigation, and the introduction of genetically superior, disease-resistant cultivars (cultivated crops).

Yet, in the midst of this plenty, the world still has 840 million chronically malnourished people, mostly women and children, while an additional one billion suffer from protein energy malnutrition.[18] Despite slower rates of population growth, grain supplies per capita have actually fallen over the past decade. The situation is critical in many poor developing countries. Between 1985 and 1995, food production lagged behind population growth in 64 out of 105 developing countries monitored by FAO.[19] Africa fared worst of all. Food production per person fell in 31 out of 46 African countries. In fact, Africa produces nearly 30 per cent less food per person now that it did in 1970.[20]

The change in direction in food availability is due to two mutually antagonistic trends: Rapid population growth and changing diets have increased demand, while higher population densities in traditional agricultural areas, fragmentation of small farmsteads, poor land management, and inappropriate agricultural and economic policies have combined to suppress supply.

Population growth, rapid urbanization, and land degradation have reduced the amount of arable land available per person. In developing countries as a whole, the average amount of arable land per person fell from about 0.3 hectares in 1961 to less than 0.2 hectares in 1992.[21] Urbanization is devouring farmland: China is losing close to one million hectares of prime agricultural land each year,[22] while urban sprawl in the United States claims nearly 400,000 hectares a year.[23]

On top of these alarming developments, nearly 2 billion hectares of the world's crop and grazing land — an area larger than the United States and Mexico combined — suffer from moderate to severe soil degradation.[24] The main causes are soil erosion, loss of nutrients, damage from inappropriate farming practices (including poorly built irrigation systems), and the misuse of agricultural chemicals. In the Philippines, for example, nearly one-quarter of all cropland has been severely degraded. According to WRI projections, by 2025 some 3 billion people, 40 per cent of the global population, will live in land-short countries, with less than 0.07 hectares of fertile land per person (roughly the size of two tennis courts).

Death by Breath: air pollution and climate change

No one disputes the simple fact that more people mean more air pollution. Population growth translates directly into more consumers of energy, more vehicles on the road, more industries, and, hence, more urban pollution. The debate, again, is over the cumulative effects of population and income growth in the developing world and the continued rise in energy consumption in industrialized countries. Today, over one billion people suffer from dangerously high air-pollution levels. Most of these people are in sprawling Third World cities where industries and power plants have few, if any, pollution controls and where traffic jams are a perpetual feature of urban life.[25] Up to 700,000 people die every year from air pollution.[26] Cities such as Bangkok, Beijing, and Manila are often entombed in a sickening pall of pollution spewed from a rapidly growing fleet of vehicles and uncontrolled industrial emissions. In these cities and seventeen others, air pollution is one of the leading causes of respiratory infections and premature death. Just breathing the air in Mexico City, for instance, has been said to have the same health-destroying effect as smoking three packs of cigarettes a day!

Currently, the richest fifth of humanity consumes close to 60 per cent of the world's energy, while the poorest fifth uses just 4 per cent. The benefits of the fossil fuel revolution have not yet reached a full third of humanity — the 2 billion people condemned to burn fuelwood for heating, cooking, and lighting.[27]

Carbon emissions, from the burning of fossil fuels, tell the tale. In 1997, according to the Worldwatch Institute, global emissions of carbon totalled 6.3 billion tons. Since 1950, world carbon emissions have increased fourfold. Although Western industrialized countries currently account for close to half of all carbon emissions, developing countries have increased their share dramatically in the past decade; collectively, they are responsible for 40 per cent of global carbon emissions. China is now the world's second largest emitter after the United States, with a 14 per cent share.[28]

The other side of our atmospheric pollution problem is climate change. When carbon is released into the atmosphere from the burning of fossil fuels — oil, coal, and gas — and wood, it combines with oxygen to form carbon dioxide, the greenhouse gas responsible for two-thirds of human-induced changes in the world's climate. Atmospheric concentrations of carbon dioxide in 1997 reached 363.6 parts per million, the highest concentration in over 160,000 years.[29] Carbon dioxide concentrations are expected to double over the course of the next century, triggering potentially devastating climatic changes on a regional and global scale. By 2100, sea levels may rise by up to one meter, inundating vast swaths of coastal land, while average surface temperatures may increase by up to 3.5 degrees Celsius.

Destabilization of the Earth's climate engine is expected to result in more intense heat waves, more severe droughts and floods, more devastating storms (tornadoes and hurricanes), and more frequent forest fires. This could have dramatic short-term results: the six months of extensive forest fires in Asia in 1997 and 1998 released more carbon into the atmosphere than Western Europe emits in an entire year.

The Ocean Planet in Decline

Life on Earth first evolved in the primordial soup of ancient seas some 3.5 billion years ago. The world ocean covers 360 million square kilometres, 70 per cent of the Earth's surface. This gigantic body of water, which wraps around the planet like an insulating blanket, literally makes life possible. The oceans are the engines that drive the world's climate, defining weather and storing huge quantities of solar energy in the process. Oceans are also the liquid heart of the Earth's hydrological cycle, which causes roughly 430,000 cubic kilometres of water to evaporate from the oceans every year.

But even this vast, watery world is coming under increasing pressure from human activities. Just over half of humanity, some 3.2 billion people, live and work within 200 kilometres (120 miles) of a seacoast, on just 10 per cent of the Earth's land area. A full two-thirds of the world's population are found within 400 kilometres of a coast.[30]

Mounting population and development pressures have taken a grim toll of coastal and ocean resources. Consider the following trends:

- The world has lost half its coastal wetlands, including mangrove swamps and salt marshes. Over the past century, mangrove forests have been decimated: 25 million hectares have been destroyed or grossly degraded.
- Seagrass beds have fared little better. Although no overall estimates of damage are available, these underwater meadows are in retreat near virtually all inhabited coastal areas.
- Coral reefs, the rainforests of the sea, are being pillaged in the name of development. Of the world's 600,000 square kilometres of reef-building corals, we could lose 60 per cent within 40 years. Over 80 per cent of the reefs in Southeast Asia are threatened with destruction.[31]
- Coastal and ocean fisheries are in serious decline. Of the world's 15 major oceanic fisheries, 11 are in decline. The catch of Atlantic cod has dropped 70 per cent since 1970, while bluefin tuna stocks have declined by 80 per cent over the same period.[32]
- Close to 70 per cent of the world's beaches are eroding at rapid rates because of human impacts.

The fivefold growth in seafood consumption since 1950 has pushed many fisheries to the brink and beyond. Between 1991 and 1995, the world's commercial fleets hauled in, on average, 84 million tons of seafood a year. Since seafood provides close to 20 per cent of the world's total animal protein intake — up to 90 per cent in the South Pacific and parts of Southeast Asia — this decline is eroding food security for a number of poor, tropical countries.[33]

One of the biggest threats to the integrity of ocean ecosystems is the tremendous over-capacity of the world's fishing fleets. Currently, 15 million square kilometres of ocean bottom are trawled each year, the marine equivalent of strip mining. Since bottom trawls are indiscriminate harvesters of marine life, the discarded, dead by-catch from these operations constitutes a horrendous waste of potential food. Every year, some 10 pounds of fish and shellfish are discarded for every person on Earth; up to 40 million tons.[34]

National governments, working together through international conventions and other agreements, will have to come to grips with the non-sustainable exploitation of the world's seas. What we need is nothing less than a revolution in the way ocean resources are utilized. Sustainable harvesting must become the norm, not the exception. Hanging in the balance is the world's richest source of "free protein," along with a host of other goods and services that the sea and its myriad creatures provide to humankind. It is time to cease treating this resource as if it were inexhaustible.

Plundering the Planet: Loss of Biodiversity

The current rate of habitat loss and species extinction is unprecedented. We live in a period of the greatest extinction of plant and animal species since the mega-extinctions of the Jurassic Period, some 65 million years ago. It has been estimated that some 50,000 plant and animal species will become extinct every year over the course of the coming decades.[35] The loss of insects and micro-organisms is incalculable. Human-induced habitat loss and the introduction of "exotic" or non-native species, has shoved the percentage of birds, mammals, fish, reptiles, and amphibians threatened with extinction into double digits.

Loss of biodiversity is not limited to wildlife. Since 1900, about three-quarters of the genetic diversity of agricultural crops has been lost, according to FAO estimates, along with half the wild gene pool of domestic animals.[36] Ecosystem destruction is so severe in the tropics that as many as 60,000 plant species, roughly one-quarter of the world's total, could be lost by the year 2025.

Increasing population density and pressure for faster economic development have played large roles in the loss of biological resources. In a study of fifty countries in Asia and Africa, UNFPA found that the loss of natural habitat was greatest in high-density areas and least in low-density areas. In the ten countries that had lost the most habitat (averaging 85 per cent), the average population density was close to 200 people per square kilometre. In the ten countries that had lost the least amount of habitat (averaging 41 per cent), the average population density was just 29 people per square kilometre.[37]

Unfortunately, population growth, coupled with the unsustainable exploitation of natural resources, is savaging prime habitat in some of the most biologically rich countries. This is bad news for the prospects of preserving "biodiversity hotspots"; i.e., ecosystems with a super-abundance of plant and animal species facing the greatest risks of destruction. So far, twenty-four of these hotspots, containing half the planet's land species, have been identified. Countless more remain to be assessed in marine areas, especially coral reefs — the rainforests of the sea — thought to contain up to one million or more species on less than one per cent of the Earth's surface. Five of the six most biologically diverse countries could see more than two-thirds of their original habitat destroyed or grossly degraded by the middle of the next century if current trends continue.[38]

Another growing threat to biodiversity is the introduction of non-native, or exotic species. Hawaii's native fauna and flora, for instance, have been decimated by introduced species. Exotics have been implicated in close to 70 per cent of all fish extinctions in the United States during the past century. Much of the Black Sea's fauna have been exterminated by a combination of over-fishing, pollution, and introduced exotics. The number of commercially valuable fish species in the Black Sea has declined from 26 to 5 in a decade.[39]

Continued population growth and the rising consumption of natural resources ensure that the loss and impoverishment of biodiversity will not only continue but will accelerate.[40]

185

Conclusion

The world is entering a precarious new millennium, filled with mounting dangers but also promising opportunities. We have a window of opportunity to make a real difference in the quality of life for future generations. But policymakers and politicians are going to have to come to grips with the spectre of continued population growth in much of the developing world (except Latin America and parts of Southeast Asia) and continued depletion of natural resources everywhere. In particular, four challenges loom: Continuing the downward trend in population growth, reaching replacement-level fertility as soon as possible; stemming the haemorrhage of biological diversity; reducing non-sustainable consumption patterns; and mitigating the worst effects of global climate change.

References

[1] Lester Brown, Gary Gardner, Brian Halweil, "Beyond Malthus: Sixteen Dimensions of the Population Problem," Worldwatch Paper No. 143, September 1998.

[2] United Nations Department of Public Information, *Changing Our Patterns of Production and Consumption to Save the Global Environment* (Special Session of the General Assembly to Review and Appraise the Implementation of Agenda 21, New York, June 23-27, 1997).

[3] A. Marcoux, *From Linkages to Policy Issues: Population and Environmental Change* (Rome: UNFPA/FAO, 1998).

[4] United Nations Population Fund, *Guidance Note on Population and Environment* (New York: UNFPA, 1998).

[5] United Nations, *Report of the International Forum for the Operational Review and Appraisal of the Implementation of the Programme of Action of the International Conference on Population and Development.* The Hague, 8-12 February 1999 (New York: United Nations, 1999): p. 9.

[6] Philippine Legislator's Committee on Population and Development, *Of all the Planet's Renewable Resources, Fresh Water, People Count* (January 1994): pp. 1-4.

[7] T. Gardner-Outlaw, R. Engelman, *Sustaining Water, Easing Scarcity: A Second Update* (Washington, D.C.: Population Action International, 1997): pp. 2-19.

[8] C. Juma, *The CBD and the Biological Diversity of Inland Waters* (Paris: International Conference of Water and Sustainable Development, March 19-21, 1998): pp. 1-4.

[9] I. A. Shiklomonov, *Assessment of Water Resources and Water Availability in the World* (Stockholm: Stockholm Environmental Institute, 1997): pp. 1-88.

[10] J. Davidson, D. Meyers, M. Chakraborty, *No Time to Waste — Poverty and the Global Environment* (Oxford: Oxfam, 1992).

[11] S. Postel, G. Daily, P. Ehrlich, *Human Appropriation of Renewable Fresh Water,* Science 271 (5250), (1996): pp. 785-788.

[12] World Bank, *Water Resource Management: A World Bank Policy Paper* (Washington, D.C.: World Bank, 1993).

[13] Dirk Bryant, Daniel Nielsen, Laura Tangley, *The Last Frontier Forests: Ecosystems and Economics on the Edge* (Washington, D.C.: World Resources Institute, 1997): pp. 6-40.

[14] Ibid.

[15] Lester Brown et. al., "Beyond Malthus: Sixteen Dimensions of the Population Problem," Worldwatch Paper No. 143, September 1998.

[16] Op. cit.: 12.

[17] Ibid.

[18] Population Coalition for Action, *Conference on Hunger and Poverty: An Overview* (Brussels, November 1995): pp. 2-24.

[19] Food and Agriculture Organization of the United Nations, *FAO Production Yearbook 1995* (Rome: FAO, 1996).

[20] Ibid.

[21] United Nations Population Fund, *Population and Sustainable Development — Five Years After Rio* (New York: UNFPA, 1997): pp. 1-36.

[22] P. Tyler, "Nature and Economic Boom Devouring China's Farmland," *New York Times*, March 27, 1994: pp. 1 & 8.

[23] B. Feder, "Sowing Preservation — Towns Are Slowing Invasion of Farms by Bulldozers," *New York Times*, March 20, 1997: pp. D1 & D19.

[24] Food and Agriculture Organization of the United Nations, *Dimensions of Need: An Atlas of Food and Agriculture* (Rome: FAO, 1995): pp. 16-98.

[25] World Health Organization, *Health and Environment in Sustainable Development — Five Years After the Earth Summit* (Geneva: WHO, 1997).

[26] Ibid.

[27] Lester Brown *et. al.*, "Beyond Malthus: Sixteen Dimensions of the Population Problem," Worldwatch Paper No. 143, September 1998.

[28] Ibid.

[29] Lester Brown *et. al.*, *Vital Signs 1998* (New York: Norton, 1998): pp. 66-67.

[30] Don Hinrichsen, *Coastal Waters of the World: Trends, Threats and Strategies* (Washington, D.C.: Island Press, 1998).

[31] Ibid.

[32] Anne Platt McGinn, "Safeguarding the Health of the Oceans," Worldwatch Paper No. 145, March 1999.

[33] Op. cit.: 29.

[34] Op. cit.: 31 and 29.

[35] United Nations Population Fund, *Population and Sustainable Development — Five Years After Rio* (New York: UNFPA, 1997).

[36] Food and Agriculture Organization of the United Nations, *Dimensions of Need: An Atlas of Food and Agriculture* (Rome: FAO, 1995).

[37] Op. cit.: 34.

[38] John Tuxill, "Losing Strands in the Web of Life: Vertebrate Declines and the Conservation of Biological Diversity," Worldwatch Paper No. 141, May 1998.

[39] Op. cit.: 29.

[40] Ed Ayres, *God's Last Offer* (New York: Four Walls Eight Windows, 1999).

Shaping Population and Development Strategies

M. Nizamuddin

Introduction

Central to the increased willingness and determination of countries and international organizations to address population issues directly has been their increased awareness, not only of the place of population factors in development processes, but also of their relationship to human well-being. Over the past thirty years, the United Nations Population Fund (UNFPA) has played a central role in promoting widespread and systematic consideration of population issues in public policy. The Fund has also made a major contribution to building the know-how — and the data sets — needed to understand how population processes interact with broader development processes and to analyse the complex relationships between human well-being and population trends.

This chapter addresses the full range of policies and programmes that bear directly on population patterns and trends and that guide and strengthen interventions in the broad field of population. While we will consider the impact of deliberate efforts to promote countries' adoption of national population policies, the adoption of formal population policies is but one facet of the much broader process of developing and implementing policies and programmes that guide and support population activities.

First we will recall key features of the situation that prevailed when UNFPA was established. At that time, there was no consensus on the appropriateness, legitimacy or usefulness of adopting and pursuing public population policies and programmes. The phrase "population and development strategies" had not yet been coined, and the term "population policy" was widely seen as a euphemism for antinatalist "family planning" programmes designed to lower population growth rates. In the late 1960s, the justification for adopting population policies and programmes was essentially macro-economic in nature; much of the debate about population issues and population programmes concerned the macro-economic effects of a reduction in the rate of population growth, with advocates of population programmes envisaging substantial gains in per capita incomes.

The next part of this chapter reviews UNFPA's response to deliberate efforts by governments to influence demographic behaviour and population trends. We will explore, in particular, how and why certain methods and approaches adopted by UNFPA responded to the situation that prevailed in the 1970s and 1980s, and review the ways that UNFPA's approach to what is now termed "population and development strategies" evolved over time in response to changes at the country

The author acknowledges the invaluable contributions of Stan Bernstein, John Herzog, and Ann Pawliczko.

level in each country's needs and constraints. We go on to comment on the extent of success that has been achieved in modifying attitudes and practices in population and development strategies (PDS).

The chapter concludes by identifying the key strategic challenges UNFPA faces at the onset of the twenty-first century. We also examine the ways in which UNFPA can respond to the challenge of unmet needs and help countries deal effectively with population issues and promote both development and human well-being.

The focus of population and development activities that UNFPA and other organizations have supported in the past was determined largely by the conditions that then prevailed. A brief overview of the assumptions about the nature of population trends and their social and economic impact, and of the interrelationship between population and development, will enhance our understanding of the needs and constraints that prevailed in the past and the changing focus of population activities. Indeed, over the past three decades, remarkable changes have taken place in perceptions of population/development relationships and their implications. These changes are reflected in the terms and phrases used to discuss population issues. Whereas in the past there was much discussion of "population growth," "family planning," "development planning," and "technical assistance projects," emphasis is now placed on "reproductive health," "stakeholders," and "well-being."

The Population and Development Policy and Programme Environment in the 1970s

When UNFPA joined the population field in 1969, there was little appreciation of the importance of population factors for well-being. Understanding the linkages between population, socio-economic development, and the environment was limited. Few countries had population policies. The population literature of the time focused on "the great debate" on population versus development. In such discussions, "development" referred broadly to efforts to improve the quality of life, but initially this was equated primarily with improving the economic aspect of life; i.e., economic development. At the centre of this debate was the question of whether, for the present and future good of the human race, the rapid rates of population growth prevalent at the time needed to be curbed, and, if so, how that should be accomplished through deliberate action, primarily by governments.

Those who were on the population side of the debate were concerned with the population problem and advocated the public provision of family planning information and services to control the fertility of interested couples and thus reduce growth rates throughout the world, especially in developing countries. Proponents of the development argument were primarily interested in development, not population, and believed that the best way to curb population growth was through economic development. To them, the basic problem was the reduction of poverty — the best contraceptive was development. The debate on population growth and macro-economic development has been going on for decades, with no clear agreement among economists on just how detrimental rapid population growth is to development.

The debate did, however, produce a more nuanced understanding in which the potential for rapid economic growth is now seen as related to the pace, not of population growth, but the relative growth of different age groups (and particularly of working age populations compared to the very young and the elderly) under changing rates of fertility and mortality.

190

When UNFPA joined the population scene, intervention in population was still controversial, and few countries considered population policy to be an integral part of their development strategy. Indeed, few countries thought it proper for governments to become involved in decisions about family size. Population concerns were at the bottom of the agendas of most countries and international organizations.

Demography emerged as a field of public policy after the 1974 World Population Conference (WPC). After the worldwide attention to population issues in Bucharest, UNFPA began to receive increasing numbers of requests for assistance in addressing concerns that many governments considered sensitive. As governments became more aware of the implications of demographic trends for the realization of development objectives, they were increasingly interested in establishing mechanisms to take such interactions into account. They turned to UNFPA for guidance and support to create and operationalize such mechanisms. UNFPA was ready to meet the challenge.

Influencing Demographic Behaviour Through Population Programmes

The case for population policies and programmes, as well as for supporting measures such as data collection, training, and institution-building, hinges on their capacity to affect demographic behaviour and trends in a predictable way. Indeed, it is important that at the time UNFPA was established, discussion of population policy issues was largely limited to advancing arguments for and against measures to discourage or delay childbearing. However, relatively few governments had adopted explicit policies on fertility or had implemented measures that deliberately encouraged or discouraged childbearing. On the other hand, it is possible that some widespread policies, such as those that discouraged extra-marital fertility or regulated marriage, reflected the will to modify fertility behaviour. In any event, relatively recent improvements in contraceptive technology almost certainly increased the scope for adopting and implementing policies and programmes that would significantly modify fertility behaviour and trends.

The extent to which voluntary family planning programmes — and, more broadly, programmes to make available more and better reproductive health services and information — have led to or accelerated declines in fertility remains the subject of much discussion and debate. In practice, even with the use of sophisticated statistical methods it is difficult to separate out the effects of a "family planning programme" from the effects of numerous concomitant development programmes and continuing socio-economic change. Broadly speaking, relatively few specialists would claim either that voluntary family planning programmes alone can induce and sustain fertility declines or that well-designed and well-managed family planning programmes have no impact on fertility levels and trends. Even if programmes alone do not create the desire for smaller families, however, they do provide the means to implement them.

Moreover, while recent discussions of reproductive health policies place much emphasis on human rights, gender equity, and the concerns of special groups, there have been many proposals to try to alter fertility behaviour by sanctioning couples who have many children and rewarding those who have few. For instance, some proponents of strong measures to discourage large families have called, for example, for limiting the frequency and duration of maternity leave and for making school fees depend on the size of the family. Severely sanctioning extra-marital fertility and trying to

191

humiliate couples who have one child after another are some of the harsher measures for discouraging early, frequent, and late childbearing.

A very different approach to bringing about declines in fertility puts the emphasis on creating conditions propitious to changes in fertility behaviour. At the time UNFPA was established, many argued that reducing infant mortality and improving access to education would foster declines in fertility. More recently, the emphasis has been on reducing gender disparities, empowering women, and promoting a rights-based approach to fertility decisions.

For a long time, governments adopted laws and regulations to reduce mortality and morbidity, ranging from regulations concerning housing, sanitation, and public health to efforts to improve standards of medical services, prevent famine, and ensure industrial safety.*

The situation with respect to migration is more ambiguous, especially as some of the measures adopted by governments prohibit or oblige persons to migrate, while other measures rely mainly on incentives or inducements. On one hand, most states restrict international migration, and many states have attempted to restrict internal migration, sometimes in connection with rules requiring families and individuals to be registered in a particular place. Moreover, a number of states have, at one time or another, adopted policies and programmes of forced migrations; while political or military motives may be paramount, such policies may aim at shifting population from areas considered heavily populated to areas considered lightly populated in relation to their economic potential.

On the other hand, despite widespread concern about the consequences of rapid urbanization, the "brain drain," and the rural exodus, and despite measures to reduce disparities that give rise to migration, on the whole most countries have not undertaken aggressive or sweeping policies and programmes to prevent or promote migration flows. Presumably the governments of many countries recognize — implicitly or explicitly — that because migration trends and patterns are shaped by fundamental economic, social, and political factors and that because the scope for modifying those factors is relatively small, there are limits to the impact of population policies and programmes on migratory flows. For instance, as long as residents of urban areas enjoy higher real incomes, better services, and more opportunities than residents of rural areas, reducing the "rural exodus" may prove very difficult.

It seems fair to say that thirty years ago, opinions regarding the ability of deliberate population policies and programmes to influence demographic behaviour and trends ranged widely. Proponents of "family planning programmes" and government policies to reduce population growth believed that modern methods of communication, economic pressures, and the availability of improved contraceptive methods meant that there was considerable scope for "engineering" substantial declines in fertility. At that time, many policymakers and development specialists counted on "development planning" to ensure the effective use of domestic and international resources, and many commentators felt that the demographic transition was under way in most of the world's "underdeveloped countries" and would continue until both fertility and mortality had fallen to relatively low levels.

The thesis that population programmes could change demographic behaviour and, especially, bring about or significantly accelerate declines in fertility was hotly contested by many groups. Many analysts stressed the strength and ubiquity of socio-cultural values that underpinned childbearing in

*Certain policies may have been adopted to prevent some individuals from engaging in practices that threatened the well-being of other individuals. However, some health, famine prevention, and sanitation policies appear to aim at reducing morbidity and mortality in society as a whole.

192

developing countries. It was often argued that in the absence of higher levels of education and sustained economic development, fertility would remain high. The phrase "development is the best Pill" was widely repeated, and calls for campaigns to change values and attitudes were decried as social engineering. Moreover, errors in the design of some early population policies and programmes attracted much attention and ridicule.

There are some who object to policies intended to alter demographic behaviour on ethical or moral grounds. For instance, some groups and individuals argue that governments have no right to modify individual behaviour by imposing life-protecting practices such as banning dangerous drinks, requiring vaccinations, or making the use of seat belts mandatory. Moral and ethical considerations are often stressed in connection with policies intended to increase or reduce fertility. Naturally, much depends on the type of policies considered: while relatively few would object to policies that aim at making prospective parents aware of their responsibilities as parents, most would object to policies that put intense pressure on unmarried women to agree to induced abortion. Consensus is not so wide regarding setting a legal age for marriage and there is even less agreement on a legal age for sexual activity. Restrictions on migration are often said to be discriminatory and unfair, while programmes of forced migration are generally deemed incompatible with human rights and human dignity.

At the time UNFPA was established, numerous objections were raised to government programmes designed to induce poor people to have fewer children and thereby accelerate development. While proponents of strong government policies maintained that all sections of the population would benefit from the anticipated acceleration of development, opponents claimed that "birth control" policies put great pressure on poor people to limit the size of their families, but that those families might not benefit significantly from any increase in the rate of economic growth or development. Indeed, their situation might deteriorate, as they might lose their most important resource. Moreover, scant attention was paid to issues of well-being and gender equity and empowerment at this time. The focus was on the pace and nature of development, and some objections to the principle of national population programmes reflected reluctance to call for changes in attitudes and behaviour at the micro level in the hopes of facilitating gains at the macro level.

Impact of Population on Development

The impact of population on development, especially the impact of an induced change in fertility, has long been the object of intense debate. At the time UNFPA was established, the thesis that a reduction in fertility would ensure more rapid economic development was hotly contested. On one hand, advocates of antinatalist policies used relatively simple macro-economic models to argue, *inter alia*, that lower rates of population growth would mean greater investment per capita and rising per capita incomes. On the other hand, opponents of such policies argued that reductions in the rate of population growth would not necessarily result in increases in per capita incomes. Not only did they refer to the advantages of economies of scale and the tendency for population pressure to stimulate innovation and technical progress, but they also questioned whether in practice the pace and nature of development was largely determined by macro-economic variables. These analysts argued that the pace of development depended on such factors as access to markets, to capital, and to technical know-how; the prices of the goods and services exported by developing countries; and the proportion of a country's national income used for the purchase of arms or luxury consumer goods, for prestigious buildings or activities, or for private transfers to foreign bank accounts. A fairly common assertion was that rich countries were promoting antinatalist policies in order to protect or enhance their ascendancy.

Commitment to Implement Effective Population Policies

Even if in a given country it is widely acknowledged that population policies and programmes can influence demographic trends and can thereby contribute to development and well-being, there is still a need for the government (and for non-governmental organizations (NGOs) and international agencies) to translate that acknowledgement into effective population policies and programmes. One indicator of the strength of commitment to addressing population issues is the level of support for building national capacity in areas crucial to formulating and implementing appropriate population policies and programmes. These areas include:

•   Collection, analysis, and dissemination of demographic, reproductive health, and socio-economic data;
•   Analysis of gender-related disparities, discrimination, and issues;
•   Training in, and support for, methods for programme planning, management, and evaluation; and mobilizing the inputs of communities and individuals, particularly of women; and
•   Structures to coordinate population activities, to mobilize resources, and to formulate and monitor population policies and programmes.

Since "national capacity" includes the capacity of NGOs (as well as of the private sector), consideration should not be limited to public-sector capacity-building activities.

Another indicator of the extent of a country's commitment to population issues and programmes is the number and content of statements by political and community leaders. If leaders recognize the importance of population issues but hesitate to speak out, their awareness may not be translated into effective policies and programmes. A related indicator is the existence of effective mechanisms for population advocacy. In most cases, there is a need for channels and methods for increasing the number and range of people who are well informed about population and development issues.

Broadly speaking, there is rather limited evidence that at the time UNFPA was established numerous governments were strongly committed to addressing population issues effectively. For instance, not many countries had established national population councils or commissions. Other than decennial censuses, the collection and analysis of population data was not a priority for most governments. The leaders of many, perhaps most, developing countries avoided making firm public statements about population issues. Expressions of strong support for policies and programmes to reduce population growth were seen as endorsements of the "capitalist" approach to development, and most leaders of developing countries preferred to avoid aligning themselves on the positions of one of the two great politico-economic blocs of the time.

Even so, a number of developing countries were, in fact, taking some steps to build foundations for addressing population issues. For instance, training in demography and related

194

subjects was being strengthened, and KAP surveys — surveys of (family planning) "knowledge, attitudes and practices" — were becoming increasingly common. Skills and experience in providing family planning information and services were increasing, and in many countries, one or more NGOs were offering limited family planning services in at least one large city.

UNFPA's Role

The situation that prevailed three decades ago makes it clear that promoting the adoption and implementation of population policies and programmes was an enormous challenge for the newly established United Nations Fund for Population Activities. While small numbers of academics, development specialists, and community leaders were calling for vigorous measures to reduce population growth (since that was expected to accelerate development), in developing countries only a comparatively small number of individuals were convinced that population policies and programmes would alter fertility behaviour and trends and would thereby make a significant contribution to the pace and structure of development. Indeed, in some quarters, there were strong objections to trying to change fertility attitudes and behaviour at all, and few governments or national leaders were inclined to endorse strong measures to bring about changes in fertility behaviour. Moreover, while a few groups saw adoption of policies and programmes to "control fertility" as the key to socio-economic development, others saw repeated calls to drive down fertility as attempts to prevent developing countries from rivalling the rich countries in power and progress.

One of UNFPA's crucial roles from the very beginning was to assist countries in integrating population concerns into national development strategies, including national policies, plans, and programmes. The Fund was well aware that partial solutions would not solve problems and could, in fact, exacerbate them. Thus, in order to solve population problems, the answer was not to focus solely on family planning activities to the exclusion of other programmes, but to seek solutions that looked at all of the parts in their total context. It is this broader view of population within the context of development that the Fund has been advocating since its inception. According to its first Executive Director, Rafael M. Salas, "UNFPA, from its very beginnings, never considered population programming as an investment for fertility control alone or as an end in itself but always considered it as one of the elements of the development strategy depending upon the special needs and circumstances prevailing in a particular country."[1] The policy of the Fund was clear: "The integration of population programmes with specific aspects of the development strategy can lead not only to an increase in general welfare but can also have a beneficial impact on population trends."[2]

It became clear that policies for moderating fertility and population growth alone could not solve the problems of development; however, population policies, in conjunction with an intensified development effort, could make a significant contribution to solving development problems. As a result, UNFPA's position was that policies and programmes designed to influence population trends, composition, and distribution should go hand in hand with development policies.

UNFPA's response to the need to further the formulation and implementation of population policies and programmes was multifaceted, and it has evolved over time. The following review of UNFPA's response to the need for conducive and supportive policies focuses on three key features of that response:

- UNFPA provided support for population activities and programmes at various levels of political organization, including, notably, programmes and activities at the global level, at regional and subregional levels, at the country level, and to a lesser extent, at subnational and community levels.

- UNFPA provided substantial and varied support for activities that helped build the foundations for a broad consensus on population issues and for planning and implementing effective population programmes.

- UNFPA made provisions that the content and form of its support would vary from country to country in light of actual needs and constraints, and also that the content and form of its support would evolve over time in light of changes in priorities and opportunities.

UNFPA's mission in the area of PDS received a broader mandate after the International Conference on Population and Development (ICPD) in 1994, which underscored the integral and mutually reinforcing links between population and development, and recommended a set of objectives as well as qualitative and quantitative goals to be attained over a twenty-year period. These included the reduction of infant, child, and maternal mortality; the provision of universal access to education, particularly for girls; and the provision of universal access to a full range of reproductive health care and family planning services.[3]

UNFPA Support for Population Activities at Different Levels

While it is mainly at the national level that population policies and programmes are adopted and implemented, UNFPA support for population activities and programmes at various levels of political organization (from the global level to subnational and community levels) helped create the environment, the broad consensus, and the momentum necessary for the adoption and implementation of national policies and programmes.

Despite their oft-discussed limitations, international and regional conferences have helped create, at all levels, the common ground that has facilitated discussing population issues in a systematic matter and identifying and implementing effective programmes. UNFPA support for global and regional conferences and associated research activities has contributed significantly to efforts to hammer out common positions and declarations on population issues and has thereby helped to foster the emergence of a consensus, not only on the interrelation between population and development, but also on policies and programmes to address population issues. Indeed, international and regional conferences appear to have facilitated the introduction of new or revised ideas and approaches and more effective collaboration.

Regional institutions have played a key role in moderating marked differences between countries in the same region. For instance, in Africa, the Organization of African Unity (OAU), together with the Economic Commission for Africa (ECA), helped narrow the gap between countries that questioned the usefulness of family planning policies and programmes and countries that had already adopted family planning policies.

It is, of course, primarily at the national level that population policies and programmes are adopted and that UNFPA efforts have been concentrated. Initially, the emphasis was on addressing those responsible for national development planning, a reflection of the then-prevailing confidence in "development planning" as the overall tool for bringing about development, but the Fund's scope has broadened gradually and now extends to many groups and many issues.

Of particular significance has been UNFPA support for programmes and activities at the national level that deal with the interrelationships between population factors and specific sectoral (or thematic) policies and programmes, such as those in the areas of education, employment, environmental management, human resources development, macro-economic planning, gender, agriculture, and regional planning. Moreover, sustained efforts to encourage and support discussion of a wider range of population and reproductive health issues — from censuses to HIV/AIDS, and from rural — urban migration to very early marriage — has helped increase the range of political and community leaders and intellectuals, including parliamentarians, government officials, business leaders and technicians, who participate in discussions of population and reproductive health matters. This expansion at the national level in the number and variety of politically acceptable population and development activities has contributed substantially to changes in the perception of population issues.

Only rarely has UNFPA become directly involved in activities at subnational levels to strengthen support for the adoption of population policies and programmes. However, many UNFPA-assisted national projects and programmes have specifically provided for the implementation of activities at provincial, district, and community levels. These activities probably did not reach a large proportion of the population of a country, but they seem to have contributed significantly to improved understanding of the diversity and severity of population issues and problems at subnational levels and the understanding of factors favouring and impeding changes in demographic behaviour.

Foundations for Consensus and for Effective Interventions

Another important feature of UNFPA's response to the difficult "policy-making" environment that prevailed at the time of its establishment was building the basis for a more balanced, more operational, and more effective approach to population issues. UNFPA's approach put the emphasis on data collection and dissemination, promoting population and development analysis, and providing training in population and development. The Fund's support for strengthening a large number of national, regional, and international organizations may also have contributed to building the foundation for designing and implementing more appropriate population policies and programmes. However, the durability of the effects of these institution-building activities has still to be tested.

Data collection and dissemination

UNFPA-supported data collection and dissemination activities have made a very important contribution to stimulating interest in population processes and to understanding their consequences. In many countries, most notably in Africa, UNFPA support for national population censuses not only increased interest in the size, growth, and composition of the population, but also led directly and indirectly to gradual strengthening of skills in analysing population trends and in determining their main consequences. Countries that planned and undertook population censuses became acutely aware that they lacked the expertise needed to take account of ongoing population changes or to

197

forecast future changes in population trends and their consequences. There was also increasing recognition of the importance of being selective in collecting and processing information. Increased emphasis on collecting the information that was most needed and seeing that it was processed and made available quickly contributed to the interest in establishing databases and management information systems (MIS).

At the same time, the empirical information that became available enabled African researchers and policymakers to see more clearly the outlines of population problems. For instance, evidence appeared that fertility levels were relatively lower and were declining among more highly educated groups; that many couples who did not want to have a child in the short-term were not using any method of family planning; that many young women began childbearing before they were fully mature; and that rates of maternal mortality were extremely high. Censuses and surveys in East Asia, however, showed that many couples were adopting family planning methods and using them effectively to lower fertility.

Although having improved information did not result at once in changes in attitudes and policies, it certainly contributed to the spread of more even-handed views of population policies. Analysts observed that fertility had remained high in some countries whose governments had endorsed strong population policies, but they also saw that, in some countries, relatively large numbers of people had begun to obtain and use methods of contraception. Indeed, wide use of contraceptives was also observed in many countries and cultures whose traditional values had been considered insurmountable barriers to a rapid decline in fertility. However, the data did not show unambiguously that marked declines in fertility — and, hence, a decline in population growth — spurred gains in per capita income.

Research supported by UNFPA helped to throw light on the causes and consequences of population trends. Although many studies drew attention to the importance of such determinants of levels and patterns of fertility as gender disparities, the level of education of the parents, and the social and economic usefulness of children, findings did not suggest that implementation of large-scale family planning programmes would soon or "automatically" result in significant improvements in reproductive health and sizeable declines in levels of childbearing and fertility.

More systematic and more comprehensive studies of the interrelationship between changes in demographic trends and the pace and characteristics of economic development showed that the economic repercussions of changes in demographic trends could be subtle, numerous, and sustained. For example, declines in fertility led to increased labour force participation rates among women, higher family incomes, and greater economic prosperity. On the other hand, comprehensive studies supported by UNFPA have yielded little unambiguous evidence of strong or universal links between demographic trends and the rate of economic development. For instance, research findings do not lend support to the thesis that, in general, population growth favours innovation and technological progress, or to its converse — that it inhibits such progress. Economic growth is not an end in itself, but a means to the larger objective of improved well-being.

Evidence that high fertility constrains economic growth does not *in itself* provide a rationale for public interventions to reduce fertility, especially if the means to reduce fertility (for example, coercive family planning programmes) compromise the well-being and rights of individuals. However, the growing evidence that high fertility exacerbates poverty and the evidence that among the poor some portion of high fertility is unintended, justifies policies and interventions that can be shown to improve the situation of poor families, including the kind of non-coercive family planning and reproductive health programmes included in the ICPD Programme of Action.

Though research findings did not lend much support to sweeping generalizations about the interrelationships between population and development and the effects of a decline in population growth, they did provide a great deal of evidence about the complex and manifold ways in which a wide range of population variables interacted with socio-economic variables. For instance, research on the benefits and costs to families of having children showed that patterns and levels of fertility and migration could be affected by the perceived returns on "investment" in the education of children, by children's rights to land, and by gender roles and discrimination. Similarly, it became clear that decisions that households and enterprises took regarding investment, savings, allocation of resources, and adoption of new contraceptive methods were influenced by population variables.

While such findings did not support sweeping generalizations about the consequences of population trends, they did help demonstrate that population processes are important, integral components of development processes and strengthened the case for seeing population policies as indispensable components of national development policies. In essence, research showed that population was not an essentially exogenous, narrowly delimited phenomenon that could be dealt with adequately by specialists. Indeed, it was increasingly recognized that population, and reproductive health in particular, should be seen as an integral and important part of development.

UNFPA-supported research apparently contributed to the gradual decline in categorical statements about the causes and consequences of population trends. Another important result of such research was a significant strengthening of the foundations of family planning programmes. Research findings threw much light on the reasons why women (and men) did or did not use family planning.

For instance, analysts came to understand better why in some settings many women and couples who did not want to have children did not use any modern method of family planning. Analysts also came to understand better that couples were not only interested in preventing pregnancies and having fewer children: they were also concerned about the number of children they would have — and, in particular, the number of boys; about their own health and the health of their children; about the attitudes of community members and health service providers; about costs; and about long-term economic security. Indeed, research showing that many potential users of family planning methods and many health-service providers preferred an integrated approach — that is, one providing for family planning information and services to be provided within the framework of general family health services and, more specifically, mother and child health services — may have contributed to the adoption of the reproductive health approach.

Research on the causes, consequences, and correlates of reproductive health (and ill health), supported by significant improvements in data collection and analysis, has undoubtedly led to improvements in policies and programmes for delivery of reproductive health information and services. What may be less apparent, but just as important, is that such research has made clear the multiple, diverse, and intense links between "reproductive health" and "development." To a significant extent, research conducted at both "micro" and "macro" levels on the determinants and consequences of reproductive health indicates that, in many countries, poor reproductive health cannot be disassociated from inadequate socio-economic development. We must work toward conditions that promote person-centred development and the development of public, private, and community means to provide access to information and services. Reproductive choice and the exercise of reproductive rights must be seen, promoted, and advanced in a full social context.

Training

Over the past three decades, the population and development activities supported by UNFPA have put considerable emphasis on training, where "training" has often included a significant component of awareness-creation. Training activities have often been justified on the grounds that they build the capacity of national institutions. Much emphasis has been given, for example, to training planners in the methods of integrating demographic variables in planning; to creating skills in analysing demographic data; to building the expertise needed to mainstream gender concerns; to training in methods of programme formulation, implementation, monitoring, and evaluation; to training of trainers; and to the development of training materials and software. Emphasis has also been placed on enhancing efficiency and facilitating the transfer of technologies to promote national "ownership" of programmes.

Although the importance of training nationals has not been challenged, there has been some criticism of actual training activities. Among the concerns expressed are that public-sector workers constitute an excessively large proportion of the beneficiaries of training programmes; that due to high rates of staff turnover in the public sector, many of those trained have little opportunity to put to use the skills and knowledge they acquired; that material benefits of participating in training programmes may result in some individuals' attending more courses and workshops than is necessary; and that, in many cases, the equipment, structures, data, or attitudes needed to put to use newly acquired skills and information are non-existent. Some observers point out that, despite considerable UNFPA support for training programmes over many years, many population institutions do not seem any better staffed than they were one or two decades ago.

While it is difficult to assess the indirect or diffuse effects of training, there are many indications of a gradual accumulation of awareness and understanding of the interrelationships between population and development and their policy implications. From early marriage to the rural exodus, from population ageing to urban unemployment, and pressure on agricultural land, numerous facets of these interrelationships are often mentioned by a wide range of policymakers, officials, development specialists, and community leaders. Although understanding of population issues remains insufficient in many respects, there has been a quiet revolution in the knowledge of population/development interrelationships.

Differentiated and Evolving Response to the Needs of Countries

The specific objectives and strategies of UNFPA-supported country programmes have differed from country to country and have evolved over time. To assess UNFPA's contribution to facilitating and promoting the adoption of appropriate and effective population policies and programmes, it is useful to focus attention on ways that country programmes have differed — both over time and from country to country.

UNFPA's approach has been to be as flexible as possible within the broad framework of the ICPD Programme of Action. The Fund has ably tailored its activities to national capacities, while seeking to broaden them. It also focused on priorities in addressing a country's needs while recognizing the need to adapt measures to reach common goals. A significant feature of UNFPA's response to widely divergent and strongly held views on the need for population policies and programmes was to identify priorities and strategies that corresponded to conditions and perspectives at the country level and to ensure that there was scope for those priorities and strategies to evolve over time. From the very beginning, the Fund adhered to three fundamental principles — neutrality, flexibility, and innovation — that have made its universally acceptable to governments of both developing and developed countries as well as to NGOs. It has operated on the basic assumption that the United Nations system does not prescribe any population policy to any country and acts only when a country requests assistance. The Fund's work was also grounded in the belief that population programmes are not substitutes for economic development efforts but are necessary complements to them.[4]

Whereas some UNFPA-supported country programmes emphasized family planning and, subsequently, reproductive health, others gave priority to activities that created or strengthened the foundations for population policies and programmes. These included activities in such areas as data collection and analysis, research on the determinants and consequences of population trends, and integration of population variables into development planning.

Over time, there have been certain changes in the focus and methods of UNFPA-assisted activities that have been evident at the global level. Among the most significant of these changes has been placing the focus on the set of needs, issues, and interventions now brought together under the term "reproductive health." Although priorities and strategies differ markedly from country to country, there has been a clear shift towards supporting analyses and interventions that are expected to result in substantial improvements in the reproductive health of the country's population. Over the past three decades, UNFPA's support for population policies and programmes has come to put far more emphasis on improving the situation and status of women and on responding to gender concerns and disparities. The Fund's support has been based on the assumption that accelerating development and enabling reproductive choice depends on fuller and mutually supportive partnerships between women and men. In many cases, UNFPA has been in the forefront of the struggle to mainstream gender concerns so that they are addressed as part-and-parcel, not only of population policies and programmes, but of all other development policies and programmes as well.

Of particular interest has been the steady but silent shift from emphasis on "development planning" and various types of sectoral and spatial planning (including human resources planning, agricultural planning, health planning, and regional planning) to an emphasis on broad themes and areas of particular concern. Among the themes and issues attention has been focused on are gender, environment, structural adjustment, human rights, and (more recently) poverty eradication, good governance, and conflict avoidance and conflict resolution. Since the ICPD, the focus of population activities has been to meet the needs of individual women and men rather than simply trying to meet demographic targets. The concept of "development" has been broadened to include strategies of sustained economic growth, long-term sustainability in production and consumption, and a more integrated approach to population and environmental concerns.

Surely one of the most extraordinary changes over the past decades has been the enormous increase in the willingness and readiness of governments to consider explicit policies and programmes that address sensitive aspects of reproductive health — from early marriage, induced abortions, and sexual and reproductive health of adolescents, to contraceptives, sexual activity, sexually transmitted diseases (STDs), and gender disparities. Although it has long been possible to raise most of these issues in some countries and although it is still not possible to raise them in others, the overall picture is one of far greater openness.

UNFPA has been sensitive to differences between countries and has taken account of changes over time in readiness to discuss openly sensitive issues and to address them explicitly. In some countries, UNFPA initially adopted a very careful — indeed, timid — approach to many reproductive health issues. Such problems as adolescent sexual activity, abortion, gender violence, male attitudes and behaviour, STDs, female genital mutilation (FGM), very early marriage, and high levels of maternal mortality and morbidity were avoided or only raised indirectly and discreetly. In other countries, UNFPA adopted a bolder approach, both by drawing attention to serious problems and by inviting leaders and specialists to consider possible solutions. Broadly speaking, with respect to raising sensitive issues and calling for the adoption of appropriate policies and programmes, UNFPA has been in the forefront of organizations and agencies; in fact, in many cases, UNFPA has been called upon to encourage and assist regional and international agencies to adopt a less timid approach.

Differences between countries and over time are also pronounced in their support for capacity building. Broadly speaking, as a nation's capacity in the field of population and reproductive health has grown, UNFPA has increasingly focused "capacity-building" efforts in areas that are critical to designing and implementing operational policies and programmes. Examples include assistance in such areas as logistics; construction, maintenance and use of databases and MIS; operational research; formation of coalitions; collaboration with NGOs and community-based organizations (CBOs); quality of services; methods of programming and management; and training strategies and methods. Assistance in such areas is generally expected to facilitate improvements in programme management and to increase efficiency.

Capacity-building has also been facilitated by changes in the way assistance is provided. For instance, the introduction of Country Support Teams (CSTs) has made it possible to reduce the use of expatriate Chief Technical Advisers (CTAs) in the design and management of UNFPA-supported activities. Higher priority has been given to capacity-building in programme management and efficiency and to building systems for monitoring and evaluation.

UNFPA has been moving towards results-based management by setting clear and focused programme priority areas and developing appropriate indicators to demonstrate the results achieved and to ensure that resources are used in the most effective and efficient way. Results-based management seeks to improve programme and management effectiveness and accountability by involving key stakeholders in defining expected results, monitoring progress towards achievement of those results, integrating lessons learned in programmes and management decisions, and reporting on performance.

Initially, in most countries, UNFPA support was concentrated at the national level, with projects and activities being designed and undertaken centrally by national institutions. However, as more central governments recognize the advantages of decentralized structures, UNFPA support is increasingly reaching institutions at the provincial, district, or even community levels. Similarly, while the extent of NGO participation in programme design and implementation varies considerably — reflecting differences not only in government policies and priorities but also in the capacities of NGOs to plan and manage population programmes — there is a tendency to enhance the role of NGOs in programme development, implementation, and evaluation.

It is also significant that over the past three decades, UNFPA has made substantial changes in the allocation of its funds between countries and between sectors. Countries are categorized in three groups according to their needs for specific types of assistance and their progress towards implementing the ICPD Programme of Action, based on seven ICPD indicators concerning reproductive health, mortality reduction, and universal primary education. UNFPA support is concentrated on Group A countries, those that are farthest from achieving ICPD goals and have the lowest levels of development. These countries have the greatest need for external assistance and the lowest capabilities for generating domestic resources. Group B and C countries, which have made more progress towards achieving ICPD goals and have higher levels of development, receive proportionately less UNFPA support. The funds made available to countries with especially low levels of health and socio-economic development have increased considerably, and a larger proportion of those funds are being allocated to efforts for activities intended to bring about improvements in reproductive health.

There have been many and varied reasons for the changes over time in the focus and methods of UNFPA-assisted activities. Major shifts in the international situation have led to far-reaching changes in development policies and strategies. With the end of the Cold War and the associated rivalry between the capitalist and socialist blocs, virtually all countries began to count on the private sector for economic expansion. In many countries, development strategies based on development planning have evolved into strategies based on macro-economic policies, market forces, deregulation, and investment incentives. Governments have come to place more importance on costs, efficacy and high-quality human resources. In many countries, there is increased concern that the government will not be able to provide adequate education and health services. There are also concerns that, on the whole, the productivity of labour in the public sector and in the informal sector is low and might be further reduced by large flows of school-leavers into the labour market.

Other far-reaching changes in the policy environment have included widespread adoption of rigorous programmes of structural adjustment; greatly increased awareness of gender disparities and their consequences; concern over the pace and consequences of environmental degradation; measures to reform the United Nations system; decentralization of government in many countries, often extending to systems for planning and implementing development activities; increased emphasis on establishing databases and MIS; and increased commitment to systematic monitoring and evaluation of development activities. The emergence of sector-wide approaches (SWAPs) signals a willingness by the international donor community and governments to enter into new partnerships that will facilitate better aid coordination at the sectoral level instead of relying on the fragmented project approach. Although UNFPA experience with SWAPs is still limited, the Fund recognizes the opportunities afforded by this modality to reduce aid fragmentation, improve coordination, strengthen national institutional capacity, and enhance the effectiveness of public sector expenditures.

Substantial changes over time in the focus and methods of UNFPA-supported programmes were also the consequence of significant changes in the adoption and implementation of population policies and programmes. These changes, many of which were brought about, partly or entirely, by previous UNFPA-supported activities, included large gains in information about and understanding of population trends; greater interest in determinants and consequences of demographic behaviour at the micro level; increased recognition of the human and developmental costs of reproductive ill health; growing concern about the consequences of the spread of HIV and AIDS; greater receptivity to considering the gender dimensions of reproductive health and population dynamics; greater willingness to address sensitive reproductive health issues; and increased awareness of the extent and complexity of interaction between population phenomena and development processes.

In essence, at the country level, perceptions of population policies have been evolving rapidly, and leaders of countries in which family planning programmes had often been described as unnecessary or irrelevant have begun to draw attention to the benefits of family planning and to the need for programmes.

Changes in the priorities and methods of UNFPA-supported programmes have also been made in response to changes at the operational level. Despite constraints and setbacks, countries have gradually acquired much of the experience and expertise needed to assume responsibility for the design and implementation of population programmes. Mechanisms for reporting and accounting have been developed and improved (although many databases and MIS failed to live up to expectations). Population and reproductive health activities have been planned and implemented within the framework of broader development programmes. Mechanisms for coordination of population activities at the country level have been established, and, although the results were sometimes disappointing, some progress was made towards avoiding duplication or fragmentation of efforts. More provision has been made for involving stakeholders in the design and implementation of policies and programmes, and the importance of finding and working with appropriate partners was increasingly recognized. In many countries, marked changes have occurred in the roles of NGOs and the private sector. Social marketing appeared and has come to play a major role in the distribution of contraceptives, especially condoms. In many countries, NGOs have taken on the daunting tasks of persuading adolescents to avoid high-risk sexual activity, of coping with the consequences of septic abortions, and of making clear the consequences of unsafe sex.

Conclusion

In reflecting on the past three decades, UNFPA can point to numerous success stories throughout the world. The Fund has been instrumental in bringing about major changes in attitudes and policies in the area of population and development in many countries. Considerable progress has been made. But so much more remains to be done. Many challenges were encountered and a wealth of lessons have been learnt. In the process, UNFPA has gained much valuable experience. It is ready to meet the challenges that lie ahead.

Lessons Learnt and Their Implications

A great many lessons have been learnt over the past three decades. Building on past experience and lessons learnt is essential to developing effective and appropriate strategies for the future. The following discussion is limited to seven lessons whose implications appear to be particularly significant.

There are substantial advantages to working at several levels. This holds true from global consultations down to subnational discussions and interventions. However, careful planning is needed if the potential benefits of the complementarity of activities at different levels are to be realized. It cannot be assumed that the mix that was appropriate in the past will be appropriate in the future. That is not to imply that increased capacity at the national level to formulate and implement population policies reduces the need for regional and global activities. Indeed, the scope for — and benefits of — global and regional collaboration may actually be greater where and when countries enjoy higher levels of expertise and have accumulated more experience.[*]

There are a number of domains in which a multilevel approach appears especially advantageous:

- UNFPA will almost certainly choose to adopt a "multi-tiered" approach in responding to the HIV/AIDS epidemic. Whereas international and regional conferences help build awareness and commitment, it is mainly at the national and subnational level that specific activities need to be designed and implemented.
- Another area that calls for a multilevel approach is taking account of the interrelationships between population and the environment. Not only do the repercussions of population/environment interactions often extend across large areas and affect the inhabitants of two or more countries, but their technical complexity is so great that there are major advantages to collaborating in the conduct of the necessary analyses. Moreover, while the effects of many population/environment interactions may be evident at the macro level — f or instance, in the decline in average crop yields, in stress on water resources, or in rising levels of pollution — there is often a need for behavioural change at the micro level. Indeed, policies and programmes often aim to change behaviour at the level of families and of rural communities.
- The case for UNFPA's continuing to pursue a multilevel approach to training is straightforward. On one hand, UNFPA is likely to find that for advanced training, international and multi-country training activities are relatively efficient: such activities may facilitate satisfactory coverage of new topics and information and may prove conducive to maintaining high standards. On the other hand, where it is necessary to train considerable numbers of persons, training activities that are designed and implemented at the national or subnational level may be more efficient, especially as it may be easier to ensure their relevance to local needs and conditions.
- UNFPA is also likely to find that a multilevel approach is well suited to supporting the introduction and use of modern methods of census enumeration, analysis, and dissemination. For instance, regional workshops may be the most suitable mechanism for building capacity in using geographic information systems (GIS) and global positioning systems (GPS) and systems for accessing information on-line, while national or subnational projects may be the most appropriate mechanisms for planning, conducting, and evaluating field operations.

UNFPA experience to date makes clear the importance of adapting priorities and strategies to the needs and constraints of specific countries, and it also demonstrates the need to make provision for priorities and strategies to evolve in response both to changes at the country level and to changes at the global level. The need for such changes may result from the needs and priorities of the country concerned or from a variety of constraints and difficulties that are encountered along the way. This is especially true in addressing issues as diverse as HIV/AIDS, the role of NGOs and the private sector, and the management of large-scale reproductive health programmes. In order to assist

---

[*]Developed countries collaborate extensively in many are as — ranging from methods of technical and vocational education to medical research and from music to meteorology. South-South initiatives such as Partners in Population and Development facilitate technical cooperation between developing countries to advance the implementation of the ICPD Programme of Action.

countries in addressing each of these areas, UNFPA will need to take account of the great differences between countries in terms of needs and resources and to determine for each country the priorities and strategies for its assistance. In addressing such issues as HIV/AIDS, for example, UNFPA must be in a position to make frequent and significant changes in the support that it provides to national programmes.

It is important to maintain a balance between activities to build foundations for long-term gains in national technical and managerial capacity, and action-oriented interventions. Often the two types of activities are complementary. More specifically, it seems likely that it will remain necessary for UNFPA to continue to promote and support both capacity-building activities with long-term objectives and other interventions that have short-term objectives. For instance, UNFPA may decide that even as it promotes research, seeks a wider range of partners, and supports long-term training, it should also continue to support large-scale information and reproductive health activities. The Fund may continue to broaden the information base and identify the subgroups within the population that are most at risk or that are deprived of access to information and services.

In the area of adolescent reproductive health, UNFPA may find that in addition to continuing to assist information, education, and communication (IEC) activities and the development of adolescent-friendly reproductive health services, it also needs to make support available for research on such topics as attitudes conducive to engaging in risky sexual activity; methods for reducing gender bias and stereotypes; and ways of reaching distinct groups, such as out-of-school youth.

Similarly, inasmuch as education of women is closely associated with gains in reproductive health, it is desirable that UNFPA continue to call for efforts to improve women's access to education. That, however, does not rule out strong support for efforts to address directly such immediate problems as unsafe abortion, FGM, the spread of HIV/AIDS, and gaps in the information needed to design and manage effective programmes. Given the human, social, and economic costs of such immediate problems, it would be difficult indeed to recommend to governments that they suspend efforts to address immediate problems and simply wait for thorough studies to be conducted.

Improving the "delivery" of technical and financial assistance for population programmes remains important. Such steps as decentralization of authority to approve projects, creation of CSTs, introduction of the logical framework approach, and expanded use of national execution have made possible substantial improvements in the delivery of technical and financial assistance. Further steps are needed, but it is essential that they be carefully planned and implemented. In the coming years, UNFPA will certainly seek to take advantage of the ongoing reform of the United Nations system. Improved collaboration of United Nations agencies, where each sister agency can capitalize on its comparative advantage, can be expected to reduce costs. The reform also has the potential to facilitate development of programmes and activities that more fully take into account the complex interrelationships among economic, demographic, and social factors.

Maintaining the efficacy of the CSTs will continue to be important. In this perspective, UNFPA may consider providing for CST specialists to undertake missions in conjunction with national consultants; making changes in the composition of the teams; and streamlining contacts between CST specialists and national decision-makers and specialists.

In conjunction with reform of the United Nations system but also in collaboration with other development partners, UNFPA may seek to make greater use of infrastructure, staff, administrative systems, and monitoring and evaluation mechanisms that were not specifically designed and put in place in order to support implementation of UNFPA-assisted activities. In other words, broadening the scope of its activities by addressing several issues at the same time can help UNFPA achieve maximum efficiency. For example, advocacy on population and reproductive health issues can be undertaken within the framework of other advocacy activities, such as those concerned with women, primary health care, or HIV/AIDS prevention.

Experience over many years, in many countries, has demonstrated the importance — as well as the difficulty — of securing the active involvement of a broad range of stakeholders. This is especially true where stakeholders include development institutions not primarily or specifically concerned with population or reproductive health issues. In essence, obtaining the interest and support of diverse stakeholders greatly increases prospects for steady and rapid progress in formulating and implementing population policies and programmes, partly because it becomes easier to overcome resource constraints and to cope with resistance or scepticism.

Despite the importance of securing the support of stakeholders, past experience has also shown that, in many situations, it is tempting to work with a small group of truly dedicated individuals and to neglect efforts to involve a wider range of individuals and groups. Securing the support of a wide range of stakeholders requires not just identifying and taking account of their concerns but also engaging in a real dialogue with them and responding to the concerns and views that they express. In most cases, simply informing stakeholders or soliciting their support is not sufficient. Experience has also shown that the support of stakeholders should never be taken for granted: maintaining a dialogue with real "give-and-take" is essential in avoiding hostile reactions and reversals in support.

Rapid changes at headquarters in priorities, procedures, and strategies can result in confusion and serious difficulties in the field. Changes that are perceived as sudden, frequent, or drastic can lead to major delays and indecision. Changes should be prepared carefully, and offices and individuals concerned should have the skills, information, and tools needed to deal with them. A more systematic approach to making major changes in execution modalities is by far the more preferable course of action.

It is of great importance that as population and reproductive health programmes increase in size, they become more efficient. This implies that costs should be considered carefully at all stages in the policy and programme process — from formulation through implementation to evaluation. Given the scale of many reproductive health programmes, it will be especially important to ensure and enhance their efficacy, possibly through improvements in the way in which health services are delivered. Efforts to increase the efficacy of other types of population programmes will also be essential. For instance, major changes in the ways in which census data are collected, processed, and disseminated may facilitate adoption of more cost-effective approaches. Similarly, steadily increasing pressure on statistical offices and research centres to market their services may lead not only to reduction in costs but also to greater responsiveness to the needs and preferences expressed by clients. Moreover, if users of statistical and research services are required to pay for the services they request, they will be inclined to specify their needs far more precisely.

There may also be a need to re-examine support for "capacity building" and to consider bringing to an end long-standing assistance to regional and national institutions, including training institutes, National Population Commissions, and Population Planning Units (PPUs). Increased emphasis on operations research, as distinct from fundamental research, may enhance the contribution of research activities to policy and programme development. For instance, the focus of UNFPA support may shift from analysing why a certain category of the population behaves in a certain way, to determining which measures are likely to have a positive and significant impact on behaviour. In the same vein, increased emphasis on building the skills needed for careful targeting of IEC activities may lead to increases in the efficacy of those activities.

Experience has also taught UNFPA the importance of making sound choices in allocating support to countries, especially in times of reduced resource levels. UNFPA has learned the importance of cost efficiency, appraising options, monitoring and evaluating programmes, and conducting follow-up of training, research, and other capacity-building activities. It has learned the risk associated with relying heavily on a single approach or strategy, which often inhibits the development of institutional arrangements that are better adapted to particular needs and constraints.

Supporting the Development of Population Policies and Programmes for the Twenty-first Century

Despite the important achievements of the past three decades, not all needs have been met and not all constraints have been overcome. It is essential to move on, steadily shifting the emphasis from the identification of needs and constraints to the design and implementation of effective programmes.

Recently completed reviews of progress in implementing the ICPD Programme of Action show that some progress has been made in several key areas, especially in gender policy, quality of reproductive health care, the provision of services for the prevention and treatment of STDs and HIV/AIDS, and strengthening civil society partnerships. In many countries, post-ICPD changes in policy and legislation provide emerging opportunities for making a real difference in the well-being of people. The reviews make it clear, however, that in many countries the gaps between actual conditions and minimal standards of reproductive health remain enormous. Moreover, in some countries, population patterns and trends impact negatively on the pace and content of development.

There are many challenges ahead. The pressing needs of the developing world must be addressed amidst dwindling resources and staff cuts. Resource flows have levelled off and total official development assistance (ODA) is decreasing. Most developing countries are unable to generate the necessary resources to cover the cost of their national population programmes. The largest incoming population of young people and the greater-than-ever numbers of elderly, each of which have their own special needs, pose equally serious challenges that must be met. HIV/AIDS has made greater inroads than was previously projected. Poverty is rampant. Gender equality and the empowerment of women remain elusive in many parts of the world.

UNFPA could effectively accomplish so much more if only it had the necessary financial and human resources at its disposal. UNFPA field offices already feel the heavy burden of insufficient funding and human resources required to support country-level initiatives. Advocacy efforts must be increased, and the greater involvement of civil society and the private sector should be encouraged. Collaboration among the agencies and organizations of the United Nations system should be enhanced. And additional resources must be mobilized to assist countries in implementing the ICPD Programme of Action.

While success in moderating views regarding population policies and programmes came relatively slowly and unevenly and required unrelenting efforts to promote a dispassionate and balanced approach to population issues, a great deal was achieved. In many respects, the role of UNFPA was pivotal in shifting the focus of public debate about population from sweeping claims and counterclaims regarding the macro-economic consequences of an induced decline in fertility, to discussions of ways to improve reproductive health through access to improved information and

208

services. To appreciate how radical have been the changes over the past three decades, one need only note that, while recent international debates have dealt with such difficult issues as abortion and access of adolescents to contraceptives, in the past, there was debate centred on "demonstrations" that fertility declines would accelerate development, on objections to public support for "family planning," and on claims that proponents of family planning had a hidden agenda.

With respect to the well-being of millions of people in many countries, what is crucial is not simply the change in the perception of the interrelationship between population and development. Perhaps UNFPA's most important achievement was helping to bring about far-reaching changes in attitudes toward policy and programme responses to population/development interrelationships. Within a remarkably short period of time, many countries that had been reluctant to consider vigorous policies and programmes in the area of population and reproductive health have now formulated, adopted, and begun to implement such policies. Indeed, there are indications that the extent of the changes that have occurred at the country level has not been fully recognized and appreciated.

References

[1] Rafael Salas, *Reflections on Population* (New York: Pergamon Press, 1984): p. 90.

[2] Ibid.

[3] Population and Development. *Programme of Action adopted at the International Conference on Population and Development,* Cairo, 5-13 September 1994. Volume I. Department for Economic and Social Information and Policy Analysis, ST/ESA/SER.A/149. (United Nations: New York, 1995): para. 1.12.

[4] Rafael Salas, *International Population Assistance: The First Decade* (Oxford: Pergamon Press, 1979): p. 3.

UNFPA's Role in the Population Field

Stafford Mousky

During its thirty-year history, a number of valuable books have been written about the United Nations Population Fund (UNFPA), both by insiders and by knowledgeable outsiders. Most of these books have been organized around broad themes, usually UNFPA's work in each of the major population areas (reproductive health and family planning; policy formulation; population information, education and communication; data collection and analyses; and programmes focused on women and adolescents); UNFPA's work in each of the five major geographic regions; its role in the three international population conferences held in 1974, 1984, and 1994; and its involvement in new initiatives and innovations.

This chapter takes a somewhat different tack. It attempts to describe UNFPA's overall role in population and development over the entire 30 years. In addition to summarizing the major accomplishments and challenges of UNFPA in each of the past three decades, it presents a number of events from each year in a chronological framework in order to chronicle and illustrate the wide variety of ways UNFPA has made and continues to make a constructive difference, including its role in many advocacy and programme activities that otherwise might never have been undertaken.

While the chapter covers the entire period, it does try to highlight some important items and subjects that were somewhat overlooked in earlier books on UNFPA. These items and subjects include the annual *State of World Population* (SWOP) reports; UNFPA-sponsored conferences in the 1970s and 1980s; population, development and the reduction of poverty in China; and the Rafael M. Salas Lecture Series. More recent developments, including UNFPA's role in the series of United Nations conferences and summits on economic and social matters in the 1990s, its active role in the various policy and programme coordinating mechanisms of the United Nations system, and UNFPA's evolving role in population and development since the International Conference on Population and Development (ICPD) in 1994 are also described in some detail.

Introduction

During the formative years of UNFPA, numerous population issues — especially those concerning family planning — were sensitive, controversial subjects that could not be discussed at the United

---

In preparing this chapter, the author has used a large number of UN and UNFPA documents that are listed at the end of the chapter.

Nations, in national legislatures or, quite often, even in private homes without putting into play matters at the core of human nature and of power: namely, sex, religion, social mores, family structures, societal arrangements, human rights, etc. Since that time, other related issues have gained prominence, including abortion, HIV/AIDS, adolescent reproductive health, women's rights and empowerment issues.

And yet over the past thirty years — despite all of these sensitivities — much has changed and changed for the better in population, in family planning, in health, including reproductive health, and in women's empowerment and rights. The work of UNFPA has contributed significantly to each of these changes for the better. Under the tutelage of two strong leaders with roots in the developing world — Rafael M. Salas from the Philippines and Dr. Nafis Sadik from Pakistan — and operating under a well-crafted, ground-breaking mandate given to it in 1973 by the Economic and Social Council of the United Nations (ECOSOC), since 1970 UNFPA has managed to mobilize and put at the service of the developing world over $4.9 billion of voluntary grant contributions (see Table 1). In keeping with the stated aims and purposes of UNFPA, the amount of $4.9 billion has been used "to promote awareness, both in developed and developing countries of the social, economic and environmental implications of national and international population problems, of the human rights aspects of family planning, and of possible strategies to deal with them in accordance with the plans and priorities of each country; [and] to extend systematic and sustained assistance to developing countries at their request in dealing with their population problems; such assistance to be afforded in forms and by means requested by the recipient countries and best suited to meet the individual country's needs" (ECOSOC Resolution 1763 (LIV) of 18 May 1973).

While huge challenges certainly remain, the "balance sheet" on population covering the period of the past 30 years is a good one, considerably better than that of nearly any other component of the human development equation. The supporting evidence is clear and encouraging:

- The world's population growth rate has fallen by one-third (from 2 per cent a year in 1970 to 1.33 per cent in 1998), and is continuing to fall;
- The total fertility rate per woman in the developing world has fallen from 6 per woman in 1970 to 2.7 per woman in 1998;
- Life expectancy in the developing world has increased from 52.2 years in 1965-1970 to 63 years in 1998;
- Both the absolute number and the percentage of married women aged 15-49 living in developing countries who are using modern contraceptive methods have increased greatly since 1969-1970 (from an estimated 40 million or 8-10 per cent of married women to an estimated 430 million, or 50 per cent, today).

The First Decade of UNFPA

Starting in early 1970 with a staff of five, $4 million in voluntary contributions, and, not surprisingly, a suspicious United Nations system to confront, Mr. Salas steadily applied the managerial and interpersonal skills he had honed in the Philippines over the previous 20 years, first in university politics and later in a series of powerful senior positions in the Marcos administration, both to grow UNFPA and to win the trust and support of donors, recipients, the United Nations system, and the population community.

Table 1. UNFPA Income (General And Supplementary), 1967-1999 (in US$ millions)

YEAR	GENERAL[a]	SUPPLEMENTARY[b]	TOTAL
1967	0.1		0.1
1968	1.0		1.0
1969	3.9		3.9
1970	14.1		14.1
1971	26.1		26.1
1972	28.4		28.4
1973	39.8		39.8
1974	57.1		57.1
1975	61.0		61.0
1976	75.1	0.56	75.66
1977	89.1	0.85	89.95
1978	104.7		104.7
1979	117.1	2.8	119.9
1980	128.7	3.6	132.3
1981	125.5	2.9	128.4
1982	130.9	5.9	136.8
1983	134.7	6.7	141.4
1984	138.6	4.9	143.5
1985	142.9	6.4	149.3
1986	140.0	3.7	143.7
1987	156.1	4.8	160.9
1988	178.0	11.8	189.8
1989	185.2	7.3	192.5
1990	212.4	11.7	224.1
1991	224.0	8.9	232.9
1992	238.2	13.1	251.3
1993	219.6	15.6	235.2
1994	265.3	10.3	275.6
1995	312.6	15.9	328.5
1996	308.8	20.2	329.0
1997	292.5	29.4	321.9
1998	277.0	30.2	307.2
1999	250.0[c]	34.0[c]	284.0
Total	4,678.50	252.51	4,930.01

RDB/27 APR 2000

---

[a]   From 1974 and onwards: includes voluntary contributions, interest income, other income, and/or other miscellaneous adjustments.

[b]   Multi-bi Programmes.

[c]   Provisional until UNFPA's official closing of 1999 accounts, does not include miscellaneous and exchange rates adjustments, and actual interest income.

Less than two years into his efforts at UNFPA, Mr. Salas had the wisdom and good fortune to recruit Dr. Sadik to take over many of UNFPA's expanding programming responsibilities. Dr. Sadik brought with her seventeen years of medical and programming experience in Pakistan, including five years with the Pakistan Central Family Planning Council, the last two years as its Director-General. Dr. Sadik was soon named to head UNFPA's fast-growing Programme Division. Halvor Gille, UNFPA's Deputy Executive Director, drawing on his long experience in social development and population work at the United Nations Secretariat, focused his attention on many of the policy concerns confronting UNFPA. He also worked to build up the Fund's capacity and to engage concerned parts of the United Nations system to assist UNFPA in responding to requests for assistance. Mr. Salas could therefore devote time and energy to things he did best, including fund-raising; making friends and allies; and devising various strategies, awareness-building instruments and events to make UNFPA better known and the work of the United Nations in the population field respected and sought-after.

On the fund-raising side, with assistance from a noted 75-year-old population activist, General William Draper, Jr., Mr. Salas increased voluntary contributions to UNFPA from under $4 million in 1969 to $14 million in 1970, $28 million in 1972, and $50 million in 1974, the year of the ground-breaking World Population Conference (WPC). In 1971-1973, Mr. Salas and General Draper used to great advantage a United States government matching-grant formula devised by General Draper, as well as a series of trips that were taken by parliamentarians from Germany and Japan to see the population needs of Asian countries first-hand. These initiatives, coupled with General Draper's excellent contacts and reputation in Germany, Japan and the United States, helped influence each of these countries to make generous voluntary contributions to UNFPA in the 1970-1974 period and beyond. Deftly building on that momentum, Mr. Salas by late 1972 had persuaded 52 countries to make voluntary contributions to UNFPA.

Largely as a result of UNFPA's fund-raising successes, the General Assembly of the United Nations, noting "that the resources of UNFPA and its scope of operations have now grown to a size that makes supervision by an inter-governmental body desirable," in December of 1972 (General Assembly resolution 3019) decided to place UNFPA under the authority of the General Assembly as a subsidiary organ of the Assembly, giving it a status comparable to those of the United Nations Development Programme (UNDP) and the United Nations Children's Fund (UNICEF). It also decided that the Governing Council of UNDP would also become the governing body of UNFPA, subject to the policy functions and conditions to be established by the ECOSOC. The same resolution "invited" the Governing Council to organize itself in effectively carrying out its functions such a way as to take "into account the separate identity" of UNFPA.

UNFPA and the UN Administrative Committee on Coordination

In the late 1970s after seven or eight years of interaction with numerous parts of the United Nations system, Mr. Salas came to the conclusion that neither UNFPA nor population would be able to take their rightful places in the day-to-day work and in the implementation of the policies and programmes of the United Nations system until UNFPA became a full member of the Administrative Committee on Coordination (ACC), the principal coordinating mechanism of the United Nations system. The membership of the ACC is made up of the executive heads of all of the specialized agencies of the United Nations system — including the World Bank and the International Monetary

Fund (IMF) — plus the executive heads of the major funds and programmes of the United Nations. Chaired by the Secretary-General, the ACC holds two or three (usually two) two-day sessions each year in order for the Secretary-General and the various heads to keep one another apprised of major developments in their respective spheres as well as to discuss and coordinate system-wide issues. The ACC also has an extensive subsidiary machinery consisting of four (now three) main committees focusing on substantive and administrative questions, plus numerous specialized subcommittees on such subjects as information, nutrition, statistics, demographic projects, etc.

Making UNFPA a full member of the ACC would not be easy to bring about, given the view of the heads of some of the major specialized agencies that they were equal with the Secretary-General of the United Nations. They did not believe that the executive heads of funds, programmes and offices of the United Nations, especially those who were appointed by the Secretary-General, as opposed to being elected, no matter how large and important the fund or programme in question might be, were their equals. They certainly did not want to add another fund to the existing list. Other subtexts included the continuing sensitivity of various population issues.

After running into one or two cul de sacs, Mr. Salas' lobbying efforts began to pay off. In 1979 the first United Nations Director-General for Development Cooperation, Mr. Kenneth Dadzie, and the Administrator of the UNDP, Mr. Bradford Morse, both made known to the Secretary-General and others that they strongly supported the view that UNFPA had grown in size, stature, and reputation to a point where it deserved full membership in the ACC. Their support, coupled with a strong "hint" in General Assembly resolution 34/104 of December 1979, which "invite[d] the Secretary-General to arrange in consultation with ACC members for UNFPA to participate in all aspects in that body and its subsidiary machinery" and for the Secretary-General to report to the next General Assembly on the implementation of the resolution, combined to carry the day. On 3 November 1980, at the invitation of the members of ACC, UNFPA became a full member of that body.

With its membership in ACC, UNFPA became a full citizen in good standing within the United Nations system and in the eyes of the Member States of the United Nations. It was no longer seen as inextricably linked to UNDP, but rather was seen as an independent subsidiary organ of the General Assembly with its own mandate and separate identity, even though UNFPA maintained close ties with UNDP on many financial and administrative matters.

UNFPA's Executive Director now had two or three opportunities each year to interact with the Secretary-General and the heads of the World Bank, IMF, and each of the United Nations specialized agencies and offices and programmes to find out their views on population matters and, as UNFPA's mandate directed, "to play a leading role in the United Nations system in promoting population programmes . . . and to promote coordination in planning and programming and to cooperate with all concerned." UNFPA staff became active in the work of the various pieces of the ACC subsidiary machinery. Given UNFPA's small size, it was not always easy, but UNFPA has acquitted itself well in the various ACC settings.

First Comprehensive Country Agreements

The first multi-year country agreement was signed with the Government of Pakistan in August 1970. The second and third such agreements, with Mauritius and Egypt, were signed in 1971. Thereafter, UNFPA's capacity to field negotiating or programming missions at the request of recipient countries continued to grow steadily, as did the number of such requests. By the end of 1973, UNFPA had entered into comprehensive country agreements with seven additional countries (Chile, Indonesia, Iran, Malaysia, Sri Lanka, Thailand, and the Dominican Republic), with five more following in 1974, namely, Bangladesh, India, the Republic of Korea, Cuba, and Turkey. Beginning in 1974, all comprehensive country agreements as well as all projects totalling over $1 million had to be submitted to the Governing Council for its approval. All other projects could be approved under the authority of the Executive Director of UNFPA.

One of the large projects approved by the Governing Council in 1974, a $2 million, four-year project with Costa Rica to assist it in consolidating the national family planning and sex education programme, is especially noteworthy as it was UNFPA's first attempt to assist a country wishing to directly execute a project itself, in this case by the Costa Rica National Population Council, located in the Ministry of Health. Given his financial accountability responsibilities for all UNFPA monies, Mr. Salas first had to assure himself that Costa Rica had the capability to execute the project. He then made his proposal to the Governing Council, which granted its approval. This innovation was something of a first in the United Nations system and was made possible because of UNFPA's enabling mandate, which explicitly stated that UNFPA "should invite countries to utilize the most appropriate implementing agents for their programmes, recognizing that the primary responsibility for implementation rests with the country concerned" (ECOSOC Resolution 1763 (LIV) of 18 May 1973).

World Population Year and the World Population Conference, 1974

In mid-1972, ECOSOC designated UNFPA as the agency responsible for the preparation of the World Population Year (WPY), planned for 1974, including setting up a temporary WPY secretariat within the Fund. Mr. Salas and UNFPA took full advantage of this golden opportunity over the following 30 months to generate a large number of national, regional and international WPY activities that aroused worldwide interest in population issues and questions like never before. Some 64 countries established national population commissions or similar authorities that held seminars, conferences and activities for specially targeted groups, including women and youth. A large number of publicity initiatives received financial assistance from UNFPA under the WPY rubric, and more than 50 major NGOs and 1,000 national groups were assisted in undertaking WPY-related activities.

All of these activities culminated in the NGO-organized, twelve-day Population Tribune attended by more than 1,400 people, and the four-day Youth Population Conference attended by 237 participants and observers. Both were held in Bucharest, Romania, in August 1974 as parallel activities to the WPC. Overall, the events held in conjunction with WPY did a great deal to build awareness of population issues and challenges. They reflected favourably on the United Nations and on UNFPA and also served to increase greatly the demand for UNFPA-assisted population programmes and activities.

By the end of WPY in December 1974, it was fair to say that the so-called promotional phase of UNFPA was over, and the Fund was well along the way to reaching one of Mr. Salas' goals — establishing a clear identity for UNFPA. By the end of 1974, UNFPA had mobilized over $175 million in voluntary contributions and supported over 1,200 projects in 92 countries. Importantly, because of the growing awareness generated by WPY activities and the growing trust in UNFPA as a desirable development partner, more and more of the requests to UNFPA were requests for projects in maternal and child health and family planning (MCH/FP) as opposed to demographic research and training. By the end of 1974, UNFPA had expanded to 42 professional and 47 general service staff at headquarters plus 20 field coordinators.

While UNFPA and its Executive Director did not play a major substantive role in the 1974 WPC — as they did for the 1984 and 1994 population conferences — UNFPA did play a key funding role, financing approximately 50 per cent of the costs of the preparatory work and the conference itself. UNFPA benefited enormously from the WPC, especially from its 109-paragraph World Population Plan of Action (WPPA), which was approved by consensus by 133 countries in Bucharest, and most especially from two paragraphs of the WPPA, namely paragraphs 14f and 105, which read as follows:

> All couples and individuals have the basic right to decide freely and responsibly the number and spacing of their children and to have the information, education and means to do so: the responsibility of couples and individuals in the exercise of this right takes into account the needs of their living and future children, and their responsibilities towards the community (United Nations, 1975: paragraph 14f);
>
> It is suggested that the expanding, but still insufficient, international assistance in population and development matters requires increased co-operation; the United Nations Fund for Population Activities is urged, in co-operation with all organizations responsible for international population assistance, to provide a guide for international assistance in population matters which would be made available to recipient countries and institutions and be revised periodically (ibid.: paragraph 105).

After urging greater development assistance in accordance with the goals of the Second United Nations Development Decade, the WPPA recognized, "in view of the magnitude of the problems and the consequent national requirements for funds, that considerable expansion of international assistance in the population field is required for the proper implementation of this Plan of Action" (ibid.: paragraph 104).

Following WPY, the International Women's Conference and Women's Year in 1975, in which UNFPA participated actively, served as springboard for a growing level of UNFPA support for a wide variety of women's activities. For example, in 1976, UNFPA issued a set of guidelines to ensure that the Fund's project formulation, implementation and evaluation activities took full account of the status of women and that women were active participants in all population matters. In 1979, within the terms of its mandate, UNFPA created a new organizational unit, the Women and Youth Section. Also in 1979, UNFPA began financially assisting the Centre for Development and Population Activities (CEDPA) in its programme to train women as family planning managers.

UNFPA Activities in the Post-World Population Conference Period

Thanks in large part to the awareness built up by WPY activities and by the wide acceptance of the WPPA, during the remainder of the 1970s, requests from developing countries and others for UNFPA assistance in confronting their various population challenges grew at a fast pace. While voluntary contributions to UNFPA more than doubled between 1974 and 1979 (growing from $50 million in 1974 to $112 million in 1979), the number and the amounts of the requests it received far exceeded the funds at its disposal.

UNFPA took numerous measures to address this growing gap between requests and resources. First, with requests for direct assistance from developing countries growing rapidly, UNFPA, with the strong support of its Governing Council, cut the proportion of programme funds going to finance regional, interregional and global projects from 60 per cent of the programme budget in 1974 to 32 per cent in 1977, with a goal of reaching 25 per cent by 1982.

UNFPA also devised a set of criteria — consisting of one economic and four demographic indicators — for allocating future resources to countries on a priority basis, with 54 countries with the most pressing problems being labelled as "priority countries" using these criteria and thus eligible to receive a greater share of the funds available to finance country programmes and projects. This formula was first proposed by UNFPA in 1977 and, with some refinements, including building in more flexibility and transition time, was approved by the Governing Council in 1978. With some major modifications made in the mid-1990s to better reflect the ICPD Programme of Action, this priority system has served UNFPA in good stead and continues to be utilized today.

The third initiative by Mr. Salas for expanding the resource base was a device called "multi-bilateral funding." In 1976 and 1977, UNFPA proposed and received Governing Council approval to use this collaboration mechanism of financing to narrow the gap between demand for multilateral population assistance and the resources available to UNFPA. The mechanism involves, with the recipient country's prior approval, adding bilateral financial support to specific projects that UNFPA is also helping to finance. Modalities and principles for such arrangements were worked out to ensure that these arrangements would in no way substitute for increased core contributions to UNFPA from donors that saw advantages in also using UNFPA's multi-bilateral mechanism. During the period from 1976 to 1998, the total bilateral assistance committed under UNFPA multi-bilateral arrangements totalled approximately $200 million. The evidence shows that donors who provide UNFPA with multi-bilateral funds have also increased their core contributions to UNFPA substantially. Another important benefit gained from these arrangements with donor countries is the considerable amount of direct contact it triggers with aid agency personnel at all levels.

State of World Population Reports

The preparation and wide dissemination of an annual *State of World Population* (SWOP) report was another Salas initiative that would be widely copied over the course of the 1980s and 1990s. In June 1978, UNFPA issued the first SWOP report. These annual reports, in addition to containing information on population trends and developments plus a series of updated population and social development indicators for each country and region of the world, gave special in-depth attention each year to a particular population subject or theme, such as women, adolescents, ageing, migration, contraception, etc. The report, along with a media package on its contents, is widely distributed and issued on a particular date in conjunction with coordinated public launches by the Executive Director and senior UNFPA officials in capital cities around the world.

Over the years, these reports have proven to be one of UNFPA's most effective instruments for promoting awareness of the need to address a whole range of national and international population issues and problems. By the early 1980s, a number of other funds, programmes and agencies of the United Nations system began issuing annual state of the world reports on a wide variety of topics. By the early 1990s it was difficult to find a single United Nations organization without such a report.

International data collection

Two additional examples of major initiatives central to answering numerous hotly debated fertility questions and to providing critical census information were the World Fertility Survey (WFS) and the African census programmes, which were financed in large part by UNFPA in the 1970s and early 1980s. It is highly unlikely that either of these important endeavours would have been carried out — certainly not in as timely and professional manner — if UNFPA had not had the wherewithal and the foresight to step forward and agree to provide steady support for an extended period of time to each of them.

Between 1972 and 1984, UNFPA provided $15 million to the International Statistical Institute (ISI) to help it meet the need for reliable, comparable, and up-to-date information on human fertility. The WFS was the world's largest social science research project of that period, covering 42 developing countries — plus 20 developed countries under separate funding arrangements — representing 30 per cent of the developing world's population. Utilizing a core questionnaire, ISI and the concerned countries produced over 100 reports, reports documenting such things as actual levels of fertility decline, the number of children wanted by mothers, preferred family size, contraceptive prevalence levels, etc. In addition to providing much-needed data, the WFS project proved to be a superb vehicle for strengthening the domestic capacities of many developing countries to undertake social science research and to train, upgrade and expand their human resource skills in conducting research and surveys.

The first UNFPA financial assistance for African census programmes (from 1970 to 1977) covered 22 countries, mostly newly independent countries that had never before undertaken a complete population census. In each of the 22 countries, reliable demographic data were urgently needed by the government and by others as a basis for socio-economic planning and for the elaboration of development programmes and projects. UNFPA provided $16 million to help finance a wide range of the required components for these 22 censuses. A few years later, another 24 national census projects in sub-Saharan Africa countries received UNFPA support for carrying out the 1980 round of censuses.

Building new constituencies

In 1979 and 1980, Mr. Salas undertook several initiatives to further UNFPA's outreach and to build additional political support for meeting population challenges.

In September 1979, parliamentarians from 58 countries attended the Colombo Conference, co-sponsored by UNFPA and the Inter-Parliamentary Union (IPU), and issued the Colombo Declaration. The declaration underlined how population and development are inextricably linked, and it cited the progress made since the 1974 WPPA, while stressing that far more had to be done. Along that line, it called for strengthening the role and functions of UNFPA, and for an increase in international population assistance to $1 billion annually by 1984. It went on to define areas of action where parliaments could supplement and enhance the population efforts of their governments.

The declaration's references to strengthening UNFPA were mentioned in General Assembly resolution 34/104, entitled "United Nations Fund for Population Activities."

The 1979 Latin American Conference on Population and Development Planning was another international gathering sponsored by UNFPA, in collaboration with the Economic Commission for Latin America and the Caribbean (ECLAC). It was the first such meeting or conference to facilitate exchanges of views and experiences on population and development among the ministers of planning of Latin American countries.

The Brandt Commission Report: UNFPA, as well as numerous other concerned entities in the United Nations system, had discussions with members of the Brandt Commission and its secretariat during 1979, prior to the release of the report "North-South: A Programme for Survival" (also called "The Report of the Independent Commission on International Development Issues") in early 1980. Although the Brandt Report certainly did not place the continuing rapid population-growth phenomenon at the centre of the numerous development, environment, peace, and quality-of-life issues that it was addressing, it made it clear that such rapid growth was one of the strongest forces shaping the future of human society and, along with excessive consumption, was a prime source of alarming ongoing ecological changes.

In 1980, UNFPA sponsored, in cooperation with the Government of Italy and the city of Rome, the International Conference on Population and the Urban Future. The objectives of the conference were: to increase the awareness and understanding of population factors in urban planning at local and national levels; to bring to the attention of planners, policymakers and administrators the results of recent experience and research on urban issues and problems; and to provide a forum for all parties involved in urban management.

The conference was attended by mayors, deputy mayors and city planners from 41 of the 60 cities whose population was projected to be five million or more by the year 2000 as well as by national planners from the 31 countries. One of the mayors who attended the conference was the mayor of Shanghai, Jiang Zemin, who went on to become president of China. At the end of the conference, the Rome Declaration on Population and Urban Future was adopted by consensus. The declaration was later officially placed by the Government of Italy before the thirty-fifth session of the General Assembly. The conference received extensive media coverage, and the participants were received and addressed by His Holiness, Pope John Paul II.

The Second Decade of UNFPA

The 1980s started on a high note when UNFPA, as discussed above, was invited to become a full member of ACC, the highest coordinating body of the United Nations system. The 1980s ended on an equally high note with the Amsterdam Forum Declaration, which was approved by 79 countries in November 1989 and positively referred to in decisions of the Governing Council of UNDP/UNFPA and in resolutions of the General Assembly. The declaration called for doubling the financial resources spent on population programmes from all sources in the 1990s. It also called for intensified advocacy on population issues and set a goal of increasing contraceptive use in developing countries by 50 per cent by the year 2000. In 1983, UNFPA reached the $1 billion mark in total voluntary contributions (it reached the $2 billion mark in core voluntary contributions in 1990). The decade also saw the establishment of an annual United Nations Population Award in

1981, and the International Conference on Population (ICP) in Mexico City in 1984. The world's population reached 5 billion in 1987, and UNFPA took advantage of that milestone to launch World Population Day, which has since been celebrated on 11 July every year, in over 150 countries around the world. For UNFPA itself, the decade was marked by a major milestone when Mr. Salas died of a massive heart attack in March, 1987. The Secretary-General of the United Nations, Javier Perez de Cuellar, in a much-applauded move in April 1987, appointed Dr. Nafis Sadik as the second Executive Director of UNFPA.

The 1980s also saw a highly significant negative development. UNFPA and population efforts around the world were adversely impacted — beginning in 1984 and lasting through 1992 — by decisions of the Reagan and Bush administrations to have the government of the United States, UNFPA's largest single donor, cease making voluntary contributions to the International Planned Parenthood Federation (IPPF) in 1984 and to UNFPA in 1986. The stated reason for cutting off the contribution was that, in light of its continuing $10 million annual programme in China, UNFPA was involved in the management of China's $1 billion a year family planning programme, which was tied to that country's one-child policy. There were also accusations that at least a few of the very large cadre of family planning personnel involved in implementing China's nation-wide population programme had resorted to coercive measures in implementing the programme. This decision was taken despite the fact that at least two U.S. government studies of the UNFPA programme in China conducted in the early-mid 1980s had explicitly found that no UNFPA funds or financially assisted programmes were in any way linked to alleged coercive measures. The decision of the U.S. Government to stop voluntary contributions to UNFPA was thus essentially a case of guilt-by-association.

The 1984 International Conference on Population (ICP) in Mexico City marked a major shift in the posture of the executive branch of the United States government towards both the nature of the population challenge and "the rules of the game" for the use of population assistance to non-governmental organizations (NGOs) working in developing countries. UNFPA took the extraordinary step for a multilateral organization of segregating the funds it received from the U.S. government so a clear paper trail could show that no U.S. funds were being spent in China. The use of a segregated account postponed the cut-off of U.S. funds to UNFPA for approximately 18 months. However, in keeping with its so-called "Mexico City Policy" of 1984, beginning in 1985 the U.S. had stopped funding for IPPF, the leading NGO in the voluntary family planning area, because some of its autonomous national affiliates in countries where abortion was legal provided, upon request, some abortion services. In 1986, however, the United States cut off all funding to UNFPA because of its continued involvement in China's family planning programme.

This decision was taken by the United States Agency for International Development (USAID), which, under considerable pressure from powerful far-right groups, finally decided that while UNFPA's programme in China was clean, UNFPA was involved in the "management" of the China population programme. For anyone to believe that a huge, proud, and powerful country, fiercely protective of its sovereignty, with 200,000 full-time family planning workers and an annual family planning budget of about $1 billion would allow UNFPA (with an international staff in China of four and sometimes five people) or anyone else to be involved in managing their population programme stretched credulity to the breaking point.

UNFPA During 1980-1986

The positive highlights of the 1980s included cumulative voluntary contributions to UNFPA exceeding the $1 billion mark by 1983; the ICP held in Mexico City in 1984, with the UNFPA Executive Director serving as the Secretary-General of the conference; the continent-wide legitimization of population issues and concerns in Africa flowing from the January 1984 Kilimanjaro Programme of Action for African Population and Self-Reliant Development; and the World Bank's decision to redouble its lending in the population, health and nutrition areas in order to slow population growth, fight pervasive poverty and accelerate development. The major negative of the period was a considerable slowing down — indeed a reduction in real terms — in the growth of voluntary contributions to UNFPA at a time when the interest in and requests for UNFPA assistance by well over one hundred developing countries continued to grow and grow. A major reason for this slowing was the United States' decision to cut off funding to UNFPA.

The 1980s actually got off to a good start for UNFPA, with a 12 per cent increase in voluntary contributions and the International Development Strategy for the Third United Nations Development Decade not only calling on all countries to strengthen their implementation of the WPPA but stressing that "population policies will be considered as an integral part of overall development policies" and that countries should continue to integrate their population measures and programmes into their social and economic goals and strategies (General Assembly resolution 35/56, Annex). However, already in February 1980, "the Report of the Independent Commission on International Development Issues" under the chairmanship of Willy Brandt noted that "international support for population policies is flagging at precisely the time when the commitment to and political acceptance of family planning is spreading in the [T]hird [W]orld." The report went on to point out "that UNFPA can meet only two-thirds of the requests it receives" and declared that "[i]nternational assistance and support of population programmes must be measured to meet the unmet needs for such aid."

In 1980, UNFPA established a new field Coordinator post in China and prepared and issued revised guidelines on women, population and development as a means for accelerating and giving priority to women-oriented population projects. At the behest of the General Assembly (resolution 35/129), UNFPA provided financial support to the preparatory work for the 1982 World Assembly on Ageing and supported the International Forum on Active Ageing held in Rome in September 1988 and sponsored by Opera Pia Alessondrini in consultation with the Holy See.

In 1981, several leaders of the developing world (including the presidents of Mexico and Indonesia, the Prime Minister of India, and the Director-General of the OPEC Fund) made statements stressing their commitment to addressing the population challenge. Also, the heads of state of the seven most prominent developed countries, meeting in Ottawa, Canada, noted their deep concern about the implications of world population growth, lauded the actions being taken by many developing countries to deal with that problem, "in ways sensitive to human values and dignity," and said they would "place greater emphasis on international efforts in these areas." However, in 1981 UNFPA experienced a decline from its 1980 level of voluntary contributions, blamed in part on sharp exchange rate fluctuations.

In April 1981 UNFPA, IPPF and the Population Council co-sponsored the International Conference on Family Planning in the 1980s in Jakarta, Indonesia. The statement issued by the conference outlined nine actions of practical and moral importance that "deserve support by political leaders, religious groups, health professionals." UNFPA also played an active role in the United

Nations Conference on the Least Developed Countries held in Paris in September. Population concerns were given due attention in the Programme of Action approved by the conference. In recognition of UNFPA's increasing recognition as the leader in population activities internationally, ECOSOC, in resolution 1981/87, requested the Secretary-General to appoint the Executive Director of UNFPA to serve as the Secretary-General of the 1984 ICP.

In 1982, the Declaration of the Seven Heads of State and Government and representatives of the European Community at the end of a June 1982 meeting in Versailles once again included "we give special encouragement . . . to programmes to address the implications of population growth."

In other items of note, in 1982 for the first time UNFPA reached the goal set by the Governing Council that two-thirds of country programme resources go to priority countries — allocations to priority countries totalled 69 per cent in 1982. In the same year, UNFPA's Governing Council approved a revision in the criteria for the designation of priority countries for UNFPA assistance, giving 53 countries priority status.

In 1983, at the inter-country level the Fund was busy assisting the worldwide Population Information Network (POPIN) designed to speed the flow of population information throughout the world.

In other items of note, UNFPA helped finance the World Health Organization's (WHO's) "Adolescent Reproductive Health: An Approach to Planning Health Service Research" published with a view to aiding communities in improving the effectiveness of health services for adolescents. UNFPA continued to make major financial contributions to support the WHO-administered Special Programme of Research Development and Research Training in Human Reproduction, which had 600 projects under way in 160 centres around the world in 1983. In January, in an update of a 1977 joint memorandum, the Administrator of UNDP and the Executive Director of UNFPA issued a co-signed memorandum elaborating and clarifying the relationship between the two organizations, especially the roles and functions of the UNDP Resident Representative and the Representative of UNFPA, and the relationship between the UNFPA Representative and the UNFPA Deputy Representative in the countries where UNFPA maintained one.

The major event of 1984 for the population community was the ICP held in Mexico City during 6-14 August. As Mr. Salas, the Secretary-General of the conference, stated, it was one of the briefest, most economical, least documented and best attended international conferences sponsored by the United Nations during the decade. The conference had some 3,500 attendees, including representatives of 146 states and 800 accredited journalists.

The conference was particularly rewarding for the future work of UNFPA in that most developing countries made it clear that, in contrast to the 1974 WPC, they now saw population as a central, cross-cutting imperative of social and economic development, an imperative that had to be addressed if they were to progress and to improve the quality of life of their citizens. Recommendation 83 of the Mexico City Conference stated that "the Fund should be strengthened further, so as to ensure the more effective delivery of population assistance, taking into account the growing needs in the field."

The year 1985 was a year of solidification for UNFPA following the Mexico City Conference, a year in which UNFPA put more emphasis on projects focusing on improving the status of women and — in keeping with 1985 being International Youth Year and recommendation 57 of the Mexico City Conference — on youth. During the year, UNFPA played an active role in the World Conference for the United Nations Decade for Women in Nairobi, including financing the participation of 36 women from developing countries and providing financial assistance for workshops held as part of an NGO forum. UNFPA also approved 30 projects with a total budget of $2 million for improving the status of women.

In 1986, as a forerunner to two conferences on urban matters that UNFPA would co-sponsor during the year, the theme of the SWOP report for 1986 was population and the urban future. The report focused on patterns of urban population structure, urban population dynamics, successes and failures of policies addressing urban problems, and some tentative recommendations for future policies and programmes.

The Fund, in collaboration with the Government of Mexico, sponsored a weeklong conference in Mexico City on Population and Small and Medium Sized Cities in Latin America and the Caribbean, which attracted participation from 22 countries. Later in the year, UNFPA joined with HABITAT, the International Union of Local and Spanish Authorities, for a weeklong international conference in Barcelona on Population and the Urban Future. The conference emphasized the need for integrated rural-urban development, forward-looking strategies, problems relating to population dynamics — including greater support for MCH/FP services — and was attended by mayors, city planners, and national planners from 54 cities in 29 countries around the world.

Despite the decision by the United States to withhold funding, voluntary contributions for 1986 to UNFPA fell by only $2.5 million from the previous year, to $133.5 million, thanks in part to exceedingly generous supplementary contributions made by Canada, Finland, and the Netherlands.

UNFPA During 1987-1989

In early March 1987, Mr. Salas died of a heart attack at the age of 59. Six weeks later, Secretary-General Perez de Cuellar appointed Dr. Sadik to be his successor.

Mr. Salas was not a health professional or a population guru; at his core he was a humanist. At an early age he had developed political, administrative and interpersonal skills that built a reputation for getting things done. These abilities shaped his professional life, first in the Philippines, and then, at the United Nations as the Executive Director of UNFPA for the last 17 years of his too-short life. In his last years he was known to be interested in pursuing new challenges if the right opportunity were to present itself.

Dr. Sadik was and is a health professional. She made herself into the most well-known, respected and influential population spokesperson — certainly concerning operational and advocacy matters — in the world. The international population and development community as a whole acknowledges that population issues and challenges would not have been so prominently factored into the nine United Nations-sponsored world conferences on economic, social, human rights and environmental questions that were held during the 1990s without her determined efforts. It is unlikely that the World Bank (including its Development Committee, which Dr. Sadik addressed shortly before Cairo), IMF, and the European Union would be giving the steadily growing level of attention and priority to the social development aspects, including the population element, and social development consequences of their projects, programmes and policies without her persistent and effective gadfly role over the course of the past decade.

From the time of the preparations for the International Forum on Population in the Twenty-first Century held in Amsterdam in November 1989, Dr. Sadik sought successfully to influence important entities (such as the United Nations ACC and the Organisation for Economic Cooperation and Development's Development Assistance Committee (OECD/DAC) and the periodic meetings of development policy leaders (such as the elite Tidewater Group of which she was a member and the far larger Society of International Development of which she was president from 1994-1997) to publicly acknowledge population issues as central to all sustainable development efforts.

Dr. Sadik's contributions are equally noteworthy in terms of improving the well-being of women within UNFPA and the United Nations system, and, more important, through programmes and projects that work to improve the health and status of women in the 160-plus countries where UNFPA is actively involved. UNFPA, under Dr. Sadik, greatly increased both the quantity and quality of the Fund's previous level of involvement in many areas such as promoting safe motherhood; building needed knowledge and statistical bases; providing leadership and livelihood skills training; and promoting reproductive health, rights and gender equality. UNFPA has also pushed vigorously into other areas of concern to women and girls such as combating female genital mutilation (FGM) and gender-based violence; providing services to women in emergency situations; working to prevent HIV/AIDS; furnishing reproductive health information and services for adolescents; and working with treaty bodies of the United Nations responsible for monitoring human rights to better integrate women's rights, including reproductive rights, into their work, including their evaluation of states' reports.

When Dr. Sadik was appointed UNFPA's Executive Director in April 1987, she was the first woman in the 41-year history of the United Nations selected to head one of its major voluntary-funded funds or programmes. Her first year was remarkably full of accomplishments. During the year UNFPA submitted, and the Governing Council approved, 31 multi-year country programmes (including 21 in the sub-Saharan Africa region), as many as had been approved over the previous four-year period. UNFPA's structure was realigned to enhance its technical and substantive capacity by consolidating technical resources into one division and by increasing the efficiency and effectiveness of limited staff resources through decentralization of authority and responsibility to the field. In December of 1987, the General Assembly approved the change in the title of UNFPA from the "United Nations Fund for Population Activities" to the "United Nations Population Fund" while retaining the acronym UNFPA (General Assembly resolution 42/430). All procurement of the supplies and equipment for UNFPA-financed activities (which had been done for UNFPA by UNICEF from 1970 until 1985) was consolidated in 1987 under the authority of the Procurement Unit. The volume of goods and services processed that year totalled $24.5 million. Because of the Procurement Unit's growing expertise in purchasing contraceptives and its proven ability to largely eliminate procurement fees, in 1987 donor countries began using the unit as their agent in procuring contraceptives for some of their bilateral population assistance programmes.

Of greatest significance to UNFPA, and the world, in 1987 was that world population passed five billion during the year. UNFPA devoted its SWOP report to the implications of a world of five billion, and declared 11 July 1987 the "Day of the Five Billion." The theme, "A Day to Celebrate, a Day to Contemplate," was taken up by over 90 countries, which marked the occasion in various ways.

The highlight of the Day of the Five Billion was the welcome by Secretary-General of the United Nations, Perez de Cuellar, to "Baby Five Billion" in Zagreb, Yugoslavia, on 11 July. A feature of the day was a television special by the Turner Broadcasting System with the participation of several heads of state, leading intellectuals and music stars that was intercut with accurate and moving documentary footage. The show was seen in over 80 countries and aired again on United Nations Day, 24 October.

In the following year, 1988, UNFPA's SWOP report entitled "Safeguarding the Future" focused on how increasing human demands are damaging the natural resource base — land, water, and air — upon which all life depends and on how high fertility and rapid population growth are contributing to the process. It focused on what is known — and unknown — about the critical links between population, environment and resources.

Also in June 1988, the Governing Council approved a new cycle of the Fund's interregional programme for 1988-1991 in the amount of $87.1 million. Almost three-quarters of this programme is executed by United Nations agencies and organizations, with WHO's Special Programme of Research, Development and Research Training in Human Reproduction receiving the largest allocation. The remaining quarter of interregional resources are for projects executed by NGOs. In Decision 88/34 the Governing Council approved 16 additional country programmes and noted "with satisfaction the new programme directions of the Fund, in particular improved substantive analysis, strategic programming and staff development and training" at the same time that it welcomed "the continued increase in both volume and percentage terms of United Nations Population Fund assistance to sub-Saharan Africa."

UNFPA convened a "Global Conference" in New York in 1988 to provide UNFPA staff and other concerned parties an opportunity to review and assess the accumulated experience of the past 20 years and to apply the lessons that had been learned to future programmes. The findings and recommendations — which incidentally focused far more on reproductive health than had earlier been the case — were printed and circulated.

The highlights of 1989 for UNFPA included a very detailed SWOP report entitled "Investing in Women: The Focus of the Nineties" as well as the successful Amsterdam Forum. "Investing in Women: The Focus of the Nineties" ends with both a long series of recommendations and a set of goals for the year 2000, many of which, with only minor modifications, would find their way into the goals approved at the Cairo and Beijing conferences. The report was translated into 22 languages. Likewise, looking ahead to the year 2000, the 79 participating countries in the forum approved by consensus the Amsterdam Declaration, whose Call to Action asked all countries to double expenditures for family planning and other major population activities from $4.5 billion in 1987 to $9 billion in 2000 in order to provide the financial resources necessary to reach the United Nations medium-variant population projection for the year 2000.

During the year, WHO/UNFPA/UNICEF jointly issued a statement, "The Reproductive Health of Adolescents: A Strategy for Action," which was widely circulated. The statement documented the commitment of the three organizations to a joint, complementary and coordinated action as well as cooperation with other United Nations bodies and governmental and NGOs in the promotion of the reproductive health of adolescents.

The Fund also stepped up its efforts to confront the growing AIDS pandemic by expanding its collaborative work with WHO, including seconding a UNFPA staff member to its Global Programme on AIDS; by integrating special components on HIV/AIDS into projects in a number of sub-Saharan Africa countries; and by promoting greater awareness of the need to integrate AIDS prevention activities into MCH/FP networks.

By the end of 1989, cumulative pledges to UNFPA totalled $2 billion from 151 donors, and UNFPA had 694 authorized budget posts comprising 167 professional and 527 general service staff. These included 100 professional and 132 general service staff at headquarters and 65 professional and 397 general service staff in the field.

China: population, development, and the reduction of poverty

Over the period 1970-1997, well over 400 million Chinese were lifted out of poverty as the country's annual per capita income increased eightfold. Never before in the annals of human history has a development transformation of such magnitude taken place in such a short period of time. Obviously, population and health factors played an important role. During the period 1970-1997, China's total fertility rate fell from 6 to less than 2; its contraceptive prevalence rate for modern methods rose to well over 80 per cent, one of the highest levels in the world; its infant mortality rate fell by more than 45 per cent; and life expectancy rose by 8 years, to 68.5 years.

Many countries and population and development experts believe that by providing assistance to China at their request (under the mandate given UNFPA by the General Assembly, all developing countries have the right to request UNFPA to provide them with population assistance), UNFPA's presence and small inputs help influence China's population programme and policies and also help promote human rights. In the past, UNFPA helped China with its censuses; in modernizing 23 contraceptive facilities; in training physicians, health workers and counsellors with a focus on individual choice and informed consent; in establishing population science curriculum in 22 Chinese universities, which utilize foreign training and visiting foreign professors; and in helping finance various projects in eleven poor provinces to promote women's status. Most of UNFPA's current, smaller, four-year $5 million a year programme in China, which began in 1998, is aimed at helping meet the unmet needs for comprehensive and integrated client-centred reproductive health services in 32 of China's poorest counties by making quality services available on a voluntary basis in line with the principles, approaches and recommendations of the ICPD Programme of Action. None of the 32 counties have birth quotas or targets.

The United Nations Population Award

In 1981, with the behind-the-scenes support of Mr. Salas, the General Assembly (in resolution 36/201) established the United Nations Population Award, the first global award of its kind and, to date, the only United Nations annual award authorized by the General Assembly. The award is presented by the Secretary-General of the United Nations at a public ceremony at United Nations Headquarters to an individual or individuals, or to an institution or institutions, or to any combinations thereof, for outstanding contributions to the awareness of population questions or to their solutions. The award consists of a diploma, a gold medal and a small monetary prize financed by voluntary contributions of Member States to a trust fund administered by UNFPA. The award ceremony has always included a special "Salas touch"; namely, live chamber music being played at the beginning and end of the ceremony. The first award laureates were chosen in 1983. Since then, through 1998, 13 organizations and 17 individuals (including four heads of state) from around the world have been chosen and honoured as laureates.

Evaluation

Already in 1971, with his strong management bent, Mr. Salas had recognized and responded to the need for UNFPA to develop good in-house monitoring, implementation and evaluation capabilities.

By 1972, as part of UNFPA's first reorganization, Mr. Salas set up a formal evaluation unit. Evaluation has maintained a prominent place at UNFPA ever since, helping to solidify the Fund's reputation as a serious, well-managed development organization. UNFPA's frank and realistic reports flowing from the many evaluations it carries out — many utilizing outside evaluators — have been widely circulated. Over the past twenty years, the Fund's periodic reports on evaluations to its Executive Board have consistently been well received. More important, these evaluations have enabled UNFPA to learn from problems encountered, correct project design shortcomings and unrealistic assumptions, and make mid-course corrections. In a related and quite recent (December 1996) evolution, UNFPA has combined evaluation and oversight functions under an independent organizational office that reports directly to the Executive Director. The Office of Oversight and Evaluation (OOE) is responsible for ensuring that the findings of all oversight mechanisms within UNFPA are acted upon and are also reflected in UNFPA's decision-making.

Programme Coordination within the United Nations system

There are numerous United Nations groups and committees that have been active over the years in facilitating programme coordination. Two such groups that UNFPA has been involved with over the years are the Joint Consultative Group on Policy (JCGP) and the Consultative Committee on Programme and Operational Questions (CCPOQ). These mechanisms have helped to ensure that population programmes and activities are full partners in the United Nations development efforts.

JCGP

The JCGP consisting of UNDP, UNICEF and UNFPA, the World Food Programme (WFP) — which joined in 1983 and the International Fund for Agricultural Development (IFAD) — which joined in 1988, was established in 1981 as a forum of information exchange. It was an important, little-known group that did much useful work before it was subsumed into the larger United Nations Development Group (UNDG) set up by Secretary-General Kofi Annan in early 1998 as part of his major reform programme and framework for change. The JCGP was most active and did its best work between 1986 and 1996. The Chair of JCGP rotated among Member agencies as did the chairs of its seven subgroups.

The first high-level meeting of JCGP executive heads and their top four or five senior staff, a meeting organized in large part by UNFPA, was held in December 1986 and had as its theme "Women and Development." The meeting triggered commitments and a series of directives designed to ensure that gender-responsiveness became an integral part of all of the mainstream development activities of each of the five organizations. The members of JCGP also agreed that staff training at senior and middle management levels was critical in order to ensure that gender issues were incorporated as meaningful elements of their programming and project work. The meeting has since been acknowledged as a "breakthrough" event at which many of those taking part finally "got it" for the first time.

CCPOQ

CCPOQ is another entity little known outside of the United Nations circles — and not that well known even within the United Nations system. It works hard in a service-oriented manner to keep all United Nations agencies, organizations, funds and programmes (including the World Bank and IMF) on the same page by assisting the ACC to promote complementarities within the United Nations system and to mobilize its analytical, normative and operational capacities for economic and social development in support of common goals and agreed strategies on such subjects as fighting poverty, special initiatives for sub-Saharan Africa, follow-up to global conferences, etc. The committee meets twice a year. Dr. Sadik was the chairperson of CCPOQ from 1994 to 1996. She was the first head of a United Nations organization ever to serve as the chair of the committee. CCPOQ has only a small (two or three persons) jointly financed secretariat to carry out its very wide-ranging terms of reference. These include preparing recommendations for consideration by the ACC, and considering and monitoring progress on measures to enhance the programming, implementation, and cost-effectiveness of operational activities.

The Rafael M. Salas Lecture Series

A memorial lecture series is sponsored by the Rafael M. Salas Endowment Fund, which was created by UNFPA, with the approval of the Governing Council, in June 1987. It was established as a response to requests from both developed and developing countries to commemorate the contributions of Mr. Salas. As of April 1999, there have been seven lectures, including two by heads of state. As Secretary-General Kofi Annan said in introducing President Fidel Ramos who gave the most recent Salas Lecture in November 1997, there are few areas as sensitive or in need of understanding as population and population-related activities.

The list of guest lecturers and the lectures themselves have been impressive. Taken together they have a remarkable consistency in their call for collective action, for a genuine international partnership to address critical aspects of population and development that cut across all borders and affect everyone. Former Japanese Foreign Minister Saburo Okita, in October 1988 emphasized the importance of taking direct measures to reduce population growth in tandem with such indirect measures as raising incomes and promoting economic development. His Royal Highness Prince Philip, Duke of Edinburgh, in March 1990 reminded us how the natural systems of the planet are being distorted both by the sheer size of the human population as well as by its activities and its insatiable demand for all kinds of resources. Robert S. McNamara, in December 1991 stressed the urgency of acting now to reduce rates of population growth and outlined a programme to do so. Captain Jacques-Yves Cousteau, in September 1992 took us on what he called the "greatest adventure of all times" — the effort to reconnect humans to nature.

Norwegian Prime Minister Gro Harlem Brundtland, in the fifth lecture given in September 1993, delivered a powerful message: Unless we accept that rapid population growth is the most serious, predictable and intractable crisis facing us today, "we shall not be able to avoid . . . the ultimate collapse of [the Earth's] vital resource base." Baroness Chalker of Wallasey, United Kingdom Minister of State for Foreign and Commonwealth Affairs and Minister for Overseas Development, in March 1996 proposed ways to rekindle support, within each country, for sound international development overseas. Philippine President Fidel Ramos in November 1997, after recalling he had known and admired Rafael Salas since high school, and after recalling the current scope of human deprivation despite the progress made over the past quarter-century, described how the Philippine population policy — in response to realities and the centrality of the family and family values — "is both pro-life and pro-choice; non-coercive but value-laden; family-centered yet socially responsible."

These very brief summaries illustrate what have become the hallmarks of the Salas Lecture — the explication of a vital issue; the appeal for understanding; the need for greater awareness; the identification of a bold plan of action; and the call for collective and concerted action to carry out that plan.

UNFPA's Third Decade

The 1990s were a highly successful decade for UNFPA and for its and others' efforts to provide desired information and services to hundreds of millions of women and adolescents. Among UNFPA's most important accomplishments of the 1990s have been: a large role in the preparations for, the holding and follow-up of the 1994 ICPD; the mobilization of over $2.76 billion in voluntary population resources, including $2.57 billion for its core programme supplemented by $190 million of multi-bilateral resources; moving the centre of gravity of more and more of its activities and decision-making to the field; establishing eight regional Country Support Teams (CSTs) located throughout the developing world and staffed with a total of 130 technical advisers mostly from the United Nations system, who are in a position to respond in a timely and effective manner to the various technical backstopping needs of national population programmes; and a great expansion in its awareness building and advocacy work.

Among the most striking and encouraging accomplishments in the population sector in the 1990s for which data are available, are the following:

- The average number of children per woman decreased from 3.3 in the 1985-1990 period to 2.7 in 1998 — a drop of 19 per cent;
- Despite an encouraging continuing increase in life expectancy, the world's population growth rate fell from 1.7 per cent a year in 1990 to the current rate of 1.3 per cent; and
- Contraceptive prevalence use continued to increase in developing countries with a large number of them increasing by at least 10 percentage points over the past 10 years (United Nations, 1999).

Secondments, Due Diligence and the United Nations Conferences of the 1990s

It became something close to common practice for each of the funds and programmes of the United Nations system, including UNFPA, to second a knowledgeable staff member or otherwise lend support to the usually severely understaffed and underfunded *ad hoc* secretariats charged with carrying out the nine major United Nations conferences of the 1990s. This was especially true of the United Nations Conference on Environment and Development (UNCED), the ICPD, the Fourth

World Conference on Women (FWCW), and the Second United Nations Conference on Human Settlements (HABITAT II).

Secondments were not only a tangible sign of interest and solidarity but brought expertise in areas that otherwise would not have received the level of up-to-date, nuanced attention they deserved. While secondments and due diligence were important to all funds and programmes of the United Nations system, it was especially true in the case of UNFPA because of the continued sensitivity of numerous population subjects and issues. Because of these sensitivities, more than a few of the concerned country representatives and organizations were prone to treat population issues and concerns with benign neglect in the interest of facilitating harmony and reaching consensus more easily, as well as to a common human disposition to leave contentious issues to others. Thus, by way of example, General Assembly resolution 44/228, an 87-paragraph resolution of December 1989 that set the 1992 UNCED in motion, mentions every issue and concern that impacts on the environment, except population or even demography.

Alerted to this lacuna and aware of the little progress made in correcting it during the first year of the UNCED preparatory process, Dr. Sadik brought the issue to the attention of the Secretary-General of the conference. In response, he requested Dr. Sadik to second one of her staff members to his secretariat to assist him in addressing the issue. The secondment began in January 1991. Thereafter, population issues were systematically reflected in the documents prepared for the second and third sessions of the UNCED PrepCom, finally resulting in a mandate to prepare a stand-alone chapter of Agenda 21 entitled "Demographic Dynamics and Sustainability." The demographic chapter was adopted by consensus at the UNCED in Rio de Janeiro with the need to "promote appropriate demographic policies" also included in Principle 8 of the Rio Declaration.

The positive results flowing from the secondment, coupled with the due diligence of Dr. Sadik and her staff during 1991-1992, were many. In the national reports prepared for UNCED, over 90 per cent of developing countries identified population dynamics as one of the three major problems they faced with regard to sustainable development. At UNCED, 24 heads of state or government, 36 heads of national delegations and 12 heads of international organizations expressed their concern and support for population issues in the framework of policies and programmes aiming at sustainable development. The Secretary-General of the conference, in outlining the rate of population growth said, "this cannot continue. Population must be stabilized, and rapidly. If we do not do it, nature will, and much more brutally." Much of this would resonate over the next 24 months and would be a major contributing factor in the crafting and approval of the ICPD Programme of Action in September 1994 in Cairo.

UNFPA, as part of its contributions to the preparations of global conferences sponsored by the United Nations, also seconded staff members to the *ad hoc* secretariats that did the bulk of the preparatory work for the World Summit for Social Development (WSSD) held in Copenhagen in March 1995, and for the FWCW held in Beijing in September 1995. In addition, UNFPA financed a senior member of the *ad hoc* secretariat charged with the preparations for HABITAT II held in Istanbul in June 1996. UNFPA also played a direct, active role in the various meetings of the Preparatory Committees (PrepComs) of each of the above-mentioned conferences as well as four other major United Nations conferences of the 1990s: namely, the World Conference on Education for All in Jomtien, Thailand, in March 1990; the World Summit for Children held in New York in September 1990; the World Conference on Human Rights held in Vienna in June 1993; and the World Food Summit held in Rome in November 1996. It is noteworthy that Dr. Sadik personally addressed eight of these world conferences.

UNFPA also did very well as a recipient of a number of valuable secondments and financial support for secretariat staff from UNDP and UNICEF in 1993 and 1994 in its own preparations for the 1994 ICPD.

Thanks to due diligence and an earned reputation for being a quietly persistent and reliable partner, and after more than a little bit of pushing, pulling and especially reminding, I am pleased to be able to state that population concerns (principally gender concerns; reproductive health; maternal, infant and child mortality; and poverty eradication) are prominently included in the declarations, platforms, plans and programmes of action, and agendas of the nine world conferences of the 1990s as well as in their highly significant follow-up mechanisms.

UNFPA Accomplishments in 1990-1993 Leading up to Cairo

The early years of the 1990s saw UNFPA building on the positive momentum generated by the Amsterdam Forum and preparing for the Cairo Conference in 1994. The UNFPA Governing Council in 1990 noted "with satisfaction" the results of the Amsterdam Forum and urged all concerned "to increase significantly their allocation to population activities in order to reach the target of $9 billion per year by the year 2000." These views were strongly endorsed by the General Assembly in resolution 45/216 of December 1990 entitled "Population and Development." The Governing Council also recommended that 11 July always be observed by the international community as "World Population Day."

The year 1990 also saw the issuance of a joint letter from the executive heads of UNFPA and IPPF to all staff, and the participation of UNFPA in two IPPF advisory panels on programme and medical issues, in order to promote more systematic cooperation between the two organizations.

The following year, 1991, marked the first full year that Dr. Sadik wore two hats: Executive Director of UNFPA and Secretary-General of the ICPD. Each assignment required a great deal of substantive, managerial, and advocacy work.

On the UNFPA front, it called for managing a $225 million programme while paying greater attention to: a) making the world better aware of the many linkages between population and environment as part of the build-up to the 1992 UNCED; b) working with WHO and others to give greater attention and financial assistance to contraceptive research; c) working with WHO and UNICEF on the role of traditional birth attendants (TBAs) in improving maternal and infant survivability; d) parent education via projects in Burundi, Liberia, Malawi, Mozambique, Panama, and Vietnam to educate parents in reproductive health and human sexuality; and e) continuing to expand UNFPA's women, population, development and advocacy work.

On the ICPD front, there was a need to: a) plan and schedule the six expert group meetings and five regional preparatory meetings authorized by ECOSOC (resolution 1991/93 of 26 July 1991), which took place in 1992 and 1993; b) organize the secretariat of the ICPD; c) ensure appropriate inter-agency participation and coordination; and d) begin the important fund-raising and awareness-building work necessary to a successful preparatory process and conference.

In 1992 a "Global Initiative on Contraceptive Requirements and Logistic Management Needs in Developing Countries in the 1990s" was launched. It was overseen by UNFPA, with the first four (of twelve) in-depth country studies looking at the contraceptive needs over the next decade of India, Nepal, Pakistan, and Zimbabwe. During the year, UNFPA also signed an agreement with the Organization of African Unity (OAU) to promote the adoption and implementation of population policies among OAU member states and participated in the United Nations Joint Collaborative Mission to the Commonwealth of Independent States (CIS) and its follow-up, which found great need for family planning assistance in the Central Asian Republics.

During 1993, UNFPA was fully immersed in the extensive preparations for the 1994 ICPD while also striving to upgrade the quality of its activities in over 100 countries and respond to requests for assistance from newly independent countries such as Kazakhstan, Kyrgyzstan, Tajikistan, Turkmenistan, Uzbekistan, as well as the Government of the Republic of Georgia. Studies in late1993 estimated that there were 399 million people in the developing world using modern contraception — a tenfold increase since 1970. At the same time, the effort to broaden the scope of the UNFPA programme to encompass a more comprehensive reproductive health-care approach was one of the notable features of the Fund's work in 1993.

In preparations for the ICPD, the ICPD PrepCom was "upgraded" to become a subsidiary body of the General Assembly (resolution 48/186). Dr. Sadik's proposal that the envisioned Programme of Action of the ICPD articulate a comprehensive approach to issues of population and development identifying a range of demographic and social goals to be achieved over a 20-year period was accepted. The final meeting of the PrepCom was wisely extended to three weeks in length, and two-day pre-conference consultations at the venue site were also approved (ECOSOC resolution 1993/76). In getting ready for the meetings of the PrepCom, the United Nations Population Division and UNFPA worked smoothly to first produce an annotated outline of the final document for discussion by the General Assembly in late 1993, and thereafter the draft final document of the conference, which was made available to all interested parties in February 1994.

On the UNFPA front, in addition to laying the foundations for programmes of assistance in six new countries, mentioned above, no table work was accomplished in producing a policy note on reproductive health care to support countries' efforts in the area of integrated reproductive health care/family planning services through primary health-care systems. The Fund also published an assessment of its experience — nine projects — with micro-enterprise projects to enhance women's economic independence. A review of UNFPA's review and assessment of programme strategies, of which 189 had been conducted between 1977 and 1993, was undertaken in order to improve the usefulness of their recommendations by making them more explicit and by establishing clearer priorities, including in light of the ICPD, placing more emphasis on reproductive health care as the linchpin of integrated programmes.

UNFPA in the Post-Cairo Period

In 1994, UNFPA celebrated its twenty-fifth anniversary in grand style with several accomplishments. It crossed the $3 billion mark in cumulative voluntary contributions. It witnessed an increase of 18 per cent in pledged assistance. Most important, the Fund played a major role in the concluding year of the three-year preparations for ICPD, seeking, successfully, to involve stakeholders at all levels in over 180 countries in a process that culminated in the adoption by consensus of the ICPD Programme of Action in September 1994, followed by its endorsement by the General Assembly in December 1994 (resolution 49/128 of 19 December 1994).

As United Nations Secretary-General Boutros-Ghali wrote in the foreword of UNFPA's 1994 Annual Report:

1994 will be remembered as the year the international community changed the way it views population issues. . . . Population is no longer seen in isolation, but as an integral part of all activity for development. . . . The Programme of Action recognizes the rights of women as a key to improving the quality of people's lives everywhere. . . . Perhaps the most important legacy of the Cairo Conference is the collaborative spirit that lives on, as UNFPA collaborates with governments, NGOs, and its partner agencies in the United Nations system to translate the ambitious goals of the Programme of Action into reality.

UNFPA came fully of age in 1994. This was recognized when the General Assembly noted "with satisfaction the positive contributions the Fund and its dedicated staff have made during its first 25 years in promoting better understanding and awareness of population and development issues, in improving the quality of human life, and in extending systematic and sustained assistance to developing countries . . ." (resolution 49/3 of 20 October 1994).

Following the ICPD, UNFPA gave priority to the substantive preparations for the FWCW in Beijing and for the WSSD in Copenhagen that would be taking place in 1995. The Fund worked to ensure that both would take explicit account of the Cairo Programme of Action, especially its clear recognition of the need to empower women and to take steps to recognize and improve their human rights, including their reproductive rights. UNFPA's strong advocacy work overcame a number of hurdles (including the reluctance of some to revisit and include sensitive subjects concerning people's reproductive rights). These efforts paid off quite handsomely, especially in the strong wording on reproductive rights and services that was contained in the Platform for Action adopted by the Beijing Conference.

Other noteworthy developments in 1994 included the establishment of a UNFPA country office in South Africa and funding a project designed to encourage consensus-building between the government and NGOs on future directions for reproductive health care/family planning. In keeping with the ICPD Programme of Action, declaring that "countries with economies in transition should receive temporary assistance for population and development in light of the difficult economic and social problems they are presently facing," UNFPA approved ten new reproductive health projects in countries with economies in transition to help address the high rates of induced abortion. It should be noted that all of the countries in transition had played an active role in ICPD and its preparatory process. The small countries of the South Pacific subregion had also played an active role in ICPD and its preparatory process. For many countries in both groups it was their first active involvement in a major world conference. In 1994 UNFPA provided assistance to 50 projects in the South Pacific subregion, with the majority being in the area of MCH/FP.

The Inter-Agency Task Force (IATF) on the Implementation of the ICPD Programme of Action

Following the endorsement by the United Nations General Assembly of the ICPD Programme of Action, the Secretary-General of the United Nations asked the Executive Director of UNFPA to convene and chair an Inter-Agency Task Force (IATF) to develop a coordinated approach for the implementation of the ICPD Programme of Action, as well as a framework for reporting on the progress of the implementation. The IATF focused the bulk of its attention on country-level cooperation. Six working groups were set up by the task force addressing the key areas for action corresponding to the goals and objectives of the Programme of Action. The working groups produced guidelines and detailed guidance notes that were sent to all United Nations Resident

Coordinators in September 1995. Copies were also made available to interested governments, to organizations of the United Nations system and to other interested parties.

The working method and outputs of the IATF on the ICPD Programme of Action were so well received throughout the United Nations system and elsewhere that in late 1995 they served as models for three ACC task forces set up by the Secretary-General. These task forces were designed to galvanize the United Nations system to meet priority goals emerging from United Nations global conferences of the 1990s on economic, social, and related issues, and to strengthen the system's follow-up mechanisms. From early 1996, the work of the IATF on ICPD would be encompassed into the work of the ACC Task Force on Basic Social Services for All. The ACC decided in late 1995 that Dr. Sadik would also chair the ACC Task Force on Basic Social Services for All (BSSA), with UNFPA as its lead agency.

The ACC Task Force on Basic Social Services for All

Eighteen United Nations organizations and agencies participated in the BSSA task force. The mandate of the task force encompassed the following key concerns: population, with special emphasis on reproductive health and family planning services; basic education; primary health care; drinking water and sanitation; shelter and social services in post-crisis situations.

From the outset, the task force focused on the need to devise a pragmatic, doable and time-bound programme of work that would clearly respond to key issues and priorities at the country level. Given the broad mandate and the limited time, the BSSA task force decided to concentrate on producing concrete outputs that would be of specific use to the United Nations Resident Coordinator system and to others in assisting countries in programme implementation.

The end products of the BSSA task force included guidelines in the five key areas of its concerns, guidance notes on international migration and development, a wall chart with twelve key indicators to assist countries in monitoring progress in meeting conference goals in the provision of basic social services, a report on donor collaboration in assistance to the social sector, three country case-studies, an advocacy card, and the *Compendium of Social Issues from the United Nations Global Conferences in the 1990s*. The BSSA task force made its final report in April 1998.

In 1995, the momentum created by the ICPD continued and intensified. The year saw voluntary contributions to UNFPA grow by 18 per cent to $313 million, with UNFPA providing support to 150 countries. This was also the first year advocacy took its rightful place (alongside of reproductive health, including family planning; and guidance in drawing up population and development strategies) as a UNFPA core programme area. Through its advocacy programmes, UNFPA actively promotes the goals of the ICPD Programme of Action, including women's equality; international consensus on population and sustainable development; early stabilization of the world's population; and mobilization of resources and political will.

The role of increased advocacy as a critical tool for enhancing interest in UNFPA and highlighting the many inextricable links between population and development was a central theme of a four-day June 1995 meeting of 240 UNFPA staff members from around the world. During the year, the Fund also initiated advocacy training for UNFPA Country Directors; issued a "how-to" handbook on public information; and launched a state-of-the-art UNFPA site on the World Wide Web (http://www.unfpa.org).

235

New initiatives and "breakthroughs" during the year to begin translating the ICPD Programme of Action into reality numbered well over one hundred. There are several that I consider to be particularly noteworthy.

The year 1995 marked the first full year of operations of UNFPA's Office of Emergency Operations, based in Geneva. The Office helps the Fund plan, coordinate, monitor and evaluate UNFPA activities in the area of reproductive health in emergency situations. Working with the UNFPA network of CSTs, the Office of the United Nations High Commissioner for Refugees (UNHCR), UNICEF and WHO, the Office helps to develop reproductive health projects for refugees, internally displaced persons, and returnees.

UNFPA reviewed and adjusted all of its operational and policy guidelines to align them with the recommendations of the ICPD Programme of Action and began preparing a report on its programme priorities and future directions (DP/1995/25) for its Executive Board. The Board endorsed the core programme areas proposed in the report and requested the Executive Director to concentrate UNFPA assistance in those areas while stressing that population policies are an integral part of a strategy for sustainable development (Executive Board decision 95/15).

While UNFPA focused much of its attention on the three core programme areas, it remained aware that countries faced a series of related challenges in the post-ICPD era deserving of the Fund's support. Demographic phenomena such as migration and the growing number of elderly people and social changes such as later marriages and earlier sexual activities received increased attention from UNFPA in 1995, especially in its interregional and NGO-supported programmes.

Lastly, the authority, prestige and visibility of UNFPA in the field was further enhanced with the change of designation of UNFPA resident Country Directors to UNFPA Representatives (Executive Board decision 95/20).

During 1996, the Fund continued to devote considerable time and energy to translating its three core programme areas into concrete activities at the country level. Each of the 47 new country programmes formulated during the year combined this substantive programming grid with the new resource allocation approach — proposed by UNFPA and approved by its Executive Board in decision 96/15 — to determine the amount and type of resources allocated to each programme as well as its strategy and focus. The percentage breakdown approved in the new resource allocation approach takes into account the various indicator and threshold levels of countries on the gaps remaining towards meeting the goals of the ICPD. It divides countries into five categories: the 60 Group A countries (those most in need of assistance to realize ICPD Goals) are to receive 67-69 per cent of country programme funds; the 39 Group B countries are to receive 22-24 per cent of funds; the 12 countries in category C are to receive 5-7 per cent of country programme funds; the 27 countries with economies in transition are to receive 3-4 per cent of country programme funds; and the 38 other countries are to receive 0.5 per cent of country programme funds.

The Executive Board also endorsed (in decision 96/28) the UNFPA Mission Statement it had asked the Fund to prepare. The seven-paragraph Mission Statement is reproduced in Box 1.

Voluntary contributions to UNFPA in 1996 once again totalled just over $300 million, with 98 per cent of the contributions coming from the Fund's fourteen major donors.

UNFPA continued to pay increased attention to adolescent reproductive health care in virtually every UNFPA country programme prepared in 1996, including factoring into each the important lessons for programming that had been learned from the recent work of a WHO/UNICEF/UNFPA study group in this area. UNFPA also worked closely with IPPF on initiatives to promote youth-to-youth counselling, the Commonwealth Medical Association (CMA) in orienting national medical associations to the importance of and need to address adolescent reproductive health, and the Working Group on Health and Population at the World Youth Forum.

Following approval by the Executive Board of the Global Contraceptive Commodity Programme (GCCP) in decision 96/3, stock holdings were collected of all primary contraceptive methods in order to respond to any emergency demand. Since its establishment through the end of 1996, over a dozen urgent requests had been received for immediate assistance.

In recognition of the HABITAT II Conference in Istanbul, the SWOP report for 1996 took as its theme population and the urban future. The report was widely covered by the international media in the context of HABITAT II and widely distributed at the conference. It also served as the centrepiece for national level coverage of HABITAT-related population issues.

In 1996, UNFPA strengthened a number of key collaborative arrangements by signing cooperation agreements with UNHCR, the International Committee of the Red Cross (ICRC), IPPF and the International Organization for Migration (IOM). After three years of active lobbying by UNFPA and its Executive Board, UNFPA was added to the UNICEF/WHO Coordinating Committee on Health.

In the Arab States a holistic approach to maternal and reproductive health was formally endorsed by the Governments of Lebanon and Sudan, and by the Palestinian Authority. In September, the UNFPA Executive Board approved a new $7.2 million programme of assistance for the Palestinian people in Gaza and the West Bank. In Egypt, in July 1996, the Minister of Health banned the practice of female genital cutting in state-run hospitals.

In addition to utilizing its own regular resources for strengthening the capacity of NGOs, UNFPA has also been entrusted with multi-bilateral funds for this purpose. For example, in the Central Asian Republics the Government of the Netherlands is supporting, through UNFPA in collaboration with IPPF, the establishment of national family planning associations (FPAs) in six countries and strengthening their capacities through the provision of equipment and training.

In 1997 UNFPA's role in population — despite an erosion in resource momentum — continued to evolve, with still greater emphasis being placed on adolescent reproductive health; on efforts to reduce maternal mortality; on HIV/AIDS prevention; on efforts to measure progress and to improve indicators to serve as markers of performance; and on technical advocacy work designed to show the Executive Board and donors the dire reproductive health consequences in the period 1995-2000 if the financial goals set down in the ICPD Programme of Action were not met. The year also saw the beginning of a process known as "ICPD+5" to assess what had been achieved since Cairo and to reinforce its message.

In addition to giving increased priority to the task of reducing maternal mortality, in many of its country activities, UNFPA also provided assistance to an innovative programme being executed by the International Federation of Gynaecology and Obstetrics called "Save the Mothers." This project is being implemented in seven countries that have high maternal mortality rates, the existence of an active obstetric/gynaecological society and a demonstrated government commitment to improving women's health. UNFPA also participated in the Safe Motherhood Technical Consultation sponsored by the Inter-Agency Group for Safe Motherhood held in Sri Lanka with over 250 delegates from 65 countries in attendance.

Box I
UNFPA MISSION STATEMENT

UNFPA extends assistance to developing countries, countries with economies in transition and other countries at their request to help them address reproductive health and population issues, and raise awareness of these issues in all countries, as it has since its inception.

UNFPA's three main areas of work are: to help ensure universal access to reproductive health, including family planning and sexual health, to all couples and individuals on or before the year 2015; to support population and development strategies that enable capacity-building in population programming; to promote awareness of population and development issues and to advocate for the mobilization of the resources and political will necessary to accomplish its areas of work.

UNFPA is guided by, and promotes, the principles of the Programme of Action of the International Conference on Population and Development (1994). In particular, UNFPA affirms its commitment to reproductive rights, gender equality and male responsibility, and to the autonomy and empowerment of women everywhere. UNFPA believes that safeguarding and promoting these rights, and promoting the well-being of children, especially girl children, are development goals in themselves. All couples and individuals have the right to decide freely and responsibly the number and spacing of their children as well as the right to the information and means to do so.

UNFPA is convinced that meeting these goals will contribute to improving the quality of life and to the universally accepted aim of stabilizing world population. We also believe that these goals are an integral part of all efforts to achieve sustained and sustainable social and economic development that meets human needs, ensures well-being and protects the natural resources on which all life depends.

UNFPA recognizes that all human rights, including the right to development, are universal, indivisible, interdependent and interrelated, as expressed in the Programme of Action of the International Conference on Population and Development, the Vienna Declaration and the Programme of Action adopted by the World Conference on Human rights, the Convention on the Elimination of All Forms of Discrimination against Women, the Programme of Action of the World Summit for Social Development, the Platform for Action of the Fourth World Conference on Women and in other internationally agreed instruments.

UNFPA, as the lead United Nations organization for the follow-up and implementation of the Programme of Action of the International Conference on Population and Development, is fully committed to working in partnership with governments, all parts of the United Nations system, development banks, bilateral aid agencies, non-governmental organizations and civil society. UNFPA strongly supports the United Nations Resident Coordinator system and the implementation of all relevant United Nations decisions.

UNFPA will assist in the mobilization of resources from both developed and developing countries, following the commitments made by all countries in the Programme of Action to ensure that the goals of the International Conference on Population and Development are met.

238

During 1997, UNFPA supported HIV/AIDS prevention activities in 132 countries with NGOs helping implement UNFPA-supported programmes in 80 of those countries. The reproductive health guidelines issued by UNFPA in 1997 specify the wide variety of types of support the Fund can provide in the area of HIV/AIDS. In a closely related area, in 1997 UNFPA provided 173 million condoms to 55 countries and procured an additional 16 million on behalf of other organizations. Female condoms were provided in two countries. Also during the year a twenty-page joint WHO/UNICEF/UNFPA Statement on Female Genital Mutilation (FGM) was issued.

In its best and strongest worded advocacy effort of the 1990s, UNFPA sent two sobering reports (DP/FPA/1997/12 and Annex, and DP/FPA/1998/CRP2) to its Executive Board in 1997 documenting the unacceptably high order of magnitude of the grave — yet avoidable — consequences over the period from 1995-2000 of large resource shortfalls in meeting the goals laid out in the ICPD Programme of Action.

These extremely well-researched and well-documented reports showed in text, charts, tables, and various scenarios that around 100 million individuals or couples who would have used modern family planning services will not be able to because insufficient funds rendered those services unavailable. A total of 130-230 million more unintended pregnancies would result over the period 1995-2000, leading to 50-90 million additional induced abortions; 3.8-7 million more women would die than otherwise, either in childbirth or while undergoing unsafe abortions; 1.3-2.4 million more children would die in their infancy or early childhood from the many millions of unintended births. The exact estimates may change as the analysis is further refined, but no one could or should doubt that the order of magnitude of these avoidable consequences will not change unless international population assistance triples quickly — from $1.9 billion in 1997 to the ICPD target of $5.7 billion for international population assistance for the year 2000.

It is fair to say that the UNFPA Executive Board had never before received such reports. The stakes involved in providing or not providing adequate population resources had never been presented so clearly and graphically to them.

Actively playing its assigned leadership role in the implementation of the ICPD Programme of Action, UNFPA's work in 1998 most notably included conducting a many-sided operational review and appraisal process of the lessons learned and the constraints encountered carried out since the Cairo Conference. The results were designed to inform The Hague Forum in February 1999 and a Special Session of the General Assembly from 30 June to 2 July 1999. Annual resources available for the UNFPA programme in 1998 totalled slightly above $300 million for the fourth year in a row, meaning that the Fund once again had to scale back the resources it could provide to country programmes and many related activities. UNFPA prospects for a higher funding level were also hurt by an October 1998 decision by the United States Congress to not include funding for UNFPA in its appropriations for the coming year as a result of the China controversy detailed above.

On the positive side, UNFPA received a three-year grant from the William H. Gates Foundation for two programmes, and it received over $17.9 million from the United Nations Foundation, financed by the Turner Foundation, for twelve projects focusing on women and advancing adolescent reproductive and sexual health. A $27.5 million initiative for reproductive health delivery programmes in Cambodia, Pakistan, Sri Lanka, and Vietnam to be implemented in cooperation with NGOs and financed by the European Commission began programme activities in earnest in 1998. In a further encouraging development, the Packard Foundation announced in November 1998 that it will be allocating more than $300 million to international population and reproductive health programmes over the next five years.

The year 1998 was proclaimed as the "Year of Safe Motherhood" by UNFPA and five other international organizations (WHO, UNICEF, the World Bank, IPPF and the Population Council) that have been involved in the field for the past decade. The aim was to bring to the world's attention that more than 600,000 women, most of them in developing countries, continue to needlessly die each year from childbirth-related illnesses and injuries. In preparation for a major event on Safe Motherhood at the World Bank headquarters on World Health Day, UNFPA collaborated on the production of "The Safe Motherhood Action Agenda: Priorities for the Next Decade."

During 1998 UNFPA was deeply immersed in various operational review and appraisal activities to access the progress made and the principal constraints encountered in the first four years of the implementation of the twenty-year (1995-2015) Programme of Action of the ICPD. This process raised a number of pertinent questions. Our language has changed, but has our behaviour? To what extent have policy changes occurred and been reflected in operational activities at the community level? Are the programmes focusing on the interventions required to reach ICPD goals and objectives?

The review and appraisal activities in 1998 included three round table meetings and four technical meetings organized by UNFPA. ICPD+5 review and appraisal meetings by the five United Nations regional commissions were held, each producing a final report that included large numbers of recommendations for key future actions required to accelerate and expand the implementation of the ICPD Programme of Action.

UNFPA conducted a global Field Inquiry on Progress in the Implementation of the ICPD Programme of Action, to which 114 developing and 18 developed countries responded. The inquiry focused on the operational dimensions of population and reproductive health programmes. The findings of the inquiry were taken into account in the preparation of the background paper by UNFPA for the February 1999 Hague Forum. A 69-page summary report on the inquiry was also submitted to the forum. Among the many findings of the inquiry were that at least 106 governments recognized the involvement of NGO/civil society in the implementation of the Programme of Action, with 57 of these permitting direct funding of NGOs from external donors.

The theme of the SWOP 1998 report was "The New Generations." The report focused attention on the one billion young people between the ages of 15 and 24, the biggest-ever generation of young people; on the large growth in ageing populations in both developed and developing countries; and on a demographic bonus in the next 15-20 years as a "bulge" of young people come into the workforce while fewer children are born. If jobs can be found for them, the workforce bulge can be a basis for more investment, greater labour productivity, and faster economic and social development. The report underlines that if the ICPD Programme of Action is successfully implemented, healthy life spans will be longer, fertility lower, and young people less numerous but healthier and better educated.

Conclusion

In addition to its being the conduit for something on the order of 20 per cent of the international population assistance extended to developing countries during the period 1969-1999, I have tried to show that UNFPA has provided a considerably larger proportion of the salt and pepper, the spices, herbs and yeast that have been so crucial over the entire thirty-year period in increasing awareness, in building up knowledge and in increasing the capacity of governments — and a large cross-section of other constituencies — to respond to national, regional and global needs and challenges in the population and reproductive health fields.

There are many little-known ways in which UNFPA has made a big difference in the population field over the past thirty years. The following brief questions and answers focus on just a few of the many cases in point.

Questions and Answers

- Question: Would the population programmes in such countries as Albania, Algeria, Cuba, Iran, Mongolia, the South Pacific island countries, Sudan, the Syrian Arab Republic, Uzbekistan, Vietnam, and Yemen — countries that received little or no international population assistance from other sources over most of the past three decades — have begun as early or made anywhere near as much progress as they have in beginning to meet the population and reproductive health needs of their peoples without the timely and sustained assistance provided to each by UNFPA?

    Answer: No.

- Question: Would the conduct, outcomes and follow-up of the 1974 WPC, the 1984 ICP, and especially the 1994 ICPD — and the implementation of their recommendations and plans and programmes of action — have been as successful and far-reaching without the major roles in each played by UNFPA?

    Answer: No.

- Question: Would the population policies, activities, awareness, acceptability and trained manpower in the 45 sub-Saharan Africa countries be anywhere near as far along as they currently are without the trusted and sustained assistance provided to each by UNFPA?

    Answer: No.

- Question: Would the nine global conferences and summits sponsored by the United Nations on economic and social development matters held during the 1990s have taken due, explicit account of the important roles played by various population factors in the development process without skilful, persistent advocacy work by UNFPA?

    Answer: No.

- Question: Would the United Nations system, including the World Bank, be as united and speaking with such a strong, clear voice on reproductive health and rights; on the importance of fully empowering women; on AIDS prevention; on health information and services for adolescents; on intensifying efforts to reduce infant, child and maternal mortality; and on

241

improving the education opportunities for girls without the support and advocacy work of UNFPA in each of these critical development and human rights areas?

Answer: No.

A Postscript

With UNFPA having played a major substantive and administrative role in its long, arduous preparatory process, the General Assembly of the United Nations met in a Special Session from 30 June to 2 July 1999 and adopted by consensus a 106-paragraph document on key actions for the further implementation of the Programme of Action of the ICPD. The document highlighted that positive progress in implementing the recommendations of the ICPD had been made over the past five years. The document called on governments to take strong measures to promote the human rights of women and girls and to encourage strengthening their ready access to reproductive and sexual health services. It also called on governments to ensure that prevention of and services for STDs and HIV/AIDS are an integral component of health programmes and that governments, with assistance from the Joint United Nations Programme on HIV/AIDS (UNAIDS) and donors, should by 2005 ensure that 90 per cent of young men and women aged 15 to 25 have access to the information, education and services necessary to develop the life skills required to reduce their vulnerability to HIV infection.

Countries were urged to substantially increase their voluntary contributions to UNFPA, as well as to other relevant United Nations organizations. And UNFPA was urged to continue to strengthen its leadership role within the United Nations system in assisting countries to take the strategic action necessary to ensure availability of reproductive health services and choice of reproductive health products, including contraceptives. This is a role that it has been playing for the last thirty years, and I can only hope that it will continue and grow in the coming years.

References

Stanley Johnson. *World Population and the United Nations: Challenge and response* (Cambridge: Cambridge University Press, 1987).

Nafis Sadik. *Population: The UNFPA Experience* (New York: New York University Press, 1984).

Nafis Sadik. *Making a Difference: Twenty-five Years of UNFPA Experience* (London: Banson, 1994).

Rafael Salas. *People: An International Choice* (Oxford: Pergamon, 1977): 2nd edition.

Rafael Salas. *International Population Assistance: The First Decade* (New York: Pergamon Press, 1979).

Rafael Salas. *Reflections on Population* (New York: Pergamon Press, 1984).

Jyoti Shankar Singh. *Creating a New Consensus on Population* (London: Earthscan, 1998).

Richard Symonds and Michael Carder. *The United Nations and the Population Question 1945-1970* (New York: McGraw-Hill Company, 1973).

United Nations. *Report of the United Nations World Population Conference, 1974, Bucharest, 19-30 August 1974* (1975: sales no. E75.XIII.3).

United Nations. *Report of the International Conference on Population, 1984, Mexico City, 6-14 August 1984* (1984: sales no. E84.XIII.8).

United Nations. *Earth Summit: Agenda 21: The United Nations Programme of Action for Sustainable Development, Rio de Janeiro, 3-12 June 1992* (1993: sales no. E.93.1.11).

United Nations. *Report of the International Conference on Population and Development: Cairo, 5-13 September 1994* (1995: sales no. E.95.XIII.18).

United Nations. *World Summit for Social Development: Copenhagen, 6-12 March 1995* (1996: sales no. 96.IV.8).

United Nations. *The Fourth World Conference on Women: Beijing, September 1995* (1996: sales no. 96.IV.13).

United Nations. *Report of the ACC Task Force on Basic Social Services for All* (1997: E/CN.9/1997/4, 7 January).

United Nations. *Meeting the goals of the ICPD: Consequences of resource shortfalls up to the year 2000* (1997: DP/FPA/1997/12, 10 July).

United Nations. Review and Appraisal of the Progress Made in Achieving the Goals and Objectives of the Programme of Action of the ICPD (New York: Population Division, 1999).

United Nations Population Fund. *UNFPA Report 1969-1972* (New York: 1973).

United Nations Population Fund. *UNFPA Annual Report 1973-1998* (New York: 1974-1999).

United Nations Population Fund. The *State of World Population* (New York: 1978-1998).

United Nations Population Fund. *Global Population Assistance Report, 1982-1985* (New York: 1988).

United Nations Population Fund. *Report of the International Forum on Population in the Twenty-First Century: Amsterdam, The Netherlands, 6-9 November 1989* (New York: 1989).

United Nations Population Fund. *Global Population Assistance Report 1982-1990* (New York: 1992).

United Nations Population Fund. *Global Population Assistance Report 1996* (New York: 1998).

UNITED
NATIONS

A

General Assembly

Distr.
GENERAL

A/RES/54/11
18 November 1999

Fifty-fourth session
Agenda item 99 *(h)*

RESOLUTION ADOPTED BY THE GENERAL ASSEMBLY

[with reference to a Main Committee (A/54/L.18 and Add.1)]

54/11.   Thirtieth anniversary of the operations of the United Nations Population Fund

The General Assembly,

Recalling its resolution 2211 (XXI) of 17 December 1966, in response to which a trust fund, subsequently named the United Nations Fund or Population Activities, was established in 1967 by the Secretary-General,

Noting that the United Nations Fund for Population Activities, renamed in 1987 as the United Nations Population Fund, began operations in 1969,

Recalling its resolutions 3019 (XXVII) of 18 December 1972, 31/170 of 21 December 1976 and 34/104 of 14 December 1979, in which it, *inter alia*, recognized the leading role and effectiveness of the Fund in the United Nations system in the population field and affirmed the Fund as a subsidiary body of the General Assembly,

Reaffirming Economic and Social Council resolutions 1763 (LIV) of 18 May 1973 and 1986/7 of 21 May 1986 stating the aims and purposes of the Fund,

1.   *Congratulates* the United Nations Population Fund on the occasion of the thirtieth anniversary of its operations;

/...

99-77521

2.   *Notes with appreciation* the positive contributions the fund and its dedicated staff have made during its thirty years in promoting better understanding and awareness of population and development issues, in improving the quality of human life and in extending systematic and sustained assistance to developing countries and countries with economies in transition, at their request, in undertaking appropriate national programmes to address their population and development needs.

40th plenary meeting
27 October 1999

ANNEX II

General Assembly Resolutions pertaining to UNFPA	
<u>3019 (XXVII)</u>	• United Nations Fund for Population Activities
<u>36/201</u>	• Establishment of the United Nations Population Award
<u>45/216</u>	• Population and Development
<u>49/128</u>	• Report of the International Conference on Population and Development
<u>1995/55</u>	• Implementation of the Programme of Action of the International Conference on Population and Development
<u>50/124</u>	• Implementation of the Programme of Action of the International Conference on Population and Development
<u>1997/42</u>	• Follow-up to the International Conference on Population and Development
<u>52/188</u>	• Population and Development
<u>53/183</u>	• Implementation of the Programme of Action of the International Conference on Population and Development

Broadening Choices: Information, Education, Communication, and Advocacy

Sylvie I. Cohen and Tevia Abrams

Introduction

Building awareness of population issues in both developed and developing countries was one of the tasks assigned to the United Nations Population Fund (UNFPA) in the Economic and Social Council of the United Nations (ECOSOC) resolution 1763 (LIV) in 1973. UNFPA's mandate reaffirmed its leadership role in promoting population programmes and in raising awareness that population and development have an integral and mutually reinforcing relationship. Around the same time, population information, education, and communication (IEC) became one of the areas the Fund supported in its programme countries to bring attention to the needs of couples, families and individuals in the areas of reproduction and population, and to prompt action to improve their well-being through broadened choices. Now every national population programme has a communication component for either advocacy, resource mobilization, partnership-building, capacity building or behaviour change. The purpose of this chapter is to explore how UNFPA's efforts in awareness-creation and IEC and advocacy have evolved in the last 30 years and how current challenges and visions will shape its future directions.

Communication has played a vital role in creating universal awareness of the benefits of family planning (FP) and the availability of services and in persuading individuals and communities to decide to use family planning. Communication can spread new values, ideas and social norms and create new understanding and practices once people have been motivated and empowered by information that they find relevant to their own situations. According to the United Nations Population Division, total fertility rates (TFRs) are coming down: the TFR of 5.0 that prevailed globally thirty years ago has been reduced by about half, to 2.4*.[1] At the same time, demographic and health surveys (DHSs) indicate near-universal awareness of the benefits of family planning. Population IEC advocates may claim with justification that their efforts share credit for such significant achievements.

Supporting the contentions that IEC interventions do work is a study undertaken recently by the Johns Hopkins University Center for Communication Programs (JHU/CCP), based on data obtained from an UNFPA-sponsored Tanzania radio drama programme in the early 1990s to increase usage of contraceptives. The study concluded that a multimedia campaign, integrated

---

* While it is true that many countries in Europe and North America have achieved rates below 2.0, and that this has given undue weight to the calculation of the global figure, the fact is that many developing nations have also made exceptional strides, notably in some of the high population countries — China, India and Indonesia, for example, where the TFRs have come down to 1.92, 3.56, and 2.90, respectively.

with a reproductive health service delivery programme, did more than influence knowledge and attitudes: it actually changed behaviour and led directly to the increased use of reproductive health facilities, acceptance of contraceptives by women, and greater discussion of family planning between husbands and wives. The findings confirmed that multiple media sources of information could reinforce and actually extend the reach of family planning services, ultimately "creating an environment where the practice of contraception is perceived as a social norm."[2]

It is indisputable that positive attitudinal changes are taking place at global, country, and, by extension, at the community and individual levels, but this did not happen overnight or in an improvised or spontaneous fashion. In the 1960s, international development initiatives realized that they were not in tune with people's interests and needs. Communication was the missing link.

Fortunately, development communication became recognized by the United Nations system as the key ingredient of international assistance to explain decisions to the communities concerned and enlist their informed involvement in the development programme — although initially this was done in a top-down fashion. This purposeful communication involved a planned and research-based process that drew from various fields such as anthropology, marketing, social psychology, social learning and persuasion theories, public relations, and political economy. Pervading such projects was the underlying assumption that cultural beliefs and values played a major role in people's reproductive preferences and practices, and that they could be positively stimulated and reinforced via the mass media, community networks, and interpersonal exchanges. This assumption — called the *ideational model* — underlined the fact that the diffusion of innovations like modern family planning methods and utilization of family planning services could be accelerated via the diffusion of ideas. Consequently, the goals of seeking social change through new ideas boosted social and educational communication as a feasible, socially acceptable and effective complement to strong family-planning service delivery systems.

Similarly, UNFPA operations gave increasing importance to systematic IEC activities to create awareness and acceptance of population and human reproduction issues. A constant of the period are the two levels of UNFPA's communication operations: the *global* arena and the *country* arena. Global efforts were directed at bolstering preparation for the international population conferences and then for implementing their agreed conclusions. The ultimate aim was to put population issues high on the global public-opinion agenda of both developed and developing countries. At the country level, communication tools, skills, and processes supported national population programmes.

During the thirty years of UNFPA's history, conceptualization of, and language on, communication has undergone significant shifts. Such shifts reflected population and development trends, international consensus, and changes in national population policies and service delivery programmes, whose directions have been extensively depicted in previous chapters. The communication components of UNFPA-supported national population projects have also evolved as the focus of the Fund's country programmes has changed over the last three decades. In his ground-breaking study on communication strategies for family planning, Rogers (1973) identified several phases in a population programme, which coincided with its growing maturity: the "clinic era," the "field era," and the "beyond-family planning" era. Remarkably, this classification remains valid today — with the operational shift since Cairo from a family planning focus towards a model based on comprehensive reproductive health.

For the first two decades, UNFPA opted for the terms "awareness creation" and "population information" to encompass institutional and social communication that aimed at creating public awareness of and interest in population issues. Awareness and public information also aimed to mobilize societies to commit their resources and demonstrate political will to help achieve the international population conference goals. On the other hand, "population communication" and "population education" covered activities that built knowledge and skills, influenced attitudes, and promoted individual behaviours to improve family well-being. These work categories received separate funding. Later, the build-up to the Cairo Conference and the paradigm shift articulated in the International Conference on Population and Development (ICPD) Programme of Action have sharpened UNFPA's focus on more political spheres — "advocacy" for reproductive health and rights. The ICPD also led IEC to be considered an integral part, mutually reinforcing and supporting elements of two new thematic areas: reproductive health, and population and development strategies.

In this chapter, we revisit, as participant-observers, how UNFPA's experience and approach in communication evolved on the road to ICPD+5. We begin by discussing the first two decades, examining first, global awareness creation and public information efforts and, second, how UNFPA addressed policymakers' information needs. We then look at pioneer work in population education, then examine how the new mindset brought about by the Cairo revolution has been translated into UNFPA's public information efforts. We then review the conceptual shift from distinct population communication and non-formal education to a more strategic country programme approach. This leads to a scrutiny of how UNFPA has embarked on rights-based advocacy work. Finally, recent changes in the international context that have affected UNFPA's overall communication vision are summed up and challenges and opportunities for the twenty-first century are spelled out.

The First Two Decades: Establishing Worldwide Prominence of Population Issues

UNFPA's priorities in awareness creation for population and development were dictated by international consensus, but it required a concerted communication effort to create that consensus. Only a few decades ago, the topic of "population" — if seen as an issue at all — attracted little concerted attention. Even when the phenomenon of the exponential growth of population was becoming clear to all — 2 per cent every thousand years in the prehistoric past; 2 per cent every year by the mid-1950s — neither governments nor assistance agencies had reached agreement on the causes, implications or actions to take.

As a result, development strategies and assistance programmes did not take "population" into account. Developing countries were reluctant to accept the notion that rapid population growth was *not* a sign of economic health.[3] Consequently, for the first two decades, UNFPA's institutional communication focused on building political will on the part of national leaders to recognize population growth as a development problem and to legitimise operational solutions that family planning pioneers had demonstrated. In the last decade, extensive efforts were geared towards creating a new consensus,[4] which culminated in the ICPD and was reaffirmed five years later during the ICPD+5 process.

As we discussed in Part II, Chapter 1, "UNFPA and the Global Conferences," UNFPA's work has been influenced by the global population conferences that took place in Bucharest in

1974, Mexico in 1984, and Cairo in 1994. However, they did not always provide a clear blueprint for "positioning" population issues. In this section, we consider how these conferences influenced the way UNFPA framed its advocacy messages. The directions of the international population movement have sometimes been controversial and the alliances unstable due to differing goals, changes in perceived benefits of the coalition, and at times, incompatible ideologies.[5]

The 1974 Bucharest Conference

The first global blueprint spelt out in the World Population Plan of Action (WPPA) in Bucharest in 1974 placed before the Fund and the community of nations a broad new agenda. While demographic issues and the need for direct responses through family planning initiatives were dominant, at the same time, issues related to family formation, sex, religion, gender roles and reproduction, which are at the core of human values, remained sensitive.

At Bucharest, representatives of some developing countries argued that "development is the best contraceptive" as a way to resist population control and fertility reduction goals. It was then widely held that economic growth would produce the "demographic transition" to smaller families, as it had in industrialized countries. This doctrine — also called the "socio-economic model" — emphasized that only changing circumstances require couples or households to adapt, and that demographic transition would automatically induce in parents a desire for smaller families.[6] Fortunately, the human rights rhetoric adopted at Bucharest both rationalized family planning and deflected criticism of imperialism; it fitted well with the consensus for improving the status of women, a language that could easily be translated into United Nations terminology.[7] For the next decade, this controversy would provide the context for the Fund's information and advocacy work.

The 1984 Mexico City Conference

As a result of the Mexico City Conference in 1984, the 1980s witnessed an expanded consensus and political commitment among political leaders of developing countries to address population issues. National leaders endorsed the necessity of improving women's status and women's health and to meet increasing demand for family planning as a health benefit for mothers and children. Also, developing countries' governments seemed to accept alliances more readily with national family planning NGOs. At the same time, conservative forces in the developed countries used controversy over abortion to disengage themselves from international population assistance.

Orchestrating international consensus

In preparing for these world population conferences, UNFPA provided assistance for a wide range of global United Nations communication initiatives. These included training seminars for mass media gatekeepers, expert group meetings on the evaluation of family planning communication programmes, and demonstration workshops and programmes for government information officers from developing countries on how to use the media in family planning and population communication. UNFPA also lent support to publications of newspapers and magazines as well as to the organization of special events by governments and NGOs, some of which resulted in the establishment of regional population information centres. For instance, in 1974, UNFPA inaugurated its magazine *"Populi."* It also produced films on UNFPA programmes and distributed them to television outlets around the world.

Following this impetus, supplying materials to the established mass media outlets has been an ongoing enterprise for UNFPA, and this continued to be stimulated by the preparations for subsequent international population conferences. As part of such services, the Fund often sends video news releases by satellite transmission (and now by Internet), with arrangements made for downloading at predetermined times by television outlets around the world. Copies are also distributed directly to the major television networks in the hope that such personalized service would encourage their use. Broadcast news items and public service announcements are made available for both television and radio. From time to time, filmed documentary specials are undertaken by independent producers or in partnership arrangements with broadcasting groups or sister donor organizations. These are also distributed to major media outlets.

Such media releases are frequently timed to coincide with important meetings or events, such as the World Population Day observances in July of each year. In July 1987, when the Day of Five Billion was marked with public events and much media attention, the UNDP/UNFPA Governing Council and the United Nations General Assembly approved the annual observance of World Population Day on 11 July. The approval reflected the recognition of the importance to the world of the growing population issue. The R. M. Salas Memorial Lectures — a fitting way to honour the dedication and lifetime achievement of UNFPA's first Executive Director, Rafael M. Salas — and the annual Population Award ceremonies are other special events that serve to highlight public concerns and perceptions about population issues.

A Centrepiece: State of the World Population Report

The Fund's centrepiece of advocacy endeavour is the annual *State of World Population* (SWOP) report, which is launched through major international and national media events. Its dual purpose is to highlight and promote important issues while expanding awareness of the Fund's programmes. Themes for the SWOP report are selected for relevance and timeliness — for example, in 1997, the report focused on reproductive health and rights, while in 1998 the report examined the causes, social consequences and policy implications of the simultaneous rapid growth of young adult and elderly populations. In 1999, it focused attention on the implications of the Day of the Six Billion. Materials are carefully researched and prepared for ease of comprehension and visual appeal.

Today, the annual media launches of SWOP reports and global observances of World Population Day are occasions for UNFPA to distribute posters and other display materials. After its initial launch and the first floods of media attention, the SWOP report continues to provide useful content throughout the year, notably for press seminars, other advocacy activities, and background materials for media representatives. Because of their consistently high substantive quality, the reports also serve as credible data and information sources for technical researchers. The most recent external assessment of the SWOP, which was carried out in 1997, gave the publication high marks for readability and for "effectively" meeting the Fund's advocacy and communication needs. The current SWOP report is UNFPA's most visited Web page.

For years, the Fund has also aimed at reaching world opinion leaders in efforts to bolster its mass media initiatives. For example, governments, field offices and interested partner organizations are regularly asked by UNFPA headquarters to create opportunities for public speaking engagements to reach opinion leaders. In addition, many countries now have parliamentary movements for population and development, united in regional and interregional groupings such as the Global Committee of Parliamentarians on Population and Development. The debates and recommendations of these parliamentary groups have both added to the body of population information and helped to communicate it. Initiatives taken by parliamentarian groups to reach out to the world's major religious leaders are a case in point. Another example is the active Inter-American Parliamentary Group on Population and Development — which includes Caribbean parliamentarians — issuing regular communications on population-related matters of importance to the region.

In some countries, non-governmental organizations (NGOs) act as lobbyists, keeping pressure on legislators and civil servants on behalf of population interests. UNFPA has provided support to the Population Institute, a Washington-based international advocacy organization, along with many other networks of interested legislators and local government officials. These groups meet in national and international settings to discuss questions of common interest and agree on action. The Population Institute has obtained good results from the preparation and international distribution of publications on ICPD issues and from its planning and sponsorship of annual World Population Awareness Week (WPAW) observances around the world. In the run-up to WPAW, which is observed in late October, the Population Institute promotes media events and interpersonal communication opportunities in many countries, building on issues explored earlier in the year by UNFPA's SWOP report.

These global media and public information activities are useful mechanisms to help create a cultural environment that is supportive of population-related programmes. Attention is also being focused on donor countries in Asia and the Pacific, notably Japan, Australia, and New Zealand; and in Europe, where there has been some erosion in public support for population assistance. An illustration of UNFPA headquarters' advocacy at work is its support to the Japanese Organization for Cooperation in Family Planning (JOICFP) for an information project to build awareness levels in Japan about world population issues and to raise government funding levels for international population programmes.

Showing that these efforts were resonating, population issues increasingly appeared on the agendas of international conferences dealing with health, food, housing, jobs, the rights and status of women, and threats to the global environment. Such meetings produced important policy and position statements from governments, development agencies and specialists, contributing to the refinement of knowledge and a greater understanding of the issues involved. Another notable development has been greater coverage of population-related issues by the mass media networks. Media coverage of population has greatly improved in recent years. In particular, it is noteworthy that news services other than those that specialize in development reporting, where population is a staple, have increased their reporting on population-related topics.

The First Two Decades: Sharing Population Knowledge For Policy Advocacy

The population community has always had a need to generate and disseminate research findings and information to formulate and refine policies and to design action plans to carry them out. Governments and population experts have worked to understand what factors govern fertility decline. The task of population advocates has been to introduce new ideas and information as a way to affect policy positions. To this effect, advocacy institutions — including UNFPA — have packaged information for decision-makers to encourage them to tackle population issues of national relevance and to help them develop options for implementing development-oriented population and family planning programmes.

UNFPA's hallmark has been to provide information on population that aimed at shaping policies that were both comprehensive and respectful of the basic human right of parents to determine freely and responsibly the number and spacing of their children, and of the country-specific sociocultural context. Therefore, in addition to operational family planning programmes, UNFPA-funded population programmes have included a large policy and institution-building component dealing with the relationship between population and development; urbanization; migration; women's status and gender equity; and building national capacities in data collection and research. Demonstrating how these complex, multisectoral aspects of population interact in development has required extensive information packaging and dissemination of research findings, all of which is necessarily quite expensive.

UNFPA population information encompassed the dissemination of both technical and more popular information to create awareness of population factors among national and international decision-makers. Much interpretation of research findings has been necessary to build a comprehensive picture of population that is convincing to governments and international agencies through dissemination of research findings about socio-cultural factors influencing demographic change, population programmes, new ideas, new technology, new services, and new behaviours that were effective in bringing about improved reproductive health. Demographic research and knowledge, attitudes, and practices (KAP) surveys were used to convince sceptical national leaders and bureaucrats that family planning was a desirable and legitimate component of health and social services. For example, the World Fertility Survey (WFS) added rapidly to the store of knowledge about population trends, their causes and their implications. They informed readers about unmet needs and the demand for family planning. This supported arguments for offering family planning as part of maternal and child health (MCH) services. Consequently, national policies were developed as a way of achieving national aims that were increasingly reflective of internationally recognized population goals.[8]

Sponsorship of Internally Recognized Publications

International as well as national NGOs are still at the forefront of awareness creation concerning population. They stimulate the development of population teaching and research programmes, considerably increasing the information base. Such organizations disseminate information through their publications and activities to local leaders and community activists in developing countries whose acceptance and promotion of the ideas that are being promoted can speed social change.

NGOs also produce regular information on particular sectors of programme design and management for information and communication activities. Many technical publishing programmes issue both regular and occasional population reports and country data sheets on demographic and related socio-economic conditions. Outstanding among UNFPA-sponsored publications of NGOs include the Population Council's *Studies in Family Planning* and *Population and Development Review*; the Alan Guttmacher Institute's *Family Planning Perspectives* and *International Family Planning Perspectives; People and the Planet*; the

Program for the Introduction and Adaptation of Contraceptive Technology's (PIACT's) periodical *Outlook*; and the International Committee for the Management of Population Programmes (ICOMP's) publications on innovative management practices.

One of the most important recent developments in population information services has been the growth of regional, subregional, and international data and information networks, which have vastly expanded the amount of information available. To a greater or lesser extent, population information centres now exist in almost every country. These centres collect, organize and disseminate scientific and technical information tailored to specific audiences, particularly policymakers, programme planners and managers. Some centres are small libraries supporting a demographic training or research unit within a larger context, such as a ministry, university or specialized agency of the United Nations. Others focus on a specific sector and are designed to support, for example, population education in schools, family planning programmes, or national statistical data management. For example, the United Nations Economic and Social Commission for Asia and the Pacific (ESCAP) has had a strong regional information programme for many years and has encouraged and assisted the establishment of national population information centres.

Supporting A Global Population Information Network

In 1979, a major development took place with the establishment by ECOSOC of POPIN, an international information network, with UNFPA support in collaboration with the United Nations Population Division. In less than seven years, it gained a membership of some 100 institutions engaged in population information activities. A primary objective of POPIN is to increase the availability of and access to Web-based information about population and reproductive health topics, with an emphasis on building information infrastructure and capacities in developing countries and regions. With UNFPA support, POPIN has initiated several innovative and creative Internet programmes, including establishment in 1993 of the first United Nations population Internet site and the coordination of Internet coverage of the ICPD in 1994.

Paying attention to population information needs in Africa, information to political leaders and decision-makers has been enhanced by the work of regional demographic centres and the Economic Commission for Africa (ECA). POPIN has also been instrumental in the creation of more than 170 websites around the world. Its largest regional network — POPIN ASEAN, has been established for countries in the Association of South-East Asian Nations (ASEAN). The POPIN Africa website hosted by ECA was launched in 1999 (http://www.un.org/undocuments /eca/fssdd/popin.org).

Establishing a Knowledge Base

As the breadth and complexity of the population field has grown, the need for specialized language and more-manageable classification schemes has become apparent, especially with the advent of computer technology. Catalogues of population literature are accessible in computerized databases established in advanced information centres through guides published by POPIN and Johns Hopkins University. The Population Information Program of JHU is also an important resource, publishing *Population Reports* and a journal on family health topics, and maintaining POPLINE, an international, computerized, bibliographic database on population. With UNFPA support, a POPLINE CD-ROM was issued and distributed to more than 300 institutions in some 79 countries; this venture was undertaken to help consolidate gains made in information networking. More recently, UNFPA produced with JHU/CCP a CD-ROM called "Condoms" to provide a gateway to worldwide condom promotion materials and research, as well as know-how on how to run a mass media campaign.

Computer modelling is now being used to promote awareness of population issues. The Futures Group in the United States has developed RAPID, a system of presentations showing the effects of rapid rates of population growth on development prospects and the natural resource base in different countries. Systems are also in place in academic institutions where future population programme managers are trained. Working in partnership with the United Nations Statistical Division, the ECA, and the International Labour Organization (ILO), UNFPA has supported the development of innovative software for population-related data processing, analysis and dissemination.

For example, at ECA, the Food Security and Sustainable Development Department has developed an integrated computerized model to enhance African leaders' understanding of the interrelationship between food security, environment, health, education and population issues. One of the resulting products, developed with the United Nations Statistical Division, is POPMAP, which enables the user to combine maps with social, economic and demographic databases. POPMAP is a valuable tool for planning and administering population activities that emphasize geographical or logistical components; it is distributed free of charge to UNFPA-supported programmes and to training institutions and government agencies in developing countries.

Over the three decades of UNFPA's work, the scope of information considered necessary for policymakers and programme administrators has broadened, partly because more information is available, partly because national programmes and projects — particularly those receiving international population assistance — need broader information on development indicators, such as health, environmental stress, gender issues and observance of reproductive rights. Emerging issues include the characteristics and problems of ageing populations, international migrations, poverty alleviation, rapid urbanization, gender-based violence, the increase in adolescent pregnancy, and the spread of AIDS.

Despite growing complexity, the global understanding of population as an integral factor in development is expanding, accompanied by the increasing involvement of governments and NGOs in developing countries' policies and programmes. A solid body of knowledge has been built up in the past three decades. This great change in population perceptions has taken place partly because countries experiencing rapid population growth and high fertility were given opportunities to study their own situations and act on them.

Even though much knowledge has been accumulated and widely disseminated, the subject of population has remained controversial. Rapid population growth is, of course, a recent phenomenon, and the implications of a world of 6 billion are already challenging development planners and political strategists. If political commitment is to be encouraged and sustained, governments will need improved databases and better research and analytical capability. The challenge of the next millennium is to improve the level of commitment, connect population information with all other areas of development information, and integrate it fully into the daily activities of governments, organizations, and individuals.

The First Two Decades: Educating for Change

Why Population Education?

The aim of population education is to increase understanding of population dynamics at both the national and world levels and, therefore, to improve an individual's ability to make informed choices.

> It is generally agreed that population education is the process of helping people understand the nature, causes and implications of population processes as they affect, and are affected by, individuals, families, communities and nations. It focuses on family and individual decisions influencing population change at the micro level, as well as on broad demographic changes. . . . A basic goal of population education should be to convince learners that they can control many of the events in their lives, including those related to reproductive behavior (e.g., when to marry, when to have the first child, how many children to have, etc.). They can take decisions, follow up with action and obtain results. Many children begin to believe early that they have no control over their fate. Schools should help them modify this attitude, and teach them that what they become in life will depend in large part on their own decisions and actions. Participatory learning is important to the accomplishment of this goal.[9]

Population education was designed to meet the needs of school-aged youth and to integrate population content into a wide range of educational channels. Through population education, the individual and social implications of population issues are studied and discussed in formal and informal education settings.

As all countries have school facilities with personnel in place, the schools were found to be logistically and organizationally appropriate for such education. In addition, when both boys and girls are exposed to population education through the school curriculum, their knowledge, attitudes, and decisions regarding gender roles can be influenced as well. Teachers, particularly those in rural areas, are often recognized community leaders so that their orientation towards population issues and their own fertility behaviour reinforce the effects of population education in school systems.

Only a few governments in the late 1960s and early 1970s had introduced national population education programmes into their school systems. By the mid-1980s, or within 15 years, more than 90 countries included population education in their schools.[10] As the leading donor in the area of population education, UNFPA has made concrete and widespread contributions to the improvement of the quality of education in this innovative field.[11] Since 1978 it has partnered with the United Nations Educational, Scientific and Cultural Organization (UNESCO) to fund pioneering work in the development of new, relevant curricula, and the introduction of participatory teaching methods and new teaching materials.

A Worldwide Pioneer Effort

The goals and content of population education have differed among regions and countries. Some countries have not perceived rapid population growth to be a major problem to be addressed through population education. In sub-Saharan Africa, for example, rapid population growth was not widely perceived as a problem in the late 1980s, and, as a result, population education programmes dealt largely with education for development, environmental issues, and family life. Other countries have given priority to the immediate need to prevent adolescent pregnancy and AIDS[12] and have emphasized human sexuality and reproduction concepts in their secondary-level school curricula. UNFPA has supported the integration of HIV/AIDS prevention modules into school and out-of-school educational programmes in all countries.[13] In addition to taking concrete action to incorporate key gender issues in education projects funded by UNFPA, the Fund has also supported reviews of a broad range of school materials in an effort to eliminate gender stereotypes.

Not only do the aims of programmes vary from country to country, but so, too, do the strategies for carrying them out. A programme may be designed as a large-scale nationwide effort or as a smaller effort in a single region or district, reflecting local characteristics. New population content may be aimed at the secondary or the primary levels, limited to a few grades, or designed for all levels at once. The content may be incorporated into a broad educational reform that includes consultations between governmental and non-governmental bodies.[14]

UNFPA-supported population education activities also devote significant attention to teacher training. This is a vital part of all major population education projects, and it needs to be reinforced to expand coverage to more teachers, provide pre-service teacher preparation, improve teaching skills, and influence teachers' attitude formation, especially in the area of gender.[15]

UNFPA has also published and disseminated state-of-the-art research and evaluation studies on population education. The establishment of clearing houses providing information to national population education projects assisted countries in building and expanding their collections of population resources, and in developing national population education networks. These efforts have also facilitated the sharing and exchange of materials and information within countries and among countries in different regions.

Over the past 30 years, population education has gradually gained acceptance as an important part of the school curriculum in most countries, largely through the efforts of UNESCO and UNFPA. Still, a great deal remains to be done to institutionalize and strengthen this relatively new field to maximize its impact over the long-term. The more than 100 population education projects currently under way have yielded several valuable lessons, not least that population education is a complex undertaking. It is often difficult to introduce, and it is typically a slow process. Like other educational innovations, population education suffers from large, cumbersome, and overburdened education systems; low quality of schooling; funding limitations; inadequately trained personnel; limited supply of materials; staff shortages; and resistance to change. Problems that have arisen specifically in introducing population education projects include the controversial nature of many of the topics as well as the intimate character of some of the issues (e.g., sexuality, contraception). Often educators themselves have serious concerns at the outset about how to teach such subjects.[16]

Population and Education for All

In the meantime, all education programmes are faced with the task of introducing new educational content that is relevant to present-day concerns of the students. The challenge has been articulated at the World Conference on Education for All (1990), the Nine High Population Countries Summit (1993), the ICPD (1994), the Fourth World Conference on Women (1995), and the worldwide AIDS conferences. Fortunately, the recommendations on population education have appeared to coalesce at these international meetings, and they are mutually supportive. They serve, moreover, to strengthen the Programme of Action by their promise of contributing to improving the quality of basic education and national capacity-building by including more relevant curricula, and promoting curriculum reform and more effective teaching techniques. An important additional feature is that many of the recommendations are concerned with keeping the education of girls and women high on the international and national agendas.

UNFPA also recognizes improvements in basic education as an important prerequisite to sustainable development and as a factor in social well-being. UNFPA promotes basic education, particularly the education of girls, to combat illiteracy and to eliminate gender disparities in access to, retention in, and support for education as part of the goals of the ICPD Programme of Action. Through the education activities it supports, the Fund aims to: (a) contribute to improvements in the quality of basic education through the introduction of more relevant (population- and development-related) curricula, and the promotion of curricular reforms and more effective teaching techniques; and (b) keep the education of girls and women high on national and international agendas.

Carrying out this vast strategy requires comprehensive and sustained advocacy efforts at global, regional, and national levels to get the full commitment and support of governments, as well as those of relevant international agencies and NGOs. At the same time, country-level programmes need to look for more effective ways to encourage community participation in support of education — both parents' support to girls' access and parent/community support for population education activities.[17]

Five years after the adoption of the Programme of Action, a note of concern was sounded about the approaching deadlines for achieving universal access to education. At a March 1999 meeting of the Commission on Population and Development, called to prepare for an upcoming General Assembly special session on the implementation of the ICPD Programme of Action, governments and the international community were urged to make special efforts to reach a number of important goals.[18] Regarding education, delegates were reminded of some important target dates: 2015, for universal access to primary education; 2002 and 2005, for closing the gender gap in primary and secondary education, respectively; 2005, for raising the net primary school enrolment rate for boys and girls to 90 per cent from an estimated 85 per cent in 2000. With deadlines closing in, the delegates were urged to study and adopt "bold and innovative initiatives" that would help "surmount the enduring poverty barrier to education in developing countries." Proposals included making use of modern information communication technology, including satellite transmission of educational content.

Non-Formal Population Education

Students are not the only beneficiaries of population education. Outreach is especially important when a target population is difficult to attract. UNFPA made its most remarkable contribution to the "field era" of family planning programmes in carrying out a large spectrum of community-oriented and informal communication projects beyond the walls of schools and health centres — so-called "non-formal population education," aimed at out-of-school youth or unschooled youth and adults, particularly girls and women. These efforts can be seen as an extension of the relationship of family planning service providers to their clients. They include: (a) providing clients with facts about family planning services; (b) encouraging clients to express their reproductive intentions and needs; and (c) supporting their efforts to obtain medical advice and care.

In carrying out such an approach to informal education, UNFPA built lasting programmatic alliances with specialized United Nations agencies such as ILO, the Food and Agriculture Organization of the United Nations (FAO), UNESCO, and the World Health Organization (WHO). Outreach activities have been integrated into governmental, non-governmental and United Nations programmes of adult education, functional literacy, vocational training, health education, special programmes for disadvantaged population groups, as well as the educational programmes of trade union organizations and employer and management groups. Agricultural extension and home economics courses, cooperatives, young farmer associations, and women's clubs and groups have also served as vehicles to introduce population education and the practice of family planning in rural areas in the context of rural development programmes. Population education has taken place in a variety of settings — such as multi-purpose youth centres, community centres, women's centres, workplaces, churches and recreation centres. Activities sponsored by UNFPA have included curriculum development, training of trainers, awareness-raising campaigns, painting and poster competitions, art exhibitions, seminars and workshops, and development and distribution of education and training materials.

Education in non-formal settings has many advantages. Providing family planning education and services through the workplace appeals to both workers and employers. Like other groups, workers benefit from learning about the importance of planning their lives and from developing decision-making skills in family welfare. The workplace often provides access to males — an important audience as far as reproductive decisions are concerned. Population education also offers women in rural and urban areas the possibility of improving their knowledge and skills in the areas of family life, family health, child spacing, nutrition, and other social and economic matters. It also helps women develop their leadership potential. It brings the activities to a place where the group is comfortable, and discussions may be more open than they would be in a school classroom. Participation is voluntary. Activities gain additional acceptance in the community when carried out by traditional and respected groups.[19]

All these pioneer outreach efforts have contributed to increasing community leaders' awareness of major population issues. A major achievement of projects in the organized sector has been changing the attitudes and behaviour of management personnel with regard to family planning for workers. When successful, this has resulted in the provision of time for population education classes and of workplace health and family planning services.

The First Two Decades: Population Communication for National Family Well-Being

Why Population Communication?

Only after the Mexico City Conference in 1984 and the Amsterdam Forum in 1989 did fertility reduction through increased contraceptive use and accessible family planning emerge as priorities in most nations' development goals. Because UNFPA support is conditioned by government policies, it was only after these shifts in priorities that the Fund's country programmes became committed to achieving explicit communication objectives concerning the utilization of family planning services.

The population communication component of UNFPA programmes was primarily aimed at married couples of childbearing age. It was meant to influence people's strongly held traditional beliefs and practices about birth and contraception and attitudes such as those favouring male offspring; to encourage people to adopt positive, health-seeking behaviour for MCH, and encourage the effective use of contraceptives; to motivate young people to delay marriage and to adopt early the practice of planning or spacing pregnancies; to encourage healthy dialogue among young adults and couples about human sexuality and fertility; and to ensure local residents' willingness to be interviewed by census enumerators.

A number of theories and models about the process of knowledge, attitudes, and behaviour changes guided communicators in their work. These theories are well documented in the professional literature.[20] One model outlined the individual's movement from a pre-awareness phase to the acceptance of a new idea, leading to action. Others outlined predisposing conditions for behavioural change. The models all required research on the profiles of different audiences. For instance, newlywed couples would need certain types of family planning information, whereas women who had already had several children would need others. Skilled management was essential in orchestrating the complex elements of population programmes with other organizations, and in adhering to budgets for programmes and projects.

A Basic Principle: Mixing Media

Mass media can be instrumental in increasing awareness, and promoting political support and community participation in family planning. Thanks to UNFPA's cooperation with donors such as the United States and Japan, mass media campaigns have probably been used more widely for family planning communication than for any other area of development work. Multimedia population communication campaigns and staff training have been conducted in all regions during the past twenty years, either as part of general MCH/FP programmes or as stand-alone projects.

However, even in areas where acceptance levels are high, people are not always using contraceptives correctly, or they are discontinuing their use because they are dissatisfied with side effects. They may also drop contraceptive usage out of suspicion, traditional myths, taboos or rumours pertaining to human sexuality, fertility, reproduction, modern family planning methods and government programmes. Closing the gap that exists between awareness of family planning and the actual practice of contraception calls for enabling informed choice through counselling and community involvement. Face-to-face communication in clinics and in the home has been a way to respond to individual needs and concerns, and it has facilitated contraceptive decision-making. Good interpersonal communication calls for service providers to have empathy and sensitivity to the needs and views of their clients, as well as to have good listening skills and to be respectful of people's rights. For these reasons, training service providers in interpersonal communication techniques has been an integral part of UNFPA-supported population communication.

In addition, to publicize the availability of reproductive health services, their location and the types of services offered, advertising has been tried on behalf of family planning programmes. "Social marketing" of contraceptives is another way of effectively expanding distribution and consumption. Commercial marketing techniques are being applied more frequently for development programmes. Such techniques are designed to influence the voluntary behaviour of audiences in order to improve their general welfare. Community-based distribution (CBD) systems, such as in Thailand or Kenya, use social marketing approaches through which distributors sell pills and condoms, keeping a small portion of the low price for themselves. Social marketing of contraceptives has expanded in some countries since the spread of AIDS has given added importance to promoting the use of condoms.

At national level, UNFPA has provided a broad range of population communication assistance, including support to needs assessment exercises, workshops, seminars and conferences, as well as to specific products such as brochures, posters, films, comic books, use of folk media, etc., training in communication skills and management, and the development of community mobilization and national campaigns. "Knowledge-attitudes-practice" studies and the evaluation of communication projects have also drawn local leaders' attention to the gap between the relatively high levels of "knowledge" of family planning and the comparatively low level of "practice," or use of the existing services. Communication projects integrated into MCH/FP service agencies have been found to be generally effective in increasing the efficacy of health personnel. Such projects have led to the creation of information-education-communication units in ministries of health and helped insert the teaching of counselling into staff training.

Outside the Health Sector

Communication campaigns have often been undertaken in projects outside the health sector in order to reinforce the messages promoting healthy behaviours. However, these projects have not always formed a coherent and ongoing multimedia programme. Another major weakness has been their piecemeal approach to diverse audiences, and a focus on training at the central level and on producing messages and materials rather than learning about people through research. Accumulated experience suggests that collaboration between communication and field service personnel is needed to ensure that media messages correspond to the reality of the service situation. Without the link between mass media campaigns, outreach personnel, and communities, there is a risk of a disconnection between demand creation and service-delivery readiness, and little opportunity for synergy and community involvement. As a result, population communication interventions have not always achieved their full potential in reducing the so-called knowledge-attitude-practice gap.[21] Improved strategies are needed.[22]

The Post-Cairo Framework

Public Relations and Media Groundwork

The dialogue and debates leading up to the Cairo Conference extended UNFPA's global public information and external relations' outreach to a dimension it had never experienced before. Ensuring that the broader language of the ICPD Programme of Action was amplified and accepted in both developed and developing countries required a major overhaul of UNFPA's public information methods. Finding "common ground" on such matters as gender equality and women's health, constructing mutual agreements on the situation of adolescents, shifting towards reproductive health, and placing population issues in the development context, all meant setting up an extensive and inclusive preparatory process.[23]   The information activities and media relations work of the ICPD Secretariat (in close collaboration with the United Nations Department of Information and UNFPA's Information and External Relations Division) ensured that the media were kept informed of the evolution of the consensus on the issues being debated on a day-to-day basis.   Such activities were an integral part of the complex orchestration of expert group meetings, regional intergovernmental conferences, round tables, the ministerial meeting, the meeting of eminent persons, and consultation meetings with economies in transition, as well as the meetings of NGOs at national, regional, and international levels.

Advocacy efforts by UNFPA and other concerned parties led to a virtual revolution — the active participation of NGOs in the preparation for the Cairo Conference and in the conference itself.[24]   Recognizing the critical advocacy role NGOs are playing in developing countries' media and other policy debate spheres, UNFPA organized media briefings for both local journalists and civil society leaders.

Another breakthrough was achieved through the use of the Internet to share the proceedings of the Cairo Conference. In 1993, UNFPA, in collaboration with POPIN, used the Internet Gopher to supplement pre-ICPD publicity efforts by disseminating information materials electronically.   At the conference itself in 1994, UNFPA supported POPIN in putting all important documents and official statements onto its Gopher site while the meeting was under way. A few weeks after the conference, the major conference publications were available via Gopher.

Using New Information and Communication Technologies

The World Wide Web offered UNFPA an inexpensive way of informing the media about breaking news and of countering misinformation about the population situation; it also provided an unequalled opportunity for inclusiveness and participation in global decision-making. Current indications are that the Internet will continue to grow rapidly in popularity and in use and that it will provide helpful alternatives in fulfilling UNFPA's information and communication outreach mission. Estimates of Internet users worldwide suggest that the numbers may have surpassed 143 million in 1999, up from 82 million just two years previously.[25] It is probably with some justification that UNFPA is attempting to view recent developments in information and communication technologies (ICTs) in a positive light, even suggesting that they offer a good potential for "encouraging social interaction among all stakeholders and stimulating public debate on population issues."[26] Other information collection and exchange programmes are now beginning to realize their potential for outreach and accessibility.

Since 1995, UNFPA has developed its Website (http://www.unfpa.org) as an integral part of the Information and External Relations Division's publications and public relations programmes. The Internet is also providing avenues for constituency-building and participation in international decision-making processes. Throughout the 1999 ICPD+5 process, UNFPA's website pioneered the use of the Web to cover the extensive preparations for The Hague Forum and other events as they happened, together with all the key documents, allowing all stakeholders with access to the Web to participate in the process. This "virtual pressroom" allowed journalists to view activities, download audio and video clips, and ask participants questions through e-mail. This coverage of The Hague Forum, preparations for the Special Session of the General Assembly, and the electronic bulletin that summarized the proceedings as they unfolded (for example, see http://www.unfpa.org/icpd/bulletins/bulletn14.htm) were widely used by governments (including many developing countries), United Nations offices, NGOs and the media to inform and involve their constituents. These efforts played a key role in getting the ICPD+5 story out to a wider world. The site was linked to many other population-related sites. UNFPA plans to increase its use of this method.

Keeping the Momentum Going

Riding the momentum generated by the ICPD, the Fund organized international poster and essay-writing competitions to tap the interest, curiosity, and creative potential of schoolchildren. In 1996, for instance, an international youth essay contest on the theme of "Promoting Responsible Reproductive Health Behaviour" provided an opportunity for young people to voice their views and concerns. UNFPA field offices worked with many local and international youth and youth-related NGOs such as the World Young Women's Christian Association, the World Association of Girl Guides and Girl Scouts, and the World Organization of the Scout Movement, medical students and young Rotarians to organize the contest. In several countries, impressive national mobilizations took place: South Africa alone had 3,000 entries. Using young people as advocates for their own needs proved to be a powerful and culturally sensitive strategy to present the situation to government policymakers and help address a controversial subject.

Similarly, in Europe in 1998, UNFPA entered into a cooperative three-year arrangement with eighteen European NGOs and three private U.S. foundations to create a "Face-to-Face" campaign advocating broader political support for international population assistance and for gender equality, women's empowerment, and global reproductive rights. The campaign has engaged the active involvement of a number of UNFPA special "goodwill ambassadors" — prominent celebrities from the world of entertainment and influential European political leaders — to help attract the attention of the media and the public.

After Cairo: The Strategic Communication Era in Country Programs

After Mexico City and during the preparations for Cairo, UNFPA adopted a three-pronged approach to communication to champion population policies for sustainable development and to meet the information and education needs of family planning clients. In her review of lessons learned in communication for family planning and reproductive health, P. T. Piotrow[27] proposed a new category — the "strategic communication era."

An Integrated Approach: IEC for Behavioural Change

In the early 1990s, UNFPA shifted from the use of distinct information, education, and communication components to a more integrated and strategic approach, tagged with the acronym IEC (information, education, and communication) and advocacy. For several years, UNFPA has included strategic planning in its population programmes that aims to develop a sense of ownership among national partners.[28] Since understanding of the interrelationship of population, gender and development, and political will has risen dramatically, national population programmes supported by UNFPA and other donors have become increasingly multisectoral and aimed at achieving measurable results. In turn, this has called for well-coordinated and well-aimed communication strategies.

An IEC strategy — a framework for action — indicates commitment to achieving measurable results. It combines a variety of mass media, group and interpersonal, entertaining, educational, and participatory approaches and channels. It involves a stepwise programming sequence based on operational research. It also defines the modalities of collaboration between different national actors, using a systems approach to information campaigns.[29] Not having an IEC strategy can result in ill-defined audiences and objectives that are difficult to measure, or *ad hoc* isolated activities that have no sustainable impact. The starting point of an IEC strategy would therefore be to identify the social groups most likely to respond to action, and to understand why they are not doing so now; i.e., what are the causes of resistance to behaviour change. Now almost all of UNFPA's country programmes invest resources in designing and revising such strategies.

The call for strategic thinking was emphasized in the Cairo Programme of Action:

> A *coordinated strategic approach to information, education and communication* should be adopted in order to maximize the impact of various information, education and communication activities, both modern and traditional, which may be undertaken on several fronts by various actors and with divers audiences. It is especially important that *IEC strategies* be linked to, and complement, national population and development policies and strategies and a full range of services in reproductive health, including family planning and sexual health, in order to enhance the use of those services and improve the quality of counselling and care.[30]

Comprehensive IEC Strategies

With UNFPA assistance, IEC strategies that involve all stakeholders concerned with the integration of population and gender issues into development and reproductive health and rights have been adopted in an increasing number of countries. Fieldworkers, service providers, and local government authorities have assumed the role of managers and staff of communication projects, while youth have acted as peer educators, and community leaders have served as change agents. The IEC strategy formulation process has created opportunities to build consensus through the involvement of all stakeholders, including NGOs, local officials, and other donors.

After the ICPD, UNFPA priorities and future directions specified which objectives these IEC strategies should be seeking. First, it was necessary to draw the attention of policymakers to the need for community-specific reproductive health and family planning services. Second, the strategies emphasized improving the knowledge of programme managers and service providers about clients' perceptions and needs and their satisfaction with the services. Third, improving the quality of reproductive health and family planning care by enhancing service providers' interpersonal communication skills was seen as a priority. Fourth, greater efforts were to be made to motivate men to share reproductive decision-making with their spouses, support their partners' reproductive choices, and adopt responsible sexual behaviour themselves. Fifth, adolescent reproductive health needed to be improved through the development of responsible attitudes towards sexuality and parenthood and the encouragement of gender-fair attitudes. Sixth, campaigns needed to be designed to help specific audiences understand the benefits of

using family planning methods and reproductive health services.[31]   Revised UNFPA programme
guidelines in 1996 called for each core programme area to include IEC "crosscutting" components.

The communication specialists from the Country Support Teams (CSTs) who, since
1992, provide technical assistance at the request of countries in all regions of the developing
world, drew lessons from their vast operational experience. For instance, in countries such as
Tanzania, Kenya and Ethiopia, attempts have been made to broaden the involvement of key
players in order to enhance acceptability and utilization of IEC strategies that go beyond the
UNFPA-supported programme. To make the process of strategy development more scientific,
the CSTs have also incorporated sociocultural research on people's aspirations, and media and
institutional research into IEC planning activities. They have tried to marry various media
approaches — traditional with modern media — in a true multimedia fashion.

In working closely with demographers and census technicians, communication advisors
have helped discover through research the existence of pockets of citizens who would otherwise
not have been willing to be counted.   Data indicated the need to make such citizens
knowledgeable about the objectives and *raison d'être* for the census, beyond top-down public
service announcement messages.[32]   In this sense, UNFPA's unique contribution was in
organizing fruitful multisectoral collaboration and in building national partners' capacities to
implement communication strategies through a programme approach.

After Cairo: The Rise of Rights-based Advocacy Programmes

Strategic planning in IEC has increased communicators' alertness to changing environments.
The current decade is witnessing rapid changes in audiences, channels, values and mandates,
organizational structures, political environments, and resources that require communication
programmes to adapt to a variety of new situations.[33]   UNFPA has responded to these
movements, specifically the advent of programme advocacy communication, through new forms
of international assistance and by using new information and communication technologies.

Why Is Advocacy Still Needed After Cairo?

Advocacy is embedded in the ICPD Programme of Action and its implementation. The Cairo
process itself came about because of the extraordinarily active participation of NGOs, and the
clear acceptance by most of the governments of the NGO contribution and its potential in the
population sector. NGOs have had to work very hard to reach this level of recognition.[34]

In terms of the outcome of Cairo, the adoption of the ICPD Programme of Action
registered a significant advance in the international consensus on gender equity and women's
empowerment and its direct relevance to population policies and programmes. It established a
number of significant goals and signposts, which an increasing majority of countries have agreed
to follow.[35]   Civil society advocacy organizations, especially advocates of women's
empowerment and reproductive rights, were at the forefront of the mobilization process for the
Cairo Conference that led to the ultimate adoption by consensus of the Programme of Action.

While the consensus on the Programme of Action was impressive in Cairo, many of the
reproductive health and rights issues are new to the population and development community. It
is one thing to endorse international agreements in conference settings, but another one to

enforce them at the country level. Some governments have attempted to revise, water down, or forget some of the key concepts they accepted at Cairo. The promotion of reproductive rights as a human right is not always understood and accepted, much less carried out. Violations may begin with clients being provided insufficient information on contraceptive methods or being provided limited time to make a decision and consent. Rights violations also occur when governments fail to enforce laws on gender-based violence or to allocate enough resources to cater to basic reproductive health service-delivery needs. Similarly, while concerns about growing teenage pregnancies and rising rates of sexually transmitted diseases (STDs) among adolescents are shared, the provision of information on sexual health and contraceptive services to young people has run against opposition from religious taboos and cultural norms.

More troubling, however, are the disruptive tactics of a small number of opposition groups who appear determined to undermine public commitment to the Programme of Action through the mass media, the Internet, and other communication channels. In some Western countries, extremely conservative bodies continue to misrepresent the population-development nexus as being a pro-abortionist influence; while in some developing nations, in the Asia region, for example, groups of activists are gaining media attention and notoriety from their absolutist objections to contraceptive practices.

Therefore, the ICPD goals need to be fully understood, promoted, and adopted at national and community levels, especially in sensitive areas such as gender-based violence, quality of reproductive health care, male involvement, and adolescent sexual and reproductive health and rights.

UNFPA's New Mission

Realizing that it will take time for the ICPD paradigm shift to a "reproductive health and rights" agenda to be fully internalized and that it is therefore necessary to continue working towards a broadly based acceptance of the Cairo goals and to strengthen the coalitions forged during the ICPD process, UNFPA has identified advocacy as one of its core programme priorities.[36] Along with reproductive health and population and development strategies (PDS), advocacy has stood as an integral component of country programmes since the 1995 meeting of the UNDP/UNFPA Executive Board.[37]

This type of communication goes hand-in-hand with substantive policymaking in population and development. It also complements IEC programmes aimed at individual behaviour change by triggering a collective response. Advocacy attempts to shape public policies, to raise global and national resources in support of population causes, and to gain political and social leadership for acceptance and commitment to these changes within a society as a whole.

The Fund is now working to bring focus, intensity, and method to the advocacy work that needs to be carried out at the country level. Policies and guidelines have been revised to institutionalize new practices. The new set of Policies and Procedures for UNFPA Programme Support, issued in 1997, includes a special section on advocacy and the areas for UNFPA programme support. These guidelines provide a strategic planning framework to develop advocacy strategies, starting with situation analyses. In searching for ways to operationalize these new guidelines, an international expert consultation[38] has pointed out the need to further build national capacity in research, monitoring, and evaluation of country-based advocacy efforts; to build partnerships with civil society organizations; and to systematically organize media advocacy and policy advocacy. In a parallel effort, global and national mechanisms for monitoring advocacy are being developed through the selection of appropriate indicators.

Programme-based advocacy brings a new dimension to the Fund's work, as well as many challenges. This work involves some basic assumptions. The advocacy that the Fund sponsors assumes people have rights and are entitled to some benefits, and that institutions work the way they should. Advocacy of the goals of the ICPD is not mere top-down propaganda; it is a transformative process that involves participation of disenfranchised groups in policymaking. Advocacy blends science, politics, and activism in the context of social values and interests. It promotes a basic balance between personal responsibility and social obligation; government intervention and private response.[39]

Generally, advocacy programmes involve special skills in: a) gathering and framing information into solid arguments to set the policy agenda; b) influencing policymakers and legislators through political lobbying; c) creating and sustaining alliances and coalitions with new partners; d) mobilizing the media; e) handling controversy and unfounded rumours; and f) organizing grass-roots advocates at community level.

Evolving Roles

Concurrently, the modalities of programme execution are evolving. Traditionally, UNFPA delegated much of its country project implementation to other United Nations specialized agencies. Now, UNFPA is more directly involved in following up with the actual formulation and implementation of programmes implemented by its national partners. However, UNFPA's role is sometimes misinterpreted as advocating its own policies rather than actually facilitating the capacity of national allies and partners to advocate in favour of national issues and policies.

Another challenge is to get the population community's clear understanding of how behaviour-change communication, IEC, and advocacy communication are complementary but distinct components in a continuum for social change. Communicators are often faced with the misunderstanding that IEC — the educational dimension — is no longer necessary if advocacy communication is built into programmes. Sound population programmes are thus learning that advocacy activities are only directed at a *broad* set of social factors — issues and causes, such as public policies, culture, economics, social environment and service-delivery systems — that may impinge on individuals' enjoyment of sexual and reproductive health and rights.[40] At the same time, an IEC campaign may be directed at encouraging service providers to be more welcoming to men, as well as at motivating men to be more supportive of their partners' reproductive choices and to avail themselves of reproductive health services.[41]

To achieve lasting results, UNFPA promotes open and frank exchange of regional experiences in advocacy and the building of regional coalitions. Thematic workshops among its CST Specialists are periodically organized to share lessons and document the best practices.[42] In Latin America, the overriding conclusion stressed by NGOs in Quito in 1997 was that more needed to be done to promote sexual and reproductive health and rights from a gender perspective. Furthermore, they noted that UNFPA needed to be more active in bringing together the women's health movement and the experience and vision of specialized NGOs to bear on government programmes and policies. In Africa, UNFPA was instrumental in organizing conferences of women ministers and parliamentarians as occasions for building a powerful network of women political leaders. The Fund also supported the gathering of African leading lawyers and representatives of family planning associations to analyse laws and policies affecting women's reproductive lives in this region.

At the international level, UNFPA has spearheaded advocacy to promote and coordinate global interagency collaboration on ICPD follow-up. International initiatives — such as gender equity, the access of girls and women to basic education, or the protection of the environment within sustainable development — are broader than UNFPA's mandate and operational capacity; however, these initiatives assist population programmes and contribute to achieving the goals of the ICPD Programme of Action. This cooperation has resulted in a common United Nations advocacy statement on the importance of population as an integral component of development strategies. UNFPA has also served as a strategic ally for broader development and system-wide initiatives of the United Nations.* Closely related to this advocacy is the mobilization of financial resources for population and development activities at the international level. An information and communication strategy[43] developed in 1997 has already served to launch an impressive number of activities at international, regional, and country levels.

New Directions for the Twenty-first Century

The coming-of-age of UNFPA's bolder advocacy stands also coincides with larger changes in its environment, such as the increased voice of new stakeholders — adolescents and older citizens — and new forms of partnership with the civil society. At the same time, the reduction in funds available for development assistance and the opportunities (and threats) provided by the information society provide a new context for UNFPA's communication work.

Changes in Stakeholders' Needs

Far too many adolescents lack access, not only to preventive services such as information and contraception, but also to youth-friendly health services, including diagnosis, treatment, information and counselling. To aggravate their situation, in many countries, girls who become pregnant are not allowed to attend school. In others, the education of boys is simply valued higher than that of girls. The result is that girls constitute two-thirds of the more than 130 million children not attending school.

A major area of UNFPA support from the beginning has been advocacy for the reproductive health needs and rights of adolescents. This has included documenting the sexual and reproductive health problems of adolescents, promoting the recognition of the rights of adolescents, and promoting the fact that the needs of adolescents should be met. Such activities played a catalytic role in the emphasis given to the sexual and reproductive health rights and needs of adolescents in the ICPD Programme of Action, and these activities continue to be vital in keeping adolescent issues on the international as well as national agendas. Increasingly, support has been also been provided to projects and programmes seeking to develop new strategies and approaches, and to identifying best practices in IEC and service delivery for

---

* The ACC Task Force on Basic Social Services for All (BSSA) ensures that common advocacy messages are agreed upon and then promoted in a coordinated fashion by the entire UN system. UNFPA actively supports this process.

adolescents. Some projects have sought in particular to meet the needs of rural adolescents, adolescent girls and adolescents in refugee situations.[44]

At the country level, UNFPA has primarily supported projects and programmes in advocacy, policy, service delivery, IEC, training, and research and data collection. Most of the UNFPA-supported projects have been carried out by governments or youth or youth-serving NGOs who have contributed significantly to the progress made in the field of adolescent sexual and reproductive health (ASRH) over the past decade.[45]

Ensuring adolescent sexual and reproductive health and rights as well as improved life opportunities, equally for girls and boys, will require much greater investment than its current level, since the largest group of adolescents in world history — with 1.1 billion persons aged 10 to 19, is at particular risk of reproductive ill health.

At the other end of the life cycle, there remains a substantial gap in knowledge and advocacy on the conditions among older persons, and the effect on them of current and future social and economic development trends. Sharing accurate information provides the basis for policies and programmes addressing the particular needs of the elderly, including their economic and social security, especially the needs of older women and the frail. Advocacy efforts also support affordable, accessible and appropriate health-care services; increased recognition of the productive and useful roles the elderly can play; and support systems to enhance the ability of families to care for their older family members.

Changes in Partnership

Major positive changes have taken place in the concept of "participation" and the processes for programme consultation. In particular, there is a general recognition of the changing roles of nation states and civil society, increasing acceptance of decentralized and community-based modalities, and improved partnership among United Nations organizations and national bodies. The ICPD marked a turning point in international policymaking. It has become synonymous with the spirit of inclusion, cooperation and consensus for a new generation of reproductive health and population-related policies: based on human rights, gender equality and equity, and partnership. The Programme of Action calls for the promotion of the full participation of civil society organizations (CSOs) and leaders. This partnership will become increasingly critical, particularly in the provision of reproductive health counselling services and the promotion of advocacy and social mobilization efforts, in order to carry forward the goals of the Programme of Action.

At the national level, UNFPA actively promotes the involvement of all stakeholders — i.e., all parties that are involved in or affected by programmes, such as community representatives, service providers, programme managers, researchers and clients — to come together in analysing their situations, setting their goals and designing supportive communication strategies. Many diverse and innovative communication methodologies and materials have been developed to empower people to act on their sexual and reproductive rights. However, the effectiveness of methodologies and materials has not always been evaluated, and the content has not always addressed the common human experience, such as sexuality and gender power relations.

Further efforts are required to build strong, dynamic partnerships at the national level. In order to establish an enabling environment for effective partnership, governments, working closely with civil society, should institute common forums for dialogue for building partnerships.

In the future, this means that one can look forward to more support's being provided directly to advocacy NGOs to strengthen legal frameworks and policies that promote and protect the human rights of women and girls, and to enforce them effectively. Civil society, especially NGOs, will also receive increasing support to reinforce their IEC campaigns among community, religious, and other public-opinion leaders as a way of changing prevailing traditional attitudes and practices.

Changes in Resources

Unfortunately, although funding for population programmes has increased since the ICPD, it did not increase enough to meet the agreed-upon target of $17 billion by the year 2000. A major obstacle to increasing resource mobilization has been the slow downward trend in official development assistance (ODA).

The reasons for this trend are several. Some donor countries have reduced aid as part of an overall drive to reduce budget deficits. There has been a loss of confidence in some countries as to the efficacy of giving them development aid. The large increases in private-sector investment in ten or twelve developing countries in the 1993-1996 period, as well as the growing belief in the centrality of market-driven development, may also have worked against ODA that is preponderantly tied to projects in the public sector.[46]

The Fund's level of commitment to action may also be measured in financial terms. Over its first thirty years, it invested a total of $4.5 billion. Some $658 million of this total was directed to communication-related activities, including extrabudgetary trust fund contributions. Unfortunately, levels of support have flattened in recent years, and this could affect the Fund's ability to pursue its mandate effectively. Increasing IEC and advocacy investments are needed to help raise awareness about the value of the Fund's mission and its programmes and to help root out ignorance about the relationship between population and sustainable development. Moreover, national capacity-building efforts must be continued in such areas as training for national information and communication personnel and media practitioners. Vigorous advocacy efforts must also be made to obtain greater financial support from traditional and non-traditional donors and from other partner organizations. If successful, these investments should translate into the required resources that are so vital to the work of the Fund.

Many developing countries have made impressive progress in realigning their domestic budgets to address ICPD goals for improving the accessibility and quality of reproductive health programmes, reducing mortality, and increasing the attention given to related social sectors. But financial crises are affecting the ability of many countries, especially developing countries and countries with economies in transition, to maintain their initial momentum towards achieving these goals. And despite noteworthy progress made since the ICPD, opposition to population programmes on traditional or cultural grounds remains an obstacle to the mobilization of resources in certain domestic contexts. At times, misinformation campaigns about the real purpose of population programmes have been used to stigmatize population activities and create adverse public opinion. UNFPA-funded IEC, training, and advocacy on population issues and their relevance to development strategies can help correct such misperceptions.

Efforts will have to be redoubled — by developing countries, donors, and multilateral organizations like UNFPA, as well as the private sector, NGOs, and other civil society representatives — to both advocate for and help provide the level of resources required for the full implementation of the ICPD Programme of Action.

Changes in Information and Communication Technologies

There is probably no arena in development that more clearly illustrates the importance of people's ability to communicate with one another than that of reproductive health and population. Individuals and societies can respond intelligently to the forces of change only if they can discuss and debate the issues among themselves. Education and information strategies must therefore focus on the complexities of choice and rights and actively strengthen the ability of individuals to enjoy rational, informed self-empowerment.

In the years since the Cairo Conference, the technological revolution in communication has swept over the globe at a pace that even in 1994 was unimaginable. Already, we can exchange information, knowledge and opinions with one another to an unprecedented extent. And this is only the beginning: within a few short decades, it is likely that virtually everyone on the planet will, in varying degrees, have the ability to link electronically with literally everyone else. The impact this will have — indeed, is already having — on the human condition and on the operation of human institutions is incalculable. So, too, is the potential this communication revolution has for improving the quality of human life in virtually every sphere.

It is now generally recognized that the population and reproductive health sector can and should fully exploit the rapidly expanding presence and potential of ICTs.[47] New ICTs offer new processes and tools for advocacy communication in support of the ICPD Programme of Action. State-of-the-art tools include interactive and interlinked Websites, the production of localized, more attractive and interactive population data, electronic archives, distance learning systems, youth or women-operated community telecentres, Websites and telephone help lines, and electronic conferences. UNFPA will increasingly work with governments as well as NGO and private-sector actors so that they avail themselves of the opportunities offered by the new participatory and open paradigm of the global information society.

Conclusion: Remaining Challenges

UNFPA's hallmark has always been a multisectoral approach to IEC. Its support has been aimed at increasing institutional capacities within governments, the media, and NGOs in population and reproductive health IEC. In Pakistan, Bangladesh, and Indonesia, for instance, the Fund has furnished support to establish and maintain specialized IEC departments or units within ministries of health, social affairs, information, agriculture, and education. They have contributed to training thousands of field staff to be more knowledgeable, comfortable, and equipped in interpersonal communication with their constituencies on sensitive issues. This has contributed to the near-universal awareness of family planning in those countries.

In the future, UNFPA will continue to work with governments to strengthen their national networks and coalitions for advocacy, targeting multiple audiences ranging from national leadership to the grass-roots level, for the goals and recommendations of the ICPD Programme of Action, in cooperation with CSOs. The Fund will nurture networks that link senders and receivers, citizens and decision-makers, public and private sectors, communication professionals, community and mass media, and opinion leaders. At the same time, advocacy efforts to increase and sustain broad-based political will for the promotion of gender equality can be accomplished through the creation of NGO coalitions and consortiums that pool their differing expertise.

272

Strong women's movements and other mass movements concerned with human rights and NGOs have proved important in ensuring progress in policy development and implementation in many parts of the world and in many areas of concern, including in creating political support for population and health policies that are rights-based.[48] NGOs, which had been genuine partners in framing the Programme of Action agreements, have become partners in its implementation. However, major threats to this partnership for development are appearing as many countries undergo rapid structural changes and those in intense political and economic stress have seen a significant increase in civil and political unrest over the last few years. Wars sparked by ethnic strife, political conflicts and economic hardship have resulted in growing public health problems and a breakdown in the infrastructure to deal formally with population and reproductive health issues. These serious situations risk diverting attention and resources to emergency relief rather than long-term developmental communication.

UNFPA, working closely with governments and civil society, will strengthen and intensify its social mobilization efforts through IEC and advocacy strategies that are bolder and more innovative than those used in the past. On the basis of socio-cultural and policy research, specific stakeholders within the broader spectrum of civil society will be encouraged to open up debates on controversial topics and cultural taboos, in a manner that is culturally sensitive and that promotes justice, peace, and health.

References

[1] United Nations, *1998 World Population Prospects*, New York: United Nations.

[2] M. N. Jato, "The Impact of Multimedia Family Planning Promotion on Contraceptive Behavior of Women in Tanzania." *International Family Planning Perspectives,* Vol. 25, No. 2 (June 1999): pp. 60 ff.

[3] *Population Policies and Programmes: Lessons Learned from Two Decades of Experience*, 1991, UNFPA New York University Press.

[4] Jyoti Shankar Singh, *Creating a New Consensus on Population* (London: Earthscan, 1998).

[5] Dennis Hodgson and Susan C. Watkins, "Feminists and Neo-Malthusians: Past and Present Alliances," in *Population and Development Review,* Sept. 1997; 23(3): 469-523.

[6] J. C. Caldwell and P. Caldwell, "The Cultural Context of High Fertility in Sub-Saharan Africa," in *Population and Development Review*, Sept. 1987; 13(3): 409-37.

[7] Dennis Hodgson and Susan C. Watkins, "Feminists and Neo-Malthusians: Past and Present Alliances," in *Population and Development Review,* Sept. 1997; 23(3): 469-523.

[8] Deborah Barrett and Ann O. Tsui, "Policy as Symbolic Statement: International Response to National Population Policies," in *Social Forces*, Sept. 1999, 78(1): 213-233.

[9] O. J. Sikes, "Reconceptualization of Population Education," 1991, *Technical Paper Number 2*, UNFPA, New York.

[10] Nafis Sadik, ed., *Population Policies and Programmes: Lessons Learned from Two Decades of Experience* (New York: UNFPA/New York University Press, 1991).

[11] UNFPA's Role in Education (briefing note), New York, 16 November 1995.

[12] Nafis Sadik, ed., *Population Policies and Programmes: Lessons Learned from Two Decades of Experience* (New York: UNFPA/New York University Press, 1991).

[13] AIDS Update, 1997, 1998 and 1999, UNFPA, New York.

[14] Nafis Sadik, ed., *Population Policies and Programmes: Lessons Learned from Two Decades of Experience* (New York: UNFPA/New York University Press, 1991).

[15] UNFPA's Role in Education (briefing note), New York, 16 November 1995.

[16] Nafis Sadik, ed., *Population Policies and Programmes: Lessons Learned from Two Decades of Experience* (New York: UNFPA/New York University Press, 1991).

[17] UNFPA's Role in Education (briefing note), 16 November 1995, New York.

[18] United Nations, *Preparations for the Special Session of the General Assembly. Revised Working Paper submitted by the Chairman:* "Proposals for Key Actions for the Further Implementation of the Programme of Action of the International Conference on Population and Development." Doc. No. E/CN.9/1999/PC/CRP.1/Rev.1 (New York: United Nations, 27 March 1999).

[19] Nafis Sadik, ed., *Population Policies and Programmes: Lessons Learned from Two Decades of Experience* (New York: UNFPA/New York University Press, 1991).

[20] P. T. Piotrow et. al., *Health Communication: Lessons from Family Planning and Reproductive Health*, (London: Praeger, 1997).

[21] "Population Information, Education and Communication," in *World Population Report, 1997*, United Nations Population Division.

[22] "The Integration of IEC with Family Planning: A Guidance Note," 1995, TED, UNFPA, New York.

[23] Jyoti Shankar Singh, *Creating a New Consensus on Population* (London: Earthscan, 1998).

[24] Ibid.

[25] "Special Report: Telecommunications," *Business Week Magazine*, 3 May 1999.

[26] United Nations Population Fund, Background Paper for The Hague Forum: "A Five-Year Review of Progress towards the Implementation of the Programme of Action of the International Conference on Population and Development" (New York: UNFPA, February 1999): para. 49.

[27] P. T. Piotrow et. al., *Health Communication: Lessons from Family Planning and Reproductive Health* (London: Praeger, 1997).

[28] The Basic Needs Assessments were replaced by Programme Review and Strategy Development, and since 1997, by the Country Population Assessment.

[29] "Developing IEC Strategies for Population Programmes," *Technical Paper Number 1*, 1993, UNFPA, New York.

[30] United Nations, *Report of the International Conference on Population and Development*, Cairo, 5-13 September 1994. Programme of Action: para. 11.19.

[31] United Nations, "Priorities and Future Directions for UNFPA After the ICPD," 1995/FPA/25.

[32] "Sharing Experiences and Lessons Learnt from the TSS System and Field Activities," 1993-1997, UNFPA Country Support Team, Addis Ababa, by Israel Sembanwe, April 1998, pp. 44-46.

[33] P. T. Piotrow, L. Kincaid, Rimon II and J. Rinehardt, *Health Communication: Lessons from Family Planning and Reproductive Health* (London: Praeger, 1997), pp. 187-188. *The Hague Forum Background Report*, 1999, UNFPA, New York, Chapter One.

[34] Jyoti Shankar Singh, *Creating a New Consensus on Population* (London: Earthscan, 1998): p. 121.

[35] Ibid.: p. 120.

[36] Ibid.: p. 175.

[37] "Programme Priorities and Future Directions for UNFPA in Light of the ICPD," DP/1995/25, UN.

[38] "Operationalizing Advocacy in Support of Population and Development Programmes at Country Level: Lessons Learned," *Technical Report number 44*, UNFPA, New York, 1998.

[39] L. Wallack and L. Dorfman, "Media Advocacy: A Strategy for Advancing Policy and Promoting Health," *Health Education Quarterly*, Vol. 23 (3), August 1996, pp. 293-317.

275

[40] N. Assifi, "Population Advocacy," in *CST Bangkok Newsletter*, 1997.

[41] O. Mensah Kumah, and M. Thuo, *Advocacy for Reproductive Health in Africa: Concepts, Strategies and Issues.* Presented at ICOMP 14th Seminar on Managing Quality Reproductive Health Programmes: After Cairo and Beyond, Addis Ababa, 2-7 December 1996.

[42] Professional Meeting of TSS/CST Advisors on Population Information, Education and Communication, 1995, *Technical Report Number 20*, UNFPA, New York. Symposium on Advocacy for Adolescent Reproductive Health, Asian Institute for Development Communication and UNFPA, Kuala Lumpur, 20-23 October 1997. *Report of the TSS System Thematic Workshop on Applications of IEC and Advocacy to Reproductive Health*, 26-30 October 1998, Geneva, Switzerland.

[43] "UNFPA Information and Communication Strategy," DP/FPA/1997/8, United Nations.

[44] "The Sexual and Reproductive Health of Adolescents: A Review of UNFPA Assistance," 1998, *Technical Report 43*, UNFPA Technical and Policy Division.

[45] Ibid.

[46] "A Five-Year Review of Progress towards the Implementation of the Programme of Action of the International Conference on Population and Development," *A Background Paper Prepared by the United Nations Population Fund (UNFPA) for the Hague Forum*, The Hague, The Netherlands, 8-12 February 1999, p. 83.

[47] "ICPD Advocacy in the Global Information and Knowledge Management Age: Creating a New Culture," *Technical Report 47*, 1999, Technical and Policy Division, UNFPA, New York.

[48] "A Five-Year Review of Progress towards the Implementation of the Programme of Action of the International Conference on Population and Development," *A Background Paper Prepared by UNFPA for The Hague Forum*, The Hague, The Netherlands, 8-12 February 1999.

CONTRIBUTORS

Tevia Abrams

Tevia Abrams worked at UNFPA for a total of 19 years, where he was a specialist in information, education and communication (IEC). Between 1990 and 1994, he was the UNFPA Representative in New Delhi, in charge of the Fund's programmes in India and Bhutan. Mr. Abrams holds a Ph.D. in communication and theatre. His doctoral research was conducted in India on the uses of traditional theatre, and he has contributed to the literature on theatre and development. Currently retired, Mr. Abrams continues his interests in both the theatre and population issues.

John Caldwell

John C. Caldwell is Emeritus Professor of Demography at the Australian National University, Canberra, and Coordinator of the University's Health Transition Centre at its National Centre for Epidemiology and Population Health. He was President of the International Union for the Scientific Study of Population, 1993-1997. He has researched global fertility transition, especially in the developing world, since an attachment to the United Nations Economic and Social Commission for Asia and the Pacific in 1959. He is the author of *Theory of Fertility Decline* as well as 20 other books.

Sylvie Cohen

Sylvie I. Cohen is Acting Chief of the Advocacy and IEC Branch of UNFPA. A French national, she combines a background in political science and development economics with additional academic training in applied communication research and sociology. In addition to UNFPA, she has worked with UNICEF, WHO, the French Ministry of Cooperation and various other development agencies in developing social mobilization campaigns, particularly in Africa. Ms. Cohen is the author of a number of technical publications, including a manual on social mobilization for UNICEF, and has contributed chapters on community mobilization to several books as well papers on IEC and advocacy in support of population and reproductive health.

Rebecca Cook

Rebecca J. Cook is Professor at the Faculty of Law, the Faculty of Medicine and the Joint Centre for Bioethics at the University of Toronto. She specializes in the international protection of human rights and in health law and ethics and co-directs the International Programme on Reproductive and Sexual Health Law. She is ethical and legal issues co-editor of *The International Journal of Gynecology and Obstetrics*, and serves on the editorial advisory boards of *Human Rights Quarterly* and *Reproductive Health Matters*. Her publications include over 100 hundred books, articles and reports in the areas of international human rights and the law relating to women's health and feminist ethics, including, most recently, *Safe Motherhood: A Woman's Human Right* (World Health Organization, 2001). She is the recipient of the Certificate of Recognition for Outstanding Contribution to Women's Health by the International Federation of Gynecology and Obstetrics, and is a Fellow of the Royal Society of Canada.

Mahmoud Fathalla

Dr. Mahmoud F. Fathalla is Professor of Obstetrics and Gynaecology and former Dean of the Medical School, Assiut University, Egypt. He is Chairman of the WHO Global Advisory Committee on Health Research. He is the past President of the International Federation of Gynecology and Obstetrics and former Chairman of the International Medical Advisory Panel of the International Planned Parenthood Federation (IPPF). Dr. Fathalla received his M.D. from the University of Cairo and has a Ph.D. from the University of Edinburgh, as well as honorary degrees from the American College of Obstetricians and Gynecologists, the Royal College of Obstetricians and Gynecologists, and the Universities of Uppsala, Helsinki, and Toronto. He is the author of more than 150 scientific publications, including *From Obstetrics and Gynaecology to Women's Health – The Road Ahead*, published in 1997.

Noeleen Heyzer

Dr. Noeleen Heyzer is the Executive Director of the United Nations Development Fund for Women (UNIFEM). Born in Singapore, Dr. Heyzer received her Ph.D. in the social sciences from Cambridge University and was a research fellow at the Institute for Development Studies, Sussex, England. She has authored and edited numerous books and articles including, most recently, *A Women's Development Agenda for the 21st Century* (UNIFEM, 1995). Dr. Heyzer became the head of UNIFEM in 1994. From 1987-1994, she served as the Director of the Gender and Development Programme of the Asia Pacific Development Center, and was a founding member of Development Alternative with Women for a New Era (DAWN) and of the Asia Pacific Women in Law and Development (APWLD).

Don Hinrichsen

Don Hinrichsen is currently a programme officer at UNFPA. Previously, he was Editor-in-Chief of *Ambio* magazine in Stockholm, the journal of the human environment published by the Royal Swedish Academy of Sciences, and Editor-in-Chief of the first two editions of the *World Resources Report*, published by the World Resources Institute in Washington D.C. Mr. Hinrichsen has written five books and close to 1,000 magazine and newspaper articles over the past 25 years. He was a former foreign correspondent for radio, newspapers and magazines based in Athens, West Berlin, Copenhagen, Stockholm and London. His latest book is *Coastal Waters of the World: Trends, Threats and Strategies*, published by Island Press in 1998.

Stafford Mousky

Stafford Mousky worked with UNFPA from 1977 through 1994, where he served as Chief of the Office of the Executive Director (1977-1987); Chief of the Governing Council, UN Liaison and External Relations Branch (1987-1992); and during 1993-1994 as a senior adviser to the secretariat of the International Conference on Population and Development (ICPD). From 1972-1977, Mr. Mousky was an adviser on population and development matters to the United States Mission to the United Nations. Since 1994, he has been a consultant to various population and migration organizations and is on the Executive Board of the U.S. Committee for the United Nations Population Fund.

Mohammad Nizamuddin

Mohammad Nizamuddin is Director of UNFPA's Asia and Pacific Division (1996-1997; 2000-present). He has also served as Director of the UNFPA Technical and Policy Division (1996-1997). He was the Country Director of the UNFPA programme in Ethiopia from 1986-1991. Prior to that, he was employed as an adviser on demography and population issues in several countries, including Egypt, Jordan, Somalia and Pakistan. He was Assistant Professor in the Department of Bio-Statistics at the University of North Carolina from 1979-1981. Mr. Nizamuddin holds a Ph.D. in Population Studies from the University of Michigan. He is the author of over 20 technical papers and publications in the field of population and is a member of several professional societies.

Nafis Sadik

Dr. Nafis I. Sadik received her M.D. from Dow Medical College (Karachi) and served an internship in gynaecology and obstetrics at City Hospital in Baltimore, Maryland. She completed further studies at The Johns Hopkins University and held the post of research fellow in physiology at Queens University, Ontario. Dr. Sadik joined UNFPA in October 1971, became Chief of its Programme Division in 1973 and was named Assistant Executive Director in 1982. She was appointed Executive Director, with the rank of Under-Secretary-General in April 1987, the first woman head of one of United Nations' major voluntarily-funded programmes. She retired in December 2000. In 1990 she was appointed Secretary-General of the ICPD. Prior to her work at UNFPA, Dr. Sadik was Director-General of the Pakistan Central Family Planning Council. She began her career as a medical officer in charge of women's and children's wards in Pakistani armed forces hospitals. On her retirement from UNFPA, Dr. Sadik was appointed as Special Adviser to the United Nations Secretary-General. She serves on several boards of directors and advisory panels of non-profit organizations and research institutions in the area of population. She has been presented with numerous honorary degrees and awards including, most recently, the United Nations Population Award for 2001.

Fred Sai

Fred Sai, a Ghanaian public health physician, is currently the President of the Ghana Academy of Arts and Sciences and Adviser on HIV/AIDS to the President of Ghana. He was formerly Senior Population Adviser at the World Bank and President of the IPPF. He has received many awards and honours in the population field and was a recipient of the 1993 United Nations Population Award. He chaired the Main Committees of both the 1984 Population Conference in Mexico and the 1994 ICPD in Cairo. His writings include advocacy for adolescent and women's rights and reproductive health.

Sara Seims

Sara Seims joined The Alan Guttmacher Institute as President in November 1999. Immediately prior to that position, she was Associate Director of Population Sciences at the Rockefeller Foundation in New York. She is also the chair of the Board of the African Population and Health Research Center. Dr. Seims serves on the Board of Directors of Management Sciences for Health in Boston, where she was Director of the Population Division. She has also been Deputy Chief of two divisions of the United States Agency for International Development (USAID). Dr. Seims received a B.A. in anthropology from Rutgers University and a Ph.D. in demography from the University of Pennsylvania. She began her career as a Senior Research Associate with The Alan Guttmacher Institute, where she contributed to research in the areas of adolescent fertility, the determinants of unintended pregnancy and the need for abortion services in the United States.

Steven W. Sinding

Steven W. Sinding is Professor of Clinical Public Health at the Mailman School of Public Health of Columbia University, a position he assumed in September 1999, and Adjunct Professor of Public Policy in Columbia's School for International and Public Affairs. He is currently directing a three-year study on the future of development cooperation and assistance, with a special emphasis on reproductive health and population programmes. From 1991 to 1999, Dr. Sinding served as Director of the Population Sciences programme at the Rockefeller Foundation. In 1994, he was a member of the United States delegation to the ICPD. Prior to joining the Rockefeller Foundation, Dr. Sinding served as Senior Population Adviser to the World Bank following a 20-year career at USAID. He is a co-author of a forthcoming book from the Oxford University Press, *Population Matters: Demographic Change, Economic Growth, and Poverty in the Developing World.* Dr. Sinding holds Ph.D. in political science from the University of North Carolina. He serves on the boards of directors of several organizations active in the population and reproductive health fields.

Jyoti Shankar Singh:

Jyoti Shankar Singh was with UNFPA from 1972 to 1996. During that period, he occupied positions of increasingly higher responsibility, including those of Director, Information and External Relations Division (1980-1990); Director, Technical and Evaluation Division (1990-1995); and Deputy Executive Director (1995-1996). He served as the Executive Coordinator of the United Nations International Conference on Population (1982-1984) and of the ICPD (1991-1994). During 1998-1999, he served as Special Adviser to the Executive Director of UNFPA on the ICPD+5 review. Currently, he is Executive Coordinator of the World Conference against Racism. He is the author of *Creating a New Consensus on Population* (Earthscan, 1998).

Bradman Weerakoon

Dr. Bradman Weerakoon is currently a national consultant to the UNFPA programme in Sri Lanka. He was Regional Director of the Indian Ocean (South Asia) region of the IPPF from 1976-1977 and then served as Secretary-General of the IPPF from 1984-1989. During his stewardship, the IPPF was awarded the United Nations Population Award (1986) and the Third World Prize (1987). He was Chairman of the IPPF Regional Programme Committee in 1997-1998. He is the author and editor of numerous reports on the population situation in Sri Lanka, including, most recently, the UNFPA-sponsored Country Population Assessment 2000.

www.ingramcontent.com/pod-product-compliance
Lightning Source LLC
Chambersburg PA
CBHW032117020426
42334CB00016B/982